DISMANTLING
DEMOCRATIC STATES

DISMANTLING
DEMOCRATIC STATES

Ezra Suleiman

PRINCETON UNIVERSITY PRESS

PRINCETON AND OXFORD

SECOND PRINTING, AND FIRST PAPERBACK PRINTING, 2005
PAPERBACK ISBN 0-691-12251-2

THE LIBRARY OF CONGRESS HAS CATALOGED THE CLOTH
EDITION OF THIS BOOK AS FOLLOWS

SULEIMAN, EZRA N.
DISMANTLING DEMOCRATIC STATES / EZRA SULEIMAN.
P.   CM.
INCLUDES BIBLIOGRAPHICAL REFERENCES AND INDEX.
ISBN 0-691-11534-6 (ALK. PAPER)
1. ORGANIZATIONAL CHANGE.   2. ADMINISTRATIVE AGENCIES—
REORGANIZATION.   3. PRIVATIZATION.   4. BUREAUCRACY.
5. DEMOCRACY.   I. TITLE.
JF1525.O73S88   2003
321.8—DC21   2002193071

BRITISH LIBRARY CATALOGING-IN-PUBLICATION DATA IS AVAILABLE

THIS BOOK HAS BEEN COMPOSED IN GALLIARD

PRINTED ON ACID-FREE PAPER. ∞

PUP.PRINCETON.EDU

PRINTED IN THE UNITED STATES OF AMERICA

3   5   7   9   10   8   6   4   2

For Juan Linz

CONTENTS

ACKNOWLEDGMENTS

A WRITER RECENTLY SUGGESTED that "acknowledgments" in books have become a "numbers game," a "form of networking," and "professional aggrandizement."[1] Certainly, what was once a paragraph or a simple page has become more elaborate. I suspect the reasons for this are themselves complex.

The criterion I follow here is a simple one: any help that I received in the course of working on this book needs to be acknowledged. This is because either, as in the case of institutions, there may be an explicit or implicit contractual obligation or, as in the case of individuals, there is a moral obligation. I leave out indirect influences on my work in general and on this book in particular. This way, I hope, acknowledging those to whom I am indebted can be done without either ulterior motives or pomposity.

Much of the work on this book was carried out at four European institutions that are especially hospitable to comparative work. I began work on this book during my year at the Wissenschaftskolleg in Berlin in 1996–1997. The work was completed during the 2000–2001 year that I spent at Nuffield College, Oxford, and at the European University Institute in Florence. During this entire period I was closely associated with the Institut d'Etudes Politiques in Paris.

We often forget that when we speak of institutions we are really referring to specific people who have the knack of facilitating scholarly work. The facilitators in my case, all distinguished by their understanding of the academic enterprise, were Wolf Lepenies, Joachim Nettlebeck, Yves Mény, Richard Descoings, Stephanie Wright, and the late Vincent Wright.

I had access to numerous libraries in a number of countries. I want to thank in particular the staffs of the Firestone Library at Princeton University, the Bodleian Library and the Nuffield College Library at Oxford, the Bibliothèque de la Fondation Nationale des Sciences Politiques in Paris, the library at the European University Institute in Florence, and the library of the Frei Universität in Berlin.

This work was made possible by the generous material support I received from the Center of International Studies and the Council on Regional Studies at Princeton University, the Wissenschaftskolleg zu Berlin and Nuffield College.

I also became indebted over these last years to a number of scholars who assisted me in this work by answering my questions and by providing me with materials. I am particularly grateful to Donald F. Kettl, Carlos Alba,

---

[1] See Mark Bauerelin, "A Thanking Task: What Acknowledgments Pages Say about Academic Life," *Times Literary Supplement*, November 9, 2001.

Sabino Cassese, Françoise Dreyfus, Jacques Chevalier, Pierre Mathiot, Koichi Nakano, and Patricia Ingraham. I suspect that my colleagues at Nuffield College, and those who passed through while I was in residence, may not be aware of how often our conversations set me off exploring issues, or how their answers to my questions often resolved a nagging problem. I owe particular thanks to David Mayhew, Ian McLean, Martin Shapiro, Edward C. Page, Teresa Curristine, Jack Hayward, David Levi-Faur, and Elisabeth Ivarsflaten. I also must thank Steffan Synnerström, the director of the OECD's PUMA Group, with which I was for a time associated, for sharing his vast knowledge with me.

Over the years, I was helped in numerous ways by several excellent graduate students: Sanford Gordon, Kimberly Morgan, Bastien Irondelle, Natalia Letki, Arang Keshavarzian, Mai'a Davis (who is responsible for the index), and Daniel Suleiman. I owe special thanks to Koichi Nakano and Elisabeth Ivarsflaten. Koichi's work as a graduate student at Princeton University often intersected with mine, and numerous were the occasions when we discussed issues of comparative (most often Japanese and European) bureaucracies. Elisabeth worked very closely with me while she was conducting her graduate studies at Nuffield College. She was not only a dogged and imaginative research assistant, but she became a wonderful colleague with whom I discussed over a period of almost two years problems of methodology and issues relating to bureaucratic reforms in several countries.

Several scholars read the entire manuscript and gave me the benefit of their critical reading. I express my gratitude to Jeff Herbst and Tony King, both friends and colleagues of many years; Bert Rockman, who despite the burden of a new position as a dean nonetheless read the manuscript with his customary thoroughness; Edward C. Page and Harvey Feigenbaum, whose criticisms and advice made me change courses and avoid traps. This is as good an occasion as any to thank Joyce Slack. She is the person I have spoken to, on a daily basis, most often over the past fifteen years. She is an extraordinary administrative assistant. She is always cheerful, always helpful, and always using her unsurpassed memory to resolve queries and problems in ways that go well beyond the call of duty.

My dedication of this book to Juan Linz is a modest expression of my thanks—and here I think I reflect the feelings of several hundred scholars the world over—to him. Juan has been a model for generations of students and scholars because of his modesty, his encyclopedic knowledge, his concern with profound issues of political life, and his basic humanity and decency. My gratitude to him is as great today as it was three decades ago when he supervised my doctoral dissertation.

There is, I suspect, a reason why this is the fourth book that I am publishing with Princeton University Press. It has preserved its standards in the face of heavy pressures of commercialization and it gives authors the pleasure of working with editors of the quality of Chuck Myers.

DISMANTLING
DEMOCRATIC STATES

INTRODUCTION

FOR WELL OVER a decade now policymakers and academics have been celebrating, each in their own way, the triumph of democratic forms of government. That politicians should wish to vaunt the inexorable march toward freedom is not surprising. That academics should wish to understand the process by which a transition is made to a democratic form of government represents merely a legitimate intellectual inquiry. What these two disparate groups have in common is the belief, or at least assumption, that once the structural bases of a democratic polity are created then the democratic system is likely to remain enduring.

Democracies, however, are capable of faltering for different reasons, which include highly polarized politics, an inability to resolve mounting societal problems, the strengthening of antidemocratic parties, and the exacerbation of ethnic or regional or religious tensions.[1] The cases involving the collapse of democracies and their replacement by authoritarian regimes are extreme. But they help to demonstrate that even "strong" or "consolidated" democracies require constant strengthening so that problems are solved on a continual basis, thereby allowing legitimacy to be preserved.

Much work has been carried out on the need for institution-building and on the foundations of legitimacy. Yet, while we analyzed the process of democratization, prioritized institutional needs, and recommended to the newly liberated societies the introduction of structures and constitutions, we in the West were at the same time undermining the institutional bases of our own democratic systems that had long been "consolidated."

The tragic events of September 11, 2001, may bring about a reevaluation of the generalized views and policies of the past twenty-five years that have been contributing to weakening our democracies. It may be that a threat to American society and the resulting preparations for a long war were necessary for the reshaping of people's views of the proper role of government. It probably need not have taken a direct attack on the United States to bring home what had long seemed obvious—that "long dead thinkers"[2] were not necessarily wrong in believing that a democratic society required a professional instrument at its disposal in order to preserve its democracy. I ought to note at once that after the initial gratitude shown to the heros of September 11—firemen, police, public officials of all sorts,

---

[1] See Juan J. Linz and Alfred Stepan, eds., *The Breakdown of Democratic Regimes* (Baltimore: Johns Hopkins University Press, 1978).

[2] David Osborne and Ted Gaebler, *Reinventing Government: How the Entrepreneurial Spirit is Transforming the Public Sector* (Reading, Mass.: Addison-Wesley, 1992).

in short, all public servants—the importance accorded public institutions diminished very sharply. Indeed, it was as if the fight against terrorism could not be entrusted to the state's own institutions and servants. President Bush's current plan, as shown in the creation of the Department of Homeland Security, is nothing less than the privatization of the federal government. The 170,000 employees of the newly created department will not receive civil service protection. In addition, more than half of the federal employees (some 850,000) will become employees of private contractors. Democratic societies are based on legitimacy, which itself is largely based on effectiveness. How can governments preserve their legitimacy if they deny themselves the means of being effective?[3] This is the central question that this book addresses.

I

In almost all democratic societies we have witnessed over the past two decades an incontestable phenomenon: relentless attacks on and denigration of the state. The public sector as a whole and the state's chief instrument—the bureaucracy—have borne the brunt of the merciless attacks. This is as true of societies, like the United States, that have always exhibited a profound mistrust of state authority as it is of societies that have historically attributed a sacrosanct status to their state.

The confusion created between the need for democratization, or greater efficiency, and the reduction in the role of the state is not an accident. One of the tasks of this work is to show that the symmetry established between achieving greater efficiency from our public institutions and reducing the role of the state in society is not accidental.

Many of the criticisms of bloated bureaucracies and the waste they engendered were, of course, highly legitimate. They inspired a number of reforms in some countries. If this is what debureaucratization and reforms of the state were all about, the issue would be unexceptional. Indeed, there would be no issue that would cause alarm about the future of the democratic polity. There would only be "technical" choices of how best to achieve greater efficiency.

Why, then, do other political institutions as central to the democratic polity as legislatures, executives, state and local governments, and the judiciary tend to give rise to low-key debates, if they inspire debate at all, while reforming the bureaucracy has tended to define what politicians and political parties stand for? In short, why has the bureaucracy served as the punching bag for so many would-be reformers?

---

[3] The distinction between and connection of "effectiveness" and "legitimacy" was first noted many years ago in Seymour Martin Lipset, *Political Man* (New York: Doubleday, 1961).

These are important questions because in seeking the answers we will come to understand why the goal of bureaucratic efficiency is achieved at considerable costs. It is paradoxical that while the most determined reformers of the state bureaucracy have argued for the importance of the reduction of the costs of bureaucracy, they have neglected to calculate the costs of achieving these efficiencies.

A state's bureaucracy is in reality but the instrument of the legitimately elected government, even if it is not a completely disinterested and selfless institution. The civilian bureaucracy is not unlike the military in that it is a professional institution serving a democratically elected political authority. Just as we hold civilian control of the military to be paramount in a democracy, so we hold that politicians are responsible for the work of the civilian bureaucracy.[4] The military bureaucracy, even while subject to political control, is also a self-interested organization preoccupied with survival, budgetary growth, influence, and autonomy.

Yet, even when the military demonstrates waste or inefficiency, such as losing a war, the consequences are generally limited. No doubt patriotism plays a role in shielding this institution from the wrath that befalls its civilian counterpart. Particularly in recent years, the civilian bureaucracy of democratic societies has not only become the object of virulent attacks; it has also had its very raison d'être questioned.

The attacks on the bureaucracy have largely come from the politicians, those democratically elected representatives who are sent by their constituents to run the political institutions and whose responsibility it is to insure delivery of services in much the same way as they are charged with seeing to it that the country is well defended against external threats. Politicians, however demagogic as they might be, are seeking to maximize their chances of election and reelection and are therefore representing political forces. What are these forces? Who do they represent? What do they represent? One has to distinguish between streamlining an institution and handing it over to the private sector.

The privatization, or outsourcing, of governmental functions is the cornerstone of the New Public Management (NPM), about which much will be said in this study. Yet, as we shall see, the belief is that what is privatized *inevitably* benefits the citizen-customer because his/her tax rate will go down as will the price he/she will pay for the service. Best of all, the service will be delivered more quickly.

This is an article of faith, but faith is not empirical proof. It must, therefore, remain a hypothesis, at best. It will be treated as such in this work.

---

[4] This theory in more explicit in societies that follow a doctrine of or akin to "ministerial responsibility." See Walter J. M. Kickert and Richard J. Stillman, *The Modern State and Its Study: New Administrative Sciences in a Changing Europe and United States* (Cheltenham, U.K.: Edward Elgar, 1999).

We need to remain mindful that the transfer of governmental functions entails costs that may be social, political, and even economic. If these costs outweigh the advantages for the society, why effect this transfer?

The virulent attacks on the state bureaucracy, particularly in the United States but in other advanced industrial societies as well, have helped to undermine politics, political involvement, and citizenship. They have in the process undermined the democratic polity by delegitimizing themselves and their political functions. In difficult times of inflation, deficits, and economic instability, the political authorities in the U.S. and in European societies found themselves severely rebuked by their citizens. To ward off attacks and to deflect criticism of their incapacity to solve society's pressing problems, they turned their wrath on their own state and on the way it was being managed. Much of course needed changing in the way the state managed its resources. But rather than instituting reforms, as generally occurs under similar circumstances in the military bureaucracy, the attacks went beyond the call for reforms.

In adopting a facile, short-term, and self-serving approach of merely deflecting criticism, they helped undermine their long-term authority. Politicians in most countries, but most particularly in the U.S., chose to forget that they were essential parts of the state. In denigrating the state which they were elected to manage, they have essentially undermined their own authority. More than two decades of unrelenting attacks on and reforms of the state have produced no change (except for the worse) in voter turnout, confidence in politicians, and respect for public institutions.[5] No discussion of bureaucratic organization, function, or reform can be divorced from a discussion of democratic governance.[6] This is the central precept that underlies this work, and it explains why this work is more about strengthening democracy than about anything that might resemble a defense of bureaucracy.

II

Whether the field of public administration has been transformed into, or absorbed by, the field of management still remains to be seen. Certainly

---

[5] In fact the number of people who think that most U.S. politicians are crooks or who find democracy wanting in European societies has been lower in the 1990s than in the previous decade. See data in chapter 4. See also Susan J. Pharr, Robert D. Putnam, and Russell J. Dalton, "Introduction: What Is Troubling the Trilateral Democracies?" in *Disaffected Democracies*, ed. Pharr and Putnam (Princeton: Princeton University Press, 2000), 3–30.

[6] Anthony King has observed that the federal government in the United States has done little to create a constituency for itself. See his chapter "Distrust of Government: Explaining American Exceptionalism," in Pharr and Putnam, *Disaffected Democracies*, 74–100. In fact, the government has accomplished the opposite: it has joined—and often led—the antigovernment forces in society.

there has been in recent years a big tug in the latter direction. For the moment, the subject of public administration continues to flounder between being an uncomfortable member of the politics family and staking claims to a territory that is largely independent of the field of politics. Some years ago Terry Moe noted that "for decades, the study of public bureaucracy has been one of the most underdeveloped areas in all political science."[7] He believed that the advances in the field would come from the applications of some of the major insights of the field of economics.

It remains the case today that the study of public bureaucracies is, like political science, pulled in different directions. The issues it confronts are both methodological and substantive in nature. The two should be kept separate, even though the attractiveness of positivistic methodology sometimes imposes questions, and hence answers.[8] The primary issue should always be the "importance" or "pertinence" of questions asked, an issue about which a certain degree of subjectivity will be inevitable.

The relevance of the questions that the field of public administration asks resides in the fact that what is raised and answered depends on where this field situates itself. Management specialists do not ask the same questions as those whose main concern happens to be the distribution of power and influence. By and large, public administration may no longer be a field looking to become a discipline.[9] It appears to have found a niche within the discipline of management. The more it has thrown its lot in with those specializing in the area of management, the less it has been able to analyze reforms and policies as the consequence of the interplay of social and political forces.[10] This has been less the case in European societies, where the field of public administration has maintained its strong link with law.

There have been vast changes in concepts, perceptions, roles, practices, and expectations of public bureaucracies. Some countries have embraced new ideas and have sought to align their public bureaucracies with the practices of the private sector. Others have manifested a willingness to introduce modest reforms in the organization of their bureaucratic structures. Still others have shown either an unwillingness or an incapacity to effect changes in these organizations. Neither globalization nor greater cooperation

[7] Terry M. Moe, "The New Economics of Organization," *American Journal of Political Science* 28, no. 4 (1984): 772.

[8] See Alfred Stepan, *Arguing Comparative Politics* (New York: Oxford University Press, 2001), 1–2.

[9] Dwight C. Waldo, *The Administrative State: A Study of the Political Theory of American Public Administration* (New York: Holmes & Meier, 1984).

[10] For a discussion of the competing and successive concerns of public administration, see Christopher Hood, "Public Administration: Lost and Empire, Not Yet Found a Role?" in *New Developments in Political Science: An International Review of Achievements and Prospects*, ed. Adrian Leftwich (Aldershot, U.K.: Edward Elgar, 1990), 105–7.

through international organizations, regimes, treaties, or the European Union seems to have produced a convergence of conceptions on how best to organize the policy-making instruments of the state.

This is a book as much about good governance as it is about bureaucratic organizations. In fact, the central question that underlies this work is: Is democratic governance hindered without an effective instrument at the hands of the legitimately elected political leadership? Some years ago such a question would likely not have been posed because the answer would have been an obvious "yes." Although lip service continues to be paid to the need for a state to balance "market forces" or to insure security from external threats, the reality is that democratic societies have moved beyond the recognition that a state and the instrument that defines it are an indispensable bulwark for a democratic order.

In almost all contemporary democratic societies we are confronted by the remarkable phenomena of the denigration of the state by political parties (left and right) and of a high-level of mistrust of politicians by citizens. Politicians continually distance themselves from the state and its institutions, all the while being an integral part of it. This may be "rational" behavior in a narrow sense, but it has not increased the respect that citizens feel toward the state or its politicians nor reduced their mistrust of the state institutions.

Contemporary democratic societies have experienced so many extraordinary changes over the last three decades in their economy, institutions, and political practices that taking a second look at what were once thought to be key institutions is scarcely objectionable. A second look does not necessarily involve a different answer to an old question, but the search for an answer is a way of evaluating an institution's contribution to the democratic polity. Such a search is the primary objective of this work.

The bureaucracy is part of an array of institutions—political parties, legislatures, executives, state and local governments, the judiciary—that strengthen or detract from the quality of democracy. The experience of countries that find themselves with incompetent or wholly politicized bureaucracies is one in which a vicious circle is created: democracy needs to be introduced, but it cannot be consolidated without an effective instrument at its disposal and such an institution cannot be created by a nondemocratic regime. No democracy is conceivable without competing political parties, nor is a democratic polity imaginable with a judicial system that administers what Weber called "kadi-justice"[11] or what Kirchheimer referred to as "political justice."[12]

---

[11] Max Weber, *Essays in Economic Sociology*, ed. Richard Swedberg (Princeton: Princeton University Press, 1999), chapter 7.

[12] Otto Kirchheimer, *Political Justice: The Use of Legal Procedures for Political Ends* (Princeton: Princeton University Press, 1965).

Is, then, the construction of a democratic polity possible without the existence of a professional bureaucratic apparatus? Weber has come under incessant attacks in recent years for his views on the organization of bureaucracies. But whether bureaucracies all have or should have particular "ideal-type" characteristics (something he insisted on) may well be debatable and may even have been a view inspired by his social, political, and national context. Modifications may well be in order.

Weber, however, was concerned not just about the organization of hierarchical bureaucracies. This was, if anything, secondary to his main preoccupation, namely, the maintenance of a democratic order, which requires a trained, nonvenal bureaucratic machine.

"Good" governance has several constitutive elements that distinguish it from "bad" democratic, or nondemocratic, forms of governance. One of the crucial elements that contributes to or detracts from responsive, accountable, effective, and legitimate government is the instrument through which all governments exercise their authority—the state bureaucracy.

It is not an accident that modern mass democracy and the development of what came to be recognized as the modern bureaucracy went hand-in-hand. The modern democratic state was built upon the bureaucratic structure that undergirds this state. Political leaders of the emerging democratic states from the early nineteenth century to the late twentieth century recognized that whatever the goals of the state—controlling a vast empire, creating an educational system, guaranteeing democratic procedures, conducting war, establishing the welfare state, collecting taxes—each necessitates a highly organized, basically nonpolitical instrument at its disposal.[13]

III

What, then, is the relationship between bureaucracy and democracy? Is the former necessary for the latter? Does bureaucracy impede a healthy democracy? Is a professional bureaucracy required for *developing* but not for *maintaining* a democratic state? Why, at this point in history, has a reform movement arisen championing the gradual dismantling of the bureaucracy? Finally, what are the consequences for democratic society of the reform movement's implacable advances in pursuit of its goal of undermining the state's governing instrument?

These are the central questions that this study seeks to address. I relate the impact of the evolution of the bureaucratic apparatus to democracy in contemporary democratic societies as well as in societies that are

[13] See Bernard S. Silberman, *Cages of Reason: The Rise of the Rational State in France, Japan, the United States, and Great Britain* (Chicago: University of Chicago Press, 1993).

struggling to develop and consolidate democratic institutions after decades of authoritarian rule. While the study has much to say about what Christopher Hood calls the linguistic shift from "public administration" to "public management,"[14] I believe that the New Public Management does not alone account for the transformations of the role of the bureaucracy in modern democratic societies.

The conclusions I draw about the impact of bureaucratic development on democratic governance and the evolution of democratic practices on the changing role of bureaucracy could only derive from the comparative method that I have adopted. None of the questions raised in this study about bureaucratic reform, about "government reinvention," about professionalization and deprofessionalization of bureaucracies, about the politicization of civil servants, about centralization and decentralization, and about responsiveness and efficiency could have been answered without resorting to comparisons among democratic societies of vastly different traditions and cultures and between democratic and democratizing societies.

I had at one point, because of a growing interest in American society and American political institutions, considered devoting a study exclusively to the evolution of the federal bureaucratic apparatus and to the impact of the NPM on effacing the gap between politics and bureaucracy. It quickly became evident that I would end up with not much more than an interesting case study, which, however fascinating and suggestive it might have been, would nonetheless have resulted in yet another illustration of the proverbial "American exceptionalism."

Comparisons are useful in providing explanations, but they can only be so if they are based on some overall understanding of the underlying basis that calls for the comparison. A theoretical underpinning to the comparison becomes indispensable for comprehending the roles that similar institutions play in democratic societies. Without a theoretical foundation we end up merely with a series of parallel case studies. These are often based on an immense amount of work and are therefore not to be denigrated. But such studies do not have as their objective either posing or answering the crucial questions of what accounts for the minor or the considerable similarities and differences in inputs or outcomes, though they can be used advantageously to such an end.[15]

The comparative method I have adopted is not the standard one generally employed in comparative analysis whereby one or more countries are compared in a consistent manner on a series of dimensions. I have chosen

---

[14] Christopher Hood, *The Art of the State: Culture, Rhetoric, and Public Management* (Oxford: Clarendon Press, 1998), 3 and 19.

[15] See Harry Eckstein, "Case Study and Theory in Political Science," in *Handbook of Political Science*, vol. 7, *Strategies of Inquiry*, ed. Fred I. Greenstein and Nelson W. Polsby (Reading, Mass.: Addison-Wesley, 1975).

instead a thematic approach in this work that allows for the use of comparisons of different countries depending on the theme being analyzed. Thus, for example, I chose to include Spain only in the discussion on bureaucratic politicization because it was important to illustrate how a society with a well-developed civil-service tradition has gradually given way to a politicization of its bureaucracy. I did not judge it important to include Spain in the discussion of state reforms. On the other hand, it seemed advisable to include Britain both in the discussion of bureaucratic reform, because it broke with a longstanding tradition of bureaucratic organization, and in the discussion of bureaucratic politicization, because it appears to be breaking with its attachment to bureaucratic neutrality. This choice of countries is intended merely to be illustrative of transformations in contemporary democratic societies.

I accord these changes considerable importance, and I analyze trends that are proceeding at different rhythms in a variety of national contexts. These trends, because they are driven by a politics of interests and because of their impact on our political institutions, in particular on the capacity of governmental institutions, are to my mind of greater significance in accounting for democratic "disaffection" than the sociocultural explanations put forward by the social capital school.

In addition to the comparative approach I have taken, and to the theoretical precepts that underlie this study, I feel naturally bound to respect historical evolutions and developments. I believe we need to be sensitive to linking historical development to particular contemporary conditions or particular reforms being undertaken in our own times. But a study such as this can only demonstrate awareness of historical developments, since it is not a historical study. Still, the historical evolution is important in understanding the sharp breaks with "tradition," as well as in understanding what Woodrow Wilson called the "strong structural likeness"[16] of governments.

This, then, is a work that tries to combine comparative and, to some extent, historical analysis with theoretical and empirical analysis. It proceeds with one objective in mind: to understand the ways in which the evolution of the bureaucratic apparatus is likely to enhance or undermine the democratic order. If we wish to preserve our democratic way of life, it will not harm us to be aware of the different parts of the institutional mosaic that make up our democracy.

One final word about the method that I have adopted in this book. I believe that the bureaucracy's role in society cannot be determined solely by bureaucratic reforms of one kind or another. The bureaucracy is affected by mores in the society as much as by cultural or sociological changes in

---

[16] Woodrow Wilson, "The Study of Administration," *Political Science Quarterly* 20, no. 2 (1887): 218.

society. If our culture more and more sees the individual as a mere consumer and undermines citizenship, the bureaucracy will be ill-equipped to step in and provide the society with a sense of itself as a collectivity. Hence, the reader should not be surprised to find linkages established between sociocultural developments and the bureaucratic function.

Second, the bureaucracy is never unaffected by politics. If politics is about conflicts and compromises relating to the distribution of power, then laws, reforms, and proposals for change in the way our institutions function need to be seen in specifically political terms. There are those who will gain and those who will be disadvantaged as a result of institutional reforms just as there are gainers and losers as a result of changes in the capital-gains tax or farm subsidies.

Politics, then, is at the center of our analysis of bureaucratic reform. To be sure, all proposals for reforming the bureaucracy are presented as being essentially apolitical and of benefit to the "general interest" (a term that is scarcely ever used in American politics today). Some reform proposals may well be of benefit to the society as a whole. Some, and often the more important ones, have little to do with the bureaucracy itself and everything to do with the distribution of resources.

For those of us with some knowledge (firsthand and/or historical) of nondemocratic orders, the fragility of the democratic order is always an issue. Even if our democracies today have little chance of collapsing because of war, military coups, or the charisma of some marginal kook, there are many ways in which they are ever-evolving. We need constantly to ask whether the changes go in the direction of strengthening or undermining the democratic order.

PART I

CHAPTER ONE

THE END OF BUREAUCRACY?

"Sociologically speaking, the modern state is an 'enterprise'
(*Betrieb*) just like a factory."
—Max Weber, *Essays in Economic Sociology*

W HAT HAS occasioned the contemporary view that the modern
bureaucracy is an outdated institution whose organizational
characteristics and whose role in society need to be overhauled?
We will have a number of occasions in the course of this work to examine
the arguments that have been advanced against public bureaucracies and
that view these institutions as obstacles to, or, worse, enemies of, democracy. That this has not always been the most widely accepted view is often
forgotten. Before I return in the next chapter to look closely at what it is
that is being overturned or revolutionized, a brief explanation of the central themes of this work is in order.

I deal in this book exclusively with the instruments of statecraft and with
the relationship of these instruments to democracy. The role of the bureaucracy in modern democratic societies has inspired a considerable literature, much of which in recent years has been of a critical nature. Yet, it is
not insignificant for our later analysis of bureaucratic reforms to observe at
this early stage that criticism of the bureaucracy has a national coloring. In
Great Britain, the bureaucracy has been seen as stifling to the entrepreneurial spirit. In Italy, it has been seen as exemplifying, or at least sanc-
tioning, corruption. In France, it has been seen as sclerotic and tentacular.
In the United States it has been seen as robbing initiative from citizens.

Much of the disaffection with democratic institutions has seemed to converge on the politicians, who have then successfully managed to transfer the
society's dissatisfactions onto the bureaucracy and have tended to offer a
sweeping condemnation of the entire bureaucratic institution. Bureaucracy, it
came to be argued, was unproductive, parasitic, wasteful, secretive, unaccountable, unresponsive, elitist, and fundamentally antithetical to democracy.

A less condemnatory, albeit defensive, argument maintains that the bureaucracy is merely an organization that needs a good dose of managerial
tinkering, or overhaul, in order to render it more useful. Once it proves
that it can function according to the rules of the public management revolution, what Hood refers to as "a millennial transformation to a new

style" of management,[1] then it can assume its role among the respected (or at least accepted) institutions of democracy.

Two transformations in the society and politics of contemporary democracies have been operating more or less separately but more or less simultaneously, and they risk changing the bureaucratic instrument beyond anything that Weber might recognize as the indispensable complement to the modern state. Both these transformations, as well as their causes, are analyzed in the chapters that follow. They concern the bureaucracy and its relationship to the market, and the deprofessionalization of the bureaucratic institution. They constitute separate but reinforcing trends and they form the raison d'être of the entire discussion that follows. This chapter introduces the twin themes of this book.

Bureaucracy and the Market

If only government or the state followed the private sector and learned the lessons of competition and customer satisfaction, we would restore trust in government and save a lot of money. This is a view that underlies the "reinvention of government" movement and that is shared by those who oppose all forms of government intervention in the United States and, to a lesser extent, in Britain. Yet, seeking to bring the public sector more in line with the private sector is neither so novel an idea nor so un-Weberian, since Weber referred to the modern state as being akin to an enterprise.[2]

In fact, Weber also administered the stinging critique of bureaucracy, and nowhere more strongly than when he compared this organization and the officials who run it with their counterparts in the private sector. He referred to the "inherent limitations of bureaucracy proper."[3] He observed that "it can easily be seen that its effectiveness has definite limitations in the public and governmental realm as well as in the private economy. The 'darting mind,' 'the moving spirit'—that of the entrepreneur here and the politician there—differs in substance from the civil service mentality of the official."[4]

Bentham, long before Weber and the contemporary disenchantment with the bureaucracy, pointed to the same inferiority of bureaucracy in comparison with private-sector organization and motivation. He wrote of

---

[1] Christopher Hood, *The Art of the State: Culture, Rhetoric, and Public Management* (Oxford: Clarendon Press, 1998), 4.

[2] Max Weber, *Essays in Economic Sociology*, 110.

[3] Ibid., 114.

[4] Ibid.

"the comparative want of personal interest, that indispensable whetstone to ingenuity and spur to interest."[5]

Yet, the innocuous-sounding criteria of performance, responsiveness, and evaluation are not without their political implications. This is because all decisions affecting the creation, abolition, and budgets of bureaucratic agencies involve choices that in one way or another distribute or redistribute resources, shift or impose burdens on one segment (or class) of society. To seek to dispossess the state of any capacity to make these choices is, in effect, to substitute the voice of a group or a class for the legitimately elected government. All this is intended to be accomplished in the name of efficiency.

We shall see why some European societies, plagued as they are by a heavy burden of taxation and by considerable bureaucratic inefficiencies, have preferred to advance more cautiously where reforming the state apparatus is concerned. In part this is because there is considerable vested interest in the status quo and in part because the social democratic states seek to insure that a capitalistic order enriches but does not destroy the public space. European societies generally refer to "state modernization" rather than to government reinvention. There is a world of difference between the two: the first refers to reducing waste, changing the attitudes of civil servants toward the citizen, doing away with secrecy and excessive bureaucratic procedures, and reducing the number of public employees and ameliorating their productivity. In the United States, reinvention means increasing competition among public agencies, creating a profit-seeking environment, and applying the entrepreneurship of the private sector to the public sector. It may also mean abolishing most of the public agencies. Are we then likely to end up with what Rhodes has called "governing without government?"[6]

The hollowing of the state may have many causes and even more imagined consequences. Among the causes are the clear political choices of having governments do less and the increasing politicization of bureaucracies. As Paul Light has noted of the U.S. federal government: "If current trends continue, the federal hierarchy may eventually resemble a circle, with very few employees at the bottom, hordes of managers, supervisors and technical analysts of one kind or another at the middle, and a vast coterie of political and career executives at the top. The rest of the traditional bureaucratic pyramid will still exist, of course, not filled by federal employees, but by those who work for the increasing number of contractors,

---

[5] Cited in L. J. Hume, *Bentham and Bureaucracy* (New York: Cambridge University Press, 1981), 136.

[6] R. Rhodes, "The New Governance: Governing without Government," *Political Studies* 44 (1996): 652–67.

nonprofits, and state and local agencies that deliver services once provided above."[7]

Among the gains that ostensibly result from the hollowing of the state is a state built on, and functioning according to, corporate principles. These principles have as their aim the protection of the market and those who produce and sell in it rather than the welfare of society as a whole. As Daniel Cohen observes: "The result has been a new elite consensus on the role of the state in society. A substantial public sector is to be maintained, but its purposes and operating values are considerably different from that which was characteristic of the Keynesian welfare. The goal is no longer to protect society from the market's demands but to protect the market from society's demands."[8]

We shall return later to the issue of political intent and societal consequences of the merging of corporate and bureaucratic culture. For the moment, it suffices to note that the introduction of new conceptions of bureaucratic organization derive from and, in turn, influence market forces. But such conceptions affect not only the internal structures of state bureaucracies but also the raison d'être, that is, what it is that bureaucracies are supposed to accomplish for the polity and for the society. Reviewing the main ideas behind reforms adopted in a number of countries, Kettl observes that "the driving idea behind this broad array of reforms has been 'managerialism': the approach that traditional bureaucratic hierarchy had become unresponsive; reformers sought to replace authority and rigidity with flexibility; the traditional preoccupation with structure with improvements to process; and the comfortable stability of government agencies and budgets with market-style competition."[9]

But changing methods of organization, as well as goals, "from demand-driven government . . . to results-driven government"[10] inevitably alters policies. And since policies are outcomes of a political process, it follows that "reinventing" the bureaucracy is a political process with political consequences. This is the first of two major themes treated in this book. The second concerns the unmistakable trend toward the deprofessionalization of the bureaucracy.

[7] Paul C. Light, *Thickening Government* (Washington, D.C.: Brookings Institution, 1995), 15. See also Rhodes, "The New Governance," and his "The Hollowing Out of the State," *Political Quarterly* 65, pp. 138–51, on the phenomenon of "hollowing" that leads to the minimal state.

[8] Daniel Cohen, "Creating Crises and Avoiding Blame: The Politics of Public Service Reform and the New Public Management in Great Britain and the United States," *Administration and Society* 29, no. 5 (November 1997): 586.

[9] Donald F. Kettl, "The Global Revolution in Public Management: Driving Themes, Missing Links," *Journal of Policy Analysis and Management* 16, no. 3 (1997): 447.

[10] Ibid., 449.

Deprofessionalization and Politicization

The transformation of public bureaucracies in democratic societies has not been taking place simply as a result of reforms willed by governments under pressure from citizens who insist on better performance. Indeed, one of the most extensive transformations that has affected all public bureaucracies has been the gradual deprofessionalization of their upper echelons.

I am not nostalgic for some bygone age of thoroughly competent, professional, and neutral public servants. Politics certainly intruded into the civil service, perhaps more openly in the American federal bureaucracy than in the European countries, and the civil service certainly did not always stay out of politics as much as doctrine and myth would have us believe. It remains nonetheless the case that the professional civil servant has been one of the main victims of the changing politics of the twentieth century.

It is a curious fact that in most sectors of society professionalization has attained a level not easily envisaged only a few decades ago. The private sector hires according to a set of specific competences. The professions have created a set of sub-professions, each with a narrower degree of specialization. Yet, what is true of the recruitment criteria in most sectors of society is less and less the case with the upper echelons of public service. Indeed, one might almost be able to conclude that there has been a sort of regression in the civil service. Political affiliation has once again become a determining criterion in appointments to top-level positions.

We shall see in part III that the general politicization of the higher civil service is not a phenomenon, as is often believed, confined to the United States, where the tradition of patronage and the drive to circumvent the laws and create "administrative" presidencies has always been powerful. We find that even in European societies with strong traditions of administrative professionalism—Germany, France, Spain, Britain—the encroachment of politics into the administrative domain has been considerable. The reinvention of government, or the introduction of a corporate culture into public administration, needs to be analyzed in conjunction with other transformative forces, some of which have no link to managerial techniques. This is the case with the phenomenon of what I have chosen to call deprofessionalization.

The tendency of democratic governments to ascribe far less importance to criteria of competence and far more to political loyalty may be understandable. What has changed has been the tendency of contemporary governments not only to resist the temptation of politicizing the bureaucracy but, on the contrary, to speed up the process. More and more governments have found only advantages in politicizing the bureaucracy, which is viewed as the instrument of the governments *of the day* rather than of governments or of the *state*.

Governments consider that the immense advantages of a loyal or pliable bureaucratic instrument far outweigh the disadvantages of a political bureaucracy. When every newly elected government thinks likewise, it follows that changes in government lead to ever greater changes in administrative personnel. Indeed, there has developed in recent years (as we will see in part III) a respectable set of intellectual arguments to support the ever-greater politicization of administrative agencies. While no bureaucracy was ever totally neutral, the premise of nonpoliticization was generally believed to be beneficial, if not indispensable, for society. At any rate, until recently few were prepared to make the argument that outright politicization carries positive consequences. Even in the United States, politicization until recently was associated with the Jacksonian and machine-politics eras and not with contemporary notions of meritocratic democracy.

Are the reforms associated with the New Public Management and the changes emanating from and involving deprofessionalization complementary or do they conflict with one another?

This book essentially argues that democratic societies have been following a path that leads to undermining, or even to destroying, one of the central institutions on which a democratic polity depends. The older democracies, which were able to develop both economically and politically, did so by developing a professional instrument of governance. Yet, today these same democracies appear to ignore their own historical experiences and encourage newly created democracies to follow a different path. For one thing, they have restricted the definition of democracy to simply include competitive elections and a certain number of freedoms, ignoring that a state's legitimacy is equally important, and that this legitimacy is very largely dependent upon how efficient and responsive a state is. Second, the message that the older democracies have sent stresses the importance of economic development and touts the market as the sole guide in the allocation of resources. In none of the postcommunist states of central Europe was the development of a state apparatus accorded the priority that it received in the comparable phase of political development in Britain, France, Germany, and even the United States. In the second decade of the transition to democracy the countries of central Europe—in particular Poland, Hungary, and the Czech Republic—have, as we will see in chapter 11, begun to recognize that democratic development and legitimate government require the assistance of a professional state apparatus.

In the analysis of political institutions considered critical to the functioning of a democracy, there is little disagreement on the basic functions of such key institutions as courts, legislatures, executives, and political parties. We know that these institutions function in different ways, possess varying degrees of influence and authority, and evolve according to different national rhythms. But there is at least universal agreement on the importance of their existence and on the minimal functions they need to perform in a democracy.

The bureaucracy, as the instrument of a state and of governments, is no longer accorded the importance it once possessed in democratic governance. Indeed, it is now considered a practically dispensable institution. We know why the political institutions exist. We judge them indispensable to democracy. We compare how they function across societies. We do all this in a rigorous manner that befits the importance we attribute to them.

Yet the study of public administration has, to a large extent unwittingly, seconded the political attacks on the bureaucratic apparatus. It remains uncertain as to how it ought to view this apparatus. Should it be viewed as a mere organization in need of greater efficiency, whether through the introduction of more rationalized procedures or through the contracting out of its functions? Or should it be analyzed as the instrument of the duly elected legislative and executive authorities? The second view accords the institution an indispensability that the first does not. If we acknowledge that the bureaucracy is an indispensable arm of the state, it then becomes legitimate to insist on its efficient operation.

No political institution has undergone the kind of virulent (and sometimes justifiable) attacks as the bureaucracy. It alone has been so undermined that its contribution to a democratic polity risks being undermined. I shall return in the following chapters to offer an explanation of this state of affairs.

For the moment, it is necessary to recognize (or concede) that it has been a long time since Weber set down the essential requirements of bureaucratic organizations. Democratic societies have evolved considerably, and even the practice of democracy is altogether different from what it was in Weber's days.

Has the Weberian model been rendered completely obsolete by the transformation of democratic societies? There are many arguments in support of this view. I am not unaware that Weber's analysis of bureaucracy has always had its critics. Some saw in his model a rigid, Prussian-inspired influence that had but a tangential relationship to reality.[11] Such a model, it was argued, bears little relationship to democratic societies where the citizen participation has increased, where the hand of the state is less heavy, where decentralization is the preferred mode of state organization,

---

[11] See Alfred Diamant, "The Bureaucratic Model: Max Weber Rejected, Rediscovered, Reformed," in *Papers in Comparative Public Administration*, ed. Ferrel Heady and S. Stokes (Ann Arbor: Institute of Public Administration, 1962), 59–96.

and where professional standards for the recruitment of public servants has tended more and more to give way to politically inspired forms of recruitment.

All these societal changes impinge on our political institutions, and they have clearly impinged on the Weberian model of state organization. Our interest in them derives from the ways in which state bureaucracies in different societies adapt themselves to new methods of organization, recruit their personnel, and relate to elected officials. Undermining the bureaucracy, whether through the transference of its functions to private bodies or through the simple abolition of agencies or through the reintroduction of a quasi-patronage system, is not an issue merely of "administrative rationalization," or "administrative efficiency." If it affects the capacity of the state to produce or to implement public policies and to deliver the services in an effective and relatively just manner, then issues of bureaucracy inevitably become issues of democracy.

CHAPTER TWO

BEYOND WEBER?

"No politician ever lost votes by denouncing bureaucracy."
—James Q. Wilson, *Bureaucracy*

POLITICIANS HAVE long seen only gains and no losses from express-
ing and encouraging what has become a nearly universal loathing of
bureaucracy. It is not clear whether this detestation reflects merely
a demonic image of bureaucratic institutions, whether it reflects a clear
understanding of what function these institutions fulfill in our societies,
or whether it merely reflects opportunistic and demagogic tendencies of
politicians.

There are scarcely any institutions left in contemporary democratic societies that elicit the general approval or respect of citizens. We now appear
condemned to live in a "popular culture of bad government." All political
institutions are considered to have weaknesses, and all are viewed with varying degrees of scorn. Yet, it is rare that proposals for overhauling or transforming political institutions, much less for "reinventing" them, are put
forward. The bureaucracy is the exception. Perhaps nowhere more so than
in the United States does one find such sacrosanct treatment of political
institutions—particularly when it comes to Congress, the political parties,
the electoral laws, the executive, the judiciary—along with such a general
willingness to reform, "reinvent," or "banish" the bureaucracy.

Despite the incessant critiques of the bureaucracy, its general lack of support in the society, and its vulnerability to external pressures, it nonetheless
remains a key institution in the functioning of democratic societies. Wilson,
no opponent of bureaucratic reform, thus concludes his classic work on
bureaucracy: "[W]e live in a country that despite its array of baffling rules
and regulations and the insatiable desire of some people to use government
to rationalize society still makes it possible to get drinkable water instantly,
put through a telephone call in seconds, deliver a letter in a day, and obtain a passport in a week. Our social security checks arrive on time. Some
state prisons, and most of the federal ones, are reasonably decent and hu-
mane institutions. . . . There are not many places where all this happens. It
is astonishing that this can be made to happen at all."[1] Doing all these

---

[1] James Q. Wilson, *Bureaucracy: What Government Agencies Do and Why They Do It* (New York:
Basic Books, 1989), 378.

mundane things makes government effective, if not efficient, and reinforces its legitimacy. We know what societies look like and how they fail to function when all these chores can't be carried out, or can only be carried out in a perfunctory way. What, then, ails the bureaucracy in democratic societies? Why has there occurred a need to speak of "reinventions" and "revolutions"? Is the bureaucracy a justified target for the outpouring of critiques and for the proposals of transformation that have taken place in most democratic societies?

Whatever politics may be about, it is certain that it involves rules and ruling, and there is more of both today than in previous centuries.[2] Governing entails not just making rules but applying them. Hence the need for states to possess instruments of governing. How these instruments should be used, how they should function, whom they should be loyal and responsive to— these are all questions that remain open to debate. But the bureaucracy has had an intimate link with both capitalism and democracy. This is no longer accepted as a self-evident postulate. Hence the widespread belief, which has given rise to the reform and reinvention movement, that capitalism and democracy are no longer dependent on the role that the bureaucratic apparatus has come to assume. Indeed, the conventional wisdom today adopts a diametrically opposite postulate: capitalism and democracy are prevented from finding their full expression by the existence of bureaucracy.[3]

This view is one that needs to be taken seriously. But, unlike the believers in and champions of reinvention, I take it as a hypothesis, not as an incontestable truth. Hence, I seek to distinguish between ideology and analysis. But it is difficult to escape the fact that an analysis depends to a very great extent on our view of how our society can and ought to be organized. Nonetheless, I believe that there is a logical difference between ideologically driven conclusions and conclusions that are based on analyses that have at least examined alternative arguments and beliefs.

The Dominance of the State

Why has the bureaucracy been important in the development of the modern state? The classic explanation is provided by Max Weber:

> In a modern state the actual ruler is necessarily and unavoidably the bureaucracy,
> since power is exercised neither through parliamentary speeches nor monarchical

---

[2] See the illuminating discussion of what politics entails and why it exists in John Dunn, *The Cunning of Unreason: Making Sense of Politics* (London: Harper Collins, 2000), 30–56. See also Max Weber's classic essay "Politics as a Vocation," in *From Max Weber: Essays in Sociology*, ed. H. H. Gerth and C. Wright Mills (New York: Oxford University Press, 1962).

[3] See Fred W. Riggs, "Why Has Bureaucracy Not Smothered Democracy in the United States?" in *Comparative Public Management: Putting U.S. Public Policy and Implementation in Context*, ed. Randall Baker (Westport, Conn.: Praeger, 1994), 37–51.

enunciations but through routines of administration. . . . Just as the so-called progress toward capitalism has been the unequivocal criterion for the modernization of the economy since medieval times, so the progress toward bureaucratic officialdom—characterized by formal employment, salary, pension, promotion, specialized training and functional division of labor, well-defined areas of jurisdiction, documentary procedures, hierarchical sub- and superordination—has been the unambiguous yardstick for the modernization of the state, whether monarchic or democratic.[4]

We know a great deal about the origins and development of the modern state. Despite the proliferation of various international organizations ("regimes," as they are sometimes called), of embryonic regional alliances, and even of supranational power centers, little has transpired to diminish the role of the state as the predominant actor in national and world affairs. Despite the impact of globalization, of the permeability of borders, or of the abandonment of many restrictions on the flows of capital, trade, and labor and the consequent compromises of sovereignty that this has entailed for individual nation-states, the nation-state remains the dominant form of societal organization.[5]

Social scientists in the United States debated over many years the "taking out" or the "bringing back in" of the state. This remained a provincial (American) debate and had no repercussions in Europe, where it was always a given that the state was an actor in its own right.[6] Despite, or indeed because of, the phenomenon of globalization, citizens more than ever look to the state to insure their security, the passage or repeal of laws, the administration of justice, the delivery of services, and protection against external threats. That globalization and interdependence have diminished a state's capacity to remain unaffected by actions and events occurring beyond its borders is beyond dispute. But citizens continue to vote for *their* parties and politicians hold *their* state responsible for resolving problems.

States may differ in philosophy and in the ways they exercise their power, in the policies they choose to adopt to deal with the problems that also confront their neighbors, in how to respond to domestic claims and internationally imposed constraints. But citizens for the most part live under a form of organization whose essential feature we refer to as the state.

[4] Weber, *Essays in Economic Sociology.*

[5] See, among others, Robert J. Holton, *Globalization and the Nation-State* (New York: St. Martin's Press, 1998).

[6] See Brian Barry, Archie Brown, and Jack Hayward, eds., *The British Study of Politics in the Twentieth Century* (Oxford: Oxford University Press, 1999); and Walter J. M. Kickert and Richard J. Stillman, *The Modern State and Its Study: New Administrative Sciences in a Changing Europe and United States* (Cheltenham, U.K.: Edward Elgar, 1999).

Even if states are "imagined communities,"[7] they rely on a panoply of instruments for the governing of these communities.

A state, as Weber observed, is not defined by its ends, since it can dedicate itself to any number of objectives, including morally reprehensible ones. It can only be defined by its means, means that no other organization can possess. Hence, the essential requirement for the existence of the state, he argued, is the possession of the exclusive means of force. A state that loses its monopoly over the means of violence compromises its authority over the territory it administers and hence ceases to be a state. Its form of organization becomes indistinguishable from other types of organization.

Weber was merely seeking to understand the distinguishing characteristic of states. He recognized that states could have different objectives, could be organized more or less democratically, and could be more or less legitimate in the eyes of their citizens. States have indeed sometimes catastrophically failed "to improve the human condition."[8] They have held their citizens hostage, exploited them, and acted with unspeakable brutality. But others have defended and served their citizens against arbitrary or lawless states.

Let us, then, stay with Weber's minimal definition, which views a state as merely the means to ends. To achieve certain ends, states need to avail themselves of an instrument. The issue is therefore not so much what states as abstractions do, how strong or weak they are, or how separate from or intertwined with society they are. It is, rather, the kinds of instruments they dispose of in order to achieve whatever goals they establish for themselves. Those instruments are indispensable, even if they are what Scott calls "the unremarkable tools of modern statecraft."[9]

Bureaucracy and the Market

Because the connotations of bureaucracy in the popular mind are negative, it is nearly impossible to tie bureaucracy to the survival of democracy. But, as we shall see in the course of this work, since bureaucracy is the instrument by which a democracy can strengthen or weaken its legitimacy, its absence or inefficiency or politicization can have extraordinary effects on the governance of society.

Is the traditional instrument of the state indispensable to the functioning of a democratic order? Is this an outdated idea? The ingenuity of the modern world would seem to make everything replaceable and nothing

[7] Benedict Anderson, *Imagined Communities: Reflections on the Origins and Spread of Nationalism* (London: Verso, 1983).

[8] James C. Scott, *Seeing Like a State: How Certain Schemes to Improve the Human Condition Have Failed* (New Haven: Yale University Press, 1998), 4.

[9] Ibid.

indispensable. Can we reinvent government so that its traditional form of organization becomes more or less obsolete? Do we now possess, thanks to political and scientific progress, new ways of thinking about the state, how it ought to be organized, what its functions ought to be, the degree of responsibility it ought to have toward society? Have citizens' expectations of their government and of their state evolved to a point where we need to reconsider how the state itself should be organized?

The view has been gaining momentum for at least the past two decades that the weakness followed by the collapse of communism has proven the triumph and the inseparability of democracy and capitalism. Urging further participation and extending the reach of capitalism in democratic states was merely a logical consequence of the collapse of communist authoritarianism. There is now a widespread belief, openly avowed in certain societies, that the state should forever be protected from the capitalist engine that has served society so well. The market economy, as we shall see, is believed to be the road to freedom and democracy, since as a matter of empirical fact all democracies lack a *dirigiste* state. But the market economy, it is argued, also renders the state's instruments of control, as well as the services rendered, superfluous. Thus, according to this new doctrine, the freedom of the marketplace affects—or should affect—not only the organization of economic enterprises but also, and in a similar fashion, the organization of all state organizations.

This is advanced as a self-evident assertion rather than as a hypothesis because the imposition of market ideology on state organizations derives from normative implications. How widespread this view is can be seen from the opinions of those who might be regarded as being on the "left" of the American political spectrum, who speak of "the performance deficit in government":

> When America's private sector began to change—to be more customer-friendly and responsive and better able to tailor responses to you—the government didn't change. So if you fast-forward 30 years, and certainly by the end of the eighties, you have a very responsive, adaptive private sector that is always anxious to meet you half-way, and to fulfill your needs for the right price. But the public sector is still pretty much on the one-size-fits-all model: do things on our own schedule, on paper, between nine and five. The disjuncture between what people see in the private sector and in the public sector has contributed to the growing distrust in government.[10]

Several issues raised by the claims for a need for a major transformation of public bureaucracies need to be disentangled. First, what are the traditional

---

[10] Elaine Kamarck, "Democracy's Prospects: A Harvard Magazine Roundtable," *Harvard Magazine* (July–August 1999): 50.

goals ascribed to public bureaucracies? Second, are these goals considered outdated today? Third, does the claim for a reinvention of government aim to transform the objectives of public bureaucracies or the means by which they carry out their objectives? Finally, what is the impact of the American claim to be spearheading the administrative reforms of other societies? I turn to the first question in this chapter. An attempt to answer the second question is the task of the next chapter, while the third and the fourth are dealt with in parts II and II.

Bureaucracy and Capitalism

The search for the foundations of democracy has come up with a variety of definitions and prerequisites. Predisposition, or culture, lost its luster some years ago but has reappeared under different guises, to be sure. Process or procedures have been seen to be critical for any form of democratic organization.[11] Trust or civicness (or civility), a proto-Tocquevillian theme, has recently assumed a considerable importance in a wide array of explanations.[12] Among the wide variety of premises that include a market economy, security (economic and physical), competitive elections, and a strong civil society, two particularly stand out: the rule of law and an operating (efficient or responsive) state.

Douglas North has distinguished between institutions and organizations. The former refer to the rules that "define the way the game is played." The latter refer to political, social, or educational bodies that constitute "groups of individuals bound by some common purpose to achieve objectives."[13] The rules determine the kinds of organizations that emerge and the role they eventually play.

The institution of democracy is dependent on rules and norms that need the state's organizations to insure their orderly implementation. Without the instrument at its disposal, the state cannot insure the rule of law.

Is the need that confronts a consolidated democracy similar to the one that confronts a society in transition to democracy? Clearly not. For the established democracy the institution of a public bureaucracy sometimes evolves in a manner that seriously diminishes its role, forces it to lose legitimacy, or undermines its professionalism by excessive politicization.

---

[11] See Amy Gutmann and Dennis Thompson, *Democracy and Disagreement* (Cambridge: Harvard University Press, 1996).

[12] Robert D. Putnam, *Making Democracy Work: Civic Traditions in Modern Italy* (Princeton: Princeton University Press, 1993).

[13] Douglas C. North, *Institutions, Institutional Change and Economic Performance* (New York: Cambridge University Press, 1990), 4–5.

For the fledgling democracy, the issue is one of creation: how to develop in the transitional phase a professional bureaucratic instrument.

Why the need for a professional apparatus? Simply because that is what distinguishes, according to Weber, a patrimonial from a rational-legal order. What Weber refers to as the "monocratic"[14] variety of bureaucracy is a development that both accompanies and undergirds a capitalistic and a democratic order. The development of bureaucracy "largely under capitalistic auspices, has created an urgent need for stable, strict, intensive, and calculable administration."[15]

Capitalism, for Weber, requires the reduction of uncertainty and the greater capacity to plan and predict on the basis of technical knowledge. That is why the development of a capitalistic order tends to go hand-in-hand with the extension of bureaucratic organizations. "On the one hand," writes Weber, "capitalism in its modern stages of development strongly tends to foster the development of bureaucracy, though both capitalism and bureaucracy have arisen from many different historical sources. Conversely, capitalism is the most rational economic basis for bureaucratic administration and enables it to develop in the most rational form, especially because, from a fiscal point of view, it supplies the necessary money resources."[16]

"Bureaucracy is superior in knowledge," observes Weber, and this explains why, with the exception of the capitalistic entrepreneur, most of the population has "tended to be organized in large-scale corporate groups which are inevitably subject to bureaucratic control."[17] Bernard Silberman attempts to understand why bureaucracies have taken on different forms and do not take on a strictly "Weberian" form. He sees more differences than similarities in the development of state bureaucracies. He maintains that "all bureaucratic roles and organizational structures did not end up alike," and he wants to understand "why a seemingly universal process results in such different forms."[18] Bureaucratic forms did not develop in response to the development of capitalism, argues Silberman. But that bureaucratic organizations did develop, even if in different forms, to temper the uncertainty of capitalism is self-evident. Weber has been chastised, by Silberman among others, for drawing up a "laundry-list"[19] of characteristics common to all legal-rational societies, when in fact there were different

[14] Max Weber, *The Theory of Social and Economic Organization* (New York: Free Press, 1964), 337.

[15] Ibid., 338.

[16] Ibid., 338–39.

[17] Ibid., 339.

[18] Bernard S. Silberman, *Cages of Reason: The Rise of the Rational State in France, Japan, the United States, and Great Britain* (Chicago: University of Chicago Press, 1993), 6.

[19] Ibid.

organizational outcomes. Silberman seeks to account for the different outcomes. Yet, he perhaps takes too literally the expectation of organizational convergence, and he does not place sufficient weight on the observable need for state organizations to fulfill functions germane to a capitalistic-democratic society. The questions Silberman raises and seeks to answer in his unique and perceptive study are valid on their own and in no way dependent on Weber's "laundry list."

Weber's "laundry list" has all too often been taken as representing an indispensable totality, or prescription, for the organization of the modern state. Hence, the absence of any one requirement on the list in a particular context is taken as a discovery that Weber's framework was wrong.[20] But a closer reading of Weber would have made clear to those who have taken issue with him that his intention was not to establish an "iron law" of bureaucratic organization.

Those who today question Weber's entire model are, paradoxically, on stronger ground than the earlier critics who merely sought to "disprove" the Weberian framework, or to "prove" that it was possible to have a running bureaucracy without the presence of all of Weber's requirements. The modern management critics of Weber are seeking to replace the foundations of the Weberian edifice rather than to modify it or adopt it to a new age.

The new school of critics wants to "banish" bureaucracy. For a starter, the defenders of the New Public Management school do not believe in the efficacy of monopolies, whether public or private. Nor do they believe in centralization, rigid hierarchies, well-defined rulers, impersonal treatment, and recruitment on the basis of objective criteria such as examinations. In short, Weber's critiques do not fault the laundry list. In fact they believe that it worked well in its time. They believe, rather, that a system "designed by a genius to be run by idiots"[21] is no longer relevant to the "modern age."[22] Imposing strict controls in an organization, regarding employees as "cogs" in a machine, and expecting workers to follow instructions blindly—these are what the NPM devotees are fighting against. As Osborne and Plastrik note: "This model served us well in its day. As long as the tasks were relatively simple and straight forward and the environment stable, it worked. But for the last 20 years it has been coming apart. In a world of rapid change, technological revolution, global economic competition demassified

---

[20] See Wolfgang J. Mommsen, *The Age of Bureaucracy: Perspectives in the Political Sociology of Max Weber* (Oxford: Blackwell, 1974); Peter Hamilton, ed., *Max Weber: Critical Assessments* (London: Routledge, 1991); and Anthony Giddens, *Politics and Sociology in the Thought of Max Weber* (London: Macmillan, 1972).

[21] David Osborne and Peter Plastrick, *Banishing Bureaucracy: The Five Strategies for Reinventing Government* (New York: Addison-Wesley, 1992), 17.

[22] This is a phrase used to justify almost anything, so what it is used for needs to be looked at closely.

markets, an educated work force, demanding customers, and severe fiscal constraints, centralized, top-down monopolies are simply too slow, too unresponsive, and too incapable of change or innovation."[23]

This is a more coherent, or convincing, attack of the Weberian bureaucracy, though it presents two problems that we shall have to deal with. First, it ignores the issues of collective interest and of the role of public power in contemporary society: the important normative issues of the public sphere, of a state's responsibilities to society, and of the relationship between state organizations and democracy. Second, this attack on the organization of public bureaucracy is justified by reference to its own laundry list of factors that may not necessarily prove that bureaucracy has had its day. They may point to the possibility that modern bureaucracies are in need of both modification and strengthening. Indeed, items on this list, impressive as they may sound, might actually be used to prove the contrary. Assertion of randomly selected societal changes is not proof enough for an institution's transformation.

In addition to the inapplicability of all of the Weberian requirements and to the irrelevance of the bureaucratic model for contemporary capitalism, a third school has arisen that views bureaucracy as inherently in conflict with democracy. In fact, the public-choice school maintains that bureaucracy and society have diametrically opposed interests. The "bureaucrat" and the "bureaus" are seen as making "choices," which they seek to "maximize" in exactly the same way that any actor seeks to do. As Niskanen observes, we do not know how to think clearly about bureaucracy because we do not have a "theory of bureaus that is consistent with an instrumental concept of the state, that is, a concept of a state which is only an instrument of the preferences of its constituents."[24] He maintains that the impediment to deriving a theory of bureaus comes from the fact that "the literature on bureaucracy, from Confucius to Weber, proceeds from an organic concept of the state, that is, a concept of a state for which the preferences of individuals are subordinate to certain organic goals of the state."[25]

The economic theory of bureaucracy takes the Weberian model to task for neglecting "the economic behavior of bureaus as it affects their performance in supplying public services."[26] Weber's concern is with the behavior within and the relationships among bureaus. For Niskanen, "any theory of the behavior of bureaus that does not incorporate the personal preferences of bureaucrats . . . will be relevant only in the most rigidly authoritarian environments. In a fundamental sense, our contemporary

[23] Osborne and Plastrick, *Banishing Bureaucracy*, 17.

[24] William A. Niskanen, Jr., *Bureaucracy and Representative Government* (Chicago: Aldine-Atherton, 1971), 4.

[25] Ibid.

[26] Ibid., 6.

confusion derives from a failure to bring bureaucracy to terms with representative government and free labor markets."[27]

The merit of the economic approach on which much of the reinvention-of-government literature and objectives are based is that it poses the issue with which this book is concerned rather starkly. Does the state have autonomous, organic objectives, or is it to be viewed as a supplier of services for which it is necessary to discover equilibrium prices? How is this question to be answered in the absence of a view of the importance of public authority?

I will return in the course of this book to the issue, which is, at bottom, a normative one. There is simply no escaping the fact that an economic theory of bureaucracy—or of anything, for that matter—does not take account of, nor is it concerned with, the normative issues that societies are called upon to decide on a daily basis through the political process. Economics and politics as disciplines confront the same fundamental issue: the allocation of scarce resources. But they part company on the resolution of the issue. Economics is guided by a neat model of resource allocation that looks to the absence of visible human conflict and to the market to determine the most efficient manner to allocate society's most scarce resources. The political approach has a harder time neglecting organizations, groups, representations, pressures, elections—the messy process of democratic politics, all of which determine how resources are allocated.

The Niskanen view of bureaucracy is based on a simple economic model: the bureaucrat and the bureaus seek to maximize their interests. In other words, they seek ever larger budgets and a continual increase in personnel. Society as a whole, which pays for these bureaus, clearly has an interest that is diametrically opposed to that of the bureaus. Hence, bureaucracy cannot be seen simply as an instrument of the state. That bureaucrats have accepted considerable budget cuts in a number of countries and that these bureaucrats may well have been "maximizing" their interests by going along with the politicians wielding the hatchet suggests how complex interests can be and how simplified is the public-choice view of bureaucracy. Dunleavy refers to this agile bureaucrat as a "bureau-shaping bureaucrat."[28]

For those who adhere to the economic model, the bureaucracy can only be seen as a "chooser," as a "maximizer," and as an institution with preferences or objectives of its own, preferences or objectives that admit little complexity and that are unvarying.[29]

---

[27] Ibid., 21.

[28] See Patrick Dunleavy, *Democracy, Bureaucracy and Public Choice* (Brighton: Harvester Wheatsheaf, 1991), 75–210.

[29] For a trenchant critique of Niskanen's model and of his empirical assertions, see Colin Campbell and Donald Naulls, "The Consequences of a Minimalist Paradigm for Governance: A Comparative Analysis," in *Agenda for Excellence: Public Service in America*, ed. Patricia

It is of some interest to note how the relative importance of institutions in the democratic polity evolves over time. It was not so long ago that scholars took pains to insist that the state was capable of acting as an independent and autonomous entity in order to justify a notion of the democratic polity that differed from both Marxists and pluralists. If the state could be shown to act independently of societal interests, if it could be shown to possess interests of its own, it would then be shown that it was not a tool of the most powerful societal forces.

Indeed, it has been fashionable—at least until this approach was abandoned recently—to classify states as "strong" and "weak" depending on their capacity to resist society's pressures. States like France and Japan were uniformly viewed as strong states because they were unitary, centralized, and possessed a well-trained bureaucratic machine ready to implement governmental decisions. The U.S., together with some underdeveloped societies, was always viewed as being a decentralized, fragmented state.[30] The implication of this dichotomy was that a strong state could determine the allocation of resources and make its decisions without being subject to the pressures brought about by the most powerful groups. A weak state could not act independently of the groups endowed with the greatest resources.

What determined, among other things, whether a state was strong or weak depended on the kind of instrument at its service. What kind of bureaucratic machine a state possesses is of quintessential importance for the way in which a democratic polity conducts itself. It was the analysis of the bureaucratic apparatus that was missing from those who credited states with strength or weakness. In reality, a state relies on its bureaucratic apparatus for the development and implementation of its policies. But even the most centralized bureaucracies are riven by internal conflicts, overlapping jurisdictions, personnel and budgetary competition. A state cannot be judged to be uniformly strong or weak by reference to an organizational chart. In fact, those that appear strongest because of administrative centralization may be the most permeable to outside pressures. And those

Ingraham and Donald F. Kettl (New York: Chatham House, 1992). For other critiques of this view, see Peter Self, *Government by the Market? The Politics of Public Choice* (London: Macmillan, 1993); and idem, *Rolling Back the Market: Economic Dogma and Political Choice* (London: Macmillan, 2000).

[30] See Stephen Krasner, *Defending the National Interest: Raw Materials, Investments and U.S. Foreign Policy* (Princeton: Princeton University Press, 1978); Peter Katzenstein, ed., *Between Power and Plenty: Foreign Economic Policies of Advanced Industrial States* (Madison: University of Wisconsin Press, 1978); Peter Evans, Dietrich Rueschemeyer, and Theda Skocpol, eds., *Bringing the State Back In* (Cambridge: Cambridge University Press, 1985); and Dietrich Rueschemeyer and Theda Skocpol, eds., *States, Social Knowledge and the Origins of Modern Social Policies* (Princeton: Princeton University Press, 1996).

that appear weakest because of the fragmentation of the state structure may be more resistant to powerful interests.[31]

The bureaucracy's relationship to a capitalist economy is a close one. Either a bureaucracy is seen as necessary in providing support for a capitalistic order, or it is seen as part of the capitalistic order and behaving in accordance with motivations that are easily recognized in a capitalistic society. To be sure, the conclusion regarding its utility to society diverges depending on the viewpoint adopted. The first renders it a necessity for capitalism. The second views it as, at best, superfluous and, at worst, nefarious.

The importance of the public-choice school has not been so much its insight, insofar as the study of bureaucracy is concerned, but its considerable contribution to shifting the emphasis that had hitherto been placed on the study of bureaucracy. The application of a simple economic model to this institution helped pave the way for proposals for reforms that were ideologically inspired.

Niskanen claimed that the really important question concerning bureaucracy—and the one his book was seeking to answer—was: "What budget and output behavior should be expected of bureaus under different conditions?"[32] He noted that previous writers on bureaucracy—Weber, von Mises, Tullock, Downs—had come within striking distance of the critical questions concerning bureaucracy without really asking them. Bureaucrats, bureaus, and bureaucracies, claims Niskanen, among others, seek to maximize their own choices, and therefore their "budget and output behavior" should be subjected to measurement.

Bureaucracy and Democracy

The bureaucracy was long considered an indispensable complement, in fact a prerequisite, for constitutional democracy.[33] Even in modernizing societies, institutional weakness (the absence of a bureaucratic instrument, to take a key example) was considered the chief impediment to the transition

---

[31] See Ezra N. Suleiman, "Self-Image, Legitimacy and the Stability of Elites: The Case of France," *British Journal of Political Science* 7 (April 1977): 191–215; Graham K. Wilson, *Interest Groups in the United States* (Oxford: Clarendon, 1981); Jack L. Walker, *Mobilizing Interest Groups in America: Patrons, Professions and Social Movements* (Ann Arbor: University of Michigan Press, 1991); and Maurice Wright, *Government-Industry Relations in Japan: The Role of the Bureaucracy* (Manchester: Manchester Statistical Society, 1989).

[32] Niskanen, *Bureaucracy and Representative Government*, 20. See also, on the problem of bureaucratic autonomy, Daniel P. Carpenter, *The Forging of Bureaucratic Autonomy: Reputations, Networks, and Policy Networks in Executive Agencies, 1862–1928* (Princeton: Princeton University Press, 2001).

[33] See Carl J. Friedrich, *Constitutional Government and Democracy* (Boston: Ginn, 1950).

to democracy.[34] The extent to which the absence of a professional bureaucratic apparatus affected the democratic transition in postcommunist east-central Europe may help shed light on the longstanding debate regarding the contribution of bureaucratic institutions to democratic development.[35]

Bureaucracy is not an unambiguous complement to democracy. Dwight Waldo observed that the two could be seen as natural antagonists. "Why would an instrument [bureaucracy] designed to be impersonal and calculating be expected to be effective in delivering sympathy and compassion?" he asked.[36] Weber himself put considerable stress on the potential for conflict between bureaucracy and democracy. "Under certain conditions," he wrote, "democracy creates obvious ruptures and blockages to bureaucratic organization."[37]

Weber anticipated some of the contemporary critiques of bureaucracy, in particular that this apparatus, once established, inevitably comes to defend its own interests, some of which run counter to the requirements of democracy. He wrote:

> The concept of the "official secret" is the specific invention of the bureaucracy, and nothing is so fanatically defended by the bureaucracy as this attitude, which cannot be substantially justified beyond these specifically qualified areas. . . . In facing a parliament, the bureaucracy, out of a sure power instinct, fights every attempt of the parliament to gain knowledge by means of its own experts or from interest groups. The so-called right of parliamentary investigation is one of the means by which parliament seeks such knowledge. Bureaucracy naturally welcomes a poorly informed and hence powerless parliament—at least insofar as ignorance somehow agrees with the bureaucracy's interests.[38]

Yet, Weber nonetheless saw a strong link between the bureaucracy and democracy. Both were necessary for preserving capitalist order. For Schumpeter, the functioning of the democratic order could not have been achieved without the state's possession of a professional bureaucratic instrument. This is the view that he returned to on more than one occasion.

---

[34] Samuel P. Huntington, *Political Order in Changing Societies* (New Haven: Yale University Press, 1968).

[35] See chapter 11. Some scholars have argued that a strong bureaucracy that arises before other political institutions might actually impede the transition to democracy. See Fred W. Riggs, "Bureaucrats and Political Development: A Paradoxical View," in *Bureaucracy and Political Development*, ed. J. Lapalombara (Princeton: Princeton University Press, 1967).

[36] Cited in Louis C. Gawthorp, *Public Service and Democracy: Ethical Imperatives for the Twenty-first Century* (New York: Chatham House, 1998), 27.

[37] Gerth and Mills, *From Max Weber: Essays in Sociology*, 231.

[38] Ibid., 233–34.

Though it may be fashionable to dismiss Weber today for having ascribed organic functions to the state, it remains the case that, for Weber, no democracy could be truly anchored or consolidated unless the state had a reliable, competent bureaucratic organization at its disposal. Contemporary antistatist ideology holds the opposite view: bureaucracy is antithetical to democracy, which is why Weber is their bête noir.

All modern states possess a trained, more or less professional civil service, operating along hierarchical lines and, in Weber's terms, according to "calculable rules and without regard for persons."[39] As Weber put it: "The more perfectly the bureaucracy is 'dehumanized,' the more completely it succeeds in eliminating from official business love, hatred, and all purely personal, irrational, and emotional elements which escape calculation. This is the specific nature of bureaucracy and it is appraised as its special virtue."[40] The uniformity that the bureaucracy dispensed, which for Weber referred above all to the rule of law, is what those who wish to "banish" bureaucracy from our landscape most detest about this institution. The new reformers want the bureaucracy to respond to *the* client's needs and not to the average need of all of its clients. The reforms adopted in different national context (particularly in the U.S., Australia, and New Zealand, but in other countries as well)[41] have sought to encourage employees "to think about citizens as 'customers' to be served instead of 'clients' to be managed."[42]

The antistatist fervor ascribes little virtue to bureaucracy. This institution is seen as being opposed to democracy, or as irrelevant or nefarious for a free society and an efficient economy. It is, in Ronald Reagan's famous words, not "part of the solution, but the problem." Although democratic and democratizing societies have sympathized with or embraced this ideological position, the empirical evidence that supports the view that amputation of the instrument of the state advances the cause of democracy or spurs economic development remains yet to be produced. Such a view has

[39] Max Weber, "Bureaucracy," in Gerth and Mills, *From Max Weber: Essays in Sociology*, 215.

[40] Ibid., 216.

[41] See Tony Verheijen and David Coombes, eds., *Innovations in Public Management: Perspectives from East and West Europe* (Cheltenham, U.K.: Edward Elgar, 1998); H.A.G.M. Bekke, J. L. Perry and T.A.J. Toonen, *Civil Service Systems in Comparative Perspective* (Bloomington: Indiana University Press, 1986); G. Scott, P. Bushnell, and N. Sallee, "Reform of the Core Public Sector: New Zealand Experience," *Governance* 3 (1990): 138–67; W. I. Jenkins, "Reshaping the Management of Government: The Next Steps Initiative in the United Kingdom," in *Rethinking Government: Reform or Revolution?* ed. L. Seidle (Quebec: Institution for Research in Public Policy, 1993); and Ingraham and Kettl, *Agenda for Excellence*.

[42] Donald F. Kettl, "The Global Revolution in Public Management," in Ingraham and Kettl, *Agenda for Excellence*, 452.

far too many practical implications for the development of societies to be left in the realm of ideology or theoretical assertions.

Weber maintained that bureaucracies are inevitable instruments in modern and modernizing societies, and that no state can function without an efficient bureaucratic instrument. Schumpeter went even further and identified bureaucracy as indispensable to democracy. He lists the existence of a professional bureaucracy as one of the five conditions necessary for a democratic order. Bureaucracy, he wrote, "is not an obstacle to democracy but an inevitable complement to it. Similarly, it is an inevitable complement to modern economic development."[43]

Schumpeter cautions, however, that "recognition of the inevitability of comprehensive bureaucratization does not solve the problems that arise out of it."[44] Nonetheless, there is no escaping the fact that no democratic society can preserve itself without a professional bureaucracy: "Democratic government in modern industrial society must be able to command . . . the services of a well-trained bureaucracy of good standing and tradition, endowed with a strong sense of duty and no less a strong *esprit de corps*."[45]

The charge that government is often unable to respond to society's needs and that it is run inefficiently has become a familiar one. Schumpeter argued that a well-trained bureaucracy "is the main answer to the argument about government by amateurs. Potentially, it is the only answer to the question so often heard in this country: democratic politics has proved itself unable to produce decent city government, how can we expect the nation to fare if everything . . . is to be handed over to it?"[46]

Ours is not the first epoch in which bureaucracies have been attacked for incompetence and for stifling freedom. It is possible—even desirable—to accept Schumpeter's and Weber's argument concerning the importance of an efficient bureaucracy for a democratic order without accepting Schumpeter's view that the bureaucracy "must be a power in its own right."[47] Indeed, it is the fear that the bureaucracy will become a "power in its own right," that its unelected officials will usurp the power of the legitimately elected representatives that has attracted many of this institution's harshest critics.[48] This was not a view that Schumpeter's elitist view of democracy was much concerned with. Yet, even while considering the bureaucracy as both indispensable and as the most efficient form of orga-

[43] Joseph Schumpeter, *Capitalism, Socialism, and Democracy*, 3rd ed. (New York: Harper, 1949), 206.

[44] Ibid.

[45] Ibid.

[46] Ibid., 293.

[47] Ibid. This, to be sure, accords with the restricted view of democracy that Schumpeter held.

[48] The critics of the European Union have used this argument incessantly. The "gnomes of Zurich" have been replaced by the "unelected bureaucrats of Brussels."

nization, Weber was keenly aware of the potential dangers this institution posed if it became—and it would seek to become—a "power in its own right." In fact, Weber made clear that bureaucracy would strive to "level those powers that stand in its way and in those areas that, in the individual case, it seeks, to occupy."[49] And he had no doubt that " 'democracy' as such is opposed to the 'rule' of bureaucracy, in spite and perhaps because of its unavoidable yet unintended promotion of bureaucratization."[50]

Weber, too, was keenly aware of how averse to transparency the bureaucracy would generally be. It would cultivate a cult of secrecy and it would deny information to those who were entitled to have it. The bureaucracy instinctively understands that knowledge is power and political institutions are generally reluctant to share their power. Thus, "the pure interest of the bureaucracy in power . . . is efficacious far beyond those areas where purely functional interests make for secrecy."[51]

Nonetheless, such fears do not obviate an intimate connection between a professional bureaucratic apparatus on the one hand and democratization and economic modernization on the other. Most of the literature on transitions leaves aside the organization of the state. Some of this literature takes the availability of adequate state structures as a given. Transitions, to be sure, can go on far long periods, even if there is always the hope of reflecting the "Spanish miracle."[52]

At the very least a consolidated democracy requires a state capable of carrying out its main functions (protection of citizens, collection of taxes, delivery of services) in an orderly, predictable, and legal manner. To do this, the state must have a capable instrument at its disposal. Juan Linz and Alfred Stepan are among the first scholars of transitions to democracy to point to the importance of a professional bureaucracy as being as critical to democratic consolidation as an independent civil society, an autonomous political society, and the rule of law. They observe that no matter how one views the state's role, a modern, professionalized bureaucracy is indispensable to democratic consolidation. Or, as Stepan puts it elsewhere, "No state, no democracy."[53]

To protect the rights of its citizens, and to deliver some other basic services that citizens demand, the democratic government needs to be able to exercise effectively its claim to the monopoly of the legitimate use of force in the territory. Even if the state had no other function than this, it would have to tax compulsorily in order to pay for police, judges, and basic services. Modern democracy, therefore, needs the effective capacity to command, regu-

---

[49] Weber, "Bureaucracy," 231.

[50] Ibid.

[51] Ibid., 233–34.

[52] See Adam Przeworski, *Democracy and the Market: Political and Economic Reforms in Eastern Europe and Latin America* (New York: Cambridge University Press, 1991), 8.

[53] Alfred Stepan, *Arguing Comparative Politics* (New York: Oxford University Press, 2001), 18.

late, and extract. For this it needs a functioning state and a state bureaucracy considered usable by the new democratic governments.[54]

Linz and Stepan have essentially updated Schumpeter or, rather, made Schumpeter relevant to the process of democratic transition and consolidation. As this process has gotten under way and been in the making for several years in a number of societies in east-central Europe, the absence of a professional bureaucracy has become rapidly evident.

The extent to which bureaucratic instruments of democratizing states need to resemble a strict Weberian model may be open to question. But that such instruments form part and parcel of a state's authority, which is indispensable to the preservation of liberties, is indisputable, even if not fully recognized.[55] Carl Friedrich, not an admirer of Weber's theory of bureaucracy, nonetheless believed that no government, and no democracy, could function without an effective bureaucracy. In his *Constitutional Government and Democracy*, he observed: "A realistic study of government has to start with an understanding of bureaucracy . . . because no government can function without it. The popular antithesis between bureaucracy and democracy is an oratorical slogan which endangers the future of democracy. For a constitutional system which cannot function effectively, which cannot act with dispatch and strength, cannot live."[56]

A critical element in democratic consolidation is a bureaucracy that begins to operate in an impersonal manner, according to known rules and regulations, and in which the officials are able (or obliged) to separate their own political and personal interests from the office they occupy. As Jacek Kochanowicz observes: "A bureaucracy plays not only a technical, but also a symbolic role. Like the flag, the national anthem, an army uniform, or a presidential mansion, it is a symbol through which the state—and the nation—is perceived. Citizens who have to deal with inefficient or corrupt officials will not respect the state, and the links tying the national community together will loosen." Kochanowicz goes on to observe that creating a new, more efficient, more autonomous bureaucracy "could be a way to strengthen the legitimacy of the state,"[57] an issue of considerable urgency in the countries of east-central Europe in the early 1990s.

---

[54] Juan Linz and Alfred Stepan, *Problems of Democratic Transition and Consolidation: Southern Europe, South America, and Eastern Europe* (Baltimore: Johns Hopkins University Press, 1996), 11.

[55] See Tony Verheijen, "NPM Reforms and Other Western Reform Strategies: The Wrong Medicine for Central and Eastern Europe?" in Verheijen and Coombes, *Innovations in Public Administration*, 407–17.

[56] Friedrich, *Constitutional Government*, 57.

[57] Jacek Kochanowicz, "Reforming Weak States and Deficient Bureaucracies," in *Intricate Links: Democratization and Market Reforms in Latin America and Eastern Europe*, ed. Joan Nelson (New Brunswick, N.J.: Transaction Publishers, 1994), 203.

State authority requires state capacities that assure state legitimacy. All this is merely a means to the protection of individual rights. As Stephen Holmes notes in a perceptive essay on the weakness of the Russian state: "Today's Russia makes excruciatingly plain that liberal values are threatened just as thoroughly by state incapacity as by despotic power. Destatization is not the true solution, it is the problem. For without a well-functioning public power of a certain kind there will be no prevention of mutual harm, no personal security. . . . The rights inscribed in the 1977 Brezhnev Constitution went unprotected because of a repressive state apparatus. The rights ascribed in the 1993 Yeltsin Constitution go unenforced because the government lacks resources and purpose."[58]

The Russian example Holmes analyzes stresses the importance of endowing a democratizing state with capacities because "authority enhances freedom." As he puts it, "If the state is to have a monopoly of violence, the monopoly must be vested only in officials whom the public can hold accountable for its use. Liberalism demands that people without guns be able to tell people with guns what to do."[59] Holmes has elaborated, together with Cass Sunstein, the linkage between citizens' rights and what they refer to as "costs" that society needs to assume in order to enjoy these rights. And these "rights and freedoms depend fundamentally on vigorous state action."[60]

Bureaucracy and Political Development

Two perspectives today dominate the way we view the allocation of resources and the decision-making process in contemporary capitalist society. One relies entirely on the capacity of the market to determine allocations; the other accepts an important role for the market but calls for the state to insure workable conditions for this market.

The issue that we need to consider here is not state vs. market in the working of the modern economy. It is, rather, whether a public sphere in a democratic society needs to be preserved and whether the public sphere should itself be subject to the rules and practices governing the private sphere. In the end, this is what the debate about the reinvention of government is all about.

A society entirely dependent on the market or one dependent on patrimonialism is one in which the state makes few demands on society. By the

---

[58] Stephen Holmes, "What Russia Teaches Us Now: How Weak States Threaten Freedom," *American Prospect* (July–August 1997): 32.

[59] Ibid., 33.

[60] Stephen Holmes and Cass Sunstein, *The Cost of Rights: Why Liberty Depends on Taxes* (New York: W. W. Norton, 1999), 14.

same token, a state that makes few demands on society is one that will lose the capacity to gain support and to undertake meaningful actions when the need arises.[61]

How is a state to make demands on society or satisfy society's demands for protection, order, or welfare? This question remains pertinent for the well-established democracies but has had particular relevance, as we shall see in chapter 11, for the newer democracies. A society must first endow itself with what Linz and Stepan call a "usable" state. But a usable state is one that possesses a professional state apparatus. It is not an accident that the British and French states in the nineteenth century developed highly trained state elites in order to be able to rule their far-flung empires. These same elites also administered their own societies.[62]

It is interesting to note that a patrimonial or sultanistic state appears, in the absence of a legal-rational order, as a "strong" state in the sense that it can decide without much opposition how society should be administered. It can provide and withdraw subsidies, welfare, and grants at will. It makes little or no extractive demands. It makes, in short, minimal demands on the society.[63] Such a state is disconnected from its society and is therefore a weak state.[64]

Does it then follow that, as Carl Friedrich observed, "it is only after the establishment of that central core of administrative government that the constitutionalizing could make real headway. It is, therefore, not a question of *either* democracy *or* bureaucracy, of *either* constitutionalism *or* efficient administration?"[65] Or, does a professional bureaucracy have to be created alongside a constitutional system?

Clearly, it becomes necessary to distinguish the importance of bureaucracy and state capacity

(1) during the transition phase to democracy,
(2) during the consolidation phase, and, finally,
(3) in well-established democracies.

Depending on the phase we are dealing with, the question relating to the importance of a professional bureaucratic apparatus changes.

In the *transition* phase, the important issue is: does the development of a bureaucratic structure aid the transition to democracy?

---

[61] On this theme, see Holmes and Sunstein, *The Cost of Rights.*

[62] See Henry Parris, *Constitutional Bureaucracy* (London: Allen and Unwin, 1969), 48.

[63] See Holmes, "What Russia Teaches Us Now."

[64] See Kiren Aziz Chaudry, *The Price of Wealth: Economies and Institutions in the Middle East* (Ithaca: Cornell University Press, 1997); and H. E. Chehabi and Juan Linz, *Sultanistic Regimes* (Baltimore: John Hopkins University Press, 1998).

[65] Friedrich, *Constitutional Government,* 386–87.

In the *consolidation* phase, the question becomes: in what ways does a growing state capacity allow for the consolidation of democratic norms?

In the *well-established democracies*, the issue becomes: is a bureaucratic structure superfluous now that democracy and democratic practices are well anchored?

All three phases of democratic development involve the creation or the protection of the market, necessary for the emergence and protection of democracy. Does the need for a professional bureaucratic structure vary with the democratic phase a society finds itself in? Or, do the market and democracy always require, not simply the preservation of a public sphere, but the protection of the state's authority?

Whoever says "state authority" says instrument of state power, for a state cannot exist without an instrument of power. There are a host of instruments that serve different types of regimes.[66] Our concern in this book is with the kind of instrument required for the preservation of a market-based democratic order. This is the type of post–New Deal, post–Great Society, post–Welfare State society that admits that all capitalistic market economies live in a constrained welfare state. Hence, it is not only the United States but all European societies, whether governed by center-right or social democratic governments, that recognize that the world of the post-1945 state has come to an end. It has, however, not ushered in a world governed purely by markets. Governments are needed to provide protection and (limited) welfare, as well as to regulate markets. The rhetoric may veer in one direction on another, but the reality, and practice, of governance at the end of the twentieth and at the beginning of the twenty-first centuries suggests that this is now what may be termed a generalized or universal reality.

Beyond this unmistakable reality, there remains the issue of how much weight to attach to the state sector and how to organize this sector. Does it need restructuring? Does it need dismantling? Does it need reforming or modifying? Does it need abolishing? Is a professional bureaucracy required for *developing* but not *maintaining* a democratic state? To these questions there have come a host of answers.

We turn now to new conceptions of government that basically challenge the belief that democracy is in any way dependent on a professional bureaucratic apparatus. Under the guise of seeking more efficient government, there lurks the danger of a dismantling of the state's instruments. Careful attention needs to be given to these new ideas in part because they have a certain appeal and logic and in part because they represent a "new" way of viewing an old problem.

---

[66] Chehabi and Linz, *Sultanistic Regimes;* Karl A. Wittvogel, *Oriental Despotism: A Comparative Survey of Total Power* (New Haven: Yale University Press, 1957).

CHAPTER THREE

NEW CONCEPTIONS OF BUREAUCRACY, DEMOCRACY, AND CITIZENSHIP

"Our goal is to make the entire federal government both less expensive and more efficient, and to change the culture of our national bureaucracy away from complacency and entitlement toward initiative and empowerment. We intend to redesign, to reinvent, to reinvigorate the entire national government."
—President Bill Clinton

"What we need most if this revolution is to succeed . . . is a new way of thinking about government—in short, a new *paradigm*."
—Osborne and Gaebler, *Reinventing Government*

An American Revolution

SHORTLY AFTER becoming president, Bill Clinton created with much fanfare the National Partnership for Reinventing Government.[1] This was to be the vehicle for the revolution in the way the federal government operated. The mission of this partnership was to create a government that "works better, costs less, and gets results Americans care about."[2] To pave the way for the accomplishment of this fairly innocuous-sounding objective, President Clinton established, in March 1993, the National Performance Review. A few hundred career civil servants were enlisted and were assigned to two teams. One of these was to review individual federal agencies, while the other was asked to review the federal government's procurement, budget, and personnel policies. The agencies were also asked to create "reinvention laboratories," whose job was to put forward recommendations.

There is little question that reforming the public sector has been an international phenomenon that had its origins in the United States. But whether this has meant a clearly identifiable package of reforms implemented

---

[1] See Clinton's remarks announcing the National Performance Review, March 3, 1993, in this chapter's epigraph.

[2] National Partnership for Reinventing Government (formerly the National Performance Review), *A Brief History* (Washington, D.C., January 1999), 1.

in a uniform manner to address common problems is a different matter that I turn to in part II. But the spearhead for reforming state structures, whatever ultimate shape they came to take in different national contexts, was the United States. As Caiden notes, the administrative reform of the 1990s was an American invention: "Most of the theories employed have originated in the United States. Most of the substantive measures advocated are drawn from American texts. Many of the experts employed by international bodies to expound the platform are Americans. Most models and sample laws are based on American sources."[3]

The United States has clearly looked on its new way to refashion or re-invent how government should work, and how it should serve society, as an ideology that is ripe for export, much as in the 1980s the market economy extolled in the U.S. came to be adopted across the globe. "The reaction across locations," noted Steven Kelman, a former administrator at the Office of Procurement Policy at the U.S. Office of Budget and Management, "has been relatively similar from a management and public administration perspective. In essentially all of the western world, the form management reinvention has taken has been de-bureaucratization, fewer rules, and empowerment";[4] hence, the tendency to refer to the "global revolution"[5] instigated by the United States.

If the United States has been leading a revolution in administrative reform, no evidence has hitherto been provided, with the exception of citing some reforms in Britain, New Zealand, and occasionally Australia. Even these reforms were quite different in nature. Moreover, instituting reforms, even when this requires some political courage, is not the same as evaluating a reform and pronouncing it a success. Indeed, as we will see, many of the reforms put into practice, even in the countries that were considered as models such as Great Britain and New Zealand, have since had their wisdom questioned.

It is not even clear that the United States itself has been so adept at administrative reform. Some scholars have argued that in the area of administrative reform the United States has almost always been a laggard: "When it comes to administrative reform, the United States has rarely moved except for some highly publicized reform programs that were gutted or compromised out of recognition from their original intentions."[6]

---

[3] Gerald E. Caiden, "Administrative Reform—American Style," *Public Administration Review* 54, no. 2 (March–April 1994): 124.

[4] Donald F. Kettl, Elaine Kamarck, Steven Kelman, and John C. Donahue, *Assessing Reinvention as a Major Reform*, Occasional Paper 3–98, John F. Kennedy School of Government, Harvard University, 8.

[5] Osborne and Gaebler, *Reinventing Government*, 328.

[6] Caiden, "American Reform—American Style," 124.

And Caiden suggests that the United States, like its scholars of public administration, has been particularly parochial, refusing to recognize administrative reforms put into practice elsewhere. Many of the ideas concerning downsizing, deregulating, and cost-efficiency "have been part of the administrative lore for at least 20 years and other countries have tried them. . . . In their parochialism, Americans too often reinvent and rediscover administrative theories, practices, and reforms long tried elsewhere."[7]

Most of the reforms or innovations that have been pointed to as altering the way government works in the United States have occurred at the local level. And even here it may be that the introduction of reforms has been praised without regard to the ultimate results. Indeed, the unpreparedness of the United States federal, state, and local governments in the wake of September 11, 2001, may well have been the result of the attempts to "reinvent" governments. At the very least, the connection between the two merits a thorough study.

Beyond Cost-Cutting: NPM

The reinvention-of-government movement has been gaining momentum for a number of years. While Marxists might have given up any notion that the state will wither away, this concept has now been embraced by the Right. In fact, certain position papers—put out by the Heritage Foundation—call for the complete dismantling of all federal departments of the U.S. bureaucracy with the possible exceptions of State, Defense, and one or two others.

All new governments promise to be efficient and to reduce waste. Every American president in the twentieth century has appointed his commission on government reorganization and on the elimination of waste. In the first half of this century alone, there have been the Commission on Department Methods (1905–1909), which came to be known as the Keep Commission; the Commission on Economy and Efficiency, which President Taft appointed; the Joint Committee on the Reorganization of the Administrative Branch of Government (1920s); the Brownlow Committee Report (1937); the First Hoover Commission (1949); and the Second Hoover Commission (1955).

Presidential Task Forces on Governmental Organization were appointed by Presidents Kennedy and Johnson. President Nixon appointed an Advisory Council on Executive Organization, under the chairmanship of Roy L. Ash. President Carter proposed, in his words, "the most sweeping reform of the civil service system since it was created nearly 100 years ago." Such a

---

[7] Ibid., 124–25.

reform was necessary, according to Carter, in order for us to have a "government that is efficient, open, and truly worthy of our people's understanding and respect."

Although Congress and the president usually agree on the need for government reorganization and are always eager to establish commissions and task forces, their respective views of what needs to be accomplished generally differ. Congress has been mostly concerned with ensuring reorganization that results in economies, whereas presidents have preferred to see rational management of the federal bureaucracy without particular regard to economies. President Reagan broke this trend, aided by the Carter initiatives, and placed the emphasis on the need to curtail the size and influence of the federal bureaucracy. This is the reason he appointed the Grace Commission, which was originally known as the Public Sector Survey on Cost Control.

Where the Clinton-Gore proposals on the reinvention of government differ from the earlier attempts at government reorganization is not only in the scope of the changes that were sought but in the embrace of norms that had hitherto been considered appropriate only for the private sector—customer orientation, entrepreneurism, competition among government agencies—and in the implicit alliance that has come to be made with social and political forces that seek to curtail the role of government for ideological or class interests.

What are the key concepts behind the new movement to transform the way governments organize themselves and why do they differ from earlier moves to reform the state's bureaucratic agencies?

1. Entrepreneurism

Management theorists and gurus have long sought to transform the way the public sector functions to resemble that of the private sector. Osborne and Gaebler state their intentions in unambiguous terms: "*To melt the fat,*" they write, "*we must change the basic incentives that drive our governments.* We must turn bureaucratic institutions into entrepreneurial institutions, ready to kill off obsolete initiatives, willing to do more with less, eager to absorb new ideas."[8]

An important aspect of cultural change inherent in the reinvention of government is *entrepreneurism.*[9] Reinvention offers an emphasis on innovation and ingenuity as things to be rewarded and encouraged, rather than to be stifled and punished. Al Gore, for example, cites a civil servant in the Department of the Interior who cut the length of the approval process for

---

[8] Osborne and Gaebler, *Reinventing Government,* 23, italics in original.
[9] Ibid.

fish ladders over dams by two years.[10] James Q. Wilson talks of managers employing "get out jail free" cards that exempted government workers in one government agency from punitive measures if the worker took an initiative contrary to procedural requirements but thought to be in the best interest of clients.[11] At the center of the entrepreneurial spirit is the idea of *flexibility*: a disdain for red tape coupled with emphasis on "getting the job done." There is also a seeming emphasis on common sense as the solution to red tape.[12] Accordingly, procedural due process, which is seen as the core legitimating concern that prompts the existence of red tape in the first place, is deemphasized in the literature on government reinvention.

2. Customer Orientation

The idea here is that the overriding concern of any agency is the satisfaction of particular client groups. This notion, it is argued, contrasts with earlier foci of public administration: strict adherence to established rules and procedures; concern over budgets and other organizational inputs; agency slack, etc. A customer orientation relates inextricably to structural and performance changes in the bureaucracy proposed by manager-advocates of the new paradigm: an emphasis on measurable output as opposed to inputs, and the devolution of authority to lower-level service providers. The idea of customer service is best summed up by Michael Barzelay: "Thinking in terms of customers and service helps public managers and overseers articulate their concern about the performance of the government operations for which they are accountable. When supplemented by analysis of how these concepts have been put into practice in other settings, reasoning about customers and service helps managers generate alternative solutions to the particular problems they have defined as meriting attention."[13]

Two additional shifts complement the notion of reorienting bureaucracies to customer orientation and entrepreneurism. If managers are to encourage entrepreneurism among their subordinates to serve customers, they must attempt to minimize purely self-motivated entrepreneurism. This, according to reinventors, is accomplished through an emphasis on *public-spiritedness*.

[10] Donald F. Kettl, "Building Lasting Reform: Enduring Questions, Missing Answers," in *Inside the Reinvention Machine: Appraising Governmental Reforms*, ed. Donald F. Kettl and John J. DiIulio (Washington, D.C.: Brookings Institution, 1995), 10–11.

[11] James Q. Wilson, "Reinventing Public Administration," *Political Science and Politics* 27, no. 4 (December 1994).

[12] Philip K. Howard, *The Death of Common Sense: How Law Is Suffocating America* (New York: Random House, 1994).

[13] Michael Barzelay, *Breaking through the Bureaucracy: A New Vision for Managing in Government* (Berkeley: University of California Press, 1992), 6.

Most important in this view is the idea that the dangers of bureaucratic discretion that are said to be concomitant with entrepreneurism are not really dangers at all if bureaucrats are motivated to serve in the public interest.[14]

3. Flattening Hierarchies

The third broad category of changes emphasized in the reinvention literature is structural. One major structural change advocated is the *flattening of hierarchies*. Innovators criticize as inefficient and counterproductive the hyperrational division of labor inherent in bureaucratic organization. Instead, they advocate merging high-level staff workers such as budgeting, procurement, and personnel management with actual policy implementation workers. This requires an emphasis on team production. Advocacy of teams seems very much in line with private-sector criticism of Fordist methods of assembly-line production, criticism that was popular in the 1970s and 1980s. Another aspect of flattening is the decreasing attention to formal rules and hierarchies that I just mentioned. Bucking the chain of command to get the job done is a central myth of American popular culture. Reinvention does not specifically advocate breaking rules; it does, however, advocate getting around them through their deemphasis. So, for example, two of the National Performance Review's accomplishments have been paperwork-reform in the Office of Personnel Management, and general procurement reform. A type of flattening is the disaggregation of large bureaucratic institutions into quasi-autonomous agencies; the extent to which such break-ups have occurred is not shown.

4. Alternative Forms of Implementation

Another major type of structural change advocated in the reinvention of government is a *reliance on alternative frameworks for implementation*. Four types of alternatives for service-provision are: downsizing the public service in absolute terms; privatization and contracting out where possible; competition between agencies performing the same function in an effort to increase efficiency (related to Niskanen's advocacy of organizational redundancy);[15] and the devolution of authority to the street level (related to flattening hierarchies) more generally.

Advocated changes in performance are captured most fully in the concept of redefining agency mission from an emphasis on *input* to one of *output*. This emphasis, of course, relates to customer orientation; it is seen in catchphrases like "results instead of rules." Advocates of planning and

---

[14] See the essays by Kettl and DiIulio in *Inside the Reinvention Machine*.
[15] Niskanen, *Bureaucracy and Representative Government*.

budgeting argue that agencies that configure their missions toward an emphasis on outputs (such as the number of clients satisfied, checks delivered, etc.) will be more easily evaluated than those that emphasize inputs (such as personnel recruitment, budgetary acquisition, and procurement).

The importance ascribed to performance evaluation is that agencies that advocate results instead of rules will be more easily evaluated, and therefore more efficiently improved. Generally, the theory of evaluation concomitant with reinvention is embodied in the idea of "Best Practices Research."[16] This type of research is inductive rather than deductive; it is positive and prescriptive. Unlike previous efforts of evaluation, which compare bureaucratic operations to variants of the Weberian ideal type, Best Practices Research is based primarily on a philosophy of pragmatism and rationality. There is considerably less normative commitment to any particular conception of what bureaucracy should do or what it should look like.

It seems clear that some of these proposed reforms are narrowly managerial in nature, but that taken as a whole the reforms aim at altogether altering the role of the bureaucracy in society. Few people can raise objections to cutting red tape, whether through a Weberian hierarchical structure or though teamwork and the absence of hierarchy. Few object to energizing officials and making them desirous of serving the public. Few would object to evaluations of performance. But at the heart of the reinvention-of-government movement lies a skepticism about the existence of a public-service institution. This may be below the surface of the proposals made by the reinvention-of-government advocates, but it remains nonetheless highly visible.[17]

Bureaucratic Reform and the Public Interest

There are many reasons generally given for the pressures on administrative reform: the fiscal crisis, declining tax revenues, higher taxes, perceived governmental waste. But there is an additional factor that is often left out of the list because it does not constitute a specific event like the oil shocks or the fiscal crisis of the 1970s. This is the changing concept of democracy. Throughout the democratic world, over the past thirty years citizens have felt less constrained by, and no doubt less respectful of, authority.

[16] E. Sam Overman and Kathy J. Boyd, "Best Practice Research and Postbureaucratic Reform," *Journal of Public Administration Research and Theory* 4, (January 1994): 67–83.

[17] H. George Frederickson, "Comparing the Reinventing of Government with the New Public Administration," *Public Administration Review* 56, no. 3, (May–June 1996): 267.

Participation, whether through voting, interest groups, a direct action, has affected the political system. No longer are people content to vote and hope for the best. They demand more of their representatives and they respect them less. Many reasons have been given for this phenomenon: growing influence of private groups, cultural shifts, and corruption and poor performance of the political leaders.

The demanding public, and their criticisms of the inability of governments to resolve problems, gave rise to the attacks on the bureaucracy. Many of the criticisms were highly justified both in the United States and in the European countries. These in turn led to the new conceptions of government. By the early 1990s it was no longer possible to get along merely by appointing yet another commission on how to reduce government waste; hence the ambition developed by Gore and Clinton to "reinvent government."

The reinvention-of-government movement that emanated from NPM has been gathering speed and gaining momentum. Even if it is no longer at the center of public debate in the United States, the values and objectives that underlie its goals have gained wide support. It is rare for politicians to propose the creation of new agencies or an increase in the number of public employees to administer new initiatives.

The view that there is little that is distinctive about the work accomplished by the federal government is no longer confined to the extreme right of American politics. Donald Kettl and John DiIulio note that the most important lesson of privatization "is that there is no function left that only the public sector can deliver. . . . Because the private sector *can* do anything, there is less certainty about what government *ought* to do."[18]

No one disputes that governments should do whatever they take on as efficiently as possible. Nor is there much disagreement about cutting waste. It is legitimate that legislatures should seek to make bureaucracies accountable for the way they spend the citizens' taxes, though only the U.S. Congress seems able to accomplish this task.

The question of whether government should be doing much of anything, or what government *ought* to be doing, is altogether different. Indeed, because it is such a central issue, there is no consensus in most societies on the answer. The attempt to substitute the norms of the market for those of a collective interest is as much a philosophical and normative issue as it is one of institutional efficiency.

Two questions are raised by the continual reduction of the public sphere and the transfer of public functions to the private sector. First, is the concept of the "public interest" wholly obsolete? Second, how does the trans-

---

[18] Kettl and DiIulio, *Inside the Reinvention Machine*, 51.

formation of the citizen into a customer guarantee efficiency and assure against atomization?

In continental Europe, the concept of the "public interest" still retains considerable force, in part because it is in many instances the raison d'être of government and in part because the application of universal norms is tied to the stability of society and to the legitimacy of government. In the United States, this concept long ago lost any force it might have had, "in part because it became so hard to define and in part because some critics wondered if the new entrepreneurial spirit might not be superior to the old notions that drove it."[19] Kettl and DiIulio, like many champions of government reinvention, place the importance of entrepreneurism, performance, and customer satisfaction above all else. They note that "[r]esurrecting the concept [of the 'general interest'] along with the old definitions clearly will not help the debate over the NPR. The classical approach does not fit an administrative world of high technology and instantaneous communication, interdependent organizations . . . and institutionalized political tension between the executive and the legislature."[20]

In the United States, the concept of the public interest to the extent that it has existed at all has had to be modified further in order to fit in with the New Public Management. In other countries, it has needed, or would require, a major transformation. Indeed, the traditional yardstick—the serving of the collective interest—by which the work of public administration was judged has now been reversed. We now decide what kind of public administration we want our state to have, and then we reformulate the concept of public interest to fit into this new requirement. Kettl and DiIulio put it starkly: "The success of the NPR depends on establishing and promoting a new definition of the public interest."[21]

This has been the most difficult aspect of the attempts to reform the public bureaucracies in continental Europe. Historically, as we shall see, the republics of the continent established a strong state whose task was to guarantee the unity of the nation and the unity and indivisibility of the republic. The republican model is therefore opposed to the democratic model in that it accords primary importance to the collectivity as opposed to the liberty of individual groups to structure their own degree of integration. Grafted onto the democratic model has been the decentralized federal system of the United States—the extreme example of the democratic model—which further exemplifies the liberty of all parts of the republic.

[19] Ibid., 52.
[20] Ibid.
[21] Ibid., 53.

Where, then, the concept of a collective interest is flexible, if at all existent, it becomes possible to argue for a diminished role for the public bureaucracy. Where, on the other hand, the republican tradition, reinforced often by a social democratic vision of how society should be organized, prevails, then the concept of a social collectivity takes on a particular importance in preventing the undoing of a strong bureaucratic tradition. This is what explains the extreme difficulty in reforming the bureaucratic structure in France. For France conceives of itself as the quintessential republic dedicated to the equality of groups before the law. Indeed, a republic does not recognize groups as such. It recognizes only citizens, and in so doing believes that this type of citizen-state relationship—the antithesis of a multicultural society—constitutes the glue that holds the nation together.[22]

It comes as no surprise that the opposition of democracy and republicanism finds the counterpart in the customer-citizen dichotomy. The absence of a "general interest" allows the reformers of the public bureaucracy in the United States to substitute the customer for the citizen. Since there are no limits to what the private sector can do and "less certainty about what government *ought* to do," it becomes possible—even logical—to argue that government should be as entrepreneurial as the private sector if it wants to survive. Both sectors should operate according to market criteria. This is the thrust of the reinvention of government.

From Citizen to Customer

The bureaucracy has long been urged to be less wasteful, more efficient, and more customer-friendly. These unobjectionable requirements have led to a questioning of the very raison d'être of a professional public service. As will be seen in chapter 8, the public services in most democratic societies have tended to suffer in the competition with the private sector for highly qualified recruits. Many factors are responsible for this state of affairs, though the onslaught launched on the public service by the reinvention-of-government movement has served only to accelerate this trend. As George Frederickson has observed, advocates of the reinvention of government lack the commitment to an "effective professional public service and the equitable implementation" that public services are intended to practice. That the reinvention of government movement is characterized by a "systematic bashing of bureaucracy" is undeniable: "Although this bash-

[22] Whether this model can offer a practical guide to dealing with a society that has in effect become multicultural remains to be seen. The recent reform that grants a degree of autonomy to Corsica may signal the end of the republican model as France has traditionally known it.

ing is denied, the public service is routinely held up to ridicule in the reinvention movement. When this is pointed out to reinvention advocates, they reply, 'We are only ridiculing *bureaucracy*, not bureaucrats. We believe that bureaucrats are good people trapped in bad systems.' However wellmeaning this distinction, it is lost on virtually all careful observers."[23]

The reinvention of government in the United States has not merely sought to make bureaucracies more responsive to customers, it has sought to maintain that all citizens are first and foremost customers. Indeed, one is more a customer of an enterprise (whether the service is provided by the state or by a private firm) than a citizen. This is at the heart of the broad movement to undermine public bureaucracies. It is worthwhile to examine this basic tenet and its implications both for the bureaucracy and the society.

The logic of the argument is uncomplicated. The state, like the private sector, provides services. It is, in this sense, a producer. The citizen pays for those services when he or she purchases a service from a provider. The collection of garbage or taxes has a price in the same way that a manufactured product or a service has in the private sector. The purchaser is entitled to the best deal, and it can only be obtained in nonmonopolistic, competitive conditions. This, in a nutshell, is the basis of the ideas that underlie the reinvention of government. "If empowering employees is the 'how' of the NPM, customer service is the 'why.' "[24]

In the NPM, the state becomes a producer with citizens as customers. The Gore Report, basing itself on Osborne and Gaebler's *Reinventing Government*, suggested that the federal government could restore its prestige by making itself more customer-friendly. Taking care of its clients would allow the federal government to become more efficient as well as more respected. As Wilson noted: "In my view, the key sentences in the report are found in the first two paragraphs of the preface and of the body of the report. 'Public confidence in the federal government has never been lower.' To remedy this, there must be created 'a new customer service contract with the American people,' one that will close the 'trust deficit.' "[25]

The emphasis on the customer is, to be sure, a change of some significance. No one will object to being treated better by the bureaucracy. But this approach is likely to entail a number of consequences for the democratic polity.

No one denies any longer that states should not provide cradle-to-grave care. This ideology is under attack to one degree or another in all European

---

[23] Frederickson, "Comparing the Reinventing Government Movement," 267.

[24] Kettl and DiIulio, *Inside the Reinvention Machine*, 53.

[25] Wilson, "Reinventing Public Administration," 669.

societies. Yet, if the changes are coming about slowly in Europe, this is because these countries are struggling with both the imperative of preserving a community on the basis of some semblance of equity and with the need to reduce the dependence of citizens on the state. All European governments have begun understanding that citizens want to see value for their taxes and that citizens need to assume a greater responsibility for their own welfare.

In the United States, for some politicians and management experts, the concept of the reinvention of government is a call for rendering the expensive government machinery more efficient and less costly. For others, government reinvention has been embraced with an ideological fervor and is not regarded merely as an innocent program for a reorganization that reduces costs and delivers services more efficiently. It is essentially a political program whose aim is to curtail the activities and duties of the government, to curtail its obligations to society, and, most important, to curtail the obligations of citizens to their own society. NPM is merely a vehicle for this ideological program.

When citizens assume that all that matters is "personal" responsibility, the result may be private militias, gated communities, private security forces, and so on. Developing a sense of responsibility for oneself is one thing; developing it to the exclusion of all else is a danger to the society in which we live.

The reinvention of government seeks to import into the public sector the methods and goals of the private sector—competition, entrepreneurship, customer orientation. The citizen thus becomes a mere customer in the society in which she lives. Just as she shops for goods, she should be able to shop for all services that the government provides. But when the customer shops for a refrigerator through the yellow pages, the article is bought without any commitment on the part of the customer to the seller.

When the citizen is transformed into a customer, why should he be concerned about other customers or about his community? If the government is looked upon as a mere deliverer of services, why should anyone care anything more than that it provides quality of services at low prices? Can a nation be made up of free-riders?

The citizen as customer clearly appeals to many groups, and politicians are scrambling to get on this bandwagon without having the slightest idea of where it is heading. It sounds good. It sounds American. But Americans are also attached to the notion of community, to the town where "everyone knows everyone and everyone helps everyone." But no politician tells them that you can't go through life as a customer and hope to create a decent community in which to live. To be a customer requires no commitments and a responsibility only to oneself. To be a citizen requires a commitment and a responsibility that goes beyond the self.

If the politicians push the idea of dismantling almost the entire federal government, as some groups have suggested would be a good idea, they may find themselves having a hard time running for office. After all, if they don't want the government to do very much, then how will they keep any promises at all? And why should the citizen vote at all, or pay taxes? After all, customers vote with their purse. That's good enough for them. Will America "reinvent" or "bury" government, destroy what sense of community it has left, and render politics superfluous?

Two important questions are raised by the more recent attempts to reinvent government. First, what objectives underlie the drive to curtail the role of government? Second, what are the consequences for a democratic political community of the objectives that seek to alter the relationship between the citizen and the state? These two questions can, for immediate purposes, be taken together. The objective is not merely to make the government more efficient; it is to adapt government to the consumer society.

The justification is alarming in its simplicity: the government delivers services for which the citizen is called upon to pay. But the citizen is a consumer and therefore should be provided with the right to pay only for what he wants. The authors of the bible of the reinvention of government, Gaebler and Osborne, suggest that government can deliver its services better and in accordance with the rules that govern private enterprise. In fact, the subtitle of the book says it all: "How the Entrepreneurial Spirit Is Transforming the Public Sector." But is the citizen a mere consumer? And is the state a mere enterprise?

There is in American political history a heritage for treating the citizen as a consumer. It was, in fact, the progressive movement that, as Michael Sandel notes, "encouraged Americans to confront the impersonal world of big business and centralized markets, not as members of traditional communities or as bearers of a new nationalism, but rather as enlightened, empowered consumers."[26]

Paradoxically, the attempt to promote the consumer and to make him central to the new democracy was an attempt to combat the cartels and the plutocrats. As Sandel observes, Walter Weyl's *New Democracy*, published in 1912, most clearly laid out this position: "In America today the unifying economic force, about which a majority, hostile to the plutocracy, is forming, is the common interest of the citizen as a consumer."[27] Sandel also quotes Boorstin's recognition of the importance of the new "consumption communities": "Now men were affiliated less by what they

---

[26] Michael J. Sandel, *Democracy's Discontent: America in Search of a Public Philosophy* (Cambridge, Mass.: Harvard University Press, 1996), 221.

[27] Cited in Sandel, *Democracy's Discontent*, 223–24.

believed than by what they consumed. . . . Men who never saw or knew one another were held together by their common use of objects so similar that they could not be distinguished even by their owners. These consumption communities were quick; they were non-ideological; they were democratic; they were public, and vague and rapidly shifting."[28]

But a community of consumers is not the same as a community of people brought together by common interests. The contemporary attempt to see the government as facing a horde of consumers that it needs to satisfy, rather than as citizens to whom it has a responsibility, differs from the consumer movement of the early part of the century.

Contemporary American politics reflects the contradiction between two incompatible objectives: the drive to make government an enterprise that deals with clients and the drive to create social and political communities. The first results in atomization; the second attempts to combat atomization.

America may be creating communities, but not necessarily the kind of democratic, participatory communities that Tocqueville admired. Indeed, the question has to be raised as to why the absence of a central authority, or the delegation of authority from the center to the periphery, leads to the absence of participation and to the unraveling of communities. The answer may lie in the need to see the citizen as a mere purchaser of services. As Dworkin noted in an article about the financing of American politics:

> [A] community can supply self-government in a more collective sense—it can encourage its members to see themselves as equal partners in a cooperative political enterprise, together governing their own affairs in the way in which the members of a college faculty or a fraternal society, for example, govern themselves. To achieve that sense of a national partnership in self-government, it is not enough for a community to treat citizens only as if they were shareholders in a company, giving them votes only in periodic elections of officials. It must design institutions, practices, and conventions that allow them to be more engaged in public life, and to make a contribution to it, even when their views do not prevail.[29]

The attempt to view the citizen as a mere consumer is the antithesis of the kind of citizenship required to sustain a democratic polity, as the American past shows well. "The shift to consumer-based reform in the twentieth century," notes Sandel, "was a shift away from the formative ambition of the republican tradition, away from the political economy of citizenship."[30]

[28] Ibid.
[29] Ronald Dworkin, "The Curse of American Politics," *New York Review of Books*, Oct. 17, 1996, 23.
[30] Sandel, *Democracy's Discontent*, 225.

The issues raised by the conversion of the citizen into a customer are both political and social. They go to the heart of the creation of a community. There is an obvious contradiction between seeking to create communities and informing citizens that they are always to be seen as customers when responding to government. A sense of community comes from a commitment of citizens to a public good or a public value. The customer is encouraged to maximize his gains when he purchases goods and services from the private sector or the government.

A Nation of Free-Riders

The concept of a general interest has never had much appeal in the United States. So it is futile to appeal to the state to defend or even to represent the interests of the collectivity. The NPM certainly cannot accommodate such a notion, if only because it might clash with the necessary entrepreneurial spirit and competition that the movement calls for. The concept of the general or public interest gradually "disappeared from most debate about public management," partly because "it became so hard to define" and partly because "some critics wondered if the new entrepreneurial spirit might not be superior to the old notions that drove it."[31]

To dismiss the idea of a collective interest is to acknowledge that

(1) citizens cannot place demands on the state,
(2) they have little commitment to the collectivity, and
(3) the state can no longer insure impartiality.

Yet, most theories of democracy stress the need for the state to arbitrate impartially among competing claims, even in the absence of a clearly articulated philosophy of the general interest: "The organization without bureaucratic rules is an organization without the means of ensuring consistency. To be unresponsive may be a weakness, but to be over-responsive may equally be a weakness as the absence of rules to enforce impartiality means that responsiveness can become partiality."[32]

Politics involves conflict, and the state creates institutions to resolve conflicts of multiple interests. But customers are not a collectivity.[33] The NPM appears as a vehicle for those forces who seek not government arbi-

[31] Kettl, "Building Lasting Reform," 52.

[32] John Stewart, "Advance or Retreat: From the Traditions of Public Administration to the New Public Management and Beyond," *Public Policy and Administration* 3, no. 4 (winter 1998): 18.

[33] Kettl, "Building Lasting Reform," 59.

tration but government representation. This can be expected to occur when the citizen becomes a customer and the state abandons its commitment to impartiality.

This is the primary political danger of the attempt to dismantle state institutions. What of the social consequences? Turning citizens into customers eliminates connection and ties and erodes trust. And this cannot bode well for democracy.

How is trust to be reestablished if the government curtails its activities and its obligations to society? More important, how can democracy be strengthened if the government also asks its citizens to curtail their obligations to the collectivity? When citizens come to assume that all that matters is "personal" responsibility, that they cannot or should not assume that they owe obligations to their government, the result is the kind of anomie or mass society phenomenon that leads to what Putnam decries in *Bowling Alone*, and to the privatization of life, whether in the form of private militias, gated communities, private security forces. Developing a sense of responsibility for oneself is one thing; developing it to the exclusion of a wider community of citizens represents a potential danger to democracy. And again, as Kettl notes, "Defining customers is much harder than it looks. Different people tend to want very different things."[34]

Statist Minimalism and Politics

The drive to reinvent government has been more than a drive to render government more efficient. It has aimed also to diminish the role of government and to make the federal government in the United States responsible only for a minimal number of functions. The reactions to the "generosity" of the federal government following the New Deal and the Great Society has thus been used not merely to render the federal bureaucracy less wasteful and more respectful of citizens' tax contributions, but in effect to render it more and more impotent. Transforming the citizen into a customer means in effect that neither the state nor the citizens can expect much from one another. The ultimate question must be: Does this advance and reinforce democracy, or does it weaken this cherished and imperfect form of government?

No greater contradiction exists between the desire to maintain a collectivity, or sense of community, and the drive to transform all citizens into customers. Robert Putnam's thesis that Tocqueville's view about the strength of American civil society and its contribution to the strength of the democratic polity may gradually be giving way to a society of indi-

---

[34] Ibid.

viduals who have lost all desire for common action has aroused great interest.[35] Whatever the cause that occasioned transforming Americans into anomic individuals who have turned their back on joining, cooperating, and participating, it becomes evident that a customer, as opposed to a citizen, is not a joiner, or rather, a society of customers cannot be the society that spurs people to engage in cooperative action.

This is one of the main dividing lines between European societies and the United States. The push to have public services be more sensitive to their clients is interpreted only in this limited sense: public services do not exist for the benefit of the civil servants and the public organization but for providing clients with efficient, courteous service. For the heavy bureaucracies of European countries, this has been a major step forward. But most of these countries are loath to develop a cult of the customer in the way the United States has. This is partly owing to weight of the civil service itself, partly owing to the power of trade unions in the public sector, and partly owing to the belief that there are only full-time citizens who happen to be momentarily customers.

Why the difference between a "full-time" customer and a "momentary" one? The essential distinction is that in the case of the momentary customer the citizen needs to be treated well when having recourse to a state service, but that is not a role he is called upon to assume permanently. The customer is above all a citizen who recognizes a public sphere, even if that public sphere has shrunk considerably in size.

The European countries have moved over the last two decades towards abandoning the state's control over most of the means of production, as well as the credit sector.[36] There remains largely a public sector that services but does not produce. And it is here that one can speak of a "European model," which refers to areas, such as the protection of rights, that are expected to remain in the public domain. The existence of a public sphere is dependent on the existence of citizenship conscientiousness in a larger community, that is, on the existence of a public sphere.[37]

To be sure, that sphere is eroding in all European societies, but no country in Europe, not even the United Kingdom (which comes closest to the U.S.), approaches the disdain of the public sphere that has been attained in the United States. In the last general election of June 2001, the two major parties in Great Britain felt it necessary to compete on which would spend

---

[35] See Robert Putnam, *Bowling Alone: The Collapse and Revival of American Community* (New York: Simon and Schuster, 2000).

[36] See chapter 5.

[37] For a summary of the principles of the republican model, see Pierre Birnbaum, *France Imagined* (New York, Hill & Wang, 2001). See also Maurizio Viroli, *Republicanism* (New York: Hill and Wang, 2002).

more public funds on public services. The competition was no longer about who could cut more but about who would invest more.

There is thus a greater link than has been avowed between the "customerization" of American citizenship and the "bowling alone" phenomenon. For Tocqueville, people joined groups, clubs, or associations because they felt part of and had a duty to the larger community. In so participating they also strengthened their communities. If this has become a thing of the past it is because the attachment is no longer to a community but to a product, and products and services do not elicit any meaningful loyalty. Putnam draws no conclusions about the role of government in strengthening democracy. Instead he documents at great length the "disconnectedness" of the American people.[38]

The withdrawal from the life of the city on the part of citizens is certainly likely to affect in numerous ways the quality of democracy. As members of a community, people are told that they will be treated as customers, and this type of relationship will characterize their interaction with their state authorities. But then they are also expected to become involved citizens, caring about and serving their communities. This is a fundamental contradiction that is difficult to reconcile. "Without effective government, American citizens would not be able to enjoy their private property in the way they do. Indeed, they would enjoy few or none of their constitutionally guaranteed individual rights. Personal liberty, as Americans value and experience it, presupposes social cooperation managed by government officials."[39]

The state's quest for minimalism has had another consequence: it has tended to render politics more and more irrelevant. Here again we confront a glaring contradiction in what the politicians demand: they insist on the minimalist state and they claim that they seek to innovate and to improve the lives of citizens. But if they wish to undermine the state, what levers will they hold? In denigrating all public functions, they have succeeded in denigrating themselves and rendering politics superfluous. Why are citizens expected to believe in politics and political choice if they are continually told that politics is bad for people's lives and that political institutions function on principles that cheat the customer?

This is the explanation for the disenchantment with politics that has now become a permanent feature of democratic societies. Politicians, having been excessively critical (demagogic?) of political institutions and of their own profession, have secured the contempt of the citizen.

---

[38] Is social capital strengthened by the strengthening of a public space, or is it strengthened by the shrinking of public space? Since both are plausible explanations, the Left and the Right have found much to feed on in Putnam's data.

[39] Stephen Holmes and Cass Sunstein, *The Cost of Right: Why Liberty Depends on Taxes* (New York: W. W. Norton, 1999), 15–16.

NPM may be a vehicle for the political program of state minimalism, but the issue of political choice and political involvement cannot be analyzed merely in terms of bureaucratic reform. NPM does not concern itself with issues related to the promotion of democracy. Yet, no responsible analyst (or citizen, for that matter) can separate issues that affect the dismantling of the central government, whether through decentralization, the abolition of government functions, the withdrawal of government responsibilities, or privatization, from the consequences this is likely to have on the quality of democracy.

PART II

CHAPTER FOUR

POPULAR DISSATISFACTION AND ADMINISTRATIVE REFORM

For some citizens, the Government has become almost like a foreign country.
—President Jimmy Carter, 1978

The Government is full of dedicated people whose hard work is being
choked off by our own bureaucracy. . . . We simply cannot allow the Federal
bureaucracy to beget more bureaucracy.
—President Bill Clinton, 1993

THERE IS widespread agreement among students of public opinion
that in the U.S. since the 1960s we observe increasing dissatisfaction
with politicians and political institutions.[1] Scholars perceived the
trend—which has been termed the "popular culture of bad government"[2]—in opposing ways. Some saw increasing distrust as undermining
political institutions and authority altogether,[3] whereas others viewed it as
a response to bad government in particular contexts.[4] Jimmy Carter
looked at public opinion polls and argued in a television speech in 1979
that "the gap between our citizens and our government has never been so
wide" and that the "crisis of confidence" made effective government difficult, if not impossible.[5] Ronald Reagan famously claimed that government is
not the solution to the problem, government *is* the problem.[6]

Studies of public opinion in Western Europe tend to conclude that the
distrust of politicians and political institutions are less strongly pronounced
there than in the U.S. but that we nonetheless have some evidence of
increasing distrust across states.[7] Such conjectures have led Inglehart to

[1] See, for example, Joseph S. Nye, Jr., Philip D. Zelikow, and David C. King, eds., *Why People Don't Trust Government* (Cambridge: Harvard University Press, 1997); Ronald Inglehart, *Modernization and Postmodernization: Cultural, Economic, and Political Change in Forty-three Societies* (Princeton: Princeton University Press, 1997); and Seymour Martin Lipset and William Schneider, *The Confidence Gap: Business, Labor, and Government in the Public Mind* (New York: Free Press, 1983).

[2] Joseph S. Nye, Jr., and Philip D. Zelikow, "Conclusion: Reflections, Conjectures, and Puzzles," in Nye, Zelikow, and King, *Why People Don't Trust Government*, 276.

[3] Inglehart, *Modernization and Postmodernization*.

[4] Lipset and Schneider, *The Confidence Gap*.

[5] Jimmy Carter, television address on energy crisis, July 15, 1979, as cited in Lipset and Schneider, *The Confidence Gap*, 13.

[6] As cited in Patricia W. Ingraham, "The Reform Agenda and National Civil Service Systems: External Stress and Internal Strains," in *Civil Service Systems in Comparative Perspective*, ed. Hans A.G.M. Bekke, James L. Perry, and Theo A. J. Toonen (Indianapolis: Indiana University Press, 1996), 247.

[7] For a comprehensive examination of available data on Western Europe, see the five-volume series *Beliefs in Government* (1995), especially Hans Dieter Klingemann and Dieter Fuchs, eds., *Citizens and the State* (Oxford: Oxford University Press, 1995); Ole Borre and Elinor Scarbrough, eds., *The Scope of Government* (Oxford: Oxford University Press, 1995);

predict that "in the long run, industrialized societies of both East and West must cope with long term changes that are making their publics less amenable to doing as they are told, and more adept at telling their governments what to do."[8] Focusing on the civil service, Ingraham concludes that "as we approach the end of the twentieth century, there is no region in the world whose nations express satisfaction with public bureaucracies and civil service systems."[9]

In this chapter I examine the apparent relationship between popular distrust of government and the current wave of administrative reform. A detailed examination of available data on a range of advanced industrialized democracies shows that trust in government is not decreasing by all measures. To the contrary, in Western European countries satisfaction is increasing by many measures. A close analysis of available data on public dissatisfaction does, in other words, not lead us to expect a growing demand for government reform in all states. Apart from the different trends across countries, it is also the case that trust in the civil services is nowhere strikingly low when we look at attitudes toward the civil service as opposed to other institutions. In other words, public opinion gives us little reason to conclude that bureaucracies should be more vulnerable targets for reform than other institutions.

Our findings challenge those accounts that explicitly or implicitly concluded that distrust in government would lead to government reform. Thus, Miller argued in 1974 that "in a democracy ... discontent may lead to political and social change" and that the "satisfaction of the unfulfilled needs which presumably led to the discontent gives testimony to the flexibility of the political system and the ability of government to manage conflict."[10] Similarly, Lipset and Schneider argued that "in order for the trends in political confidence to reverse, things will not just have to get better; they will have to get better in such a clear and palpable way that the public will pay no attention to the inevitable voices of cynicism and disbelief."[11] The adoption of Proposition 13, which curbed growth in property taxes in California in 1978, has been seen as a reform that directly followed from growing dissatisfaction with government. Following this line of reasoning, Sears and Citrin argued that "the popular disdain for public officials ... contributed to the success of the tax revolt."[12] In 1997, Nye

---

and Max Kaase and Kenneth Newton, eds., *Beliefs in Government* (Oxford: Oxford University Press, 1995). See also Inglehart, *Modernization and Postmodernization*.

[8] Inglehart, *Modernization and Postmodernization*, 323.

[9] Ingraham, "Reform Agenda," 247.

[10] Arthur H. Miller, "Political Issues and Trust in Government: 1964–1970," *American Political Science Review* 68 (1974): 951.

[11] Lipset and Schneider, *The Confidence Gap*, 352.

[12] David O. Sears and Jack Citrin, "Tax Revolt: Proposition 13 in California and Its Aftermath," in *Bureaucratic Power in National Policy Making*, 4th ed., ed. Francis E. Rourke (Boston: Little, Brown, 1988), 279.

and Zelikow continued the interpretation of government reform as a response to public dissatisfaction when they concluded that: "Responding to the first and second industrial revolutions, the answer of the developed democracies was: more government. The answer is now engulfed in a rising tide of public distrust and distance from institutions. Responding to the new challenges associated with a third revolution in commerce and society, our project must next focus on how to understand and give another answer: different governance."[13]

Our main reason for doubting a strong causal link between public distrust and administrative reform is, however, neither the lack of a general pattern of declining trust or satisfaction in most Western European states nor the lack of evidence that bureaucracies are more distrusted than nongovernmental or other governmental institutions. Rather, it is that the patterns of distrust or dissatisfaction with government in general and bureaucracies in particular through time and across countries do not correspond with the pattern of New Public Management reform that we observe. In countries where dissatisfaction with government and bureaucracies runs high, such as in Italy, Japan, and to some extent France, or where it has increased sharply in the 1990s, such as in Germany, there have been only limited attempts at NPM reforms. In other states where there has been no increase in dissatisfaction with democracy, such as in Britain, or where there has been declining dissatisfaction, such as in Denmark and the Netherlands, NPM reforms have been adopted extensively during the last two decades. In the end, the U.S. is the only state where the extensive adoption of NPM reforms follows a strong growth in distrust of government. Whereas other parts of the book will examine how government reforms have been adopted in different countries, this chapter focuses on the widespread and uniformly accepted argument that public dissatisfaction and distrust in government is causing the contemporary wave of administrative reform. As a guideline for the argument in this chapter, table 4.1 provides a crude typology of the adoption of NPM reforms in advanced industrialized democracies.[14]

Evidence from the U.S. of the kind that is provided in figure 4.1 has led to the belief that there exists a growing "popular culture of bad government." Figure 4.1 shows that distrust in the federal government has increased between 1958 and 1998 to such an extent that whereas only 24 percent distrusted the federal government in 1958, as many as 60 percent did so thirty years later. Robert Putnam's work, which traces the decline of

---

[13] Nye and Zelikow, "Conclusion: Reflections, Conjectures, and Puzzles," 281.

[14] For other examples of such typologies, see Christopher Hood, "Exploring Variations in Public Management Reform of the 1980s," in *Civil Service Systems*, ed. Bekke, Perry, and Toonen, 268–87.

TABLE 4.1
Typology of the Adoption of New Public Management
Reforms in Advanced Industrialized Democracies

	NPM Reform	
	Extensive	*Limited*
	United States	Germany
	Great Britain	Spain
	New Zealand	Japan
Country	Australia	Austria
	Canada	Norway
	Sweden	Finland
	Netherlands	Italy
	Denmark	France

American social capital, contributes to the general perception that people care less and less about public institutions.[15] Declining trust in government institutions and disengagement from public life are not, however, two sides of the same coin. It is perfectly possible that someone who is deeply engaged in political life may be more cynical in her evaluation of political institutions than someone who spends several hours watching television and is oblivious to public activity. Nonetheless, empirical evidence from the U.S. shows similar trends for distrust in government and for disengagement from public life, and they lend support to Putnam's proposition that "the performance of our democratic institutions depends in measurable ways upon social capital."[16] It would seem from these accounts of decline of social capital and the evidence of declining trust in government that democracy is fundamentally threatened. Is not government reform a reasonable response to such overwhelming evidence?

There are two main problems connected with using this evidence as an indicator of a growing "popular culture of bad government." The first problem is that the trend is much more clear-cut in the United States than elsewhere. The compiled measure of dissatisfaction with democracy in member

---

[15] Robert D. Putnam, *Bowling Alone: The Collapse and Revival of American Community* (New York: Simon and Schuster, 2001). Other works discussed here that use these data include Nye, Zelikow, and King, *Why People Don't Trust Government*; Russell J. Dalton, *Citizen Politics: Public Opinion and Political Parties in Advanced Industrial Democracies*, 2nd ed. (Chatham, N.J.: Chatham House, 1996); and Lipset and Schneider, *The Confidence Gap*.

[16] Putnam, *Bowling Alone*, 349.

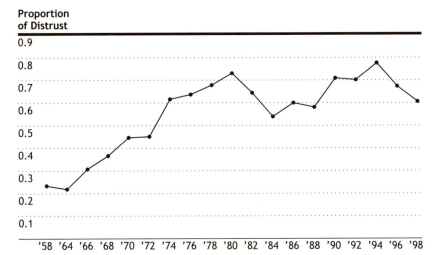

Figure 4.1.   Distrust in the federal government in the U.S., 1958–1998.
Source: American Election Survey.

states of the European Union between 1973 and 1999 shows no trend over time toward less satisfaction. As figure 4.2 makes clear, a little less than 45 percent of the respondents were dissatisfied with democracy in the mid-1970s, and a little more than 45 percent were so twenty years later. In other words, changes in satisfaction with democracy in member states of the European Union have been minimal during the last three decades. There are some problems connected to the compiled measure of satisfaction with democracy in Europe, and the measure of satisfaction with democracy is different from the measure of trust in government. We will address these problems further below. For now, the comparison of the trend in the U.S. and in Europe serves as an indication that we should not consider increasing distrust of government to be a given in all countries.

The other problem connected to the interpretation of the data in figure 4.1 and figure 4.2 on trust and satisfaction is that they represent a narrow measure of what constitutes the public's view of government. To get a good understanding of this view, we need to look not only at how government or the functioning of democracy is perceived but also at what people expect governments to do. When we examine the public's view of government in this broader context, we find that the desire for reduction of government involvement is quite ambiguous, and that by most measures people across states—and this includes the U.S.—favor extensive government activities. The pattern of differences in views of government that arises from the broader measure further strengthens the argument that the growth of dis-

Percent

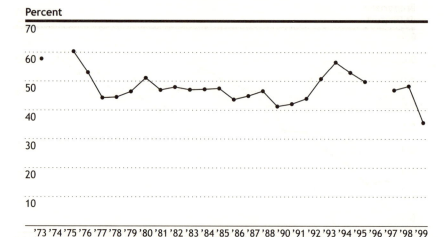

Figure 4.2.   Not satisfied with democracy in EU member states, 1973–1999.
Source: Eurobarometer.

trust of government tells us very little about the extent to which states have adopted administrative reforms in the 1980s and the 1990s.

Popular Support for Government Involvement

The number of tasks that governments assumed responsibility for increased continually in the period from the 1930s to the 1970s.[17] With the New Deal in the U.S. and the introduction of welfare programs everywhere in Europe, all governments assumed major roles in, and increased their sphere of influence over, citizens' lives. To be sure, the expansion of the scope of government was not uniform across states, but it is fair to say that the increase was significant in all advanced industrialized economies.[18] From around 1979 and 1980 when Thatcher and Reagan each took office, there began to come about a change in rhetoric and a move toward retrenchment of the scope of state responsibilities aimed at reversing the uninterrupted trend set in motion during the 1930s and, in particular,

[17] For discussions about the growing scope of government activities and public opinion, see Borre and Scarbrough, *The Scope of Government*. See also Ernest R. May, "The Evolving Scope of Government" in Nye, Zelikow, and King, *Why People Don't Trust Government*, 21–54.

[18] For an influential typology of welfare states, see Gøsta Esping-Andersen, *Social Foundations of Postindustrial Economies* (Oxford: Oxford University Press, 1999); and Gøsta Esping-Andersen, *The Three Worlds of Welfare Capitalism* (Cambridge: Polity Press, 1990).

after World War II.[19] The move toward retrenchment did not take place until the 1990s in states such as Sweden and France, but by then the change in rhetoric about and the approach to public sector expansion had taken place across the advanced industrialized world.

The diminishing scope of state responsibilities has on the whole not been unambiguously supported by public opinion. When asked in the 1980s and 1990s about particular programs or sectors, a majority of the public appeared to want the government to continue being responsible for a wide range of activities. A majority of respondents in most advanced industrialized democracies even desired an increase in government spending when they were questioned about the desirability of government involvement in particular sectors. Nonetheless, substantial majorities favored cuts in government spending in general terms. Dalton thus was correct to argue that "the attitudes of Americans and Europeans remain an ambiguous mix of support and denial of government action."[20]

Theories about democratic overload, popular in the 1970s and early 1980s, held that the demand from citizens would continue to grow while the capacity of the state to satisfy them would diminish. Armed with this theory, the prediction of a crisis of democracy, as foreseen by Jürgen Habermas, Samuel Huntington, or Claus Offe, followed logically.[21] An analysis of public opinion surveys shows that across states the extent of the public's demand for government responsibility remained high in the last two decades, but, contrary to the prediction of the theories of democratic overload and crisis, it did not grow.

Table 4.2 shows the proportion of citizens in nineteen industrialized countries who indicated that the government "probably should be" or "definitely should be" responsible for protecting the environment, for health care, caring for the elderly, financial aid for students from poor families, price control, helping industry grow, providing decent housing, unemployment benefits, jobs, and for reducing income inequalities. This snapshot of public opinion in 1996 supports the view that the desire for government involvement remained high across the board. Even in the

[19] For discussions about welfare retrenchment, see Paul Pierson, *Dismantling the Welfare State? Reagan, Thatcher, and the Politics of Retrenchment* (Cambridge: Cambridge University Press, 1994). See also Paul Pierson, "The New Politics of the Welfare State," *World Politics* 48, no. 2 (1996): 143–79.

[20] Dalton, *Citizen Politics*, 119.

[21] Jürgen Habermas, *Legitimation Crisis*, trans. Thomas McCarthy (London: Heinemann, 1976); Samuel Huntington, *American Politics: The Promise of Disharmony* (Cambridge: Harvard University Press, 1981); Claus Offe, *Contradictions of the Welfare State* (Cambridge: MIT Press, 1981); Michel Crozier, Samuel Huntington, and Jöji Watanuk, *The Crisis of Democracy: Report on the Governability of Democracies to the Trilateral Commission* (New York: New York University Press, 1995).

TABLE 4.2
Support for Government Responsibilities According to Types of Programs and States, 1996

	Environment	Care for Elderly	Health Care	Financial Aid to Students	Price Control	Help Industry Grow	Provide Decent Housing	Unemployment Benefits	Provide Jobs	Reduce Income Differences	Average
Spain	0.97	0.99	0.99	0.99	0.92	0.96	0.98	0.94	0.91	0.90	0.95
Russia	0.97	0.99	0.98	0.96	0.95	0.92	0.94	0.81	0.93	0.81	0.93
Slovenia	0.95	0.96	0.97	0.97	0.90	0.93	0.91	0.86	0.89	0.85	0.92
Poland	0.96	0.99	0.98	0.96	0.84	0.91	0.91	0.81	0.90	0.84	0.91
Germany (East)	0.98	0.98	0.99	0.95	0.87	0.73	0.91	0.92	0.92	0.84	0.91
Bulgaria	0.98	0.98	0.97	0.90	0.87	0.94	0.80	0.88	0.81	0.77	0.89
Italy	0.97	0.98	0.99	0.94	0.93	0.80	0.88	0.75	0.77	0.75	0.88
Hungary	0.97	0.98	0.99	0.91	0.88	0.89	0.76	0.63	0.87	0.79	0.87
U.K.	0.95	0.98	0.99	0.90	0.86	0.93	0.89	0.79	0.69	0.68	0.87
Norway	0.94	0.99	0.99	0.79	0.90	0.80	0.74	0.93	0.81	0.73	0.86
Sweden	0.94	0.98	0.96	0.79	0.86	0.80	0.82	0.90	0.65	0.71	0.84
France	0.95	0.92	0.89	0.94	0.76	0.82	0.87	0.81	0.69	0.74	0.84
Czech Republic	0.97	0.97	0.97	0.93	0.82	0.82	0.80	0.45	0.76	0.62	0.81
Germany (West)	0.96	0.96	0.97	0.87	0.71	0.64	0.78	0.80	0.75	0.63	0.81
New Zealand	0.97	0.94	0.97	0.87	0.74	0.85	0.78	0.64	0.55	0.47	0.78
Australia	0.96	0.94	0.94	0.88	0.81	0.87	0.76	0.65	0.44	0.52	0.78
Japan	0.94	0.91	0.90	0.64	0.96	0.75	0.60	0.73	0.63	0.65	0.77
Canada	0.93	0.90	0.94	0.85	0.64	0.75	0.72	0.66	0.37	0.51	0.73
U.S.	0.89	0.87	0.85	0.85	0.69	0.66	0.67	0.48	0.39	0.48	0.68
Average	0.96	0.96	0.96	0.89	0.84	0.83	0.82	0.76	0.72	0.70	

Source: The International Social Survey Program, 1996.
Missing data have been excluded.

U.S., where expectations were the lowest, an average of 68 percent of the respondents supported government responsibility for this wide array of activities. As expected, this crossnational comparison shows that support for state intervention is, on the whole, stronger in Europe than in the U.S., Japan, Australia, New Zealand, and Canada. The high support for state responsibilities in all Central and Eastern European countries suggests that desire for government involvement persists even in radically different political, economic, and social contexts.

The responses to these same questions at three points in time between 1985 and 1996 suggest that attitudes did not change much during this decade. As figure 4.3 shows, changes over time as well as among countries were small with regard to support for government responsibility for health care. The same minimal change in attitudes applies to support for public care for the elderly. On the issues where there are more differences among countries, such as job provision, there was a slight decrease in support for government involvement, as shown by figure 4.4. However, in Great Britain and Australia, support for government provision of jobs grew slightly between 1990 and 1996. In most sectors, therefore, expectations of governments remained high, and there is no convincing overall trend of decline of expectations. Moreover, support for government involvement was by some measure growing in two of the countries that adopted NPM reforms extensively.

The trend showing that expectations in each sector tend to remain relatively high, but not necessarily growing, is consistent with what Lipset and

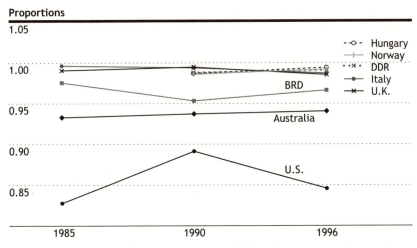

Figure 4.3. Support for government responsibility for health care, 1985, 1990, and 1996. Source: International Social Survey Program.

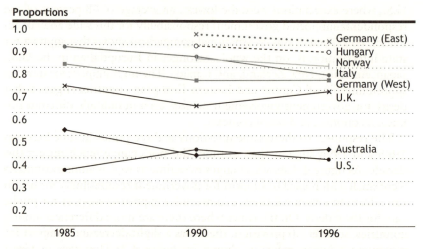

Figure 4.4. Support for government responsibility for providing jobs, 1985, 1990, and 1996. Source: International Social Survey Program.

Schneider found in the case of the U.S. in the 1970s. Citing various surveys where Americans expressed their support for government responsibilities in that decade, they concluded that "the desire for the government to intervene in beneficent ways has not diminished."[22] Recently, Orren agreed that not much has changed with regards to Americans' expectations and that "the wish list of programs and services is long and growing."[23] With regards to Europe, Dalton notes that "support for government action to resolve social need is a core element of the European political culture."[24]

Table 4.3 suggests, contrary to common belief, often inferred from the so-called tax revolt in the U.S., that when asked about particular sectors people do *not* want to cut spending. Less than 10 percent of those asked by the International Social Survey Program said they thought the government should "spend less" or "spend much less" in the sectors of healthcare, pensions, protection of the environment, education, and the police. In general, people in longstanding democracies wanted cuts in spending to be limited to the military, culture and the arts, and unemployment benefits, whereas people in the Central and Eastern European countries did not want to cut spending on anything except, in some cases, unemployment benefits. Noticeably, the respondents from the U.S. did not stand out as being more

[22] Lipset and Schneider, *The Confidence Gap*, 346.

[23] Gary Orren, "Fall from Grace: The Public's Loss of Faith in Government," in Nye, Zelikow, and King, *Why People Don't Trust Government*, 100.

[24] Dalton, *Citizen Politics*, 115.

TABLE 4.3

Proportion Desiring Cuts in Government Spending According to Sectors in Nineteen Countries, 1996

	Military	Culture	Unemployment	Police	Environment	Pensions	Health	Education	Average
France	0.66	0.40	0.33	0.13	0.11	0.10	0.13	0.08	0.24
Canada	0.61	0.39	0.31	0.12	0.10	0.11	0.07	0.04	0.22
Italy	0.73	0.15	0.21	0.23	0.10	0.07	0.05	0.05	0.20
Germany (West)	0.66	0.41	0.18	0.06	0.06	0.05	0.07	0.07	0.20
New Zealand	0.43	0.42	0.47	0.01	0.08	0.05	0.01	0.01	0.18
Norway	0.50	0.59	0.19	0.03	0.07	0.02	0.01	0.04	0.18
U.S.	0.33	0.46	0.22	0.07	0.14	0.10	0.07	0.05	0.18
U.K.	0.33	0.65	0.20	0.02	0.06	0.01	0.00	0.01	0.16
Australia	0.25	0.43	0.40	0.02	0.09	0.03	0.02	0.03	0.16
Sweden	0.50	0.44	0.15	0.06	0.04	0.03	0.01	0.03	0.16
Czech Republic	0.47	0.14	0.38	0.13	0.03	0.03	0.02	0.03	0.15
Germany (East)	0.75	0.21	0.05	0.04	0.06	0.02	0.02	0.02	0.15
Japan	0.49	0.11	0.11	0.12	0.03	0.04	0.07	0.06	0.13
Slovenia	0.36	0.09	0.17	0.18	0.03	0.07	0.02	0.01	0.12
Spain	0.55	0.10	0.10	0.04	0.05	0.02	0.01	0.02	0.11
Hungary	0.31	0.08	0.31	0.08	0.05	0.02	0.01	0.01	0.11
Poland	0.10	0.10	0.20	0.05	0.02	0.02	0.02	0.02	0.07
Russia	0.06	0.05	0.07	0.20	0.01	0.01	0.01	0.01	0.05
Bulgaria	0.05	0.12	0.08	0.04	0.06	0.02	0.01	0.02	0.05
Average	0.43	0.28	0.22	0.09	0.06	0.04	0.03	0.03	

Source: The International Social Survey Program, 1996.
Missing data have been excluded.

willing to cut spending on social programs or less willing to cut military expenditure than people in France or Germany.

Finding that most people do not want cuts in government spending in such a wide range of sectors may be surprising and goes against conventional wisdom. Are people really satisfied with the amount of taxes that they pay, and do they mostly expect that governments will put their money to good use? Table 4.4 suggests that we should avoid rash conclusions. It shows the proportion of people who answered that they were either

TABLE 4.4
Proportion "In Favor of" or "Strongly in Favor of" Cuts in Government Spending

	1985	1990	1996
France			0.91
Hungary		0.82	0.90
Germany (West)	0.77	0.76	0.85
Spain			0.85
Slovenia			0.85
U.S.	0.82	0.78	0.83
Germany (East)		0.71	0.82
Canada			0.80
Japan			0.78
New Zealand			0.71
Russia			0.70
Italy	0.68	0.70	0.70
Poland			0.69
Australia	0.75	0.75	0.68
Norway		0.71	0.66
Sweden			0.58
Czech Republic			0.55
Bulgaria			0.50
U.K.	0.38	0.42	0.45

Source: The International Social Survey Program, 1996.
Missing data have been excluded.

"in favor of" or "strongly in favor of" cuts in government spending. When the question is phrased in this general way without connecting the cuts to any particular programs or sectors, most people favored cuts in government spending. However, we should notice that it was not in the U.S. but in France that people were most keen on cuts in 1996. The U.K. stood out with the lowest number of people desiring cuts in government spending in the decade from 1985 to 1996.

Whereas on the whole less than 10 percent favored cuts in spending on particular social programs, more than half of those asked—and as many as 90 percent in France and 80 percent in Germany, the U.S., Canada, Spain, Slovenia, and Hungary—favored cuts in spending on the whole. There is no marked difference regarding attitudes to overall cuts between respondents in Eastern and Central European states and those in the other states included in our study. In some longstanding democracies where cuts had been exercised widely in the 1980s or in the early 1990s, there was relatively low support for further cuts, especially in Britain but also in Australia and Sweden in 1996. As table 4.4 shows, Australians even joined oil-rich Norwegians in showing declining support for cuts in government spending between 1990 and 1996.

These data on support for government involvement show that even in the U.S. public opinion is supportive of extensive government responsibilities. The strong demand for less government involvement that often is assumed in discussions about administrative reforms is therefore not unambiguously supported by our analysis. Moreover, the indication that the French favored tax cuts more than the Americans, and that support for less government spending has been decreasing in Great Britain, Australia, and Sweden, plainly contradicts the overall pattern of adoption of administrative reform that we showed in table 4.1. It is thus not evident that there is a direct causal relationship between the strength of the demand for cuts in government spending or the extent to which citizens want to limit government involvement and the scope and comprehensiveness of administrative reform. To investigate the questions that this evidence raises, we turn to a discussion of how governments are perceived when we compare across countries.

Popular Distrust of Government

A number of scholars have tried to probe the confidence people have in institutions, the degree to which they trust government, the degree of satisfaction that they feel with their political system, and the extent to which they believe in democracy.[25] All these questions may be related, but using

---

[25] We used two such measures in the introduction to this chapter. See table 4.2 and table 4.3.

Percent

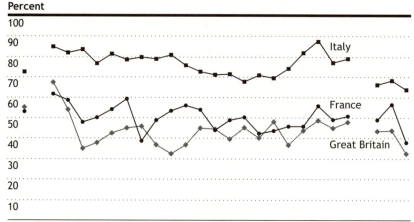

Figure 4.5. Not satisfied with democracy in Great Britain, France, and Italy, 1973–1999. Source: Eurobarometer.

different words (such as trust, confidence, belief, and satisfaction) in survey questions can influence responses greatly. Moreover, as Nye suggests, it is useful to distinguish between different dimensions of the political system to understand whether people distrust particular groups of individuals, particular institutions, the political system as a whole, or democracy and the nation-state in general.[26]

For the long-term member states of the European Union, the Eurobarometer provides a good set of data over time that shows the extent to which people are satisfied with democracy in their country. However, as Inglehart has pointed out, this question is a hybrid, which can be difficult to interpret. When asked about satisfaction with democracy, he explains, people are likely to report both how much they support the system of government in their country—and this measure has been shown to depend strongly on economic factors—and how critical they are of the current specific government.[27] But, since we are most interested not in the causes of public opinion but in how public opinion can be linked to administrative reform, this set of data is valuable, because it allows us to compare across countries over a period of almost three decades.

The time-series in figures 4.5 and 4.6 are striking, because they show few clear-cut trends and because those patterns that we can distinguish are

[26] Joseph S. Nye, Jr., "Introduction: The Decline of Confidence in Government," in Nye, Zelikow, and King, *Why People Don't Trust Government*, 1–18.

[27] P. R. Abramson and Ronald Inglehart, "Review: Beliefs in Government," *American Political Science Review* 92, no. 1 (March 1998): 185–90.

Percent

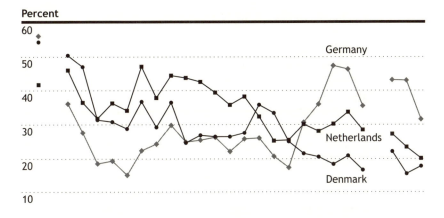

Figure 4.6.   Not satisfied with democracy in Germany, the Netherlands, and Denmark, 1973–1999. Source: Eurobarometer.

divergent. In Great Britain, France, and Italy, dissatisfaction with democracy has remained around the same level from the mid-1970s until the end of the 1990s. In Britain, dissatisfaction remained around 40 percent, and thus the British were on average less dissatisfied than the French. In France, dissatisfaction remained around 50 percent. Dissatisfaction in Italy is, not unexpectedly, in a league of its own, since between 70 and 80 percent of the respondents remained dissatisfied with the way democracy works in their country. The Italian example furnishes the occasion for viewing the impact of specific political scandals on public opinion. The *Tagentopoli* investigations began on February 17, 1992, with the arrest of Mario Chiesa, the director of the Milanese home for the elderly, Pio Albergo Trivulzio, and they revealed extensive bribery and corruption in Italian political parties specifically, and in the public sector more generally. As figure 4.5 shows, dissatisfaction with democracy peaked at close to 90 percent in 1992–1993, thus clearly indicating our measure is sensitive to major political events. Moreover, after the electoral reforms and the reforms of party finance laws in 1993, public dissatisfaction with democracy decreased in Italy. By the late 1990s, the level of dissatisfaction reached its lowest point, below 70 percent, since the surveys began in the 1970s. But even after the introduction of reforms, Italy remained the country with the highest level of citizen dissatisfaction with democracy in Europe throughout the thirty-year period.

In Germany, the Netherlands, and Denmark the trends of dissatisfaction have diverged in the 1990s. In the Netherlands and Denmark, dissatisfaction declined from around 45 percent in the early 1970s to around 20 percent at the end of the 1990s. By contrast, dissatisfaction increased in Germany following unification in 1990. The level of dissatisfaction in Germany increased from around 25 percent in the 1980s to around 45 percent in the 1990s.

The examination of trends of dissatisfaction with democracy in some European states suggests that there is little justification for the widespread view that there is a sweeping trend of dissatisfaction directed toward all government institutions everywhere. As these figures make clear, such trends have been absent with regard to dissatisfaction with democracy in Europe, with the exception of Germany after unification. Moreover, it would be wrong to think of administrative reform as a response to broad-based dissatisfaction in European countries. In those countries where dissatisfaction has been the highest or growing, such as in Italy, France, and Germany, administrative reform has been limited. In those countries where dissatisfaction has been the lowest or declining, as in Great Britain, the Netherlands, and Denmark, the adoption of NPM reforms have been more extensive.

In contrast to the data from the Eurobarometer on dissatisfaction with democracy in Europe, table 4.5 shows that, on the measure of lack of

TABLE 4.5
Lack of Confidence in National Governments
(around 1996)

Country	Percent
Germany (West)	74.3
Spain	67
U.S.	69.4
Japan	69.1
Australia	73.6
Norway	33.6
Sweden	56.4
Finland	65.6
Poland	56.7
Germany (East)	80.5

Source: World Values Survey.

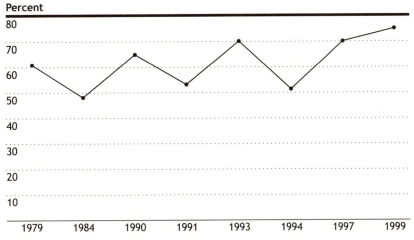

Figure 4.7.   Dissatisfaction with politics in Japan, 1979–1999. Source: *Asahi Shinbun.*

confidence in national governments, there was much that European states had in common in 1996. Only in Norway did a majority of respondents report that they had confidence in the national government. Lack of confidence in the national government in the U.S. reached almost 70 percent, but this result was by no means outstanding in a comparative context. In most of the other countries for which we have similar data from the World Value Survey—Germany, Spain, Japan, Australia, and Finland—confidence in national government was as low as in the U.S.

Distrust in government in Japan has been high and by most measures growing during the last two decades (see figure 4.7). Unlike the U.S., however, there have been only limited attempts at administrative reform in Japan. Susan Pharr shows in a study of Japanese perceptions of government that no more than 25 percent of the Japanese people persistently thought that national policy reflected the will of the people well or to some extent during the 1980s and early 1990s. Moreover, when asked about how they perceived those who ran the country in 1992, 74 percent of the Japanese respondents answered that they thought there were "many dishonest people" among them, and less than 1 percent thought that there were "no dishonest people in government." These perceptions contrast sharply with those expressed in 1976 and 1983, when a much lower number of the respondents—44 percent—thought that there were many dishonest people in government. However, a very modest number of respondents—less than 4 percent—thought there were no dishonest people in government in these earlier polls. This similarity between the early and late surveys suggests that skepticism toward government has deep roots in Japan.[28] Still, administrative reform in Japan has been limited.

Listhaug's study of small European countries shows that by some measures trust in politicians and parties has declined, but that the trends are less persuasive than in the U.S. and Japan. In the Netherlands, the number of people who believe that politicians keep their promises was low and declined from 25 percent in 1977 to 10 percent in 1989. The number of those who believed that cabinet ministers and vice-ministers only looked after their own interest was high, around 70 percent, but the trend was declining between 1977 and 1989. In Denmark, a decreasing number of people thought that political leaders would be able to make the right decisions. Whereas 60 percent thought so in 1971, only 40 percent had the same opinion a decade later. In Sweden between 1968 and 1988, there was a decline in trust in both political leaders and parliamentarians. In Norway, however, trust in political leaders stayed well above 80 percent during the same period. Trust in parliamentarians and parties, however, decreased from 1973 to 1989.[29] Listhaug's study thus suggests that there has been some limited movement toward distrust of governments in small European countries. His conclu-

TABLE 4.6
Dissatisfaction with Current
Government (around 1996)

Country	Percent
Germany (West)	65.9
Spain	74.2
U.S.	52.3
Japan	90.5
Australia	54.7
Norway	14.1
Sweden	52.3
Finland	58.7
Poland	58.6
Germany (East)	68.5

Source: World Values Survey.

[28] Susan J. Pharr, "Public Trust and Democracy in Japan," in Nye, Zelikow, and King, *Why People Don't Trust Government*, 240–41.

[29] Pla Listhaug, "The Dynamics of Trust in Politicians," in Klingemann and Fuchs, *Citizens and the State*, 273–76.

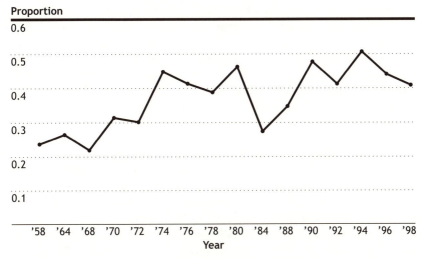

Figure 4.8.   Are U.S. government officials crooks? 1958–1998. Source: American Election Survey.

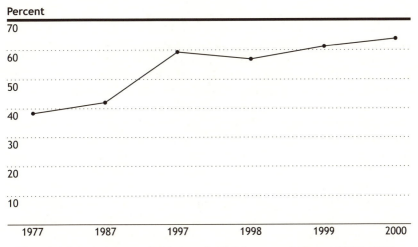

Figure 4.9.   Are most politicians and officials corrupt? France, 1977–2000. Source: SOFRES, "Les français, la politique et la représentation."

sions correspond with adoption of NPM reform. In the Netherlands, Denmark, and Sweden, where distrust has been more strongly pronounced than in Norway, reforms have been most extensive.

The correspondence between the trends Listhaug found for the small European countries and the adoption of NPM reform, is, however, contradicted when we include data about a larger number of countries. The lack of correspondence between the strength of dissatisfaction with government and the extent to which NPM reform has been undertaken is clear in table 4.6, which shows that dissatisfaction with the government was highest in those states that had only implemented limited NPM reform. Thus, by this measure of satisfaction with government, again from the World Value Survey, Japan, Spain, and Germany stand out as the places where dissatisfaction was highest. In the U.S., Australia, and Sweden dissatisfaction was much lower. About three in four respondents were dissatisfied in Germany, Spain, and Japan, but only about half of the respondents were dissatisfied in the U.S., Australia, and Sweden. The data in table 4.5 and table 4.6 might lead us to think that public opinion is responding to administrative reform in a favorable way. However as other measures of distrust show, particularly in the U.S., there is little evidence to suggest that the trend toward increasing distrust has been reversed as a response to extensive adoption of administrative reform.

One measure that has been recorded over a long time-period shows this lack of reversal of the distrust in government found in the U.S. Figure 4.8 shows that, whereas only about 30 percent of the respondents in the early 1970s to the American Election Survey thought that U.S. government officials were "crooks," between 40 and 50 percent thought so in the 1990s. This increasing trend, despite the dip in the early 1980s that can be interpreted as a short-term response to government reform, shows that extensive adoption of NPM reform certainly did not manage to reverse the perception of about 40 percent of the respondents in the U.S. that government officials are crooks. To the contrary, the number of respondents who perceived U.S. officials as crooks was on average higher in the 1990s than in the 1980s.

In France we discern a similar growth in the perception that government is corrupt between 1977 and 2000. Figure 4.9 shows that while 38 percent of the respondents thought that politicians and officials were corrupt in 1977, 42 percent did so ten years later. Continuing the increasing trend of distrust, as many as 59 percent thought that most politicians and bureaucrats were corrupt in 1977. Figure 4.9 also shows that the large percentage who distrust government in France continued to increase after 1977, so that by 2000, 64 percent of the respondents thought politicians and bureaucrats were corrupt. France, like Japan, is a case where patterns of distrust seem similar to those in the U.S. Still, the patterns of adoption of NPM reforms in the three countries are not similar. While in the U.S. there have been extensive reforms, there have been few such reforms in Japan, and only feeble attempts at reform in France.[30]

A wider comparison of perceptions of the extent to which corruption takes place in government, as seen in table 4.7, shows that the number of Americans who believed officials were corrupt in 1996 was high compared

---

[30] See chapter 7.

TABLE 4.7
Are Most or All Government
Officials Corrupt? (around 1996)

Country	Percent
Britain	37.4
Germany (West)	44
Spain	59.7
U.S.	48.9
Australia	27.7
Norway	18.8
Sweden	38.3
Finland	25.6
Poland	61.2
Germany (East)	47.8

Source: World Values Survey.

to other states for which we have data from the World Value Survey. However, the belief that officials are corrupt was more prevalent in Spain, where a majority of the respondents in 1996 thought that government was corrupt. Consistent with the argument of this chapter, we note that in states like Spain and Germany, where NPM reforms have been adopted to a limited extent, we find stronger evidence of distrust than in many of the states where NPM reforms have been adopted more extensively. Thus, in Australia the belief that officials were corrupt was held by less than 30 percent of the respondents, and in the U.K. the same belief was held by less than 40 percent of the respondents. These figures contrast with those from Germany and Spain, where more than 40 percent and close to 60 percent of the respondents, respectively, believed that corruption was widespread in 1996.

The data on public distrust in government contains some ambiguity. Although the time-series from the Eurobarometer give us reason to be skeptical that trends seen in the U.S. also take place in Europe, we have some evidence that lack of confidence in and dissatisfaction with government as well as the belief that government officials are corrupt were as common in some European countries as they were in the U.S. The differences in the level of distrust among countries have, as we noted, very weak connections with the pattern of administrative reform that we have observed. More distrust does not lead to more NPM reforms. Moreover, the trends we have been able to trace over time, such as the belief that officials are crooks in the U.S. and satisfaction with democracy in Europe, suggest that a causal link in the opposite direction—that government reform has had an impact on popular perception of government—is very weak. The data argue against a direct causal link between popular distrust of government and the extent to which NPM reforms have been adopted. We turn now to a final examination. We will observe that distrust of bureaucracies has not been particularly pronounced when compared to distrust of other institutions. Consequently, it would be inaccurate to conclude that public distrust has made bureaucracies the main target of the public's wrath and hence of NPM reforms.

Bureaucracies and Distrust

Some students of public opinion view the declining trust in politicians, parties, and officials as connected to a more general decline in interpersonal trust. Studying trends in the U.S., Orren concludes that "the generality of the trend towards mistrust is impressive,"[31] and a multi-authored article on changing social attitudes in the U.S. argues that "the problem of public confidence is not unique to government but has been a broader societal phenomenon."[32] In opposition to those who see distrust as a sweeping trend, Inglehart does not find evidence that the number of people who agree that "generally speaking, most people can be trusted" decreased in the 1981–1991 decade. Even in the U.S. and Japan, where distrust of politicians has increased in particular, there is, according to Inglehart, a trend toward more trust in other people rather than less.[33] He suggests that "the decline of confidence in established institutions and of trust in government does not represent a broad withdrawal of trust concerning people in general: it is specifically a withdrawal of confidence from authoritative institutions."[34] The World Value Surveys tend to support Inglehart's hypothesis.

Measures of confidence in the civil service generally suggest that bureaucracies are subject to the same lack of confidence that we observed with regard to national governments. Table 4.8 shows that the statement that people everywhere are dissatisfied with their bureaucracies holds true for most advanced industrialized democracies most of the time. Yet, the dissatisfied

---

[31] Orren, *"Fall from Grace,"* 82.

[32] Robert J. Blendon, John M. Benson, Richard Morin, Drew E. Altman, Mollyann Brodie, Mario Brossard, and Matt James, "Changing Attitudes in America," in *Why People Don't Trust Government*, ed. Nye, Zelikow, and King, 212.

[33] Inglehart, *Modernization and Postmodernization*, 306.

[34] Ronald Inglehart, "Postmaterialist Values and the Erosion of Institutional Authority," in *Why People Don't Trust Government*, ed. Nye, Zelikow, and King, 231.

TABLE 4.8
Not Much Confidence in the Civil Service

	1981	1990	1996
France	46.9	50.9	—
Britain	51.2	55.6	—
Germany (West)	64.8	61.4	50.8
Italy	73.4	74.9	—
Netherlands	56.5	54.0	—
Denmark	53.7	48.7	—
Belgium	54.2	57.4	—
Spain	60.0	64.8	55.3
U.S.	43.2	39.6	48.2
Canada	48.8	49.9	—
Japan	68.5	66.5	62.8
Hungary	25.8	50.4	—
Australia	52.8	—	61.8
Norway	41.8	56.4	48.6
Sweden	54.9	56.0	50.2
Finland	52.6	66.8	63.1
Poland	—	21.2	57.7
Czech Republic	—	69.4	—
Germany (East)	—	81.9	57.0

Source: World Values Survey.

majority is not large, and people do not appear to have been the most dissatisfied in the countries where NPM reforms have been most extensive. Only in Italy, Spain, Germany, Australia, Japan, Finland, and the Czech Republic does lack of confidence in the civil service cross the 60 percent mark in 1981, 1990, or 1996. In the U.S., Britain, France, the Netherlands, Denmark, Canada, and Sweden lack of confidence was rarely higher than 55 percent at these three points in time. Noticeably, confidence in the civil service was particularly high in the U.S., and confidence in the U.S. remained higher than that expressed in France in both 1981 and 1990. Canada is another example of a country where extensive adoption of NPM reform does not seem to have been driven by lack of confidence in the bureaucracy, since a slight majority of Canadian respondents, like a larger majority of American respondents, expressed confidence in their civil services.

Moreover, confidence in the civil service is not particularly low when we compare it to other institutions, as can be seen from the data in table 4.9, which show lack of confidence in the civil service, labor unions, the press, big companies, and the legal system in 1990. The figures show that in most countries people have more confidence in the civil service than in

TABLE 4.9
Not Much Confidence in Various Institutions, 1990

	Civil Service	Labor Unions	Press	Big Companies	Legal System
France	50.9	68.1	61.7	33.4	42.4
Britain	55.6	74.0	75.2	51.8	46.4
Germany (West)	61.4	64.0	65.7	61.7	34.6
Italy	74.9	66.9	60.7	38.1	68.3
Netherlands	54.0	45.9	65.8	52.0	36.0
Denmark	48.7	53.6	68.8	61.9	20.5
Belgium	57.4	62.7	55.7	49.8	55.4
Spain	64.8	60.4	52.0	54.2	52.8
U.S.	39.6	66.8	44.3	48.6	43.1
Canada	49.9	65.1	53.6	48.6	45.6
Japan	66.5	74.3	44.5	72.3	37.6
Hungary	50.4	70.0	60.1	66.0	40.4
Australia	61.8	74.5	83.3	41.0	65.0
Norway	56.4	41.0	56.6	47.4	24.8
Sweden	56.0	59.8	67.2	47.2	44.1
Finland	66.8	68.1	62.4	58.9	33.7
Poland	21.2	76.8	53.2	29.5	51.6
Czech Republic	69.4	71.6	53.6	75.0	54.4
Germany (East)	81.9	72.2	78.9	67.3	58.6

Source: World Values Survey.

labor unions, the press, and, more often than not, big companies. By contrast, most people have more confidence in the legal system than in the civil service. Again, people in the countries that adopted extensive NPM reform do not exhibit less confidence in the civil service. In the U.S., around 40 percent of the respondents lacked confidence in the civil service, around 65 percent lacked trust in the labor unions, around 50 percent lacked confidence in big companies, around 45 percent lacked confidence in the press, and around 45 percent lacked confidence in the legal system. Americans thus, in fact, showed most confidence in the civil service. In Australia, we lack data for 1990, but data from 1996 show that around 60 percent lacked confidence in the civil service, around 50 percent lacked confidence in the labor unions, around 80 percent lacked confidence in the press, around 65 percent lacked confidence in the legal system, but only around 40 percent lacked confidence in big companies. Confidence in the civil service in Australia was thus second-highest among the institutions that we are looking at. Finally, in Great Britain, around 55 percent lacked confidence in the civil service, around 75 percent lacked confidence in labor unions and in the press, around 50 percent lacked confidence in big companies, and only 45 percent lacked confidence in the legal system. The civil service was thus placed in the middle among the institutions we have looked at with regard to the level of confidence that the British expressed in the World Values Survey.

It is not insignificant to note that in all countries for which we have data from the mid 1990s, people expressed less confidence in the national government than they did in the civil service.[35] So although we may say that people in advanced industrial democracies in general have low confidence in the bureaucracy, we cannot conclude that they have particularly low confidence in the bureaucracy when compared to other governmental and nongovernmental institutions. On the contrary, the examples of the U.S., Great Britain, and Australia, where NPM reforms have been widespread, show that confidence in the civil service in 1990 was surprisingly high when compared to other institutions. Our own examination thus tends to support Inglehart's hypothesis that there is a widespread lack of confidence in institutions in general and that the civil service takes part in this trend. However, popular distrust cannot help us explain why bureaucracies have been targeted in particular in attempts to reform governments during the last two decades.

---

[35] In some instances, distrust of political institutions can sometimes spill over to distrust of the bureaucracy. For the case of Japan, see Susan J. Pharr, "Officials' Misconduct and Public Distrust: Japan and the Trilateral Democracies," in *Disaffected Democracies: What's Troubling the Trilateral Countries*, ed. Susan J. Pharr and Robert D. Putnam (Princeton: Princeton University Press, 2000), 173–201.

Conclusion

Data on public distrust do not adequately explain why reforms have been more comprehensive in some states than in others. There seems to be a higher level of dissatisfaction with the government in the U.S. than in the U.K., but reforms in the U.K. have by some measures been more comprehensive than those in the United States. Moreover, although public opinion seems to be particularly favorable to reforms in France, we have not seen as comprehensive attempts to alter the administration there as in the U.K., the United States, Australia, and New Zealand. Nor does our data on public distrust explain the timing of reforms particularly well. The drop in confidence in government in the 1970s may explain why Reagan became so popular in the early 1980s, but it does not explain why reforms took place elsewhere in the absence of similar downturns in public confidence, such as in the U.K. Moreover, it does not explain why they did not take place where the decline in confidence was similar to that in the United States, such as in Japan.

The problem of predicting the timing and scope of reforms on the basis of public sentiment is connected to a larger issue, namely, the relationship between "the popular culture of bad government" and administrative reform. Insofar as public opinion is an expression of the public's desire that politicians pay attention to particular issues, it needs to be remembered that the public also responds to opinion polls that ask people to respond to policies that have been implemented. There is thus strong interaction between the two variables, and it is often hard to tell the extent to which attempts at reform are responding to public opinion or if public opinion is responding to what politicians do. The analysis becomes even more complicated when we take into account the fact that the public is not only influenced by politics when answering questions about the government but is also influenced by general economic circumstances and particular events. We should therefore be cautious about establishing a causal relationship or direct link between public distrust of government and administrative reform. Determining the causes of administrative reform requires consideration of a variety of factors that we will discuss in later chapters.

CHAPTER FIVE

UNIVERSALISTIC REFORMS

"As far as administrative functions are concerned, all governments have a strong structural likeness: more than that, if they
are to be uniformly useful and efficient, they *must* have a
strong structural likeness."
—Woodrow Wilson, "The Study of Administration"

T HE ORGANIZATION of democratic states suggests that institutions
have a remarkable similarity across national contexts. This is what
might be called the wide-angled view of government organization.
A closer look at how institutions originate suggests that the manner of
their birth accounts for the considerable variations in organization, ethos,
power, and capacity for adaptation. Woodrow Wilson was not wrong when
he suggested that administrative organizations are bound to and need to
resemble one another. The fact remains that they do not.

If the origins of administrative institutions (as of other political institutions) explain their diverse forms across democratic societies, is it then
conceivable that a blueprint can be developed that be equally useful to all
democratic and democratizing societies? Christopher Hood has suggested
that the receptivity to implementing the strictures of the New Public
Management is a consequence of the "public service bargains" that were
struck by individual societies. "Focusing on public service bargains can
help us to understand who did what kind of new public management and
why."[1]

Yet, there remains sufficient cause for entertaining the notion that NPM
constitutes a blueprint applicable to all societies. This chapter concentrates
on programs and measures undertaken across a wide variety of societies
that led to the belief that a new paradigm of administrative organization
had been developed and was susceptible to implementation irrespective of
a society's "public service bargain" and historical underpinnings. The following chapter explains why the paradigmatic shift in administrative organization in general, and NPM in particular, encountered terrains whose
hospitality to such reforms varied markedly.

[1] Christopher Hood, "Public Service Bargains and Public Service Reform," in *Politicians,
Bureaucrats, and Administrative Reform*, ed. B. Guy Peters and Jon Pierre (New York:
Routledge, 2001), 13.

An American Blueprint

In January 1999, the then vice president, Al Gore, organized an international conference in Washington, D.C., on government reinvention. Government delegations included some heads of government, a number of ministers, and many high-ranking government officials. All came to tell of their experiences with reforms set in motion in the planning stage that reflected the basic tenets of the America-inspired revolution of the organization of governments. Al Gore, one might add, was in his element as both the "father" of this grandiosely titled revolution and as the representative of the country that was showing the way to the world on how it ought to organize its governments.

What this international conference demonstrated and what many analysts have come to believe is, first, that the organization of governance has experienced a paradigmatic shift and, second, that this shift is universal in impact. Once again, a global revolution was set in motion by the United States, and other countries were assumed to be rushing to import and implement its blueprint.

There is no denying that the massive attacks on the state and on the bureaucracy that have been a staple of American politics for the last three decades were emulated in many, though by no means all, countries. More important, it seems equally evident that a few of the guiding principles of the drive toward "rolling back the state" in favor of the market have had an important influence in most countries.[2] The spread of ideas, which sometimes travel with remarkable speed, may be more important than the ultimate results derived from their implementation.[3]

All this, however, scarcely permits us to draw the conclusion that the way that governments are organized has entailed a "revolution" or that this paradigmatic shift has been universal in conception, implementation, or impact. In order to understand whether NPM has constituted an inexorable movement that is transforming the organization of bureaucracies and the way industrial democratic states organize themselves, it is not sufficient to rely on the spread of ideas and on the debates that these ideas may generate in these states. A more painstaking empirical approach is called for, one that allows us to answer three critical questions. First, to what extent have the reforms adopted been common to a variety of societies? Second, to what extent are these reforms due to a new ideology, or paradigm of state governance, and to what extent would they have been implemented in the

---

[2] See Ezra Suleiman and John Waterbury, eds., *The Political Economy of Public Sector Reform and Privatization* (Boulder, Colo.: Westview Press, 1990).

[3] John G. Ikenberry, "The International Spread of Privatization Policies: Inducements, Learning, and 'Policy Bandwagoning,'" in *Political Economy*, ed. Suleiman and Waterbury, 88–110.

absence of an articulated set of principles of organization (NPM); and third, to what extent are administrative structures likely to experience uniformization—that is, are they likely to resemble each other after the reforms more than they did in their more traditional, Weberian guise?

The impact of NPM cannot be merely asserted or assumed. By raising and attempting to answer these questions we can begin to make an assessment of the real impact of the "reinvention revolution," as well as begin to understand what the future structure of the bureaucracy is likely to resemble in democratic societies.

It bears noting at this point, though I will return to this at a later stage, that bureaucracies are not isolated institutions that merely submit to reforms. Historically, they have evolved in response to exogenous forces. Hence, they may converge in their structures in response, not to new principles of organization or a new ideology, but, rather, in response to evolutions in democratic politics. The degree of convergence or divergence in the exogenous changes will affect the degree to which bureaucracies will come to resemble one another.

Lest it be forgotten, even Weber's ideal type did not carry the implication that all bureaucracies would develop and would be organized in a strictly uniform manner. The fact that bureaucracies develop for the purpose of managing complex societies is sufficient reason that they will end up with important similarities. But while the proponents of NPM believe themselves to be overturning the Weberian paradigm, they have forgotten that Weber always recognized that societies would endow bureaucratic organizations with their own variety of "ideal type."

Privatization

Privatization programs have appeared on government agendas across the world in the last two decades. Students of what has been called the "privatization movement" have used strong language to capture its comprehensiveness and importance. Some see privatization as a "wave," "sweeping through the world," "a fascinating phenomenon of deep significance in transforming mainstream political economy."[4] Others are surprised by the "seeming breadth and forcefulness of the international movement towards privatization"[5] or by "how widely and quickly privatization . . . has spread among developed and developing countries."[6] There is wide agreement

---

[4] Thomas Clarke and Christos Pitelis, eds., *The Political Economy of Privatization* (London: Routledge, 1993), 26 and 205.

[5] Harvey B. Feigenbaum and Jeffrey R. Henig, "The Political Underpinnings of Privatization: A Typology," *World Politics* 46 (January 1994): 185.

[6] Ikenberry, "The International Spread of Privatization Policies," 88.

that the 1980s "will be remembered as the decade of privatization and deregulation"[7] or that it will "no doubt be associated with the selling by states of public assets, much as the 1970s has come to be associated with the impact of the petrol shocks caused by the OPEC cartel."[8] At the end of the 1990s it was similarly argued that "the overall scale of privatization is impressive by any standards" and moreover that "the pace of privatization throughout the 1990s has clearly accelerated."[9]

That privatization became a widespread movement is undeniable. However, to understand the reform of state ownership better I begin, not by assuming that it was universal, but, rather, by asking what evidence has led to the general belief that privatization has been and continues to be an attractive policy for so many governments. Confining our comparisons to the advanced industrialized countries, we will not only document the privatization movement but we will also ask what inspired this movement and caused it to spread. Moreover, helped by the comparative approach we will aim to explain how privatization programs vary among countries. Finally, we will evaluate competing accounts for why privatization programs were adopted everywhere in the last two decades.

As Paul Starr observed, "Privatization has acquired both a general and a specific use in public policy discussion."[10] The general use is also referred to as the broad definition, which holds that privatization "involves that wide range of policies designed to reduce the scope, limit the functions and generally weaken the influence of the public sector."[11] Privatization as a concept understood so broadly includes most (if not all) of the public policy reforms—everything from tax cuts to efforts to treat citizens as customers. In some contexts, thinking about privatization in such broad terms can be useful. Here, however, we will limit our definition of privatization to mean the transfer from the public to the private sector of the ownership of assets and production of goods and services. This definition allows us to distinguish privatization of public assets from the gamut of public policy reforms.

Privatization narrowly defined is not necessarily the outright sale of public firms to the private sector. Although such privatization initiatives have been pursued, other ways of selling public property are more common, and they sometimes blur the question of public or private ownership.

---

[7] Giandomenico Majone, "Paradoxes of Privatization and Deregulation," *Journal of European Public Policy* 1, no. 1 (June 1994): 54.

[8] Suleiman and Waterbury, introduction to *Political Economy*, 3.

[9] Vincent Wright and Luisa Perrotti, eds., *Privatization and Public Policy*, vol. 1 (Cheltenham, U.K.: Edward Elgar, 2000), xv.

[10] Paul Starr, "The New Life of the Liberal State: Privatization and the Restructuring of State-Society Relations," in *Political Economy*, ed. Suleiman and Waterbury, 27.

[11] Wright and Perotti, *Privatization and Public Policy*, xv.

Most often states sell not whole companies, but shares in publicly owned companies. The role of the government in a company after privatization depends upon whether it sells a majority of the shares, a minority of them, or in other ways manages to hold a controlling majority. States may also choose to sell only subsidiaries of larger state-owned enterprises and thus retain control over the core production or service delivery. Just as the degree of state-withdrawal may vary, the ways in which the shares are offered for sale also differ. Sometimes shares are offered openly to the public on the international financial markets. Other times sales are more restricted and take place as off-market sales of shares or selective sales of entire enterprises to groups fulfilling certain criteria.

The Privatization Movement

To understand the scope of the privatization movement in the advanced industrialized countries, we will examine the phenomenon from two different angles. First, we look at the aggregate proceeds that have been generated from privatization over time. Second, we will scrutinize the proceeds from privatization by countries over time to see where most of the privatization activity has taken place and how this activity changes over time. In addition we briefly look at the proceeds from privatization by sector to find out in which sectors the majority of sales take place, and we ask how the sectoral pattern has changed. For measures of the proceeds from privatization, we rely mostly, but not exclusively, on data from the OECD (Organization for Economic Cooperation and Development). We do so because the OECD data are authoritative and easily comparable across states, sectors, and time.

Figure 5.1 shows the U.S. dollar equivalent of the amounts that governments in nineteen OECD countries raised from privatization from 1990 to 1998. The trend rose sharply between 1992 and 1993, and there is a general rise in the proceeds from privatization during the whole period. Whereas in 1990 about $20 billion was earned from privatization, in 1998 $60 billion was earned in the nineteen countries represented. For all OECD countries a total of $600 billion was generated from privatization between 1990 and 1999. At least two-thirds of all privatization activity took place in OECD countries and the majority of proceeds came from countries within the European Union.[12]

The rapid increase in proceeds from privatization in advanced industrialized states in the 1990s is the result of programs that were for the most part started in the 1980s. However, at no point in the 1980s did the revenues raised from privatization exceed those of the 1990s, 1997 being the

[12] OECD, "Recent Privatisation Trends," *Financial Market Trends* 76 (June 2000): 44–45.

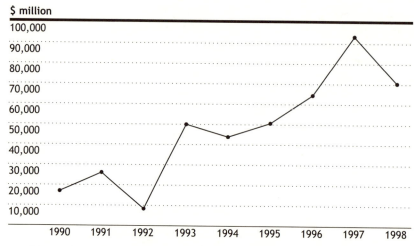

Figure 5.1. Privatization trends in the 1990s. Source: OECD, "Recent Privatisation Trends," 2000.

peak year. The U.K. and Japan alone generated over $130 billion from privatization in the 1980s and thus account for most of the proceeds in that decade.[13] There was then a rapid increase in revenues from privatization in Britain from 1983 as well as large proceeds in Japan between 1985 and 1988 when the state sold shares in the Nippon Telegraph and Telephone Company (NTT), Japan Air Lines, and the Japan National Railways. These sales account for the increasing revenues from privatization in the 1980s.[14]

A World Bank study estimates that 180 companies were privatized in OECD countries between 1980 and 1991,[15] and not all of these sales took place in Britain or Japan. Table 5.1 shows the distribution of proceeds from privatization in twelve individual OECD countries. In addition to the dominance of Japan and Great Britain, privatization efforts in New Zealand stand out in the 1980s when proceeds are measured as a percentage of GDP. New Zealand's results should not come as a surprise in view of the fact that the period since Labour's accession to power in 1984 has been viewed as one of "intensive change," characterized by "the magnitude of reform, the breadth of the reforms, the longevity of the process

[13] Clarke and Pitelis, *The Political Economy of Privatization*, 8.

[14] Kent E. Calder, "Public Corporations and Privatization in Modern Japan," in *Political Economy*, ed. Suleiman and Waterbury, 165.

[15] Sunita Kikeri, John Nellis, and Mary Shirley, *Privatization: The Lessons of Experience* (Washington, D.C.: World Bank, 1992), 22.

TABLE 5.1
Privatization in Twelve OECD Countries, 1980–1991

	Privatization Period	Proceeds (£ billion)	Percent of GDP
Austria	1987–90	0.6	0.9
Canada	1984–90	1.6	0.6
France	1983–91	8.2	1.5
Germany (West)	1984–90	3.2	0.5
Italy	1983–91	6.3	1.4
Japan	1986–88	47.8	3.1
Netherlands	1987–91	1.5	1.0
New Zealand	1987–91	3.0	14.1
Portugal	1989–91	1.5	4.3
Spain	1986–90	1.2	0.5
Sweden	1987–90	1.3	1.2
U.K.	1979–91	44.5	11.9

Source: Clarke and Pitelis, *The Political Economy of Privatization*, 8.

and the importance of the changes."[16] In addition, the French and Italian privatization programs generated significantly higher proceeds in the 1980s than in most of the other states. In the French case, the high level of proceeds was a consequence of the ambitious and high-speed privatization program introduced by the center-right government led by Jacques Chirac in 1986. In Italy, the relatively high proceeds came from a gradual form of privatization beginning in 1983 and involving half a dozen major state-owned enterprises, particularly the large-scale sale of Alfa Romeo to Fiat in 1986.

Figure 5.2 shows how proceeds from privatization have differed in nineteen OECD countries in the 1990s. Notably, the picture for the 1990s is very similar to that of the 1980s. The U.K., Japan, France, and Italy are still among the countries that raised the highest proceeds from privatization.

[16] John Halligan, "New Public Sector Models: Reform in Australia and New Zealand," in *Public Sector Reform: Rationale, Trends and Problems*, ed. Jan-Erik Lane (London: Sage, 1996), 17.

$ million

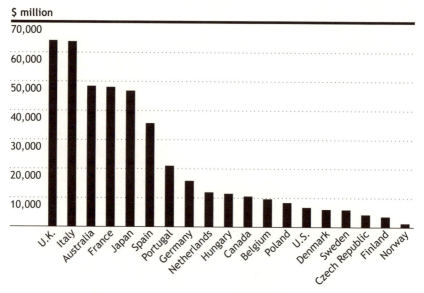

Figure 5.2. Privatization in nineteen countries, 1990–1998. Source: OECD, "Recent Privatisation Trends," 2000.

In the 1990s, over 50 percent of the proceeds generated in OECD countries came from the U.K., Italy, Australia, France, Japan, and Spain. Of the nineteen countries represented in the table, these six countries generated over 70 percent of the proceeds.

Looking at the sectors in which privatization took place, we observe the same pattern in most of the advanced industrialized countries. In the initial stage, governments sold firms providing goods and services of a purely commercial nature and operating in competitive sectors of the economy. In the latter stage, they privatized their public utilities, including telecommunications and transport sectors. The explanation for the growing proceeds in the 1990s as compared to the 1980s is not only the spread of privatization programs to Eastern Europe but that the second wave of privatization—that of public utilities and especially telecommunication companies—began in most Western European countries.

Origins of Privatization

Margaret Thatcher did not invent privatization. Before she came to power in the U.K. in 1979, Konrad Adenauer's government in West Germany had launched a significant program of denationalization. The German government privatized Preussag in 1959. In 1961 it sold a majority stake in Volkswagen, and in 1965 it sold shares in VEBA, the mining and heavy industry company. According to Megginson, Nash, and Randenborg, "a remarkable aspect of the official motivations expressed by the Adenauer government in launching its privatization program is how similar they are to the objectives expressed by the Thatcher government two decades later."[17] It was not only the German government that engaged in privatization. The Austrian government sold 40 percent of the shares of two nationalized banks in the 1950s, and in 1972 it sold a majority of its shares in Siemens-Austria to Siemens in Germany. Even in the U.K., before Thatcher, the Labour government started privatizing British Petroleum in 1977. Vincent Wright and John Vickers, however, distinguish between the similarities of the early privatization programs and those undertaken by the Conservative British government after 1979. The preceding sales, they argue, were "sporadic and limited, with no ideological roots, no political implications and belonging to no overall industrial strategy. It was not until the 1980s that privatization was to assume its wide-ranging and politically significant form."[18]

Ideologically, private ownership is at the core of liberalism as advocated by both John Locke and Adam Smith. However, the recent privatization movement has often been viewed as less firmly underpinned by a coherent set of ideas than was, for instance, the spread of Keynesian demand management. In the case of Britain, Veljanovski argues that privatization "was an idea stirred by the Conservative Party's traditional support for private property and by a growing disillusionment with the performance of the nationalised industries."[19] Debating the effects of knowledge and learning on the spread of privatization, Ikenberry concludes that "in the area of privatization, a question remains concerning what constitutes the new knowledge."[20]

The works of a number of scholars, many associated with the economics department at the University of Chicago, with their strong preference for the market over the dictates of the state, can be seen as providing the intellectual basis and inspiration for the privatization movement. These scholars, guided in particular by the work of Milton Friedman, questioned the dilemma that economists and politicians had pondered since Adam Smith,

---

[17] William L. Megginson, Robert C. Nash, and Matthias van Randenborgh, "The Financial and Operating Performance of Newly Privatized Firms: An International Empirical Analysis," in *The Privatization Process: A Worldwide Perspective*, ed. Terry L. Anderson and Peter J. Hill (Latham, Md.: Rowman and Littlefield, 1996), 18.

[18] John Vickers and Vincent Wright, "The Politics of Industrial Privatisation in Western Europe: An Overview," in *The Politics of Privatization in Western Europe*, ed. John Vickers and Vincent Wright (London: Frank Cass, 1989), 4.

[19] Cento Veljanovski, *Selling the State: Privatisation in Britain* (London: Weidenfeld and Nicolson, 1987), 7.

[20] Ikenberry, "International Spread of Privatization Policies," 107.

namely, how governments could prevent or ameliorate market failures.[21] Instead, they argued, we should ask how we could prevent or reverse "government failure." Their solution was a strategy of deregulation, privatization, and marketization (DPM). They recommended diminishing the role of the state and enhancing the mechanisms of the market; or diminishing the public sector in favor of the private one. In the case of privatization in Chile, many of the recommendations of these economists had been seen as especially influential. The Chilean case is so particular with regard to privatization that it warrants some comment although it falls outside of our comparative scope. The case is particularly important when considering the origins of the recent privatization movement. In Chile, the first stages of sales took place right after the coup (more precisely in 1973 and in 1978), before Thatcher came to power in Britain. While Pinochet controlled the Chilean government, the privatization program was by some measures carried further than even in Britain. Moreover, as Paul Sigmund argues, "the ideological commitment has come from the small group of economists known—from the university at which many did graduate work—as the 'Chicago boys.' "[22] Thus, the mix of ideas from the Chicago School with the political power of the military dictatorship of the Pinochet government gave particular resonance to the Chilean example of privatization.

Although Thatcher's Britain cannot be said to have introduced a major innovation in the sale of public assets, the British example nonetheless merits special attention in any discussions of the origins of the privatization movement. The British privatization program between 1979 and 1993 is outlined in table 5.2. We should not underestimate the importance of the British Telecom (BT) sale in November 1984, which at the time was by far the largest one of its kind in history. The privatization of BT was met with strong demand both at home and abroad, and the regulatory framework for the privatized company was initially at least perceived as reasonable and workable for consumers, investors, and the company itself. Thus, the BT sale demonstrated how successful large-scale privatizations could be.

Two factors account for the differences in the privatization programs in OECD countries. First is the difference in the initial size of the public sector. All OECD states owned enterprises, but the extent to which they did so varied and formed a natural limit to the scope of the privatization programs. A second source of difference came from the timing of the privatization programs. Some states, like Britain, started early, and thus arguably

---

[21] See, for example, Milton Friedman, *Capitalism and Freedom* (Chicago: University of Chicago Press, 1959); and Milton Friedman and R. Friedman, *Free to Choose* (New York: Harcourt Brace Jovanovich, 1980).

[22] Paul E. Sigmund, "Chile: Privatization, Reprivatization, Hyperprivatization," in *Political Economy*, ed. Suleiman and Waterbury, 346.

TABLE 5.2
The U.K. Privatization Program from 1979 to 1995

Company	Date of IPO	Proceeds (£ million)	2nd Tranche	3rd Tranche
British Petroleum	Nov-79	284	Sep-81	Oct-87
British Aerospace	Feb-81	43	May-85	—
Cable and Wireless	Oct-81	181	Dec-83	Dec-85
Amersham International	Feb-82	64	—	—
Britoil	Oct-82	334	Aug-95	—
Assoc. British Ports	Feb-83	46	Apr-84	—
Enterprise Oil	Jun-84	384	—	—
Jaguar	Jul-84	297	—	—
British Telecom	Nov-84	3,685	Dec-91	Jul-93
British Gas	Dec-86	3,691	Jul-90	—
British Airways	Feb-87	858	—	—
Rolls Royce	May-87	1,032	—	—
British Airport Authority	Jul-87	1,223	—	—
British Steel	Dec-88	2,425	—	—
10 Water Companies	Dec-89	3,395	—	—
12 Regional Electricity Companies	Dec-90	3,395	—	—
National Power	Mar-91	1,341	Mar-95	—
PowerGen	Mar-91	822	Mar-95	—
Scottish Hydro-Electric	Jun-91	920	—	—
Scottish Power	Jun-91	1,955	—	—
N. Ireland Electricity	Jun-93	684	—	—

Source: OECD, "Corporate Governance, State-Owned Enterprises and Privatization," 1998.

needed both to experiment more and have a stronger political foundation for their privatization programs than those that started privatization programs later. Remarkably, the ideology of the party in power does not seem to have been an important source of difference in privatization programs among the OECD countries.

When we examine public ownership in the OECD countries in 1980, we observe that public holdings in the U.S. and in Japan were much more limited than in all other OECD countries. However, in both states postal services were state-owned. In addition, the Japanese state owned the entire telecommunications sector, a large share of the railways, and a limited share in airlines. In the U.S. a quarter of the railways services was publicly owned, and the same held true for the electricity sector. In all other OECD states, public ownership was much more prominent. Among those states with the largest shares of public ownership, Austria, Britain, and France stand out. In all these states the postal service, telecommunications, electricity, gas, coal, and railways were completely state-owned.

If we look at public ownership by sector in 1980, we observe that postal services, telecommunications, and railways were completely state-owned in most OECD countries. The exceptions for telecommunications are the U.S., where telecommunications were entirely privately owned, Canada, where the state owned 25 percent, and, finally, Spain, where the state owned half of the telecommunication services. With regard to railways, the exceptions were the U.S. government, which owned a limited 25 percent, and the Canadian and Japanese states, which owned three-quarters of the railways services. Other public utility sectors such as electricity and gas were also completely state-owned in a majority of OECD states in the 1980s. However, in addition to the U.S. and Japan, where state ownership was limited, Belgium, Canada, and Spain had limited state ownership of public utilities. In Belgium the state owned only 25 percent of the electricity and gas companies, in Canada the state owned no part of gas but all of electricity, whereas in Spain the state did not own electricity but owned 75 percent of gas. In addition, the Swedish state owned only half of the electricity sector.

In the transport sector, ownership was, as noted, high in the railways sector, and state ownership of airlines was also significant. In OECD countries, only the U.S. had no public ownership of airlines. In Australia, Japan, and Switzerland the states owned only 25 percent of the airlines. Tradable goods such as coal, steel, oil, cars, and ships were less dominated by state ownership, but a significant number of states owned these sectors as well. Coal production was mainly state-owned in Britain, France, and Austria. In addition, the West German and the Spanish states owned half of the coal sector. The motor industry was fully state-owned in Austria, and in Britain, France, and the Netherlands, the states owned half of the car industry. In addition, the West German and Italian states owned a small part of the motor industry in the 1980s.

The timing of the sale of state-owned enterprises also influenced how extensive the privatization movement was in individual countries. Britain started especially early, followed by France, Portugal, Italy, Japan, New Zealand, and Australia, all of which began their privatization programs in the 1980s. Germany, Spain, the Netherlands, Belgium, the Scandinavian states, and Greece did not establish comprehensive privatization programs until the 1990s.

It seems evident that there are many more similarities in the privatization efforts than there are differences. Public sectors were, in general, large at the outset of the privatization movement. There was a difference in timing, but the extent to which the transfer of ownership from the state to the private sector caught on is much more impressive than the extent to which some governments refrained from privatizing in the beginning. Finally, it is not insignificant to note that privatization has been pursued both by parties of the Left and by parties of the Right.

Decentralization

The transfer of political authority within the public sector from central to subnational levels of government—decentralization—appears to be a less sweeping reform movement than the transfer of ownership from the public sector to the private one. Different conclusions in studies of decentralization reflect the more ambiguous nature of the trend. Some authors see decentralization as a theme dominating governments' agendas. Thus, Sharpe refers to the establishment of what he calls "meso government" as a "near-universal phenomenon over the last twenty years or so in the Western European state."[23] Others emphasize the variability of the phenomenon. In Keating's words, "Regional government has moved forward slowly and hesitatingly, and has been institutionalized in diverse ways and to very different extents in the countries of Western Europe."[24]

There is little doubt that programs as different as Reagan's "New Federalism," the Defferre reforms in France under Mitterrand, and Blair's devolution program in Britain have placed the theme of decentralization firmly on the political reform agenda across the advanced and less advanced industrialized states over the past two decades. It is difficult to find a clear shift in the center of gravity of authority from central to

---

[23] L. J. Sharpe, ed., *The Rise of Meso Government in Europe* (London: Sage, 1993), 1.

[24] Micheal Keating, *The New Regionalism in Western Europe: Territorial Restructuring and Political Change* (Cheltenham, U.K.: Edgward Elgar, 1998), 61.

subnational levels of government in all advanced industrialized states to the same extent that we found a shift in ownership from the government to the private sector in the case of privatization. Nonetheless, decentralization has come to be generally associated with democracy. In some cases, decentralization efforts have led to substantial transfers of political authority and financial autonomy to subnational levels of governments—Belgium and Spain are examples where such substantial transfer has taken place. In other cases, decentralization efforts have meant the establishment of elected councils on the regional level, but the transfer of authority and autonomy have been more modest—such as in France, the U.K., and Italy. In yet other cases, decentralization has meant the mere establishment of subnational administrative units without significant authority and autonomy—such as in Ireland, Greece, and Finland. Most important, the debate about decentralization is alive and well in all advanced industrialized states, and any categorization of efforts to decentralize as substantial, asymmetrical, or administrative is passionately discussed by politicians and academics alike.

Decentralization efforts have varied more among countries than has privatization, because the perception of problems connected to the centralization of the state has differed in advanced industrialized states. As we saw in the previous section, privatization programs converged to a large extent in OECD countries because of the adoption of similar solutions to what were perceived as similar problems. Decentralization has also to some extent involved the adoption of similar solutions to similar problems. However, unlike the problems perceived regarding to state ownership, the problems connected to central authority have often not been perceived as being the same in countries with as different territorial structures and linguistic and national composition as Belgium, France, Germany, and the U.K. In addition, the ability of regional groups and governments to argue for decentralization reforms has differed significantly both among and within countries. When seeking to understand the reforms to decentralize government structures in this context we face two problems. First, we will need to explain the principal differences among the efforts to decentralize. Second, we also need to ask why decentralization appears to be a dominant, if not uniform, trend in advanced industrialized democracies.

The main sources of difference arise from the varying pressures from below—from the differing ability of ethnic, nationalist, or regionalist groups to organize and form parties within countries to promote their interests. The ability of political elites to form coalitions in support of decentralization reforms has also differed. In addition, the emphasis on the regional levels within the EU has led to a promotion of the regional level in EU member states that has not been present in non–EU member states. Regardless of the important differences among countries and the many splits within them, there are indications in a number of countries of political coalitions convinced of the functional need for a more powerful subnational level of government. Strong regions are seen by these coalitions as a means to enhance the competitiveness of the state in a globalized economy and to improve democratic representation and participation. We turn now to a discussion of concrete programs that evidence the tug-of-war between centripetal and centrifugal forces. Why are decentralization reforms so different? And why is decentralization the dominant trend even though the reforms differ?

Decentralization and Democracy

The tales of the violent Basque nationalists forming the ETA movement, the Corsican separatists, the never-ending conflict in Northern Ireland, the aggrieved Flemish-speaking majority in Belgium, and the Scottish Nationalist Party have become familiar in the last decade. If we add ethnic nationalist movements elsewhere—for example, in the former Yugoslavia, the Caucasus, and Turkey—we seem to have ample evidence of a rise of ethnic, nationalist, or regionalist conflicts. We will not examine the causes of this "politicization of ethnicity," but we will discuss how pressures for decentralization from regionalist and ethnic organizations and parties have triggered and shaped the decentralization reforms to a large extent in some countries, but not as much as in others.

Belgium is probably the country in Europe where decentralization has gone furthest in response to ethnic or linguistic regionalist pressures. After a final breakthrough in 1992, known as the Saint-Michel Agreement, Belgium formally achieved status as a federal state in 1994. The final state architecture, although clearly a transfer of power from the central level to the subnational, is complex, reflecting both identities based on the three language communities and geographical identity based in Wallonnia, Flanders, and Brussels. The Belgian state now has regional levels, which can be seen as "constituent states in a federal system, with all the features connected with such status—namely, parliamentary assembly, government and above all powers and legal standards that are not subordinate to the national Parliament nor to the national government."[25] The federalization of the Belgian state cannot be separated from the linguistic and regional movements led by parties such as *Volksunie*, based in Flanders, and the *Front Democratique des Francophones*, based in Wallonia. Michael O'Neill captures the bottom-up dynamic of the Belgian reforms when he describes Belgian decentralization reform not as a "classical experience" of "enlightened

[25] Frank Delmartino, "Belgium: In Search of the Meso Level," in *Rise of Meso Government*, ed. Sharpe, 54.

constitutional craftsmen" in a "shared moral endeavour," but rather as "protracted hard-won accommodation between politicians who engaged in the project because failure threatened an even less palatable outcome."[26]

In Spain, as in Belgium, there has been a rapid and substantive decentralization process that is closely connected to the demands raised by regional parties. In the Spanish case, however, there was also a strong element of political opportunity for change caused by the establishment of a new democratic regime following the French regime. Cuchillo argues that when making the 1978 constitution, "the problem posed by the existence of a number of regions with a linguistic, historical, cultural and social identity that was quite distinct from the rest of the state was one of the questions which was considered in the process."[27] The historic territories of Catalonia, the Basque Country, Galicia, and eventually Andalucia received status as autonomous communities before other regions. There was no provision in the constitution requiring that all of the Spanish territory be divided into regions. However, by 1983, seventeen autonomous communities had been established with a constitutionally required unicameral elected legislative body, a council, and president, and an administrative corps. Table 5.3 shows the growth of government employment on the regional level between 1984 and 1998. In the last year, a larger portion of government employment was held at the regional than at the central level. The importance of regionalist organization for the decentralization process is suggested by the asymmetrical decentralization trends within Spain. The governments of the strongly mobilized regions Catalonia and the Basque Country have reached special agreements about transfer of authority to their regions, and they are also responsible for two-thirds of all challenges brought to the Constitutional Court from the autonomous regions.[28]

The third and final example of a decentralization process that has been highly influenced by well-organized nationalist groups is the devolution process in the United Kingdom. At the end of 1997, Tony Blair's Labour government passed laws that called for referenda on establishing a Scottish Parliament and a Welsh Assembly. In September 1997, referenda were held in Wales and Scotland on the establishment of these parliaments. In May 1998, a referendum was held on the establishment of the Greater London Authority, and in May 1998 the first election in the semiau-

[26] Michael O'Neill, "Re-imagining Belgium: New Federalism and Political Management of Cultural Diversity," *Parliamentary Affairs* 51, no. 2 (1998): 243.

[27] Montserrat Cuchillo, "The Autonomous Communities and the Spanish Meso," in Sharpe, *Rise of Meso Government*, 213.

[28] Robert Agranoff and Juan Antonio Ramos Gaalarin, "Toward Federal Democracy in Spain: An Examination of Intergovernmental Relations," *Publius: The Journal of Federalism* 27, no. 4 (1997): 1–38. See also Michael Keating, *New Regionalism*, 65–67.

TABLE 5.3

The Structure of Government Employment in Spain, 1984–1998
(as percent of total government employment)

	Central	Region	Local	Health	Other
1984	31.9	14.5	15.3	12.4	3.4
1989	27.8	20.1	18.0	14.0	0.2
1994	26.2	24.9	19.2	14.2	0.2
1998	25.6	28.5	20.5	15.6	0.2

Source: C. Alba and C. Navarro, n.d., "Public Employment in Spain: A Preliminary Analysis," unpublished comparative public service project, Department of Political Science, Universidad Autonoma, Madrid.

tonomous Assembly in Northern Ireland was held. In May 1999, the first elections to the Scottish Parliament and the Welsh National Assembly were held. In May 2000, the first election for the mayor of London and for the London Assembly was held. The last four years have thus completely altered the previously centralized British state, which during the 1980s was treated as a clear case of deviation from the decentralizing trend elsewhere in Europe.[29] Vernon Bogdanor describes the change as more profound in political terms than in constitutional ones. He argues that "Westminster . . . will be transformed into a domestic parliament for England, part of a domestic parliament for Wales, and a federal parliament for Northern Ireland and Scotland."[30] Especially difficult, he thinks, will be the relationship between Westminster and the Scottish Parliament, since the Scottish Nationalist Party is strong.

The demand from regionalist movements and their ability to organize have thus without doubt played an important role in shaping the decentralization reform in Belgium; they have affected the development of the constitutional compromise in Spain, and, if Bogdanor is right, the Scottish Nationalist Party will shape the development of decentralization in Britain in the future. Cases involving the granting of considerable degrees of autonomy to regions in this way involve the strong organization of sub-nationalist movements. When this is the case, the distribution of power between the center and the periphery becomes a question of the preservation of democracy. Juan Linz has argued that it is no longer logical or possible to

[29] See, for example, Yves Mèny and Vincent Wright, *Centre-Periphery Relations in Western Europe* (London: Allen and Urwin, 1985).

[30] Vernon Bogdanor, "Devolution: Decentralisation or Disintegration?" *Political Quarterly* (1999): 189.

separate discussion of federalism, nationalism, and democracy, because all three are intimately linked in binational or multinational states. The cases of growing autonomy for regions (Belgium, Spain, Britain) result precisely from this type of state, but the outcome of decentralization in these states have varied so far. Belgium has become a federal state, Spain is federalizing in an asymmetrical way, while the U.K. is not by any measure approaching a federal structure. France is another example of a state that remains unitary but that has been edging over the past decade toward the recognition of the "Corsican people" and toward granting a degree of autonomy that, to many, violates the foundation of the republican state.[31]

The association of democracy with decentralization has been described as "inevitable" in "those states that endured the long night of fascist centralization."[32] The West German, Austrian, Italian, and Spanish constitutions and their emphasis on decentralized power are in part an outcome of such associations, although the federal structures have deeper historical roots. In the Italian case, the constitutional provisions for regional governments failed to be instituted until the 1970s, except in the cases of the special-status borderline and island regions, which received their regional status in the 1950s and 1960s. Between 1970 and 1977, however, the process of regionalization started in Italy, and fifteen ordinary regions—a new, elected regional level of government—were created. By then, the link between the fascist past and decentralization in Italy had weakened substantially. In fact, Cassese and Torchia argue that it was a break with the dominant culture of the central administration, which had its roots in the fascist period, that made the reforms of the 1970s possible. Italy, unlike Germany and Austria, remained a unitary state, and the relationship between the regions and central government has been conflict-ridden. In the words of Cassesse and Torchia, "The contradiction between extending regional functions and reducing regional financial autonomy is a typical example of the continuous tension characteristic of the Italian situation."[33]

Discussions about decentralization and federalization of Italy were revived in the 1990s in the wake of large-scale corruption scandals and the electoral success of *Lega Nord*, the populist regionalist party led by Umberto Bossi. The most important decentralization effort was formulated in four laws that were passed in 1997–98 and known as "the Bassanini laws," after the minister for adminstrative reform and local gov-

---

[31] See, for example, Helen Hintjens, John Loughlin, and Claude Olivesi, "The Status of Maritime and Insular France: The DOM-TOM and Corsica," in *The End of the French Unitary State? Ten Years of Regionalization in France (1982–1992)*, ed. John Loughlin and Sonia Mazey (London: Frank Cass, 1995), 110–31.

[32] Sharpe, *Rise of Meso Government*, 14.

[33] Sabino Cassese and Luisa Torchia, "The Meso Level in Italy," in *Rise of Meso Government*, ed. Sharpe, 106.

ernment under the Prodi government, Franco Bassanini. The attempt led by Bassanini to devolve a considerable number of political functions, including financial autonomy, to the regions has been termed "administrative federalism." Bassanini himself considered these reforms to be nothing short of a "silent revolution"—"the first structural reform of the organization of the central state since 1865."[34] Other commentators have viewed the decentralization efforts with much less enthusiasm. In the words of one of them, "All in all, in institutional terms the reforms to local government initiated between March 1997 and March 1998 should be characterized as a mutation in a slowly evolving process of decentralisation rather than a leap into the federalist dark."[35]

Regionalism and a Modern, Manageable State

There have been strong movements toward decentralization even in the absence of strong regionalist movements. Decentralization has been seen by politicians and administrators not only as a way to make the state more democratic but also as a means of modernizing it and of improving its efficiency. This has been referred to as a "functionalist logic."[36] Support for both the democratic ideal and the functionalist logic of decentralization has been present within political parties and elites in all countries since the late 1960s. Still, only in some countries, and at particular points in time, have politicians been able to institute significant decentralization reform. A discussion of the 1982 Defferre laws in France helps us pin down factors that facilitate substantial decentralization reform from the point of view of the center. The lessons from that case study are that decentralization reform is facilitated, first, by a major change in government and, second, by a strategy that, rightly or wrongly, links electoral advantage and improved economic development to decentralization. Arguably, the timing of the British devolution reforms can be explained by reference to similar factors.

Together with the nationalization of industries and banks, the decentralization reform in France that was named after the minister of the interior and decentralization, Gaston Defferre, constituted, together with the nationalization program, the most important part of the program of the socialists, led by François Mitterrand, when they took power in 1981. The reforms aimed to substantially transfer political authority to the already ex-

[34] Franco Bassanini, "Italie: Notre revolution silencieuse," in *Notre Etat*, ed. Roger Fauroux and Bernard Spitz (Paris: Robert Laffont, 2000), 153.

[35] Mark Gilbert, "The Bassanini Laws: A Half-Way House in Local Government Reform," in *Italian Politics: The Return to Politics*, ed. David Hine and Salvatore Vassallo (New York: Berghahn Books), 140.

[36] For a discussion of the functionalist logic of regionalism, see Keating, *New Regionalism*, chap. 3.

isting twenty-six regions by calling for directly elected councils in the regions, the freeing of regional and departmental budget decisions from the dominance of the representatives of the central administration in the regions and departments, and the limiting of the central administration's oversight function *(tutelage)* over the communes.[37]

In the debate that has followed these initial reforms, many students have deemphasized the break they created with the past by insisting that power in France was never as centralized as the Jacobin myth suggested.[38] Through the arrangement whereby politicians could and to a large degree did hold multiple offices simultaneously *(cumul des mandats)* and through clientalism, some local leaders were able to develop extensive networks and acquire important influence before 1982. Moreover, from the late 1950s there was an ongoing debate about decentralization, which culminated in Charles de Gaulle's resignation after he lost the 1969 referendum—a loss that is commonly interpreted as a vote of no confidence in de Gaulle rather than an opposition to the regional reform in question. Simultaneously, as the Gaullists attempted to institute deconcentration reforms, decentralization acquired increasing support within different fractions of the Left—from the many among them who promoted self-management *(autogestion)* to Michel Rocard, the leader of the *Parti socialiste unifié* (PSU), who argued that the provinces needed to be decolonized.[39] Notably, as early as in 1965, Gaston Defferre published a proposal to establish elected assemblies in the regions that should be able to take on executive powers if they proved successful.[40]

It would be wrong, however, to think of the decentralization reform of 1982 as anything but an important break with the past. The Jacobin myth, which held that national unity, equality, and a centralized state are necessarily closely connected, was widely believed and supported not only among parts of the general public but also within Mitterrand's government. The resignation of Jean-Pierre Chevènement from Lionel Jospin's left-of-center government over the issue of granting Corsica a great degree of autonomy is an example of how deep the split between traditional centralists and

[37] For accounts of the content of the initial reforms, see Vivien A. Schmidt, *Democratizing France: The Political and Administrative History of Decentralization* (Cambridge: Cambridge University Press, 1990); and Loughlin and Mazey, *End of the French Unitary State?*

[38] See, for example, Sonia Mazey, "Power Outside Paris," in *Developments in French Politics,* rev. ed., ed. Peter A. Hall, Jack Hayward, and Howard Machin (London: Macmillan, 1994), 152–70; and Bernard Bouve, "France: From the Regionalized State to the Emergence of Regional Governance?" in *The Political Economy of Regionalism,* ed. Michael Keating and John Loughlin (London: Frank Cass, 1997), 347–69.

[39] Michel Rocard, "Décoloniser la province," report to the Congress at Grenoble, May 1, 1966.

[40] Schmidt, *Democratizing France,* 87.

decentralists run. In addition to these long-lasting splits within the Left itself, the powerful multiple officeholders were at the time opposed to the reforms that they rightfully saw as undermining their base of power. The reforms represented a break with the past in that they led to an initial agreement on a legal framework for a substantial transfer of power from the center to the periphery—and thus ended thirty years of much talk but little action about decentralization.

Decentralization was not achieved through one vote on March 2, 1982. Rather, the framework that was decided then has formed the backdrop for subsequent developments. Importantly, it was a framework that transferred power to the regions, departments, and communes and limited the influence of the representatives of the central administration—the prefects—but left decisions on transfers of authority and responsibilities from the center to the periphery to be worked out at later stages. Without doubt, the eagerness with which the reforms were proposed—on the very first day of the new government's legislative term and without taking time to negotiate the details—had its roots in the Left's being in opposition for over two decades. Not only had the socialists used that time to develop a policy on decentralization, but they also wanted to change a structure that had repeatedly returned parties of the Right to power.

As it turns out, the Left has not done particularly well in the regional elections, which have occurred three times since they first were held in 1986. Moreover, the elections have hardly spurred a wave of regional enthusiasm and democratic vigor. In the 1998 election, as many as 42 percent of those eligible to vote did not do so.[41] In light of such developments, those who argued early that the decentralization reforms would change the structure of support to the advantage of the Left and also "revolutionize center-periphery relations"[42] have been contradicted by those who argue that the Defferre reforms were only a limited accomplishment and that the possibility for recentralization should not be underestimated. Richard Balme, while recognizing the special developments in the insular regions (Corsica and the four overseas territories), goes so far as to argue that "the region in the top-down perspective, appears to be a mere springboard for state action."[43]

The reasons for this perceived failure of the decentralization reforms are manifold. The inability of the Socialist Party to create a coalition of support for abolishing the departments and limiting the number of communes has

[41] Gino G. Raymond, "Decentralizing or Deconstructing the Republic?" in *Structures of Power in Modern France*, ed. Gino G. Raymond (London: Macmillan, 2000), 175.

[42] Schmidt, *Democratizing France*, 182.

[43] Richard Balme, "The French Region as a Space for Public Policy," in *Regions in Europe*, ed. Patrick Le Galès and Christian Lequesne (London: Routledge, 1998), 181.

been seen as a major weakness of the decentralization effort that undermined the possibility for regional autonomy from the outset.[44] Furthermore, as Dupoirier points out, the setup of the first regional elections was such that "it is hard to imagine a more effective combination of obstacles to the creation of a specifically regional electoral market."[45] It was held at the same time as the elections for the National Assembly, and people voted within departmental voting districts, which discouraged the development of specific regional political programs. As another sign of how insignificant the regions were, those politicians who had to choose between seats in the regions and the departments, following the law of 1985 that limited the right of politicians to hold several offices at the same time, overwhelmingly opted for the position in the departments. As Bernard Jouve reports, "Out of 84 elected officials opting either for a seat in a regional council or for a seat on a departmental council, 64 chose the second."[46] On top of this weak initial standing of the regions as independent electoral areas and attractive political arenas, there has since 1986 been evidence that the prefects are regaining power, and, as an event of symbolic importance, the prefects got their name, which had been changed in 1982, back again in 1987.[47]

In spite of the ongoing fight for authority and financial resources between the center and different subnational units in France and despite the evidence that the Defferre reforms failed to meet many of its stated objectives, we should not underestimate the significant transfer of authority that began to be institutionalized with the Defferre reforms of 1982. Importantly, the center-right government did not change the decentralization policy of the socialists, as they did with many of their other policies, when they took office in 1986. Moreover, the establishment of the elected councils on the regional level, together with the 1985 law limiting the holding of multiple offices, did shake up established networks and create room for new political elites. As the Dupoirier study showed, elites attached to their regions did form during the first five years after the 1986 election, despite institutional obstacles.[48] Moreover, when people were asked what they considered to be the administrative and political unit of the future, three times as many chose the regions rather than the departments in 1991, and the number favoring the regions increased during the first five years following the first regional elections.[49] It is difficult therefore to rule out the long-

[44] See Jean-Claude Douence, "The Evolution of the 1982 Regional Reforms: An Overview," in *End of the French Unitary State?* ed. Loughlin and Mazey, 10–24.

[45] Elisabeth Dupoirier, "The First Regional Political Elites in France (1986–1992): A Profile," in *End of the French Unitary State?* ed. Loughlin and Mazey, 25.

[46] Bouve, "France: From the Regionalized State," 357.

[47] For further discussion of the rebalancing of power toward the center, see Loughlin and Mazey, introduction to *End of the French Unitary State?* 1–9.

[48] Dupoirier, "First Regional Political Elites," 25–33.

[49] Bouve, "France: From the Regionalized State," 352.

term effects of the decentralization reforms in France, even in the absence of strong regional demands from those other than the Corsicans, the Bretons, and the Basques.

Like the decentralization reforms in France, devolution in Britain benefited from the eagerness of a government that had been out of office for a considerable period to change the political and administrative structure in a way that was seen as benefiting the Labour Party electorally,[50] and British democracy and the economy generally. Sweden is another case where the functional logic has played an important role in recent decentralization attempts. Unlike in France and the U.K., the decentralization program was, however, not brought about by a government that had been out of power for a long time, but rather by the Social Democratic Party, which has held power in Sweden during most of the postwar period. This difference can account for the limited and experimental nature of the Swedish decentralization program, which consisted of four pilot regions established in Skåne, Västra Götaland, Kalmar, and Gotland in 1999.[51] The reasons for the timing of the Swedish experiment are closely tied to incentives from the EU level to promote regional autonomy in the EU member states. We now turn to a brief discussion of the impact that the EU can be seen to have on the trend toward decentralization.

"Europe of the Regions"

European integration cannot be understood as a powerful and uniform supranational force weakening European states and transforming them into assemblies of strong and dynamic units that cooperate with the European level.[52] As Keating and Pintaris point out, we should rather think about the relationship between regions and Europe as "a complex idea, dependent on what Europe and what regions we are discussing. Both are evolving and the future of both are uncertain."[53] However, when looking at the approach adopted by the European commission toward regions, and in the organization of regions at the European level, we observe that

---

[50] For a discussion of the long preparation of devolution within the Labour Party, see Michael Keating, "Reforging the Union: Devolution and Constitutional Change," *Publius: The Journal of Federalism* 28, no. 1 (1998): 217–34.

[51] A collection of newspaper articles on the Swedish pilot regions has been gathered on the Internet at: http://www.sireneast.com/forum/ind_reg.htm#vg

[52] However, for discussion of this vision of Europe, see Keating, *New Regionalism*, 161–64; and John Loughlin, " 'Europe of the Regions' and the Federalization of Europe," *Publius: The Journal of Federalism* 26, no. 4 (1996): 141–62.

[53] Michael Keating and Sylvia Pintaris, "Europe and the Regions: Past, Present, and Future," *Comparative Social Research* 17 (1998):

the last fifteen years have brought about significant changes that benefit strong subnational units. The most important evidence of an increased influence of subnational governments in Europe is the establishment in 1994 of the Committee of the Regions offering institutionalized representation to the subnational units of government in Europe. Incentives from the EU–level have, on the one hand, intensified activity within and sometimes among existing regional movements and, on the other hand, encouraged the creation of regional administrations in countries where these did not previously exist, especially in what have been called the "cohesion countries"[54] such as Ireland and Greece. But developments within the EU cannot help us account for the variety in the outcomes of decentralization reforms, though they are a significant part of the explanation of why decentralization reforms have been more frequent in Europe in the last two decades than in non-European unitary states such as New Zealand and Japan.

It has been argued that "with all its limitations, the Committee of the Regions does indicate the importance of regionalism in the current period of European history. It also represents a 'breakthrough' in terms of political representation in Europe."[55] We should be careful not to overstate the importance of the Committee of the Regions in the decision-making process in Europe, which is still very much dominated by the Council of Ministers. Nonetheless, the Committee of the Regions is a part of the formal decision-making process in that it has to be consulted on legislation that falls within its sphere of influence as described in the Maastricht Treaty. However, the formal powers of the Committee of the Regions are not its most important contribution to the decentralization process in Europe. Much more important are the opportunities it has created for regional politicians to voice their concerns and the impetus it has given to states with little demand for decentralization to establish regional administrative levels nonetheless.

In those states that already had decentralized authority, the European level became an important focal point for cooperation and the voicing of interest. Arguably, the French regions have benefited from representation on the European level in their attempt to establish a presence in the French politico-administrative landscape.[56] The profile of the Committee of the Regions has been significantly strengthened by the fact that it has attracted significant regional politicians from the German Länder, Bel-

---

[54] John Bacthler, "New Dimensions of Regional Policy in Western Europe," in Keating and Loughlin, *Political Economy of Regionalism*, 83.

[55] Loughlin, " 'Europe of the Regions,' " 155.

[56] For discussion of the French regions and the EU, see, for example, Sonia Mazey, "French Regions and the European Union," in Loughlin and Mazey, *End of the French Unitary State?* 132–57; and Raymond, "Decentralizing or Deconstructing the Republic?" 165–80.

gium, France, and Spain. In addition, the regional lobby in Europe has developed considerably over the last fifteen years so that most regions now have permanent offices in Brussels. Moreover, regions have started to cooperate with each other, forming groups such as "The Four Motors of Europe" (Baden-Wüttenberg, Catalonia, Lombardy, and Rhône-Alpes). These four regions have come together to set an example for how Europe in the future can be driven by economically and politically powerful regions. More modest associations include the "Atlantic Arc," the "Latin Arc," and the "Northern Mediterranean rim."[57]

A renewed focus on regions in the last fifteen years in Europe helps us explain why administrative deconcentration has taken place in Greece, Ireland, and Portugal. Regional levels were needed to distribute the structural funds made available by the EU. Moreover, the initiatives of the European level help us understand the common trends in decentralization reforms. Based on our discussion regarding the experiences of decentralization in Europe, it should be expected that pressures for decentralization should be stronger not only in those countries where modernization of the state or enhancement of democracy have been dominant themes and where regionalist movements have been particularly strong. We should also expect that member states in the EU would experience stronger pressures to decentralize than nonmembers. The particular mix of factors in each country explains to a large extent the particular decentralization reforms that have been chosen. Since some of the factors are present in nearly all states, decentralization has been a dominant trend across most advanced industrialized states.

Reduction in State Employment

Reforms aimed at reducing the number of public employees are not unrelated to the two other types of broad reforms that we have discussed—privatization and decentralization. Privatization and reductions in government employment seem to be two sides of the same coin. It is clear that as governments cease to own businesses, they will in effect also reduce the number of people they employ. However, as Majone notes, privatization has led to increased regulatory activity and the institution of regulatory agencies, and this activity has caused renewed demand for employees.[58] Christopher Hood and his colleagues found that there had developed in the U.K. a very substantial regulatory bureaucracy in the aftermath of privatization. Their research discovered "not less than 135 separate bodies

---

[57] Loughlin, " 'Europe of the Regions,' " 157.
[58] Majone, "Paradoxes of Privatization," 272–88.

regulating the UK public sector at national-government level. Those organizations directly employed almost 14,000 staff, and cost £776m to run in 1995—just over 30 pence in every £100 UK government spent at that time."[59] Decentralization and reduction in employment are less clearly connected. The insertion of a new level of government may lead to demand for more government employment at the subnational levels. This in part accounts for the increase in state employment in Spain and France in the last two decades. Elsewhere, however, efforts to offload to the periphery in response to tight government budgets are directly related to reduction in staff. Not all governments have had staff reductions as stated reform programs, but many administrative units have chosen to lay off staff in response to stricter budgetary constraints.

In spite of its intricate connections with other types of reforms, reductions in staff should be treated as a separate attempt at reforming the state. As we discussed above, it is not entirely clear which trend we should expect based on other reforms. In some ways they seem to call for more government employment, whereas in other ways they go hand-in-hand with reductions. It should therefore not come as a surprise that those states, such as the U.S., New Zealand, Australia, Sweden, and Finland, that have set staff reductions as a clearly defined goal have achieved the starkest reductions. In other states a less pronounced but equally significant trend has evolved: whereas government employment until the 1980s grew steadily in all advanced industrialized states, growth has declined, ended, or been reversed in the last two decades. I now turn briefly to an examination of these trends.

Downsizing Government

Reforms aimed at "downsizing" or "rightsizing" governments are, argues Ingraham, "strongly anchored in both economic reality and political ideology."[60] In her view, complaining about the size of staff and expenditure of government is nothing new. In a sense, therefore, politicians in advanced industrialized nations today are only following an age-old tradition when they promise to improve government by cutting staff and reducing expenditure. The difference between the continuous complaints and unfulfilled promises about "rightsizing government" and the reform attempts of the last two decades is that we have actually seen the beginning of a reversal of the steady increase in government staff that took place from the end of

---

[59] Christopher Hood, O. James, G. Jones, C. Scott, and T. Travers, "Bureaucratic Gamekeeping: Regulation of UK Public Administration, 1976–1996," in *Transforming British Government*, vol. 1, *Changing Institutions*, ed. R.A.W. Rhodes (London: Macmillan, 1999), 83.

[60] Ingraham, "Reform Agenda," 258.

TABLE 5.4

General Government Employment as a Percentage of Total Employment

	1970	1975	1980	1985	1990	1995	1997
Australia	11.8	15.4	15.9	17.2	16.3	15.8	15.4
Belgium	13.6	15.6	18.7	20.2	19.5	19.0	18.6
Canada	20.4	22.2	20.0	21.2	21.0	21.5	20.6
Czech Republic	—	—	—	—	—	5.2	5.8
Denmark	17.0	23.3	28.0	29.3	29.6	30.2	30.3
Finland	12.1	14.8	17.3	19.2	20.5	23.3	23.4
France	18.0	19.2	20.2	22.8	22.6	24.6	24.9
Germany	11.2	13.8	14.6	15.5	15.1	15.5	15.3
Greece	7.9	8.8	9.5	10.7	12.3	12.2	12.7
Hungary	—	—	—	—	—	7.3	7.2
Ireland	10.4	12.4	14.2	15.6	13.7	13.2	—
Italy	12.2	14.4	15.4	16.7	17.3	17.9	17.5
Japan	7.7	8.7	8.8	8.7	8.1	8.3	8.3
Netherlands	11.5	12.9	13.8	17.8	13.2	12.0	11.9
New Zealand	15.7	17.1	17.8	16.2	16.6	14.1	13.7
Norway	17.7	21.4	24.1	25.7	28.6	31.2	31.1
Poland	—	—	—	—	16.1	18.0	—
Portugal	8.0	8.6	10.9	13.2	14.7	18.4	—
Spain	4.9	6.8	9.3	12.2	13.8	15.5	15.6
Sweden	20.9	25.7	30.7	33.3	32.0	32.1	31.5
U.K.	18.1	20.8	21.2	21.6	19.5	14.2	—
U.S.	16.0	17.1	16.4	15.3	15.4	15.4	15.1

Source: OECD, analytical databank.

World War II to the late 1970s.

Table 5.4 shows general government employment in twenty-two OECD countries as a percentage of total employment between 1970 and 1997. If we compare the numbers in 1980 and 1995, we find that for most countries the level of government employment has stagnated.

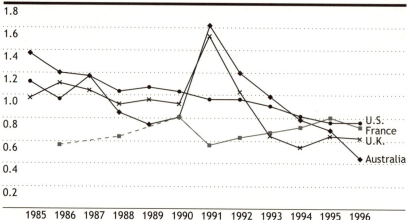

**Ratio
Inflows/Outflows**

Figure 5.3. Change in civil service employment. Source: OECD, "Structure of the Civil Service Employment in Seven OECD Countries," 1999.

The exceptions are France, Spain, Portugal, Finland, and Norway, where the level of government employment grew significantly between 1980 and 1995. If we look at the five-year period from 1990 to 1995, we still find that the level of government employment in those five countries has risen, but the rate of growth is much smaller in the first five years of the 1990s.

Figure 5.3 shows that the rate of inflows to the civil services compared to the rate of outflows has declined in Australia, the U.K., the U.S., and Sweden between 1985 and 1996. The rate in France has not declined between 1985 and 1996, but we can see that it is well below 1, which is the rate of perfect replacement in the whole period. The low replacement rate in France as shown in figure 5.3 is a bit surprising when we compare it with the numbers in table 5.4, which show that the level of government employment has gone up in France. This disparity between the different measures of government size suggests, as Goldsmith and Page observed, that the size of government that we observe depends on the definitions that we use.[61]

Table 5.5 shows the change in civil service employment, public sector employment, and overall employment in the periods from 1985 to 1990 and from 1990 to 1997. This table confirms the growing level of govern-

[61] Michael J. Goldsmith and Edward C. Page, "Farewell to the British State?" in Lane, *Public Sector Reform*, 154.

TABLE 5.5
Percentage Change in Civil Service Employment, Public Sector,
and Economy as a Whole, 1985–1997

	Civil Service		Public Sector		Overall Employment	
	1985–1990	1990–1997	1985–1990	1990–1997	1985–1990	1990–1997
Australia	−7.1	−22.0	—	−2.7	16.2	—
Canada	6.2	−19.0	9.9	−4.7	8.8	15.2
Spain	—	−2.0	18.1	9.4	13.2	5.0
U.S.	1.7	−17.0	11.7	5.3	13.2	12.1
France	1.9	6.3	2.3	−4.4	3.8	2.9
U.K.	−5.8	16.1	−2.6	−12.9	9.9	9.2
Sweden	−28.9	−38.0	5.4	−18.1	4.9	−11.0

Source: OECD, "Structure of the Civil Service Employment in Seven OECD countries," 1999.

ment employment in France, since France is the only country in our study that does not show a decline in the level of civil servants employed in any of the periods shown. There was an uninterrupted rise of the number of civil servants in France over the past three decades. The surprising growth in number of civil servants in Britain between 1990 and 1997 is heavily dependent on the choice of time period in that country. If we look at the fifteen-year period from 1981 to 1995 in Britain, we find that there has been decline on all levels of government employment, as well as the civil services.[62]

Our comparative analysis of government employment shows the direction and types of change in government employment in the last twenty years. For most of the countries, the last two decades have been a period of stagnation or decline with regard to public employment in general, and civil service employment in particular. However, for individual countries, the data does not always support unequivocal conclusions. This data becomes more useful when it is combined with case studies of programs specifically designed to effect cuts in public employment.

Specific Programs

In the last two decades, countries as different in traditional attitudes to public employment as the U.S. and Sweden have, alongside New Zealand and Finland, been those states that have implemented the strongest reforms aimed at reducing government employment. In all four countries, the efforts have shown a considerable degree of success, since the number

[62] Ibid., 155.

of civil servants has declined, in some cases rather sharply. Even in the absence of stated government goals of cutting employment, some countries have nonetheless experienced reductions in civil service employment either through rationalization programs, cuts in budgets, or early retirement schemes. In states where government employment has not declined, such as France, the general cuts in staff in some agencies have been compensated for by job creations elsewhere. France is also one of the states where reduction of government employment has not been a stated goal of the government.

The U.S. Congress in 1994 passed legislation calling for a 12 percent cut in the total number of federal civil service employees by 1999. By 1998 the reductions had already exceeded the target. Between 1993 and 1998, according to OECD the federal workforce had a net reduction of 355,500 employees, or 16.2 percent of its workforce. Ideas adopted by then vice-president Gore as leader of the National Performance Review played an important role for the American reform attempts to cut government staff. These ideas were written down in the so-called Gore Report, *Creating a Government That Works Better and Costs Less*, which was produced with Ted Gaebler as a consultant.[63] The reduction program in the U.S. was further aided by the end of the Cold War and the lessened demand for employment in the Defense Department. Almost two-thirds of the reduction occurred in the ranks of civilian personnel there. Overall, the Defense Department reduced its civilian workforce by 21.4 percent. Most of the cuts in staff in the U.S. were achieved with voluntary departure programs or so-called buy-outs, transferring some redundant workers through a re-deployment scheme, and laying off 37,000 employees.[64]

In Sweden, where a third of the population in 1980 was employed in the public sector and where most job-creation in the 1970s was due to growth in public employment, the last two decades have been marked by reforms intended to reduce the public sector. Due to a variety of programs, such as discontinuing the activity of state agencies, restructuring the ministries, and shrinking the Defense Department, the state-employed workforce in Sweden was halved from 400,000 to 200,000 by 1995. In neighboring Finland, cuts in state-sector employees were just as important. Between 1987 and 1996 the number of state-sector employees decreased by 40 percent, from 214,268 in 1987 to 122,300 in 1996. The rapid and dramatic cuts in staff in the two Nordic countries were not so much motivated by ideas about reinventing government. They were, rather, reactions

[63] Linda DeLeon, "Administrative Reform and Democratic Accountability," in *Public Management and Administrative Reform in Western Europe*, ed. Walter J. M. Kickert (Cheltenham, U.K.: Edward Elgar, 1997), 238.

[64] Vernon Dale Jones, "The Pursuit of Better Government: Federal Government Downsizing in the United States," *OECD*, 1998, 3.

TABLE 5.6
Changes in Public Service Staff in
New Zealand and Australia

	New Zealand	*Australia*
1983	—	162,200
1984	85,738	169,517
1985	85,423	173,664
1986	88,507	180,893
1987	72,417	177,677
1988	60,940	171,912
1989	58,830	165,883
1990	55,016	161,833
1991	46,337	163,220
1992	44,371	164,332
1993	36,156	166,062
1994	34,675	160,513
1995	33,263	146,165
1996	32,917	143,305

Source: John Halligan, "New Public Sector Models: Reform in Australia and New Zealand," in *Public Sector Reform: Rationale, Trends and Problem*, ed. Jan-Erik Lane (London: Sage, 1996), 29 and 39.

to what came to be seen in times of deep financial crisis as irresponsible growth in the public sector.

Reforms aimed at cutting public employment were also remarkable in New Zealand. As table 5.6 shows, the government cut staff by 60 percent in the first decade of reform between 1984 and 1996. From employing 85,738 people in 1984, the government in New Zealand employed only 32,917 in 1996. Table 5.6 also shows that, unlike the cuts in public service in New Zealand, the cuts in staff in Australia were much more modest. The public-service staff in Australia was cut by about 20,000 between 1983 and 1996. In both states, however, the efficiency objective has been a strong motivation for cutting government staff. The much more dramatic results in New Zealand can be explained by the extensive programs to outsource government services, which the labor government in New Zealand started in 1984. This program was not particularly aimed at cutting staff but, rather, to modernize the state and make service delivery more efficient. Cutting staff was a secondary objective, which worked in tandem with the rest of the program. In Australia, the coalition government has since 1996 introduced more reforms aimed at cutting government staff.[65] The U.K. has like Australia seen significant cuts in civil service employment. According to Hood, more than one civil servant in five disappeared between 1979 and 1990.[66] Goldsmith and Page see the decline of public employment in the U.K. as resulting from privatization and the declining number of employees in the armed forces.[67]

In states such as France and Spain, which have experienced significant decentralization reforms, the picture is somewhat different. Luc Rouban sees the French deviant case as resulting from the important role that public employment played in the Keynesian demand management of the economy until 1983. He also argues that the decentralization reforms created new demand for bureaucrats, and thus there was no perceived pressure for cuts in staff in France in the period when other states were reducing their public employment level.[68] An OECD study concludes that France has no large-scale workforce reduction plan. Cutbacks have been achieved in some ministries, but eliminations of posts in some sectors have tended to be offset by post creations in priority sectors. In Spain employment plans were introduced for the postal and telecommunications service, the employment agency, the tax agency, and the Defense Department, and early retirement has become possible from age 60.[69] Reductions in staff have, however, been limited, and some data show a slight increase in total government employment in the 1990s. The deviance of the Spanish case places it in a category with the French case and can be explained by the growth of government employment on the regional level. Whereas central government employment decreased or stagnated, regional employment grew from 254,500 in 1984 to 629,600 in 1998. Moreover, in 1998 employment on the regional level superseded that on the central level, which capped at 564,100.[70]

[65] John Halligan, "New Public Sector Models," 29 and 39.

[66] Christopher Hood, "Depriviling the UK Civil Service in the 1980s: Dream or Reality?" in *Bureaucracy in the Modern State*, ed. Jon Pierre (Cheltenham, U.K.: Edward Elgar, 1995), 96.

[67] Goldsmith and Page, "Farewell to the British State?" 155–56.

[68] Luc Rouban, "Public Administration at the Crossroads: The End of the French Specificity?" in Pierre, *Bureaucracy in the Modern State*.

[69] OECD, *Structure of the Civil Service Employment in Seven OECD Countries*, 1999.

[70] Carlos R. Alba and Carlos Navarro, "Public Employment in Spain: A Preliminary Analysis," unpublished and undated comparative public service project, Department of Political Science, Universidad Autonoma, Madrid.

The specific programs in particular countries to reduce public employ-ment mostly underline the general trends that we found above. If anything, the case studies make clear that in some countries the reforms to reduce government employment have been especially successful. Those states that have emphasized reforms to cut staff have achieved substantial cuts, with numbers as high as 60 percent in New Zealand and 50 percent in Sweden. The United States achieved cuts more extensive than planned and sooner than required. Not all states have been as strongly committed to reducing government employment as the U.K. and the U.S. In Sweden the budg-etary crisis and reaction to previously expansive public employment seem to have played a more important role. In New Zealand the cuts in staff have come not as a first priority but as a result of radical administrative and public sector reform. In other states, such as France and Spain, attempts to cut staff have been weak and offset by job creation following decentraliza-tion reforms. The objective of cutting public employment generally accom-panies other reforms of the state that aim at achieving efficiency, even if other reforms, in particular decentralization and deregulation, oftentimes seem to require an increase in the staff of public agencies.

Conclusion

A series of reforms aimed at changing the impact of the public sector in the economy and society have occurred in a large number of countries. There have been wide variations in the scope and impact of these reforms. There have also been wide divergences in the ultimate objectives sought by individ-ual governments. Some sought to downgrade the role of the public sector as much as possible. Some sought merely to curb the growth of the state's deficits. Some sought to achieve savings for the public purse. Some sought to emphasize the democratic goals of the reforms.

The differences in the scope and in the ultimate objectives of the reforms have been clouded by the initial seemingly universal drive to privatize, de-centralize, and reduce the level of public employment. It is nonetheless undeniable that in broad outline these reforms were adopted, even if in a variety of ways, by a remarkable number of countries with different traditions, organizational cultures, and economies.

The similarities in reforms across societies are impressive, but they do not constitute a bold new paradigm on how states should organize them-selves. For some, the new "organizational culture" begins and ends with the central state shedding some of its economic and political weight. For others, this is merely the beginning of a "reinvention of government." NPM has been presented as a universal revolution, as the Gore conference of January 1999 seemed eager to project. But NPM involves more that privatization, decentralization, and reduction in the level of public employment. And in this drive to transform, or dismantle, the authority of the central state, few states have seemed eager to follow the trail blazed by the United States, Australia, and New Zealand.

CHAPTER SIX

EMULATING THE PRIVATE SECTOR

"[This] conviction that administration is a realm of business . . .
came to be shared by practically all reformers and by educated
people generally. . . . By the first decade of this century administration is business had become a creed, a shibboleth."
—Dwight Waldo, *The Administrative State*

IN HIS MASTERFUL SURVEY of the political theory of public administration, Dwight Waldo showed that the attempts to construe the public
sector as a private enterprise have a long history.[1] The "administration is
business" precept did not have to wait to be discovered by the devotees of the
New Public Management. It was simply an outgrowth of the movement of
scientific management and, subsequently, of market ideology.

An influence, however, scarcely constitutes a program. The universality of
the types of reforms that we examined in the previous chapter—privatization,
territorial decentralization, and reduction in the scope of government—
undoubtedly conveyed the impression that a convergence process was under
way in both reform methods and in the ways that states would henceforth
be organized.

The belief that states both must converge and are converging on a new
form of organization is reinforced by the umbrella under which the subsequent reforms have found both their justification and their rationale. This
umbrella is the New Public Management (NPM), which basically seeks to
align organizational methods of the public sector to those of the private
sector.

Even universally adopted reforms, such as privatization, decentralization,
and reduction in the scope of government have been put into practice in a
variety of ways with a diversity of results. There is therefore no a priori reason
to suppose that a set of reforms covering an ambitious agenda will experience
a universal and rigid application. The name intended to identify the reforms
becomes more important than the reforms themselves. In the case of NPM,
any and all reforms began to fall under its umbrella, so that NPM became not
only an agenda for reform but also a symbol of change and even a myth.

---

[1] Dwight Waldo, *The Administrative State: A Study of the Political Theory of Public
Administration*, 2nd ed. (New York: Holmes and Meier, 1984). The quotation in this chapter's epigraph is on p. 38.

NPM has tended to become more of a political program than a rigorous paradigm. It is varied and broad, perhaps so much so that it may well already have ceased being a useful concept for analysis of contemporary administrative change.[2] The debate about whether or not state administrations have moved from one outmoded administrative paradigm to a new and better one is far from settled. There was not formerly one old paradigm, and NPM has certainly not proved to be the panacea that cured all ills. This argument will be developed in the first and second sections of this chapter. We first return briefly to certain aspects of the NPM before analyzing and comparing the components of public administration in New Zealand, the U.S., Germany, Sweden, and the U.K. around 1980.

It will become evident that NPM contained a forceful rhetorical dimension, one that many governments and scholars at the start of the 1980s believed held the solution to most administrative ills. Yet, as we will see, the administrative ills in the 1980s were far from identical in different advanced industrialized democracies. For NPM to become equally useful and applicable across a wide range of advanced industrial societies, it would have to address a set of uniform problems.

In the early 1980s, state administrations were in a situation that can be characterized as a classic battle between exogenous influences, in the form of the NPM agenda, and endogenous influences, in the form of distinct problems of distinct administrative organizations within distinct political systems. The outcomes of this battle are also the subject of this chapter. An examination of the grand strategies will suggest that endogenous politico-institutional factors remained salient. In short, the degree of centralization of political power mattered both for the strategies that were chosen and the results that were obtained. The centralized majority government in the small state of New Zealand, with its tight-knit network of elites, was able to push through a radical reform program. The U.S. government, on the other hand, has time and again tried to implement radical administrative reform, but these efforts were mostly doomed to fail in its fragmented system built on checks and balances.

The impact of endogenous politico-institutional constraints tells only half the story, and it conceals the most surprising aspect of the outcome of this battle for influence between NPM ideas and existing institutions. While many with hindsight—and some even with foresight—argued that the NPM agenda was flawed, could not be implemented, or "misdiagnosed

---

[2] See for example, Christopher Hood, "Contemporary Public Management: A New Global Paradigm?" *Public Policy and Administration* 10, no. 2 (summer 1995): 104–17; Christopher Pollitt and Geert Bouckaert, *Public Management Reform: A Comparative Analysis* (Oxford: Oxford University Press, 2000); and James Q. Wilson, "Reinventing Public Administration," *PS: Political Science and Politics* 27, no. 4 (December 1994): 667–73.

the patient,"[3] the governments in as wide a variety of advanced industrialized democracies as the U.S., the U.K., New Zealand, Sweden, and Germany did promote strikingly similar reform themes under the NPM label. They viewed these reforms as an important and considerable effort to modernize their state. In the final part of this chapter, we turn to an empirical comparison of the pursuit of the most prominent of these reform themes.

The lessons from these two decades under the spell of New Public Management are multiple. First, governments were indeed very susceptible to exogenous influences in the form of ideas and rhetoric about change. Second, when such ideas caught on, variations in existing administrative structures did not seem to matter much. Third, different governments chose different strategies to pursue change and their respective achievements varied considerably. This variation was largely predictable on the basis of what we know about the importance of politico-institutional variables.

The Rhetoric and Reality of New Public Management

Writing in 1994, Vincent Wright argued that New Public Management "has become a new policy fashion or fad, a pervasive zeitgeist diffused by international bodies (such as the OECD), national governments, business schools, armies of consultants and research institutes."[4] These observations came after a decade of emulation of private sector practices in New Zealand, where the government undertook an intense and comprehensive reform program. Similar doctrines had inspired the dividing up and restructuring of large parts of the British state sector into Next Steps agencies. A Citizen's Charter was adopted in Britain to guide the actions of the newly reformed British state. The British Citizen's Charter preceded the publication of two documents that served similar functions in the U.S., namely, *Reinventing Government*, by Osborne and Gaebler,[5] and the 1993 government report *From Red Tape to Results: Making a Government That Works Better and Costs Less*. Even in Sweden, the conservative government had in the early 1990s advocated cuts and market-based solutions as a way of salvaging its cherished welfare state.[6] Still, the reforms themselves inspired immense fears, and Swedish voters brought the Social Democrats back into government in

---

[3] B. Guy Peters and Donald J. Savoie, "Civil Service Reform: Misdiagnosing the Patient," *Public Administration Review* 54, no. 5 (September/October 1994): 418.

[4] Vincent Wright, "Reshaping the State: The Implications for Public Administration," *West European Politics* 17 (1994): 108.

[5] David E. Osborne and Ted Gaebler, *Reinventing Government: How the Entrepreneurial Spirit Is Transforming Government* (New York: Plume, 1992).

[6] Rune Premfors, "Reshaping the Democratic State: Swedish Experiences in a Comparative Perspective," *Public Administration* 76 (spring 1998): 152.

1994. By the mid-1990s the German federal administration was the only one in our group of countries that had not sought to adopt a reform program that aimed to emulate the private sector. But even Germany was not immune. Pilot projects at local and Länder levels tried out many of the private sector methods.[7] Since the mid-1990s, the German federal administration has adopted or is planning to adopt several of those.

A number of analysts have emphasized the paradoxes inherent in the NPM agenda. A leading British academic, Christopher Hood, has been a major voice in the choir of skeptics of the New Public Management agenda. In his book *The Art of the State*, he traced and categorized administrative doctrines from the Han Dynasty (A.D. 206–220) on the territory of today's China to the New Public Management agenda of today. He used that analysis to effectively demolish the view that he saw as prevalent in the New Public Management agenda, namely, that "societies worldwide are seen to be moving down a one-way street from outmoded tradition to managerial modernity."[8] Each possible way of organizing the administration has its strengths and its weaknesses, he argues, and the appeal of the NPM agenda is not its promises to solve administrative problems once and for all (it will solve some, but create others), but rather its powerful rhetorical dimension. As Hood put it: "Like most successful slogans, 'public management' is ambiguous, able to convey mixed and multiple messages. Put the stress on 'public', and the term appeals to those who think there is something quite distinctive about government and public services, needing its own special knowledge and practice. Put the stress on 'management', on the other hand, and the term appeals to those who think government and public services are just one more sphere of applying management methodologies from the business-school repertoire."[9]

The two best-selling American texts, the aforementioned *Reinventing Government*, by Osborne and Gaebler, and the government report *From Red Tape to Results: Making a Government That Works Better and Costs Less*, are frequently picked out as examples showing both the overstated rhetoric and the inconsistencies of the NPM agenda. It has been argued that making a government that works better probably does not cost less, but more. The examples of New Zealand and the U.K. show in practice that some of the private-sector-emulating reforms are very expensive, in the short run at

---

[7] See Arthur Benz and Klaus H. Goetz, "The German Public Sector: National Priorities and the International Reform Agenda," in *A New German Public Sector? Reform, Adaptation and Stability*, ed. Arthur Benz and Klaus H. Goetz (Aldershot: Dartmouth, 1996), 1–26.

[8] Christopher Hood, *The Art of the State: Culture, Rhetoric, and Public Management* (Oxford: Clarendon Press, 2000), 4.

[9] Ibid., 3–4.

least, but probably also in the longer run.[10] In the case of the U.S., it is now commonly understood that the Democratic government, unlike the Republican governments that preceded it in the 1980s, managed to minimize government quite successfully, but that nothing approaching a radical transformation of public sector practices was achieved. Ingraham concluded in her analyses of the effort of the Democratic government that came to office in 1993 that "it is clear at this early point of reinvention that both the White House and the Congress have backed away from their role in creating some of the conditions necessary for success. If they back away from support of lower level changes as well, reinvention may be better called *déjà vu*."[11] On a note of similar disappointment about the gap between rhetoric and reality in the U.S., Garvey found that "as it gradually becomes clear how much less there is in the NPR than meets the eye, the Gore effort bodes to become not the fundamental transformation that the 'reinventing' tag promises, but a modest move towards better public management, based on welcome applications of common sense."[12]

The general criticism of and disappointment with the American National Performance Review (NPR) experience can not, however, be taken alone as a final and inevitable outcome of the wide variety of attempts that have been undertaken to make the public sector operate more like the private sector. The American agenda is not the only blueprint available. Governments elsewhere have made their own promises of change, and they sometimes have brought about significant reform. Nonetheless, Christopher Pollitt and Gert Bouckaert concluded a recent book-length analysis of public management reform in ten countries by pointing out that "reform-watching in public management can be a sobering pastime. The gaps between rhetoric and actions, and between the view from the top and the experience at the grassroots are frequently so wide as to provoke skepticism or—according to taste—cynicism."[13]

It appears clear that the NPM agenda is indeed problem-ridden. Its claim to be a new and modern solution that will cure all ills does not stand up against empirical and analytical tests, and it loses much of its grandeur when measured against historical comparisons. Even when we strip the

[10] See, for example, Jeremy Richardson, "Doing Less by Doing More: British Government: 1979–1993," *West European Politics* 17, no. 3 (1994): 178–97; Wright, "Reshaping the State"; Jonathan Boston, John Martin, June Pallot, and Pat Walsh, *Public Management: The New Zealand Model* (Oxford: Oxford University Press, 1996), especially 350–65.

[11] Patricia W. Ingraham, "Reinventing the American Federal Government: Reform Redux or Real Change?" *LSE Public Policy Group Paper*, second series no. 3 (London: Public Policy Group, LSE, January 1997), 19.

[12] Gerald Garvey, "False Promises: The NPR in Historical Perspective," in *Inside the Reinvention Machine: Appraising Governmental Reform*, ed. Donald F. Kettl and John J. DiIulio (Washington, D.C.: Brookings Institution, 1995), 106.

[13] Pollitt and Bouckaert, *Public Management Reform*, 189.

NPM agenda to something approaching its bare essentials and view it as a mere attempt to align the public sector with the private sector, it remains a highly problematic concept. The problems emerge when we reflect on the following two questions: What was the public sector method of administration prior to reforms? What does the contemporary private sector method of public management look like now?

For one thing, there was no coherent public sector method of delivering services. The misuse of the Weberian ideal type to stand for the public sector method and everything that is wrong with it has been prevalent in NPM rhetoric. Likewise, assuming the existence of one coherent private sector method of delivering services is also little more than a mirage, or a rhetorical device of the advocates of the NPM agenda. The types of administrations that existed in 1980 prior to the rise of the NPM agenda do not need to be constructed as ideal types or thought of as adhering rigidly to one model in all countries. Rather, they can be usefully compared and distinguished both from one another and from various ideal types. Finding out what kinds of private sector methods that have been selected and put into practice with success can likewise be examined empirically.

An Ideal Administration?

Max Weber's prediction that modern societies would develop similar needs and that these similar needs would lead their bureaucratic structures to converge on a rational-legal model does not fit the empirical reality of the bureaucracies in today's advanced industrialized democracies. Hierarchy, career, specialization, differentiation, and expertise were the essential building blocks of the Weberian rational-legal ideal type.[14] Weber's prediction of convergence was only partially realized, and it provides an interesting parallel to today's claims of convergence made by advocates of the NPM agenda. Much of the rhetoric about the virtues of the new management agenda assumes that administrations across states all operated in like manner, shared the same ills, and would benefit in identical ways after adopting the ideal solution.

Weber's prediction of convergence toward one similar bureaucratic model remained a theory to which Weber added a number of qualifications. Specifically, of course, a perfect convergence in administrative organizations and efficiency did not occur. Silberman, in *Cages of Reason*, did not argue that Weber was wrong when he hypothesized that the rational-legal bureaucratic type was technically superior to other administrative forms.

---

[14] Max Weber, *Economy and Society*, 2 vols., ed. Guenther Roth and Claus Wittich (Berkeley: University of California Press, 1978).

Rather, he maintained that the convergence theory was wrong because "organizational rationalization in public and private realms occurred through a process of *ad hoc* strategic responses of political and organizational leaders to persisting problems of incumbency."[15] What Silberman is concerned to show is that the administrations of the highly modern societies in France, the U.K., the U.S., and Japan evolved in ways that differed markedly from each other and from the Weberian rational-legal type.

Similarly, after the initial infatuation with the seemingly fresh ideas of the NPM agenda, scholars are increasingly viewing adoption of reforms that seek to emulate the private sector as political responses to differing administrative structures, rather than as the impartial application of techniques that regardless of starting point are both better and more "modern." Hood argues that "rather than convergence on a business model, it seems to have been the politics of reaction against an institutional *status quo* that was different in each case that dominated the process. Business practice may have served some vague rhetorical purpose, but was not the prime motor in the detailed shaping of reform."[16]

We thus have two competing accounts of why and how reforms that seek to emulate the market have been adopted: the highly contextual account on the one hand, and the convergence theory on the other. Which of these is best able to account for what has actually taken place? This question cannot be answered without first answering the following question: To what extent were national administrations similar in 1980, and to what extent did governing elites perceive them as having similar ills? Put differently, how large was the variation, real and perceived, among the existing administrative regimes?

There is no doubt that there were important variations among administrations in different advanced industrial democracies in 1980. It has been recognized that it is "dazzlingly clear" that "for many years now there has not been just one type of administrative regime in existence, but several."[17] The issue is not so much showing what differences exist or existed. It is about organizing the analysis of these differences in a useful way so as to illuminate the reactions to, and the adoption of, reforms. Using the categories constituting Weber's rational-legal type is one way of organizing a comparison of bureaucracies.[18] For our analysis, such an organization has two

[15] Bernard S. Silberman, *Cages of Reason: The Rise of the Rational State in France, Japan, the United States, and Britain* (Chicago and London: University of Chicago Press, 1993), 425.

[16] Christopher Hood, "Individualized Contracts for Top Public Servants: Copying Business, Path-Dependent Political Re-Engineering—or Trobiand Cricket?" *Governance* 11, no. 4 (October 1998), 451.

[17] Pollitt and Bouckaert, *Public Management Reform*, 60.

[18] For an example of such an effort, see Edward C. Page, *Political Authority and Bureaucratic Power: A Comparative Analysis* (Kent, U.K.: Wheatsheaf Books, 1985). For other ways of

distinct advantages. First, Weber's description of the rational-legal type emphasizes the aspects of the bureaucracy that many of the NPM advocates see as negative. Second, the NPM agenda attempted to change the normative view of what a modern bureaucracy is. Wright pointed out that although all of the characteristics of the Weberian rational-legal type never existed all at the same time, "in some countries they remained important, and in most they provided a normative framework."[19] The purpose here is not to determine if any of the administrative systems fulfill all the criteria of the Weberian rational-legal type but to compare the administrative systems in the countries in a manner that is susceptible to shedding light on the issue of convergence.

One of the most important characteristics of the Weberian rational-legal type is the career-based system. In practice, this involves a highly regularized system of recruitment and promotion procedures as well as a requirement of professionalism and neutrality. In this respect, the administrative systems in the U.K. and New Zealand operated in 1980 according to the rational-legal principles. The administrative systems in Sweden and Germany operated less so. They allowed for a group of elite civil servants that was explicitly appointed from outside the administrative sphere. Moreover, in Germany civil servants were allowed to be members of political parties. The United States is the country in our group that was farthest from the career-criteria, since, as Heclo noted in 1977, it had a large group of political appointees.[20]

Another characteristic of Weber's rational-legal model is the specialized training that is required of career bureaucrats. In the group of countries under consideration, the German system came closest to that ideal in the 1980s, since most of the federal civil servants had legal training. The United States approximated the German model, with its preference for civil servants that were trained in law and technical sciences. By contrast, in the U.K. generalists were more often preferred.[21] Sweden and New Zealand resembled the U.K. in this respect. However, in all countries in our study most civil servants had university degrees.

Weber also emphasized that the rational-legal type was characterized by a clearly hierarchical organization. Germany is the state that comes closest to fulfilling that criterion, since it is organized as a regulated hierarchy.

---

organizing such comparisons, see Ferrel Heady, "Configurations of Civil Service Systems," in *Civil Service Systems in Comparative Perspective*, ed. Hans A.G.M. Brekke, James L. Perry, and Theo A. J. Toonen (Bloomington: Indiana University Press, 1996), 207–26; and Jon Pierre, "A Framework of Comparative Public Administration" (Brookfield, Vt.: Edward Elgar, 1995), 205–18.

[19] Wright, "Reshaping the State," 124.

[20] H. Heclo, *A Government of Strangers* (Washington, D.C.: Brookings Institution, 1977), 38.

[21] J. D. Aberbach, R. D. Putnam, and B. A. Rockman, *Bureaucrats and Politicians in Western Democracies* (Cambridge: Harvard University Press, 1981).

As highly centralized and unified career systems, the U.K. and New Zealand also constituted hierarchical systems. The U.K. was especially known for its doctrine of ministerial responsibility, which firmly placed responsibility for decisions at the apex of the organizational hierarchy. Sweden had as part of its constitution highly independent public agencies. They were highly independent in the sense that ministers had no direct responsibility for the decisions of the agencies and could not reverse them. The agencies were controlled by administrative courts and a system of ombudsmen. Their existence made the administrative hierarchy in Sweden less clear-cut.[22] The United States had the least clear hierarchy, as its administration was highly fragmented. Two scholars noted in the case of the United States that, "during the twentieth century a patchwork of departments and agencies grew up, which successive attempts at reform only partly succeeded in rationalizing."[23]

The requirement of a clear-cut hierarchy in the rational-legal bureaucracy can be at odds with two other characteristics of this type of organization, namely, specialization and differentiation. In all five states arrangements to facilitate the execution of specialized and differentiated tasks had developed by 1980. The arrangements to achieve specialization and differentiation were, however, not the same in each state. The centralized British and the New Zealand administrations were mainly divided according to sectoral lines. By contrast, in Sweden and Germany a distinction was made between the central ministries, which rarely provided any services, and agencies, local governments, and even private providers that did most of the service delivery in practice. In the federal systems, Germany and the United States, the apportioning of functions among different levels of the government was both a regulated and politicized process.

Specialization and differentiation imply that a rational-legal bureaucracy has to be relatively large. Before 1980 state-administrations grew in all five countries. Table 6.1 shows public spending as a percentage of GDP in all five countries between 1970 and 1999. In all countries except the United States, spending grew as a percentage of GDP between 1970 and 1988. But there were still wide variations in terms of the size of the state. The contrast between Sweden and the United States was stark, especially with regard to public social spending, as shown in table 6.2, with Sweden having the highest percentage of spending of GDP, while the U.S. had the lowest around 1980. Table 6.3 shows taxes as a percentage of the average wage for a single person. All these indicators make up a coherent picture.

---

[22] Torben Beck Jørgensen, "From Continental Law to Anglo-Saxon Behaviorism: Scandinavian Public Administration," *Public Administration Review* 56, no. 1 (January/February 1996): 95.

[23] Pollitt and Bouckaert, *Public Management Reform*, 281.

TABLE 6.1
Government Final Consumption Expenditure as a Percentage of GDP

	1970	1974	1988	1994	1999	Average 1970–99
Germany	15.9	19.5	19.9	19.7	19.0	19.5
New Zealand	13.4	14.7	16.6	14.5	15.8	15.7
Sweden	22.0	23.8	26.3	27.4	26.9	26.9
U.K.	18.0	20.5	19.7	20.1	18.4	20.3
U.S.	18.3	17.4	17.2	15.6	14.2	16.8

Source: OECD, "Historical Statistics, 2000."

TABLE 6.2
Social Expenditure on Public Programs as a Percentage of GDP

	1980	1983	1986	1989	1992	1995	1997
Germany	23.4	23.9	24.2	23.6	26.5	27.2	26.6
New Zealand	19.2	18.8	19.5	22.0	21.9	19.1	20.7
Sweden	29.8	31.3	31.2	31.4	37.5	34.3	33.3
U.K.	18.4	21.0	21.3	18.9	23.3	23.1	21.6
U.S.	13.5	14.5	13.8	13.9	16.0	16.4	16.0

Source: OECD Social Expenditure Database, "Common Programmes—Public Programmes vol. 2001, release 01," February 2001.

TABLE 6.3
Total Tax Wedge Including Employer's Social Security Contributions
(average rate in percent for singles)

	1979	1985	1989	1994	1999
Germany	40.8	44.5	45.5	48.3	51.9
New Zealand	26	27.9	23.4	24.3	19.4
Sweden	50.7	50.9	52.7	46.8	50.5
U.K.	36.1	37.8	34.2	33.3	32
U.S.	31.9	33.6	31.1	31.2	31.1

Source: OECD Taxing Wages Statistics, "Taxing Wages—Historical vol. 2000, release 01," November 2000.

Germany and Sweden both possessed a large public sector in these respects, whereas the U.K. and New Zealand were more like the United States.

To sum up, the five administrative systems differed with regard to their employment policies, the degree of hierarchical organization, their emphasis on expertise rather than a generalist-type competence, the way in which tasks had been divided, and the pattern of organizational fragmentation. In light of this evidence we should expect that the criticisms directed at and solutions proposed to the problems of state administrations would differ quite extensively in the five states.

What occurred was quite different. Strikingly, it was the three states with the comparatively smallest public sectors that saw the strongest attacks on the size of their administrations. Thatcher and Reagan's criticisms of the big state are by now well known. According to one critic, Reagan "was denigrating government service and bashing public-sector bureaucrats."[24] The Thatcher government has been described in this respect as believing that "the civil service was too privileged and complacent and that the state was too big and too interventionist."[25] In both Sweden and Germany, attacks on the bureaucracies by government politicians remained more modest and were phrased more carefully in terms of economic necessity and projections of increasing demand for government services due to unemployment and demographic and sociocultural change. They looked to their administrations to achieve savings, but they did not resort to Thatcher- and Reagan-style bureaucrat-bashing. In the view of one observer, the Social Democrats in Sweden were "keen on modernizing their public administrations, not denigrating and dismantling them."[26] In the case of Germany, Schröter and Wollmann note that "the Federal Cabinet . . . has so far refrained from any type of 'bureaucrat-bashing' that has become an integral part of the political rhetoric of many Anglo-American protagonists of public sector reform."[27]

The view that the bureaucratic organization by 1980 had become unwieldy was more common, but the governments in Sweden, Germany, the U.K., the U.S., and New Zealand constructed different rationales about the causes and consequences of this unwieldiness. In Germany, the first Kohl administration seized upon the complexity of the state's system of rules when it established an Independent Commission to Simplify Law

---

[24] Garvey, "False Promises," 102.

[25] Pollitt and Bouckaert, *Public Management Reform*, 271.

[26] Wright, "Reshaping the State," 119.

[27] Eckhard Schröter and Hellmut Wollmann, "Public Sector Reforms in Germany: Whence and Where? A Case of Ambivalence," unpublished paper prepared for the annual conference of the European Group of Public Administration, Rotterdam, September 6–9, 1995, p. 17.

and Administration in 1983. In the U.K. and the U.S., systematic waste of money was the favored theme.

A telling contrast between views of bureaucratic inertia can be seen if we compare the lessons that the Social Democratic Party in Sweden and the Labour Party in New Zealand drew from their experiences in government in the 1970s. In New Zealand, members of the third Labour government (1972–1975) argued that the civil service was conservatively inclined and thus worked against the Labour government. They viewed the civil service culture as a whole and the senior civil servants in particular as conservative and non-responsive to the Labour Party's policies. Before the election in 1984, senior figures within the Labour party talked about "loyalty tests" of public servants to improve the accountability of officials to ministers.[28] In Sweden, by contrast, when the Social Democratic Party was voted out of office in 1976, some of its leaders thought that one of the reasons why the party had fallen out of favor was that it had become too closely associated with bureaucratic inertia. Their agenda, when the Social Democrats, led by Oluf Palme, took office in 1982, became "to change their image in this respect, and to make the state machine more responsive and accessible to the ordinary citizen."[29]

The above examples should not lead us to conclude that administrative ills do not really exist but are invented to suit the reform agenda of the day. Like the British bureaucracy, the Italian one is highly centralized. Like the German civil service, the Italian counterpart is characterized by a highly legalistic culture. But unlike any of the bureaucracies we have considered so far, there was (as the Tagentopoli investigations made glaringly clear) overwhelming corruption and widespread goal-displacement within the Italian public sector. Donatella della Porta, in particular, has painted a grim picture of the participation of the public administration in the corruption of Italian politics: "The 'bureaucrat loyal to the politician' performs, in effect, an important role for the survival of the corrupt system. Not only does he often act as an intermediary between politicians and entrepreneurs, but, moreover, his connivance reduces the chance of anyone checking on the activities of politicians. . . . In exchange for their connivance, the protected bureaucrats often obtain a share in the collection of bribes, as delegates of their political party, or in their own right (in general, bribes of lesser nature, often linked to the collection of payment orders)."[30]

Italian public employees were not averse to participating in outright corruption, but in many instances they lost all concept of what constitutes public service. "In effect," argues Cananea, "the administration [in Italy]

---

[28] Boston et al., *Public Management*, 56.

[29] Pollitt and Bouckaert, *Public Management Reform*, 264.

[30] Donatella della Porta, "The Vicious Circles of Corruption in Italy," in *Democracy and Corruption in Europe*, ed. Donatella della Porta and Yves Meny (London: Pinter, 1997), 38.

has come to perform the social function of guaranteeing employment, rather than providing services."[31] In Italy, the particularly strong culture of emphasizing job security rather than career-ambition among public employees is part of a vicious circle of corruption and declining social standing of the civil service career. One example of how this vicious circle worked is the way the normal recruitment procedure to the civil service was bypassed. The Italian constitution requires that civil servants pass an official exam. However, hiring outsiders who did not have to go through the exam became an increasingly frequent tool for the Christian Democrats when they wished to bolster their political support. Politicians initially would offer their supporters temporary positions, and after a while they would pass a law which made temporary positions permanent. Sabino Cassese argues that such ways of hiring personnel were used widely for the big departments of post office, education, health, finance, defense, and also in autonomous administrations and local bodies. Moreover, as an estimate of how widespread the malpractice was, he argues that "in 1973–90, about 350,000 people were recruited without entrance exams, and then had their posts made permanent by 12 special laws. In the same period, in the same administrations, about 250,000 people were recruited through regular exams."[32] It is no wonder therefore that when the Italian government finally began to reform its public services in the 1990s, ending specific malpractices was the top priority of the reformers.

Different assessments were made in a number of countries of the ills that needed to be addressed. In general, the Italians wanted to make the bureaucracy more efficient and more professional. The British and U.S. governments paid more attention to what they saw as the elevated costs of an outdated system of management. However, these variations in assessments of bureaucratic deficiencies in 1980 were, especially in New Zealand, Britain, and the U.S., and much less so in Italy, Germany, and France, overshadowed by a new organizational theory. We now turn to a comparison of the strategies of reforms that have been pursued in the 1980s and 1990s and the extent to which they came to be realized.

Government Strategies of Reform

A comparative examination of the strategies within which a multiplicity of reforms have been pursued in the U.K., New Zealand, the U.S., Germany, and Sweden in the 1980s and 1990s is highly revealing. Among the five

[31] Giacinto della Cananea, "The Reform of Finance and Administration in Italy: Contrasting Achievements," *West European Politics* 20, no. 1 (January 1997): 195.

[32] Sabino Cassese, "Hypotheses on the Italian Administrative System," *West European Politics* 16, no. 3 (1993): 325. Perhaps to show how serious the Ciampi government in 1993–1994

countries there was extensive variation at the strategic and programmatic level. Some reform programs were sweeping, others developed gradually. The type and number of actors involved in shaping the reform process also varied greatly. Finally, the extent to which the programs were centrally imposed or experimentally tested in a decentralized setting varied.

By every conceivable measure, the reform program in New Zealand was the most comprehensive, both in comparison to the countries we are looking at and in comparison with other advanced democracies. The program was radical and sweeping, both when we look at administrative reform specifically and when we look at government reform more generally. The broader reforms included deregulation of the financial sector, the removal of subsidies and tariffs, tax reform, and labor market deregulation. The administrative reforms have been described as representing "a paradigmatic shift or a fundamental recasting of the instruments of governance."[33] Although there was no white paper published by the New Zealand government announcing its reforms, the Treasury gave a briefing paper, entitled "Economic Management," to the Labour government when it took office in 1984. This paper voiced concerns about the accountability of bureaucrats, the effectiveness and efficiency of the public sector, worries that public ownership was an impediment to the operation of both the bureaucracy and state-owned enterprises, and finally a concern for how bicultural issues had been treated.

The Treasury, under Roger Douglas, by issuing this report took a strong lead in formulating the reform program. Their way of looking at organizations and the public sector was strongly influenced by a particular set of economic and managerial theories. Public choice theory, agency theory, transaction-cost economics, and new public management ideas were the most important of those.[34] At the beginning of Labour's second term in office in 1987, when the most radical changes took place, the Treasury again produced a briefing paper, entitled "Government Management," and it reads like a programmatic, theoretical statement of how the public sector should operate and how the government should go about achieving those goals. Analysts have generally been impressed by the extent to which the reform program was carried forth by an apparently theoretically inspired, consistent, and coherent program. Kettl observed: "Modern public management reform had its true start in New Zealand. Indeed, no

---

was about reforming the bureaucracy, it appointed Sabino Cassese as the minister responsible for administrative reform. Cassese had been a strong critic of the business-as-usual attitude of the Italian bureaucracy.

[33] Boston et al., *Public Management*, 351.

[34] For a summary and evaluation of these theoretical approaches and how they were used in the New Zealand context, see Ibid., 16–40.

government has traveled farther or faster in reshaping its public programs or the administrative systems supporting them, the changes not only were enormous but also had an uncommon starting point: they resulted from a carefully thought-out plan of what the reformers wanted to do and how they could accomplish it."[35]

The Thatcherite reforms in the U.K. have been characterized as "imposed radicalism" and "sustained frenzy,"[36] and there is little doubt that by the end of the Conservative term in 1997 the British state had, like New Zealand, gone through a sweeping and comprehensive program of reforms. There was, however, much less of a sense of a clear reform strategy in the approach of the British Conservative Party. Pollitt argues that "different theories were fed to ministers through a variety of right-wing think-tanks, and, when it came to policy formulation, were often mixed together in a fairly inconsistent way."[37] Several observers have noted that the reforms under Thatcher became more radical after the initial success of the housing reforms and the electoral victories in 1984 and 1988. At a more profound level, however, Wright argues that "the programme has assumed a coherence and rationalization which is embedded in that wider set of anti-state instincts and prejudices which have informed the British Conservative government since 1979."[38] The Thatcher government's biases toward a minimal and efficient government became clear from the outset as Mrs. Thatcher put an end to all recruitment to the civil service when she came into office in 1979. Shortly after, she appointed a director of the department store Marks and Spencer, Derek Rayner, to head the government's efficiency unit, which was created by the Thatcher government. The efficiency unit produced what became known as the "Rayner Scrutinies," a report that proposed the Financial Management Initiative.[39] In comparison to the New Zealand program, however, the British reforms took place in a more evolutionary, contingent, and prudent fashion, and it was not until the start of its third term in office that the Thatcher government produced its most radical administrative reform proposal, "Improving Management in Government: The Next Steps." That report proposed a complete restructuring of the British civil service. Most radically, it argued for the cre-

---

[35] Donald F. Kettl, *The Global Public Management Revolution: A Report on the Transformation of Governance* (Washington, D.C.: Brookings Institution, 2000), 8.

[36] Wright, "Reshaping the State," 117–18.

[37] Christopher Pollitt, "Antistatist Reforms and New Administrative Directions: Public Administration in the United Kingdom," *Public Administration Review* 56, no. 1 (January/February 1996): 84.

[38] Wright, "Reshaping the State," 109.

[39] Barry J. O'Toole and Grant Jordan, "The Next Steps: Origins and Destinations," in *Next Steps: Improving Management in Government*, ed. O'Toole and Jordan (Aldershot: Dartmouth, 1995), 3.

ation of a functional separation of policy-making, which was to take place in government departments, and the delivery of government services, which was to take place in agencies that were supposed to operate outside of the regular bureaucratic structure. The agencies were to function in the same way as a private sector enterprises.

In the United States, President Reagan led a high-profile attempt at reforming the federal administration. The private sector as a model for the public sector figured prominently in his speeches during his first couple of years in office. He emphasized initiatives led by the private sectors at eighty-four public events during his first twenty-two months in office.[40] The president's management improvement program, "Reform '88," was inaugurated in 1982 together with the establishment of the Cabinet Council on Management and Administration. The most high-profile initiative was the 1984 Grace Report, named after the chairman J. Peter Grace. This commission was composed of task forces headed by 161 top private-sector executives.[41] The resulting report was described by Garvey as being the most far-reaching of all such reports: "The report of the Grace commission . . . represented the most combative (and credulous) espousal to date of private-sector managerial techniques in government. . . . To public administrators who had been brought up on Wallace Sayre's apothegm about the public and private sectors' similarity 'in all unimportant respects,' the Grace commission approach must have represented the most extreme form of rejection of the classical traditions."[42]

President Reagan's spectacular, if not necessarily theoretically motivated, attempt at administrative reform did not in the end produce radical results. As two observers put it, "In proportion to the size of the effort (and of the fanfare . . .) it left only a small trace."[43] Or as Benda and Levine admitted, the administrative reforms in the end amounted to no more than "penny pinching."[44] The evaluations of the more recent and even more high-profile effort at "reinventing government" are strikingly similar, although most scholars emphasize that the reforms in the 1990s produced more change than the Reagan attempt did. Again, the effort of preparing a large-scale report and launching the highly publicized reform in 1993 has been described as sweeping, impressive, and successful. However, DiIulio notes

[40] Peters and Savoie, "Civil Service Reform," 419.

[41] Peter M. Benda and Charles H. Levine, "Reagan and the Bureaucracy: The Bequest, the Promise, and the Legacy," in *The Reagan Legacy: Promise and Performance*, ed. Charles O. Jones (Chatham, N.J.: Chatham House, 1988), 127.

[42] Garvey, "False Promises," 100.

[43] Pollitt and Bouckaert, *Public Management Reform*, 282.

[44] Benda and Levine, "Reagan and the Bureaucracy," 130.

that "politically the rush to reinvention began to stall just two months after the NPR report was released with such great political fanfare."[45]

In contrast to the Reagan effort (and also to the U.K. and New Zealand experiences), the NPR report proposed a decentralized implementation of the suggestions it contained. In Ingraham's view this decentralized implementation strategy was a major weakness of the effort: "Given the many different kinds of recommendations contained in the [NPR] report and the different priorities and activities they represent, lack of a central strategy can be seen either as naive or as indicative of a lack of commitment to serious reinvention."[46] When we compare the U.S. efforts to those of the U.K. and New Zealand, we observe a very distinct gap between initial rhetoric and promises and the actual possibilities for implementation. As we shall discuss below, there are clear institutional reasons why this might be an expected difference between these three political systems.

In the cases of Sweden and Germany, the main strategy for reform has been incremental change. On the topic of incrementalism, Pollitt and Bouckaert note that "from an incrementalist perspective . . . the nature of public management reform is 'bitty,' ad hoc and specific, not strategic, comprehensive, and driven by generic models. Models may sometimes play a headline role, but from this perspective, they are being used as a 'selling angle' for something much more modest, or as a post hoc rationalization for the same."[47]

Germany is the most extreme case of such incrementalism. Wollmann notes that administrative reform has received a higher profile since the late 1980s, but he argues that the (West) German administrative reforms from 1970 to 1995 were "continuous . . . incremental, [and] vertically and horizontally fragmented."[48] However, incrementalism and lack of high profile does not mean that important change does not take place. Two German scholars note that "administrative modernization of the 1990s has to be interpreted as a big qualitative jump in the history of administrative reforms in post-war Germany. The current modernization introduces economic thinking and a different kind of rationale into public organizations whereas past reforms did not touch the inner logic of the

---

[45] John J. DiIulio, Jr., "Works Better and Costs Less? Sweet and Sour Perspectives on NPR," in *Inside the Reinvention Machine: Appraising Governmental Reform*, ed. Donald F. Kettl and John J. DiIulio (Washington, D.C.: Brookings Institution, 1995), 4.

[46] Ingraham, "Reinventing the American Federal Government," 12.

[47] Pollitt and Bouckaert, *Public Management Reform*, 185.

[48] Hellmut Wollmann, "Modernization of the Public Sector and Public Administration in the Federal Republic of Germany—(Mostly): A Story of Fragmented Incrementalism," in *State and Administration in Japan and Germany*, ed. Michio Muramatsu and Frieder Naschold (Berlin and New York: De Gruyter, 1997), 98.

bureaucratic organization."[49] Although the reforms in Germany mainly occurred in the absence of a central administrative reform plan, a main road map was provided by the initiative named the "new steering model." It contained elements that were similar to the NPM recommendations. The big strategic difference, however, was that this program was recommended to local governments not by the federal state but by a not-for-profit consulting agency in Cologne (KGSt). It was funded by voluntary membership of cities and counties, and its suggestions were not imposed on the administration as a whole.

There is general consensus that the Swedish reform program has been less comprehensive than those in the United States, Britain, and New Zealand. Premfors notes that "reform talk has certainly contained ideas of marketization and privatization, but the impact has been small, passing or almost negligible. Ideas of welfare and local democracy have survived and flourished even in hard economic times."[50] Elements of the incremental approach have been present as some key reforms have been tried out as pilot projects on the local or agency levels before they were adopted more generally.[51]

We should, however, not draw the parallel between the German and the Swedish strategies of administrative reforms too far. Unlike in Germany, a central strategy for reform was developed early on by the Swedish Social Democrats, who came back into power in 1982 after a brief period in the opposition. The government created a new department to work on public sector reform led by Bo Holmberg, who was leading what Premfors has termed the "decentralist faction" within the Social Democratic Party.[52] The report, entitled "A Program for Reshaping and Developing the Public Sector," was published in 1984. It recommended some elements of the NPM agenda such as decentralization, more active steering, deregulation, and relaxation of sectoral divisions, but it had a much stronger focus than reports in the U.S., the U.K., and New Zealand on customer service and consumer choice, customer participation, and democratization.[53]

In Sweden, although the Social Democratic Party did adopt some NPM practices, business emulation remained a highly contested issue within a Social Democratic Party that was split between those who, like Bo Holmberg, believed that decentralization was the way forward and who put more emphasis on efficiency and a smaller state, and those who wanted to pursue

---

[49] Helmut Klages and Elke Löffler, "Administrative Modernization in Germany—A Big Qualitative Jump in Small Steps," *International Review of Administrative Sciences* 61 (1995): 375.

[50] Premfors, "Reshaping the Democratic State," 158.

[51] Pollitt and Bouckaert, *Public Management Reform*, 265.

[52] Premfors, "Reshaping the Democratic State," 150.

[53] The information on the Swedish report is from Stig Montin, "New Public Management på svenska," *Politica: Tidsskrift for Politisk Videnskap* 29, no. 3 (1997): 263.

an agenda of traditional welfare policy focus.[54] Those wanting efficiency tended to gain strength in tough economic times, but the others remained strong and continued to argue for a focus on citizen participation and maintenance of comprehensive welfare services. In line with the latter pressures, the Social Democratic government adopted an action plan, entitled "Public Administration Serving Democracy," in 1998. This Swedish reform strategy is similar to Germany's in that it focuses on experimentation and remains highly selective in the parts of the NPM agenda that it promotes. The modest tone represents a further similarity between the two reform strategies.

The Politics of Reform

The governments in the countries that we are examining do not only vary with regard to the extent to which they have tried to adopt radical sweeping reforms or reforms of the more incremental kind. They also vary highly with regard to the obstacles that they faced when they tried to implement the reforms. In this politico-institutional respect, we find New Zealand and the U.K. at one extreme and Germany and the U.S. at the other. Sweden is a case somewhere in between, but the Swedish experience sheds an interesting light as a contrast to the New Zealand case. In both Sweden and New Zealand, the reform programs were proposed by traditionally left-of-center parties. In Sweden, the result of the Social Democratic leadership was deradicalization of the administrative reforms, but in New Zealand radicalization seems to have been the (desired) outcome.

The extent to which the New Zealand system lacked institutional checks on the powers of government in 1984 is impressive. The electoral system insured majority governments who in the imported Westminister system of centralized, unitary, parliamentary democracy could, if internal party struggles allowed for it, freely impose their political agenda in between elections. During its six years in government, New Zealand's Labour Party, and especially the powerful Treasury led by Roger Douglas, was able to put a radical model of administrative change into effect relatively unchecked. A strategy of keeping a low profile made the powers of the government even stronger. Boston and Uhr describe Douglas's strategy as "involving less publicised policy development which could then be 'fast-tracked' in order to minimise the scope of opposition, including that

---

[54] See Rune Premfors, "The 'Swedish Model' and Public Sector Reform," *West European Politics* 14, no. 3 (July 1991): 83–95.

within the governing party."[55] In such an institutional setting and with the tight-knit governing structure in a country of only 3.6 million people, it is in the end not so surprising that radical reform can be achieved.

It is more surprising that the most radical business-emulating reforms in the world were instituted by a Labour government. Analysts, who have studied the reform programs of the Labour governments in Australia and New Zealand in the 1980s, argue that "what made policy transformation in Australia and New Zealand in the 1980s so comprehensive in character was precisely the fact that in these countries, and in these countries alone, it was carried out under Labour auspices."[56] In their view, the stronger inclination toward social engineering and public sector reform traditionally found in parties of the Left insured that the administrative reforms were made comprehensive—including straightforward attempts at downsizing.

Their argument holds some truth, and it lends credence to those who argue that NPM reforms have been promoted both by the Left and by the Right. It conceals, however, the disunity within New Zealand's Labour Party that became evident at the end of the 1980s. Especially important for the image of disunity in the Labour Party was the split that developed between Prime Minister David Lange and Treasurer Roger Douglas over a flat-tax proposal in 1988 that ended with the resignation of the prime minister after he had unsuccessfully tried to dismiss Douglas from the cabinet.[57] It also fails to take into consideration the deeply felt unease in New Zealand's population about the extremity of the power of the governing party. This feeling certainly contributed to creating the majority that voted for changing the electoral system in New Zealand in a referendum in 1993. Since 1996, the electoral system has been based on mixed-member proportional representation (MMP), and this arrangement produces minority or coalition governments that has led to frequent changes in governments. As a result of this reform, changes as radical as those seen in New Zealand in the 1980s are unlikely to ever happen again. An unintended result of the change of electoral system is that the reforms already instituted by 1996 are politically more difficult to change now than they would otherwise have been.

---

[55] Jonathan Boston and John Uhr, "Reshaping the Mechanics of Government," in *The Great Experiment: Labour Parties and Public Policy Transformation in Australia and New Zealand*, ed. Francis Castles, Rolf Gerritsen, and Jack Vowles (St. Leonards, Australia: Allen and Unwin, 1996), 56.

[56] Francis Castles, Rolf Gerritsen, and Jack Vowles, "Conclusion: The Great Experiment in Perspective," in *The Great Experiment*, ed. Castles, Gerritsen, and Vowles, 216.

[57] Jack Vowles and Ian McAllister, "Electoral Foundations and Electoral Consequences: From Convergence to Divergence," in *The Great Experiment*, ed. Castles, Gerritsen, and Vowles, 202–3.

In contrast to what is often concluded on the basis of the New Zealand case, the left-of-center party had a deradicalizing effect on reforms in Sweden. It did so not only in the sense that internal splits in the Social Democratic Party prevented the reform program from being as radical as some of the most ardent promoters of efficiency would have liked. It did so also in the sense that the Social Democratic Party was markedly less radical in its business-emulating proposals than the right-of-center party in Sweden. The Conservative government that came to power in Sweden in 1991 and was sent back out again in 1994 announced a program that was abiding NPM doctrine. The program was promoted against a backdrop of deep economic crisis, but nonetheless the ideological bent was noticeable as the government focused strictly on economy and efficiency. As Premfors notes, "The reform talk could have been borrowed from New Zealand or the United Kingdom—and it largely was."[58]

More conclusive evidence of the effect of the party political influence in the Swedish case is found when we compare the period of Conservative government with the subsequent period of Social Democratic government. Instead of continuing and building on the Conservative agenda of business emulation in government, the Social Democrats have been described as slowing down the efforts to privatize and emulate the private sector.[59] Moreover, they returned to the focus on citizen empowerment even more strongly, as is shown in their 1998 action plan, "Public Administration Serving Democracy."

Similar patterns of party-political influence on the adoption of reforms can arguably also be seen in the other countries in our group. As would be expected of a government of the Right, the National Party that took over after Labour in New Zealand by most measures continued and even further radicalized the reform program. Moreover, in Germany and the U.K. the Social Democrats and Labour, respectively, have put more emphasis on the possible dangers of reducing the public sector. Even the Democrats in the U.S., at the outset of the reinvention reforms, distanced themselves from the Reagan rhetoric in particular by pointing out at the very beginning of the NPR report that they were not in principle hostile to bureaucrats: "The problem is not lazy or incompetent people; it is red tape and regulation so suffocating that they stifle every ounce of creativity."[60]

The United States is a strong candidate for the role as a polar opposite of New Zealand with regard to politico-institutional obstacles to instituting reform. Like Labour in New Zealand, the Democrats set out not only to change but to transform government. Moreover, in both countries

---

[58] Premfors, "Reshaping the Democratic State," 151.
[59] Ibid., 152.
[60] NPR, *From Red Tape to Results*, as cited in Garvey, "False Promises," 101.

there was a notion of a blueprint for reform. The New Zealand leaders relied on economic and managerial theory; the Democrats in the United
States had found their recipe for change in the proposals of Osborne and
Gaebler. However, the similarities between the efforts stop at the level of
rhetoric. It is simply not possible in a system carefully crafted on the principles of checks and balances and in a country with more than fifty times
as many people as in New Zealand to accumulate sufficient power to push
through such an extreme program. In all fairness, Gore and his team never
tried to achieve as much change as Labour in New Zealand, but even the
more limited attempt at reinvention that the U.S. government made
largely failed.

One major obstacle to the adoption of reform in the U.S. arose when
the Republicans took over Congress after the 1994 midterm elections. In
the words of Kettl, they started launching a "frenzied bidding war to
shrink government radically."[61] As a response to pressures from Congress,
the NPR reforms took a sharp bend in the direction of focusing on the
downsizing aspect rather than improvement of the quality of government
services. The NPR promised to permanently eliminate 252,000 federal
employees. Congress later raised that number to 272,900, and the objective was achieved before the scheduled time. Another problem with the
reform was that political appointees had mainly been given the responsibility for running them. This gave the reforms high profile, but it also in
many cases led to a premature death of the effort as the attention of the
political appointee was caught by more immediate concerns or they simply
left the administration.[62] As a result of the fragmented U.S. political system
and the difficulty of pushing reform efforts through Congress, the NPR
reforms' successes were very different from those in New Zealand.
Whereas the Labour government in New Zealand could point to comprehensive change, the only truly innovative and successful aspect of the NPR
reforms was the Reinvention Laboratories, which were established to solve
administrative problems in creative ways. The results varied considerably
among departments. The Department of Education, the Department of
Agriculture, the Department of Interior's Bureau of Reclamation, the
Treasury, the Department of Defense, and the Internal Revenue Service
are examples of departments and agencies that have perceived themselves
and have been evaluated as having instituted important reform.[63]

In the other federal system of our group of countries, a more extreme
variant of decentralized reforms was attempted. In contrast to the United
States, reforms in Germany were at first only tried at the local level.

---

[61] Kettl, *The Global Public Management Revolution*, 17.
[62] Ingraham, "Reinventing the American Federal Government," 9.
[63] Ibid., 7.

Schröter and Wollmann note, "Lacking a single, possibly centrally located, powerful protagonist and trend-setter in public sector reform matters and, instead, disposing of a multitude of arenas and actors each acting in its own right, it almost follows from the 'logic' of the FRG's federal system that public sector reform activities are bound to proceed in a disjointed and incrementalist rather than a comprehensive and wholesale manner."[64] A further aspect that favors incrementalism in Germany is the party system, which at least until the Greens entered government in 1998 ensured that the Social Democrats and the Christian Democrats remained moderate parties competing for the middle-voter and entering into coalitions with the small party at the center, FPD. The well-entrenched neocorporatist arrangements for arriving at political decisions also have moderating effects on the decision-making system.[65] In addition, it should not be forgotten that the German central administration was busy preparing for unification and thus had a different focus from the rest of the administrations in our group. Seibel argues that when the German government decided that the constitution, as well as the political and economic order that it was based on, should be extended to the Eastern Länder, "public administration had to be reconstructed in East Germany literally from scratch."[66]

Independent of this need, the weight of the institutional factors in Germany meant that the more radical aspects of the NPM agenda never received a sympathetic welcome. Why at the federal level "the preachers of the new public management gospel have been received in an even frostier atmosphere" than the general reception accorded the variety of market-oriented and managerial proposals is well explained by Schröter: "Although successive government coalitions led by Christian Democrats or Social Democrats have paid lip service to the need for more efficient management in the federal bureaucracy, political leaders have not seriously subscribed to a comprehensive 'reinvention' programme aiming at a paradigmatic shift in public management. In fact, it appears that every effort has been taken [*sic*] to keep any organizational change as compatible as possible with the existing machinery of government."[67]

In contrast to the German experience, the British way of adopting reform under Margaret Thatcher takes us back again to a system where radical change is facilitated to a significant extent. Decision-making capacity is highly centralized within the political system as a whole—that was the case

---

[64] Schröter and Wollmann, "Public Sector Reforms in Germany," 6.

[65] See Wollmann, "Modernization of the Public Sector," 100.

[66] Wolfgang Seibel, "Administrative Science as Reform: German Public Administration," *Public Administration Review* 56, no. 1 (January/February 1996): 78.

[67] Eckhard Schröter, "A Solid Rock in Rough Seas? Institutional Change and Continuity in the German Federal Bureaucracy," in *Politicians, Bureaucrats, and Administrative Reform*, ed. B. Guy Peters and Jon Pierre (New York: Routledge, 2001), 72.

in a more extreme sense before devolution—and the parties themselves are centralized. These two features, coupled with the electoral system that insures a solid government majority, make the cabinet in the U.K. particularly powerful. Traditionally, however, labor union organizations were seen as strong impediments to radical change, but the Conservative government ended that belief as the government under Thatcher effectively defeated the unions. Thatcher's personality and her uncompromising style are also frequently mentioned as aspects that facilitated radical reforms in the U.K. in the 1980s. Rhodes notes the impact of political leadership and suggests that Prime Minister Blair is continuing in the same vein as Mrs. Thatcher when he argues that "Margaret Thatcher used her position to push through reforms of the civil service, providing strong, directive, and above all, persistent, executive leadership. 'The Blair Presidency' continues the tradition."[68]

As in the case of New Zealand, however, it is unclear whether an extremely radical program like the one Thatcher managed to adopt is viable in the longer term, since the Thatcher legacy has proved at least as damaging for the Tories in Britain as the legacy of "Rogeronomics" has to Labour in New Zealand. The extraordinarily poor performance of the Conservative Party in the 2001 general election and the subsequent leadership struggle that ended with the election of the very conservative candidate Iain Duncan Smith show that the party has still not recovered from its spell of radical political influence. Some institutional change in Britain under Labour, like the adoption of the Charter of Human Rights and devolution, may lead to minor constraints on executive power in Britain. However, unlike in New Zealand, there has not been a reform that institutionally hinders radical reform of the type that Margaret Thatcher's government led from taking place again.

Kinds of Business-Emulating Reform

When we change focus from the larger picture and investigate the types of business-emulating practices that were sought and adopted during the 1980s and 1990s, it is not these large-scale differences but, rather, small-scale similarities that strike us. Of the different existing business or administrative practices that could have been selected as ideals, those that were in fact chosen were surprisingly similar across countries. Although the reform programs varied in ambition, emphasis, and outcome, the detailed initiatives that were pursued contained a striking number of similarities. These

---

[68] R.A.W. Rhodes, "New Labour's Civil Service: Summing-up Joining-up," *Political Quarterly* 71 no. 2 (April–June 2000): 28–29.

similarities are apparent in the themes of decentralized employment contracts, diversification of organizational structures, performance accounting, budgeting, auditing, and customer service.

Decentralized Employment Contracts

Individual contracts to regulate the relationship between the government as an employer and the civil servant as an employee have been most radically introduced in New Zealand. The State Sector Act of 1988 ended the tenure-until-retirement arrangements for senior public sector managers and placed them on contracts for a fixed term of five years. The annual general adjustment of pay and the public-service-wide negotiation of non-pay conditions were simultaneously abolished. In 1991, the Employment Contracts Act established that there should be no difference in the regulations governing private and public sector employers. Following the act of 1991, half of the public sector employees were on individual employment contracts. Collective contracts were mostly decentralized to department and agency levels as the State Services Commission delegated its responsibilities to individual chief executives. In August 2000, an Employment Relations Bill was passed that aimed to mildly reverse the extreme trend away from collectivism in the New Zealand employment system. The bill opened up more union representation and allowed bargaining beyond the reach of one single chief executive. It maintained, however, that there should be no difference between the state and the private sector in terms of employment relations. The bill underlined that a return to central bargaining was not desirable.

In the United States, individual merit pay has been a feature of the public services since the 1978 Civil Service Reform Act. The NPR initiative sought to further individualize employment contracts, and agencies were given more freedom in how they wished to classify and pay their employees. As a symbolic act that received some public attention, the Office of Personnel Management abolished the *Federal Personnel Manual* in January 1994.

In the U.K., the Next Steps initiative did not end the centralized approach to employment relations. However, in the white paper of 1994, Continuity and Change, the Conservative government argued for delegation of the full responsibility for pay and grading systems to agencies and departments. The recommendation took effect in April 1996. The Office of Public Services' tasks changed from regulating employment relations to monitoring them. The Labour government set out in the action plan of 1999, Modernizing Government, that it would make "changes to systems to ensure pay is used more creatively to provide effective incentives."[69]

---

[69] U.K. Cabinet Office, http://www.cabinet-office.gov.uk/moderngov/action/miles.htm

In a 1994 radical reform, the responsibility for pay and the general terms of employment of public workers in Sweden was taken away from the government and Parliament. The new arrangements allowed agencies to determine their own level of pay and the differentiation of pay within the agencies. The Swedish government reported to the OECD in 1998 that 90 percent of its employees had individualized pay as a result of the devolution of employer policy.[70]

In Germany, the Act to Reform the Law on the Civil Service *(Dienstrechtsreformgesetz)* of July 1, 1997, introduced important changes to the life tenure system. According to the outgoing center-right government, "the aim of the Act is to strengthen the performance principle, to increase personnel mobility, to make remuneration more flexible, and to better fill management positions by assigning functions for longer periods."[71] The government of the Left that entered office in 1998 did not emphasize individual pay of civil servants as one of their concrete goals. They preferred a less radical stand, stating that "a decisive factor for the success of all such [modernization] projects is the motivation of staff members, since the willingness to perform and capability of playing an active part will determine the efficiency of the public administration in the end."[72]

Diversification of Organizational Structures

The most far-reaching of the diversification initiatives took place in New Zealand and in the U.K. The Next Steps reforms of 1988 in the U.K. aimed to separate those civil servants who provided policy advice from the large majority who were involved in service delivery. Service delivery, or the executive functions, was moved away from the ministries to agencies run by powerful chief executives. By introducing semiautonomous agencies, the Next Steps program in effect ended the unified civil service in Britain. The program has been described as "the most radical, extensive, and vital part" of the British managerial "revolution."[73] According to Rhodes, the program was close to complete in the late 1990s, with 138 agencies employing 77 percent of the British Civil Service.[74]

---

[70] OECD, http://www.oecd.org/puma/focus/compend/se.htm#Decentralised Personnel Management and Centralised Monitoring.

[71] OECD, http://www.oecd.org/puma/gvrnance/surveys/report98/surv98de.htm#D

[72] OECD, http://www.oecd.org/puma/focus/compend/de.htm

[73] Barry J. O'Toole and Grant Jordan, "The Next Steps to Market Testing," in O'Toole and Jordan, *Next Steps*, 178. See also Tony Butcher, "A New Civil Service? The Next Steps Agencies," in *Governing the UK in the 1990's,* ed. Robert Pyper and Lynton Robins (Basingtoke, U.K.: Macmillan, 1995), 61–81; and Peter Kemp, "Next Steps for the British Civil Service," *Governance* 3 (1990): 186–96.

[74] Rhodes, "New Labour's Civil Service," 154.

Although the British Next Steps program received considerable attention as the most far-reaching civil service reform in the U.K., the restructuring of the government departments in New Zealand was by most measures more radical. As Boston puts it: "When compared with developments in some other parts of the world, the Next Steps reforms appear to be relatively modest and restrained. Certainly, they have been less radical and comprehensive than the recent public sector reforms in New Zealand."[75] In the decade following 1984, twenty-six new departments were created and twenty-three were abolished, corporatized, or privatized. The remaining departments were reorganized.[76] The new departments were smaller than their predecessors, and most of them had their role as a service provider abolished. It is especially noteworthy that the agencies in New Zealand were not, as in the U.K., maintained within the boundaries of the different ministries. Moreover, the employment relations were devolved to the agencies to a larger extent in the case of New Zealand than in the U.K. The divisions, for better and for worse, were therefore clearer between departments and agencies in New Zealand than in the U.K.

In the U.S., the government introduced its program to establish performance-based organizations (PBO) as the American version of Next Steps in 1996. In an address to the National Press Club in 1996, Al Gore proposed that the performance-based organizations in the federal administration would "be run by chief executives who sign contracts and will be personally accountable for delivering results."[77] In 1998, President Clinton signed a law making the Department of Education the first federal performance-based organization. Preceding the PBO reform, thirty-two federal agencies had been labeled "high impact agencies" in recognition of the fact that they were responsible for 90 percent of the administration's contact with citizens. These agencies were especially encouraged to survey and improve their delivery of services.[78]

In Germany, the federal administration's move from Bonn to Berlin was used to promote a streamlining of the federal ministries. These have become smaller and more focused on their policy-advice functions, whereas what are called "executive tasks" have been transferred to agencies and bodies at other levels of government. A survey from 1997 conducted by the Local Government Management Board (KGSt) showed that 60 percent of local governments had already changed the organizational structure to delegate responsibility for results and the use of resources.

[75] Jonathan Boston, "Lessons from the Antipodes," in O'Toole and Jordan, *Next Steps*, 161.
[76] Boston et al., *Public Management*, 78.
[77] U.S. Government, NPR, http://govinfo.library.unt.edu/npr/library/announc/100798.html
[78] U.S. Government, NPR, http://govinfo.library.unt.edu/npr/library/announc/hiapage3.html

About 90 percent of those asked reported that they would like to become more active with regard to modernization of their organization.[79]

In Sweden, agencies were a defining feature of the government administration inscribed in the constitution, and did not result from the current wave of reforms. Still, the Swedish government reported to the OECD in 2000 that "the rate of change in the state sector has been very rapid since the beginning of the 1990s. Such changes have involved abolishing, amalgamating and corporatising government agencies."[80] In the 1990s, state regulation was changed so that it became possible for municipalities to contract the provision of education, childcare, and care for the elderly out to private enterprises. These services had previously been provided by the municipalities only. Some municipalities have contracted out some service provision, while others have not.

Performance and Results: Budgeting, Accounting, and Auditing

During the last two decades governments have sought to keep track of the results of their operations. This idea has been especially influential in the area of budgeting and accounting, but it is also evident in the establishment or reform of auditing bodies, and in various performance-review initiatives.

Major reforms to facilitate the performance focus of budgeting—often called performance-oriented budgeting—have been implemented in New Zealand, Sweden, and the U.K. With the improvement-of-performance focus in mind, they have changed not only their budget documents but also the procedure and timing of the budget process.[81] The U.S. has made less drastic changes, but has changed the format of budget documents and started displaying more performance documentation. The Government Performance and Results Act (GPRA) from 1993 required that by 1997 all federal agencies should adopt five-year strategic plans, annual performance plans, and a report on performance. Agencies were thus to be forced to focus not only on how much funding they had available but on the results that they wished to achieve. The German federal government has started to include some performance information, but the changes have been modest compared to those in the other four countries.[82] However, in 1995 several acts were passed with the intention of finding "leaner, more flexible ways of managing public funds."[83]

All five governments have also made significant accounting reforms.

[79] OECD, http://www.oecd.org/puma/gvrnance/surveys/report98/surv98de.htm#F
[80] OECD, http://www.oecd.org/puma/country/Surveys2000/surv2000se.htm#I
[81] Pollitt and Bouckaert, *Public Management Reform*, 66.
[82] Ibid., 67.
[83] OECD, http://www.oecd.org/puma/gvrnance/surveys/report98/surv98de.htm#E

Sweden, the U.K., and New Zealand have adopted accruals accounting, which is seen to be the most common private sector method these days. It means that the total amount of money needed for a project is written down when the commitment is made, not when the money is paid out. This technique is meant to facilitate monitoring of performance. In the U.K., accruals accounting was introduced in the NHS before it was introduced at the central level.[84] Germany is now adopting what the German government calls cost to results accounting (CRA), which has been planned since 1997. This reform is one of the few administrative reforms in Germany that is implemented on a nationwide scale. The reform will leave Germany with a system of accounting similar to that in Sweden, the U.K., and New Zealand. The U.S. has adopted a system of double-entry bookkeeping. This is a system that is meant to facilitate the idea that each department or agency is a separate business, and that no money is a "free allowance" but a resource that is credited from one account and debited to another. The U.S. system is generally considered less radical than that adopted in the other four countries.

Reforms of external audit to increase attention paid to performance have been extensive in New Zealand, the U.S., the U.K., and Sweden. In all these countries performance auditing has been established as a separate activity, with its own procedures and staff. On the federal level in Germany, such audit reforms have been more limited. However, both the government that left office in 1998 and the government that came into office after it emphasized auditing as part of their strategy to improve the performance of the federal administration in Germany.[85]

Customer Service

Governments also looked to private sector practices for measures to improve their relationship with citizens as customers of public services. The concept of customer service figured prominently in the Swedish reform program. In 1998, the bill Central Government Administration in the Citizens' Service was passed. It emphasized among other things that the central government's administration should be "accessible and obliging towards the public" and that it should "have the citizens' full confidence."[86] The bill suggested that the Swedish administration should seek lessons from abroad and across agencies within Sweden in order to "be in

---

[84] Pollitt and Bouckaert, *Public Management Reform*, 69.

[85] OECD, http://www.oecd.org/puma/focus/compend/de.htm#Managing Quality

[86] OECD, http://www.oecd.org/puma/focus/compend/se.htm#Central Government Administration in the Citizens' Service" (Government Bill 1997/98:136): A Summary.

the front line internationally regarding quality in central government administration."[87] Implementing the 1998 bill, the Swedish government adopted the action plan titled Public Administration Serving Democracy in 2000. In addition, like most governments of OECD countries, Sweden recently announced that it intended to use the internet to improve service to citizens. The Parliament resolution to the government bill was entitled An Information Society for All, and it was passed in 2000.

In the U.K. the most famous initiative to improve the relationship between citizens and the administration was the Citizen's Charter, which was introduced in July 1991. Labour relaunched the Citizen Charter in 1998 and called it Service First. The Service First initiative put more emphasis on the Charter Marks Awards Scheme. This scheme provides prizes for civil servants who, among other things, can show that their users think that they "provide a really good service."[88] Part of the program is publication of league tables for schools, universities, and hospitals and the publication of performance goals and means for issuing complaints on the Internet. Prime Minister Tony Blair stated that a quarter of all contacts between government and citizens should be happening electronically by 2000.

In the U.S. in 1993, the Clinton administration stated that it would provide the American people with a quality of service "equal to the best in business."[89] Agencies were encouraged to set customer service standards, survey their customers, and develop feedback systems. The thirty-two high-impact agencies that dealt most frequently with the citizens were particularly encouraged to focus on customer satisfaction. In 1998, a renamed initiative, the National Partnership for Reinventing Government, developed a new slogan, "America @ Its Best." As the slogan suggested, one of the goals was that the use of information technology should be improved.

In New Zealand the emphasis on customer service has been downplayed. Instead the purchaser-provider division and strict performance auditing was intended to create incentives for government agencies to transact much like commercial buyers and sellers.[90] In Germany, although the notion of performance and quality management has been promoted, the idea that the citizens should be treated as customers is not commonly emphasized.

---

[87] Ibid.

[88] U.K. Government, Service First, http://www.servicefirst.gov.uk/2000/chartermark/whatare.htm

[89] PUMA, http://www.oecd.org/puma/focus/compend/us.htm#Customer satisfaction survey

[90] See Allen Schick, *Spirit of Reform: Managing the New Zealand State Sector in a Time of Change*, August 1996, http://www.ssc.govt.nz/Documents/Reform1.htm

Between Ideas and Institutions

Considering the variety of administrative practices that existed in 1980, it is striking that the governments in all five of the countries we have examined advocated similar reforms. These similarities have only to a limited extent arisen from problems endogenous to the national administrative systems. Most of them are not problem-driven but, rather, driven by ideas. The diversified structures have been adopted not because the national administrations had similar organizational structures with similar problems but because of the idea that a division between policy advice and service delivery would improve any administration regardless of context.

The international community of think tanks, experts, and academics in disciplines such as economics, accounting, business, management, and administration has played an important role in transmitting and informing about ideas and practices. Moreover, the Internet sites of organizations such as the OECD and the World Bank have also facilitated discussions and emulations across geographical boarders. It is probably fair to say that never before have governments and administrations across the world been so intensely aware of the way other governments and administrations function. In such an interconnected world, thinking about new practices does not necessarily come after a problem is experienced but, rather, as a result of an awareness that another country adopted a practice that seemed to have produced positive results.

Meanwhile, the costs of the new administrative practice, or the difficulty of pushing a reform through the political system, differ widely and may not be immediately apparent. Thus, solutions that are very similar have not led to a convergence of administrative practices, because these reforms are sought in political systems that react to and obstruct change differently. The contextual account is correct therefore in emphasizing the different macro- and microinstitutional contexts in which reform takes place. This does not negate that there is a strong degree of cross-border, uncritical borrowing of administrative practices. This has been a particular feature of the NPM reforms of the last two decades.

The ease with which practices across the world can be compared may make administrations more prone to adopt fashionable solutions to problems that may be perceived as real, or minor. One may hope that governments learn and become more critical about which practices they wish to adopt both from the private sector and from other public administrations. There is little evidence to suggest that this has happened. A stop-and-go process of continuous reform is likely as governments strive to be modern and administrations digest the newest fad. Reform fatigue may be an element that stops reform in some countries where political checks are not strong. Elsewhere, the realization that change is costly may cool down some of the reform frenzy. The initial infatuation with everything labeled NPM has ended, but many government officials and others subscribe to the view that private organizations are more modern and better adapted to the world of today than public administrations. Little evidence suggests that governments will seize upon being open to exogenous influences in the form of internationally transmitted ideas about how public organization can make use of private sector practices. But, as the evidence presented in this chapter shows, only in some political systems can radical and rapid change be expected to happen.

CHAPTER SEVEN

THE RELUCTANT REFORMERS: JAPAN AND FRANCE

REFORMING OR MODERNIZING the state is generally taken to mean a reform of the bureaucracy. We have seen that this theme is more important in some countries than in others and that it is exploited by politicians in some countries more than in others. At any rate, we have found that in all countries politicians can exploit the call for bureaucratic or civil service reform with impunity, in part because it affects a less popular institution and in part because it never implicates political institutions and practices. Hence, politicians and political parties are almost always able to use the bureaucracy to reflect a reformist image of themselves.

Yet, the call for reforms or the unpopularity of the bureaucracy do not always insure that bureaucratic reforms will follow. Nor, as we have seen, does the relative absence of criticism mean that reforms of a rather radical nature will not follow. Mrs. Thatcher began by attacking the stranglehold of the trade unions on British politics and society, but she finished with a restructuring of the most respected part of the state.

The bureaucratic machines of Japan and France share many similarities, and a reputation grew in both countries that the state could more easily act in the public interest because of its impermeability to outside forces.[1] Both bureaucracies were prestigious institutions. Both recruited in a highly competitive manner. Both have long been considered the epitome of the elitist system as a result of the narrow channels through which the top officials were recruited.[2] And, not insignificantly, both have been credited with a considerable degree of integrity and efficiency, in marked contrast to the political elites that have governed the two countries since the end of World War II.

---

[1] See Chalmers Johnson, *MITI and the Japanese Miracle: The Growth of Industrial Policy, 1925–1975* (Stanford: Stanford University Press, 1982); and Peter J. Katzenstein, ed., *Between Power and Plenty: Foreign Economic Policies of Advanced Industrial States* (Madison: University of Wisconsin Press, 1978).

[2] See John A. Armstrong, *The Administrative Elite* (Princeton: Princeton University Press, 1970); and Bernard A. Silberman, *Cages of Reason: The Rise of the Rational State in France, Japan, the United States, and Great Britain* (Chicago: University of Chicago Press, 1993).

Percent

	1984	1988	1990	1991	1993	1997	1999
Other/No Answer	5	5	4	4	4	1	3
Defense	1	1	1	1	0	1	0
Economy	15	5	4	6	19	37	32
Education	5	5	4	4	3	3	3
Administrative Reform	7	5	8	7	7	8	11
Land/Housing	2	9	10	12	6	1	2
Cleaner Politics	6	12	12	10	20	10	10
Cost of Living	20	13	17	17	11	8	7
Social Welfare	11	15	19	20	14	13	15
Tax Cut	28	30	21	19	16	18	17

Figure 7.1. What is the most important political issue for you? Source: *Asahi Shinbun*, various editions.

Neither country has escaped the criticism that its once-vaunted bureaucracy has followed the ways of the other political institutions. It could no longer assume responsibility as a "solver" of society's problems, and it had to fight charges of waste, privilege, and elitism. Yet, neither government has manifested an alacrity for bureaucratic reform.

Japan

Centrality of Administrative Reform as a Political Issue

Administrative reform has been a rather important issue in Japan in recent years. Although it has not necessarily been considered an urgent issue in the popular mind, it has occupied a prominent position on the political

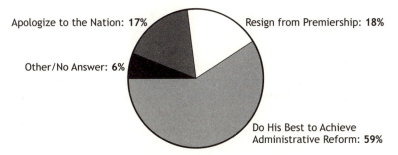

Figure 7.2. What should the prime minister do to take responsibility?
Source: *Asahi Shinbun*, September 21, 1997.

agenda, especially since 1994. A *Yomiuri Shinbun* survey found 77 percent of the respondents in favor of some kind of administrative reform in June 1994.[3]

The *Asahi* survey results since the mid-1980s have shown that administrative reform has more or less constantly been considered by around 7 to 8 percent of the people as "the most important" political issue. It almost always ranked higher than education or defense (figure 7.1).[4] Indeed, in 1999, with 11 percent of the interviewees claiming that administrative reform was the most important issue, administrative reform was ranked fourth, after the economy (32 percent), tax cut (17 percent), and social welfare (15 percent). This survey result seems to indicate that if administrative reform has not been considered by most people as the single most important political issue, this is not because it is regarded as irrelevant but because some other issues were of more pressing concern. This is to say that, on the one hand, the prolonged economic stagnation of the 1990s means that a greater number of Japanese naturally continue to think that economic growth is the most pressing issue, while, on the other hand, the changing demographics (i.e., Japan's rapidly aging—fastest among the advanced industrialized countries) have made many people anxious about the viability of public pensions, health insurance, nursing care, and so forth.

That the Japanese have desired that administrative reform be pursued was apparent in a survey following a government crisis in the midst of the Hashimoto reform efforts. In a cabinet reshuffle in 1997, Hashimoto made the political misjudgment of appointing a senior politician who had previously been convicted of corruption as the minister in charge of administrative reform. Bowing to a popular uproar and to the discontent of

---

[3] *Yomiuri Shinbun*, June 5, 1994.

[4] The data are drawn from *Asahi Shinbun*'s annual surveys, which are published in the January 1 edition of each year.

LDP's coalition partners, the new minister was forced to resign within days of his appointment. While 84 percent of the respondents considered it "a matter of course" that the minister was forced to quit and 76 percent thought that Hashimoto was "heavily responsible" for having appointed him in the first place,[5] when asked what the premier should do to take responsibility, well over a majority (59 percent) of the interviewees replied that they wanted him to do his best in achieving administrative reform, rather than resigning as prime minister or apologizing to the nation (figure 7.2).[6]

The Size of the Japanese State

Figure 7.3 shows the trends in the volume of public expenditure and nominal GDP since 1983.[7] The 1980s witnessed a sharp drop in the public spending/GDP ratio due to a combination of administrative reform efforts (Nakasone's *Rincho* reforms) and generally favorable economic climate. This downward trend, however, was reversed in the 1990s following the burst of the economic bubble. In fact, as Japan entered the new millennium the size of its public debt was at a historic high, with no immediate means of improvement in sight.

Figure 7.4 gives a rough breakdown of the national budget in selected years since 1980. The relative weight of social security and defense remained fairly constant, whereas education and science came to receive a shrinking share. The portion of the budget spent on public works seems to have gotten somewhat smaller in recent years as far as the regular budget is concerned, but we have to bear in mind that this figure reflects only part of the total of public money allotted for public works. In the meantime, the percentage of the budget that goes to servicing the interest on government bonds grew twofold since 1980—a rather clear indication of the terrible fiscal situation that Japan is in.

The Japanese government has been much more successful at keeping a lid on the organizational growth of the bureaucratic empire. The strict application of the principle of "scrap and build"[8] insured that the overall total of the number of bureaus within central ministries was kept constant (figure 7.5). The total number of national civil servants fluctuated somewhat more, but since the Nakasone reforms of the mid-1980s, it was not allowed to rise above a specified level.

The number of para-state organizations was kept under control throughout the 1980s and 1990s, after their proliferation during the period of

---

[5] *Asahi Shinbun*, September 21, 1997.

[6] Ibid.

[7] Public Management Research Center, *Administrative Data Book of Japan*, 1999.

[8] This principle was instituted in the 1960s.

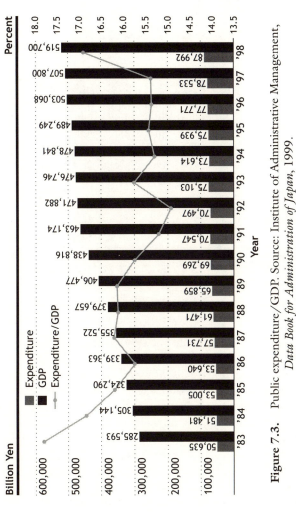

Figure 7.3.   Public expenditure/GDP. Source: Institute of Administrative Management, *Data Book for Administration of Japan,* 1999.

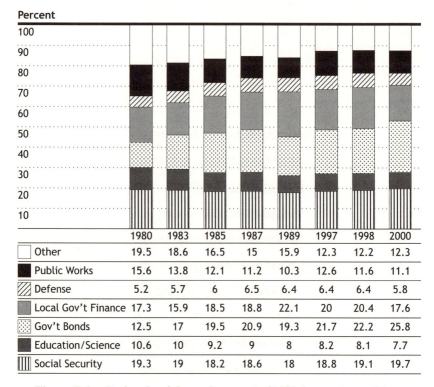

Percent								
	1980	1983	1985	1987	1989	1997	1998	2000
Other	19.5	18.6	16.5	15	15.9	12.3	12.2	12.3
Public Works	15.6	13.8	12.1	11.2	10.3	12.6	11.6	11.1
Defense	5.2	5.7	6	6.5	6.4	6.4	6.4	5.8
Local Gov't Finance	17.3	15.9	18.5	18.8	22.1	20	20.4	17.6
Gov't Bonds	12.5	17	19.5	20.9	19.3	21.7	22.2	25.8
Education/Science	10.6	10	9.2	9	8	8.2	8.1	7.7
Social Security	19.3	19	18.2	18.6	18	18.8	19.1	19.7

Figure 7.4. Budget breakdown. Source: *Asahi Shinbun*, various editions.

high-speed economic growth in the 1960s and 1970s (figure 7.6).[9] The same can be said about the number of officials employed at those quasi-governmental organizations. This, however, does not necessarily mean that those that exist have obvious grounds to justify their continuous existence. Many of these semipublic institutions dispense public money, and on that front, and paralleling similar tendencies in the state proper, combating waste has been a rather elusive goal.

The comparatively small size of the state, in terms of the number of public servants, has been a prime characteristic of Japan (figure 7.7).[10] In fact, as we will see in some detail below, despite the already small size of the state bureaucracy, an even smaller government continued to be advocated

[9] This figure, however, covers only one specific category of quasi-governmental organizations called special corporations. There are other types of semi-official organizations, which receive and dispense public money, that fall outside this category, and therefore do not appear in this count.

[10] Public Management Research Center, *Administrative Data Book of Japan*, 1999, 67.

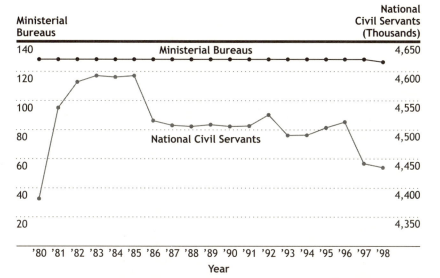

Figure 7.5. Ministerial bureaus and national civil servant numbers. Sources: Management and Coordination Agency, *White Paper on Management and Coordination*, various years; and National Personnel Authority, *White Paper on Public Servants*, various years.

during the reform efforts of the 1990s under the LDP. Together with "fiscal reconstruction without tax increase," "simple and efficient government" was the most central slogan of Nakasone's Rincho reforms of the 1980s. The Ad Hoc Council on Administrative Reform (*Rincho*) was set up in 1981 and issued five reports during its two years of existence. The last segment of its main reform proposals was implemented around 1987.[11]

The Rincho reforms are commonly credited with two major "successes." First, the Rincho did indeed succeed in solving the problem of mounting public debt by putting a break on government spending, even though its task was made considerably easier by the booming economy. Second, Nakasone's other major triumph was the privatization of three public corporations: Japan National Railways (JNR), NTT, and Japan Tobacco. The privatization of the JNR in particular was widely considered to be a special achievement because (1) from the fiscal viewpoint, JNR was a huge drain on the national coffer, and (2) politically its trade unions were among the

---

[11] For a detailed account of the Rincho reforms, see Hideo Otake, *Jiyushugiteki kaikaku no jidai* (Tokyo: Chuo Koronsha, 1994); *Gyokaku no hasso* (Tokyo: TBS Britannica, 1997); and also Jun Iio, *Mineika no seiji katei: Rinchogata Kaikaku no seika to genkai* (Tokyo: Tokyo Daigaku Shuppankai, 1993). I am grateful to Koichi Nakano for bringing these works to my attention and for helping me to understand the essentials of their contents.

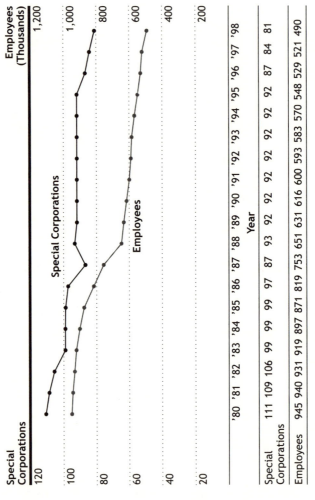

Figure 7.6. Special corporations and employees. Source: Management and Coordination Agency, *Yearbook of Special Corporations*, various years.

	'80	'81	'82	'83	'84	'85	'86	'87	'88	'89	'90	'91	'92	'93	'94	'95	'96	'97	'98
Special Corporations	111	109	106	99	99	99	97	97	93	92	92	92	92	92	92	92	87	84	81
Employees	945	940	931	919	897	871	819	753	651	631	616	600	593	583	570	548	529	521	490

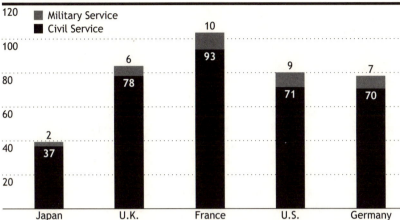

Figure 7.7.   Public servant numbers per thousand nationals. Source: Institute of Administrative Management, *Data Book for Administration of Japan*, 1999.

most militant as well as the strongest supporters of the opposition parties. Coinciding with the economic bubble, the flotation of NTT shares, on the other hand, helped the cause of fiscal reconstruction.

Nakasone was rather more frustrated by other issues of institutional reforms. His efforts to cut down the so-called special corporations did not go very far. Also, his attempts to modernize the central state, especially in order to improve cross-ministerial policy coordination, met bureaucratic obstacles.[12] These issues were to be taken up again by Hashimoto in the late 1990s.

Institutional frameworks for the further pursuit of administrative reforms were maintained after the dissolution of the Rincho in the form of three successive Ad Hoc Councils for the Promotion of Administrative Reform (*Gyokakushin*),[13] but there was little actual reform that resulted to justify their existence. On the one hand, the urgency for reform was much less palpable now that the *Rincho* redressed state finance. On the other, the economic boom leading to the speculative bubble of the late 1980s and early 1990s drew popular attention away from the reform of the public sector.

It was after the alternation in power in 1993, which brought to power under the premiership of Hosokawa the first non-LDP government in thirty-eight years, that administrative reform was reintroduced as a pressing

[12] The Management and Coordination Agency did get reorganized, and there were some intraministerial institutional reforms as well.

[13] The first *Gyokakushin* existed from 1983 to 1986; the second 1987–1990; and the third 1990–1993.

political issue.[14] Since then, administrative reform has remained among the most important items on the political agenda.

Although the reform of the electoral rules was arguably the only raison d'être that bound the otherwise disparate, seven-party coalition behind Hosokawa, his government underlined the importance of administrative reform, most notably decentralization and deregulation. These and other issues were to be taken up by the administrations that followed.

Decentralization received a boost under the Murayama government, which set up a Decentralization Promotion Commission in 1995. The commission made an early decision not to pursue devolution of new powers to local governments or the redefinition of local government units; instead, it focused on what it perceived as a more realizable goal of putting an end to the system of "administrative delegation" that had placed the nominally autonomous local governments under central control.[15] In the absence of consistent political leadership, the reform outcome ended up being rather less conclusive than the commission's initial ambition, but the reform measures were enacted in 1999 and implemented in the following year. More recently there have been renewed efforts, sponsored by the Ministry of Home Affairs, to promote municipal mergers. Similarly, the institutional framework for the pursuit of deregulation was instituted under the Murayama government in the form of a high-profile Administrative Reform Commission in 1994. This commission lasted for three years (until the end of 1997), issuing several reports and supervising the implementation of government deregulation programs during the course of its life. Even though critics have always charged that deregulation never went far enough, the concept of deregulation itself has come under challenge in recent years, and today a lesser regulatory reform committee handles the issue of regulatory reform rather than deregulation.

The other principal task of the Administrative Reform Commission was to deliberate on a government information disclosure bill. A subcommittee was established in 1995 with a mission to formulate concrete proposals. Although the commission submitted its final report by the end of 1996, it left the crucial details to be determined by government officials. Information disclosure had the widest popular support among the administrative reform issues (figure 7.8), but, not surprisingly, neither the bureaucrats nor the LDP were in a hurry to enact sweeping measures.[16] It was in May 1999 that the Diet finally had a chance to legislate, and it was in April 2001 that the law was finally implemented.

---

[14] See Koichi Nakano, "The Politics of Administrative Reform in Japan, 1993–1998: Toward a More Accountable Government?" *Asian Survey* 38, no. 3 (March 1998): esp. 293–96, for the background of the reform efforts.

[15] Not unlike the *tutelle* in France.

[16] Nakano, "The Politics of Administrative Reform," 304–5.

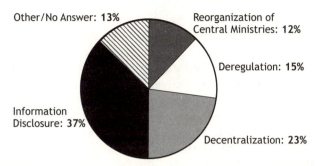

Figure 7.8. What would you like administrative reform to achieve the most? (multiple choice). Source: *Asahi Shinbun*, December 12, 1996.

The Murayama government was also responsible for launching renewed efforts to cut down the number of para-state special corporations in 1995. Progress was slow since these quasi-governmental institutions are generally deeply intertwined with political and bureaucratic vested interests, in terms of both money and personnel.[17] Since then, sixteen special corporations have been merged into eight, and an additional five have been, or are to be, either abolished or privatized. The common perception, however, is still that there are too many of them, and the most costly ones have not been much affected.

Hashimoto succeeded Murayama as prime minister in January 1996, and when he formed his second cabinet at the end of that year as an LDP-only government, he set up an Administrative Reform Conference with a view to making administrative reform a centerpiece of his government program. By the time the conference (which, unusually, the premier himself chaired) issued its final report in December 1997, it was decided that there were to be four main pillars to the Hashimoto reform. The legislative process took up much of 1998 and 1999, even though Hashimoto was forced to resign in summer 1998. The actual implementation of the reforms has been taking place since January 2001.[18]

Perhaps the most eye-catching item of the reforms is the reorganization of central ministries, even though this has never enthused the Japanese people (see figure 7.8). Intense ministerial turf wars have long been considered to be a malady of public administration in Japan. In fact, there is an oft-used term, "the ills of vertical administration," to refer to the symptoms

---

[17] Many of them channel public money into various activities, public works and otherwise. These organizations more or less invariably provide cushy and well-paid postretirement *(amakudari)* positions for elite bureaucrats as well.

[18] Some more details of these reforms are given in the section on politicization. See chapter 9.

of this problem.[19] Hashimoto believed that by merging ministries he would be able to cut waste and overlap as well as to facilitate more strategic policy coordination (even though fewer ministries inevitably also meant bigger ministries). He was initially keen on reducing the number of central ministries to a single digit for symbolic value, but had to content himself with thirteen ministries and agencies out of twenty-three in the status quo ante.[20] As yet, it is much too soon to tell whether any of the anticipated benefits of the reform will actually be reaped. The Japanese remain decidedly unconvinced: a recent survey by the *Asahi* found 78 percent of the respondents expected no change resulting from the ministerial reorganization, as opposed to 13 percent predicting change.[21]

For Hashimoto, no less important was the attempt to reinforce central coordination and prime ministerial leadership. This was done by (1) explicitly granting the prime minister the right to make proposals on the basic directions of core policies; (2) transforming the existing Prime Minister's Office into a stronger Cabinet Office; and (3) setting up an Economic and Fiscal Council, in the Cabinet Office and under the prime minister, which will set the basic framework of the budget formation. These reforms were accompanied by an effort to boost political control in other ministries as well.[22] Many consider it unfortunate that the actual implementation of these potentially effective reforms coincided with a rather weak and incompetent prime minister who showed no interest in taking the leadership.

The third pillar of the Hashimoto reforms was the downsizing and outsourcing of some state functions. More concretely, this has taken the form of agencification, even though the initial ambitions were rather different.[23] As it stands, the new "agencies" that were created in April 2001 have nothing to do with "policy implementation,"[24] but are mostly already detached organs of the likes of research and test institutes, hospitals, and

---

[19] In Japan, the ministries and agencies are set up by specific laws (and therefore that much harder for politicians to tinker with). Moreover, bureaucrats are recruited by each ministry (even though successful candidates have to first pass unified civil service exams) and basically promoted within that ministry. These practices lead to strong loyalty and identity on the part of the bureaucrats, resulting in intense ministerial sectionalism.

[20] Separately and preceding the wholesale reorganization, the Ministry of Finance came under scrutiny in the mid-1990s due to its failure to adequately regulate the financial sector. A Financial Supervisory Agency was separated off in 1998, and it was further consolidated into a Financial Services Agency in summer 2000. See Nakano, "The Politics of Administrative Reform in Japan," 306–7, for the background on this reform.

[21] *Asahi Shinbun*, January 23, 2001.

[22] Some more details of these reforms are given in the section on politicization. See chapter 9.

[23] See Koichi Nakano, "Cross-border Transfer of Policy Ideas: Agencification in Britain and Japan," unpublished manuscript presented at the Twelfth International Conference of Europeanists, Chicago, March 31, 2000, for details.

[24] The original concept of agencification is based on the separation of policy formation and policy implementation in order to maximize the delivery of public service.

museums. There are ongoing discussions about the agencification of national universities.

Finally, the LDP government had promised to cut down the number of national civil servants by 25 percent in ten years (by 2010). The underlying idea was, of course, to cut public expenditure by cutting the government's payroll. One may question the wisdom and feasibility of this reform proposal in view of the fact that Japan already has a rather small bureaucracy (figure 7.7). Indeed, one of the reasons why the government is eager to turn national universities into agencies is that by doing so it can nominally remove the many employees of national universities from the total, even though they are most likely to continue to be paid by the state and retain virtual civil servant status (this is what happened with most of the first-round agencies). The huge postal service is the next target for agencification for the same reason, but since it is politically powerful only the most optimistic expect the change, should it ever happen, to be anything other than nominal.

Other, perhaps lesser, administrative reform items in recent years include: plans to cut down the number of government councils; the introduction of self-evaluation policies; and the legislation of a civil service ethics law in 1999.[25] Yet other reforms were discussed, without leading to any significant outcome so far: proposals to strengthen the Diet's institutional capacity to keep the executive branch accountable;[26] some kind of restrictions on the practice of *amakudari* (descent from heaven);[27] and recommendations to make the police more accountable.[28]

As of now, the LDP government is once again talking about engaging itself in another round of administrative reform. Symbolically, Hashimoto is back in the cabinet as the minister in charge of administrative reform. The issues raised include: the reform of the civil service (including promotion and *amakudari*) and the reforms of quasi-government organs (including special corporations). Much of what has been said, however, remains vague and even unrealistic. Skeptics point out that this may well have been mere posturing by the deeply unpopular Mori government using the popular issue of administrative reform in a desperate attempt to prop up its support in the run-up to the crucial Upper House election in summer 2001.[29] Indeed, it was not the first time that the LDP had tried to play this trick.[30]

---

[25] This was in response to a string of corruption scandals that rocked the bureaucracy in the 1990s.

[26] Nakano, "The Politics of Administrative Reform," 302–4.

[27] This issue is perpetually debated seemingly without any lasting or fundamental change.

[28] The police received massive criticisms in the late 1990s after a series of scandals came to light. A government council was set up and submitted recommendations in 2000, but nothing really happened since.

[29] See, for instance, *Asahi Shinbun*, January 9, 2001.

[30] Nakano, "The Politics of Administrative Reform," 302–4.

But the "trick" of promising major administrative reforms that will not only result in greater efficiency and responsiveness but also lead to a less elitist system is one that has been played by other politicians in other contexts.[31] Nonetheless, there are also fundamental reasons—societal unity, egalitarianism, the protection of the public arena, as well as the vestiges of the bureaucracy's reputation for efficiency—that explain why the political class has been reluctant to undertake reforms that would transform the bureaucratic apparatus beyond recognition.

In an article entitled "In Defense of Japanese Bureaucrats," Peter Drucker acknowledged the incompetence and corruption that had touched the bureaucratic elite. He observed that, like all elites, the Japanese bureaucratic elite clings to power; and with no replacement in sight, the elite is able to hold on to power.[32] Why?

Drucker's answer is that the Japanese bureaucracy is a prime example of Japan's placing the society above the economy. Americans, Drucker argues, have trouble understanding Japanese inaction in the face of, say, their disastrous banking crisis. They tend to see inaction as cowardice. But they fail to grasp that "the Japanese—and by no means the bureaucracy alone—accord primacy to society."[33] Contrary to outsiders who see Japanese society as cohesive and strong, the Japanese see their society as extremely fragile. "But while hardly uniquely Japanese, giving pride of place to society is more important to the Japanese than to most other developed countries, save perhaps France."[34] Consequently, Drucker concluded, if Americans were to grasp the priority the Japanese accord to the society over the economy, "they might cling less to myths about the uselessness of the Japanese bureaucracy."[35]

The bureaucracy, according to the Japanese conception of this institution, is not there to undermine society in any way. It is a bulwark against social disintegration, and as such can perhaps be allowed to cost more than it ought to.

France

The panoply of NPM reforms are often viewed as constituting part of a more or less coherent movement that has culminated in the "end of history." The retreat of government from regulation, the faith in the market

---

[31] See the following section on France's struggles with bureaucratic reforms.

[32] Peter Drucker, "In Defense of Japanese Bureaucrats," *Foreign Affairs*, September–October 1998.

[33] Ibid., 79.

[34] Ibid., 80.

[35] Ibid.

as the distributor of resources, the decentralization of decision making, and the empowerment of civil society have been seen to affect the role that the bureaucracy has traditionally played in society.

Yet, one looks in vain for a set of universally applicable reforms that could constitute a program for the organization of governmental bureaucracies. Even the reforms that were embraced in many societies—privatization, decentralization, and the reduction of government employment—differed markedly in their scope as well as in their application.

In the previous chapter we saw that a number of countries that were eager and ready to undertake far-reaching reforms did so without regard for a predetermined set of "necessary" reforms. Each country appeared to determine for itself the "major" reforms it was in need of implementing.

In between countries that undertook far-reaching reforms and those that took few steps in reforming their bureaucracies was a third set of countries whose reforms may be called "tinkering." Here the society believes that reforms of the kind that NPM calls for are either not necessary or not feasible, or simply contrary to the balance that has been established between the state and civil society. Few countries fit the description of the "reluctant reformer" better than Japan and France. There are, to be sure, reasons why Japan and France have seemed allergic to reforming their state apparatus. Yet, even if Japan and France are not representative cases, they nonetheless help to explain the caution of the group of less than enthusiastic reformers.

Reforming the State

France has not escaped the universal call for state reform. In fact, those responsible for the conduct of the state's affairs have been the state's most vehement critics. Whereas Ronald Reagan could believe that the federal bureaucracy was *the* problem and could not be part of the solution, French politicians have generally been eager while campaigning to proclaim the bureaucracy as handicapping development and democracy, and while in office to act as though it is the solution.

Nor is the attack on the way the state is steered and managed confined to any political movement. What Poujade proclaimed in the 1950s in his denunciation of French society has its parallels in the denunciations of establishment political figures across the political spectrum. "France," declared Poujade, "suffers from an over-abundance of educated people—*polytechniciens*, economists, philosophers, and others who have lost all contact with the real world."[36] Similar attacks have been made by Jean-

---

[36] Cited in Betrand le Gendre, "M. Chirac contre les experts," *Le Monde*, January 2, 1995.

Pierre Chevènement,[37] Le Pen, and Laurent Fabius, who went so far as to call for the abolition of the National School of Administration.

In the 1995 presidential campaign, Jacques Chirac, as part of a populist campaign strategy, undertook a relentless attack on the governing elite that had "confiscated power," an elite that was "out of touch with reality."[38] He promised to give power back to the people. Few—sympathizers or opponents—failed to note that Chirac has spent his entire life inside the *nomenklatura* he was denouncing. Still, the fact that so many politicians in France seize on the bureaucracy and on its elitist type of hierarchy suggests that not only is it a theme that plays well but that, if it strikes such a chord, there must be something that needs reforming.

It has become something of a tradition for newly formed governments to appoint commissions on the reform of the state.[39] The reports they issue are taken not less, and certainly not more, seriously than the countless commission reports that American presidents request. At the very least they suggest recognition of a problem, even if they do not always indicate a clear solution.

The projects for reform generally come under two headings: *la modernisation de l'Etat* (or *de l'administration*), that is, the modernization of the state or the administration, and *la réforme de l'Etat* (the reform of the state). Jean Picq, himself the author of a widely debated report on state reform, explains the distinction thus: "The modernization of the administration is a technical matter, while state reform affects the quality of life of the nation. That is why it is serious, urgent, necessary. At the hour of the European Union and of decentralization, we can no longer govern France with an administration or a state built upon the 1960s model."[40]

There may be something to Picq's distinction, though he does not define it. Moreover, every reform considered to be of a "technical" nature has proven to be, as we shall see, highly politically charged. Nonetheless, what the distinction in terminology seeks to get at is that administrative modernization encompasses managerial issues of efficiency, costs, and number of employees, whereas state reform encompasses reforms of more general practices and habits of the state, such as the way it deals with its clients, the

---

[37] See Jacques Mandrin, *L'Enarchie, ou les Mandarins de la Société Bourgeoise* (Paris: La Table Ronde du Combat, 1967).

[38] See le Gendre, "M. Chirac contre les experts."

[39] François de Closets, *Le Pari de la Responsabilité* (Paris: La Documentation Française, 1989); Christian Blanc, *Pour un Etat Stratège, Garant de l'Intérêt Général* (Paris: La Documentation Française, 1994); Rapport au Ministre de la Fonction Publique et des Réformes Administratives, *Comment Réformer l'Etat* (Paris: La Documentation Française, 1998); Denoix de Saint Marc, *Le Service Public* (Paris: La Documentation Française, 1997); Jean Picq, *L'Etat en France: Servir une Nation Ouverte au Monde*, Rapport de la mission sur les responsabilités et l'organisation de l'Etat (Paris: La Documentation Française, 1994).

[40] Cited in Rafaële Rivais, "Le monopole du pouvoir," *Le Monde*, June 26, 1998.

cumul des mandats (the holding of several elective offices simultaneously), and issues of accountability, transparency, and decentralization.

Over the last decade France has not been inactive in seeking to modernize its public service sector. It came to acknowledge the need for reform rather late, in part because the budgetary constraints on France were less severe than those imposed on other governments. As long as tax rates could remain relatively high, the state authorities did not feel a pressing need to impose drastic cuts and greater efficiency, particularly as any government would face both political and ideological-cultural constraints.

By the late 1980s, however, it became apparent that while other countries (and not only those far enough away to be considered either geographically distant or culturally different—such as Australia, the U.S., Great Britain, New Zealand—but also Holland, Italy, and Spain) had embarked on programs aimed at modernizing their public service sector, France had done relatively little. The Rocard government took the initiative of proposing, through the publication of a *Chartes des services publics*, a set of reforms that aimed at "humanizing" the state and putting it at the service of its users, making it more efficient through better management, decentralizing decision-making and pinpointing responsibility for the decisions, and the evaluation of performance.

The Rocard government sought to put its ideas into practice. A number of initiatives were undertaken to insure that regional services would negotiate, manage, and account for their own budgets and resources. The most important innovation was the creation of "centers of responsibility" to evaluate the performance of the targets that were established. These initiatives were followed up by the Balladur (1993–1995) and Juppé (1995–1997) governments, both of which, in particular the latter, sought to devolve managerial responsibility to the operational level, to improve the quality of public service, to increase responsibility of the operational levels, to call for evaluations of performance, and to link salaries to performance.

It is possible to see Rocard's approach of relying more on the civil servants themselves to carry out and propose reforms as a "bottom-up" approach, while Juppé's approach, which relied more on the setting of national criteria for change, was a "top-down" one. It is nonetheless clear that these reforms shared important characteristics: "increasing the speed, effectiveness and efficiency of public service provision, giving to individual units defined objectives and responsibility for achieving those targets, providing both civil servants and citizens with clear definitions of standards expected in public services and mobilizing civil servants by better training, career management and job involvement."[41] These are important objectives for a

---

[41] Alain Guyomarch, " 'Public Service,' 'Public Management,' and the Modernization of French Public Administration," *Public Administration* 77, no. 1 (spring 1999): 174.

country where the state has allocated to itself the noble role of guardian of the general interest. Most analysts of the state, and of the tradition on which it is based, have generally pointed out its reluctance to be accountable or even to be evaluated.

But one needs to recognize that it was only in 1981 that France, still bent on increasing the state's role in the economy, went on a renationalization binge. After 1984, and particularly after 1986, the state began first deregulating the economy and then selling its prized assets, the nationalized industries. It had already taken the important decentralization measures in 1981. For a decade, then, privatization, which inevitably meant a reduction in the state's control over the economy, and decentralization, which meant a diminished hierarchy and reduced central command, became synonymous with administrative reform.

A decade after the Socialists came to power in 1981, it came to be realized that as crucial as the twin measures of privatization and decentralization were, they would not suffice. The state would have to trim itself down and would need to operate more efficiently; hence the efforts of the Rocard, Balladur, Juppé, and to some extent Jospin, governments. In fact, in urging reform of a part of the Ministry of Finance, the then minister, Dominique Strauss-Kahn, spoke of the state "being in danger."[42]

Before showing the reluctance of France to transform its public sector at least to the point where it comes to operate more efficiently and more openly, we need to bear in mind that continuous, if modest, efforts have been made over the past two decades to introduce reforms. It may well be that there will be a cumulative effect of these reforms, even if there will be spectacular failures, such as the one we will be describing in the pages that follow.

For the past forty years, thirty-six efforts have been made to render the state's budget transparent (and even understandable), to give civil servants some control over expenditures, and to grant Parliament a greater oversight over the budgetary process. A law passed on July 25, 2001, finally succeeded in making these reforms a reality. One minister described this reform, perhaps with a bit of hyperbole, as a "real Copernican revolution."[43]

While most other democratic societies have long recognized that both efficiency and democracy necessitated these kinds of measures, France has always been slower to move in this direction. This has often had more to do with politicians' conservatism, which derived from their unwillingness to cede any authority, as well as with civil servants who naturally distrusted the prying of elected officials. We need to bear in mind, therefore, that reforming the bureaucracy runs up against political and bureaucratic obstacles,

---

[42] Dominique Strauss-Kahn, "Engager une prudente réforme de Bercy," *Le Monde*, April 15, 1999.

[43] *Le Monde*, July 28, 2001.

as well as cultural or value-laden obstacles. This no doubt explains why reforms such as the recent changes in the budgetary process are seen as "Copernican."

France is one of those countries that has rejected the underlying philosophy of NPM largely for the same reasons that it was not considered to have much relevance in Japan. The underlying rationale for resisting reforms has to do with the belief that not only is the state necessary, but it is there to sustain elemental values. Whether these functions and values are, or have become, rationalizations for sustaining the status quo is an issue that needs to be examined.

Economy and Society

When the former socialist prime minister Lionel Jospin said, "Yes to a market economy, no to a market society," he meant no more than that the economy must remain at the service of the society and not the other way around. It matters little whether the phrase has a tight logic about it; what matters is that it conveys that the government does not intend to allow competition and profit-seeking into all institutions.

This makes more intelligible the French and Japanese approaches to administrative reform: efficiency, transparency, accountability, responsibility, and even evaluation are acceptable; competition, entrepreneurship, and abandonment of security of employment are not. If the criterion of solidarity is transgressed, no reform becomes acceptable.[44]

There is, of course, no clear line that can be drawn between what the government considers reforms that contribute to rendering the state bureaucracy more efficient and those that inflict damage on the principles of cohesiveness and solidarity. The latter are often used by state employees as a means of defending their specific group interests. Nonetheless, the bureaucracy is a fairly efficient instrument of political power, and no attempt to reform it that appears revolutionary is likely to be undertaken by any government.

Republicanism vs. Democracy

Associated with the value of solidarity and societal cohesion is the republican principle, which holds not only that France is "one and indivisible" but also that egalitarianism is the underlying core philosophy of all democratic

[44] See J.-M. Belorgey, "Les services publics: Instruments de solidarité," *Echanges et Projets* 74 (July 1995): 53–61. See also Philippe Bezes, "Les hauts fonctionnaires croient-ils à leurs mythes? L'apport des approches cognitives à l'analyse des engagements dans les politiques de réforme de l'État; quelques exemples français (1988–1997), *Revue Française de Science Politique* 50, no. 2 (April 2000): 307–32.

governments. Put simply, republicanism implies that the state treats all citizens equally, that it recognizes no distinctions among its citizens, and that all citizens have equal access to the services and to the protection provided by the state.

The other side of this model is that citizens do not claim rights based on identities that depart from the equality imposed by the republican principle. Hence, gender, race, ethnic, and regional identities do not have claims to legitimacy and are antithetical to republicanism. The bureaucracy has always been considered as the instrument by which republicanism applies its measures to society.[45] The state is no mere arbiter in the republican model. By its neutrality, by its representation of the "general will" or the "general interest," it stands above society's conflicts and thus insures equality: "The equality and neutrality of the state forms an important part of the French republican tradition. There is a widespread positive connotation of the state as an instrument of public service, as an agent of economic development and as a guarantor of equality between French citizens."[46]

The republican model is, to some degree, at odds with modern concepts of democracy that allow for freedom of speech and expression of differences. The expression and claims of groups based on cultural, religious, sexual, gender, ethnic, and regional identities are both accepted and contested in Anglo-Saxon democratic models. Unlike republicanism, the democratic model is at one with the concept of democratic representation.

France has had a difficult time reconciling its attachment to republicanism with the growing participation of, and claims by, groups in the society. Individual groups adhere to the view that their specific interest calls for legitimate representation that is sanctioned by representative democracy. They do not adhere to an abstract principle of republicanism.

Yet, the French state has gradually moved to recognize the specificity of interests and has passed laws granting rights to groups that contravene the republican principles.[47] The most spectacular confirmation of the modification of the republican state has been the Jospin government's passage of the law granting a considerable degree of local autonomy to Corsica.

[45] For discussions on the republican bases of democracy, see Laurence Engel, *Le Mépris du Droit* (Paris: Hachette Littératures, 2000), 17–24.

[46] Alistair Cole, "The *Service Public* under Stress," *West European Politics* 22, no. 4 (October 1999): 168.

[47] See Janine Mossuz-Lavau, *Femmes/Hommes: Pour la Parité* (Paris: Presses de Sciences Po, 1998), and "La parité en politique: Histoire et premier bilan," *Travail, Genre et Société* 7 (February 2000); Daniel Borrillo and Pierre Lascoumes, *Amours Egales? Le Pacs, les Homosexuels et la Gauche* (Paris: La Decouverte, 2002); Mariette Sineau, *Profession: Femmes Politiques, Sexe et Pouvoir sous la Cinquième République* (Paris: Presses de Sciences Po, 2001); and Daniel Borrillo and Eric Fassin, eds., *Au-delà du Pacs* (Paris: Presses Universitaires de France, 1999).

The law sets up a Corsican parliament and even permits the use of the Corsican language in schools. Under the weight of democracy, participation, claims of rights, claims of righting previous wrongs, and representation of differences, the French state has gradually, if reluctantly, succumbed to a form of representation that contravenes its original republican principles.

Egalitarianism

The central objective of republicanism is the imposition of equality in society. Ostensibly, only the state can insure this. In order to do this, the state needs to rely on a vast bureaucratic apparatus that multiplies rules and regulations that lead to control in the service of republican egalitarianism.

The bureaucracy is not just the instrument for implementing actions according to republican principles. It has erected a very substantial edifice that stands and is supported and legitimized by these principles. This has always been one of the lines of defense against overhauling the bureaucracy's methods of work, and it has also served as a rampart against attacks on bureaucratic growth, waste, and privileges.[48]

At the core of republican ideology is a belief, then, that mostly runs counter to a rational economic view of the services that the state provides. Should the state provide postal service in remote rural areas? Should trains continue to stop at stations that have been deserted by most of their passengers? Should schools that once housed many children continue to function after most families have left for the cities? France has made enormous strides in moving toward closing down facilities in areas that have been depopulated. To be sure, the egalitarian principle in France does not compare with its rigid application in Japan, where a country school can be kept open at an enormous cost because it has one child to educate.[49]

France has found ways to cut economically unjustified services without discarding its egalitarian commitments. Railways, telephones, postal services, and educational institutions (particularly primary ones) have all been reformed without abandoning the principle of access. The security of employment of civil servants is intimately tied to the egalitarianism principle of access to public services. Civil servants not only need to have security of employment based on the 1946 Statute of Civil Servants, but they need to cover the entire national territory so as to insure equality of access to state services. The concept of equality has thus served as a powerful tool with which to block reforms of the bureaucracy.

[48] See Engel, *Le Mépris du Droit*, 178–92.
[49] See Nicholas D. Kristof, "Japanese Are Torn between Efficiency and Egalitarian Values," *New York Times*, October 26, 1998.

The Need for Reform

There are not many bipartisan agreements in France. Reforming or modernizing the state constitutes that rare issue on which harmony reigns. Yet, despite this agreement among the (center) Left and (center) Right, all governments once in power tread timidly where the issue of administrative reform is concerned. Many years of promising to modernize the state and doing little to effect any meaningful changes have made France a laggard in this area.

We saw in chapter 5 that while the number of civil servants has been stabilized or lowered in most industrial countries, it has increased in France by 25 percent over the past fifteen years. According to OECD figures, public employment as a percentage of total employment in 1996 was 24.7 percent in France, while in Germany it was 15.7 percent, in the U.K. 14 percent, in Italy 17.7 percent, and in the United States 15.4 percent. With regard to the number of civil servants as a percentage of the total population, here again France, with 9.5 percent, occupies the top place. The comparable figure for Italy is 6.2 percent, for Germany 6.6 percent, and for the U.K. 6.3 percent.[50]

Even with such a large proportion of the workforce employed by the state, the French state is unable to account for the precise number of civil servants it employs. Jean Picq, the author of a government report on state reform, noted that France simply does not know how many people it employs. He writes: "No one in the state can answer any of the following questions with precision, despite their simplicity and importance: How many people does the state employ? How many functionaries work in each region, in each department? What is the precise breakdown among workers in central agencies, public institutions and decentralized agencies? What is the role of a functionary? According to the existing definition, there are at least 50 exact answers to how many people work in each ministry."[51]

That the state, which devotes over 40 percent of its budget to salaries, is unable or unwilling to account for the precise number of people it employs may be attributed to convenient ignorance. The state has not appeared eager to be open about the exact salaries of its civil servants, either. Time and again, the *Cour des Comptes* has requested that the ministries furnish it with the salary information of their employees. Some, believing themselves to be on the lower rung of the salary scale, have been eager to provide the amounts of their salaries and bonuses. Others, notably the Ministry of Finance, have always found such requests unnecessary and intrusive.[52]

[50] Picq, *L'Etat en France*, 36.

[51] Ibid., 146.

[52] See Cour des Comptes, *La Fonction Publique: Rapport Public Particulier* (Paris: Editions des Journaux Officiels, 1999).

When Jean Artuis was minister of finance (1995–1997), he thought he was making a simple request when he asked his staff to obtain for him the data on the salaries of the highest officials in his ministry. It turned out, as he learned, that he was seen as requesting state secrets to which he was not entitled.[53]

Despite the employment of about 6.5 million people in the public sector, France has not proceeded to curb the rise in state employment nor particularly to move in the direction of reforms that are inspired by NPM. A number of institutions have seen their functions reduced or modified, yet the number of employees has not diminished. Since the Bank of France lost its independence to the European Central Bank, it has continued to employ 17,000 people, whereas the Bank of England employs 2,660 people. One study has calculated that it takes 1,600 employees in France to print 1.2 billion banknotes per year, at a cost of 1 franc per note. The Bank of England, on the other hand, produces 1.3 billion notes, at a cost of 29 centimes per note, with 600 employees.[54]

Writing of the Ministry of Education, Claude Allègre, who was its minister from 1997 to 2000, noted with his customary hyperbole, "With respect to bureaucracy, we are in a pre-Soviet situation."[55] He had earlier referred to the educational enterprise as a "mammoth" that needed containment, a characterization that was to cost him dearly. But Allègre, possibly aided by his scientific training, was appalled by the basic statistics concerning his ministry. He observed that the total budget for education was approximately 600 billion francs, of which 350 billion went to the Ministry of National Education (95 percent of which went for salaries).[56] Allègre observed that this budget had increased over the past ten years by 100 billion francs, while the number of students went down by 400,000 and while the number of class days had been reduced by 50 per year since 1960.[57] The concept of productivity was simply left out of any calculations.

There are numerous examples of institutions that have seen their workloads decrease, the number of their employees remain stable or even increase, the number of hours worked decrease, and the salaries increase. On the other side of the ledger, one observes only a reduction in efficiency.[58]

[53] Jean Artuis, *Dans les Coulisses de Bercy* (Paris: Albin Michel, 1998).

[54] Bernard Zimmer, *Les Profiteurs de l'Etat* (Paris: Plon, 2001), 67. See also Jacques Marseille, *Le Grand Gaspillage: Les Vrais Comptes de l'Etat* (Paris: Plon, 2002).

[55] Claude Allègre, *Toute Vérité Est Bonne à Dire* (Paris: Laffont, 2000), 182.

[56] Ibid.

[57] Ibid.

[58] See the examples and calculations of production costs provided in Zimmer, *Les Profiteurs de L'Etat*. See also Marseille, *Le Grand Gaspillage* for an analysis of how the organization of the bureaucracy leads to increasing costs without any corresponding increase in efficiency.

Trying to understand why France has been unable to overcome even its most flagrant cases of the inefficient use of resources, we turn briefly to an examination of a failed attempt to reform a critical aspect of the Ministry of Finance. Few objective analysts or politicians could be found to argue that the reform was irrational or unnecessary.

Reforming the Tax Bureaucracy

The proposed reform was needed for the sake of rationalizing a complex, costly, and inefficient system of collecting taxes. The government and opposition had no discernible differences among them with regard to the wisdom of the reform. Finally, the reform concerned the very ministry (of finance) that had become the champion of state modernization and economic efficiency. The credibility of state reform at the very least supposed that the Ministry of Finance apply to itself the standards that it sought to impose on the rest of the state apparatus.

The French tax collection system is of a complexity not found in any other industrial society. The taxpayer has found himself, in the words of a Ministry of Finance official, becoming a "ping-pong ball when he asks for a decision or some information." In fact, all the studies conducted by the Ministry of Finance show that "almost no one understands the reality, much less the justifications, of our tax system."[59] That the system of taxation in France is the most confusing of all known systems of comparable countries is more than adequately demonstrated by a study conducted by the Ministry of Finance itself.[60] Whereas a few countries (Spain, Portugal) had only in recent years rationalized or restructured their tax bureaucracy, others had integrated reforms and changes over the years in an effort to keep in tune with the changing needs of citizens and with a general drive toward greater efficiency in public services. This is the situation faced by a French taxpayer:

> French taxpayers, individuals and businesses alike, pay various agencies, which are themselves at the very least proliferating, if not incoherent. This means there is a large number of administrators who handle, in a haphazard way, the dossiers of taxpayers. An individual will therefore declare his taxable income at the tax center that has jurisdiction over his primary residence; here there will be a check upon the amount he says he owes. This center is dependent upon the *Direction*

---

[59] Thierry Bert, "La réforme de Bercy: paralysie ou suicide collectif?" in *Notre Etat: Le Livre Vérité de la Fonction Publique*, ed. Roger Fauroux and Bernard Spitz (Paris: Robert Laffont, 2000), 127.

[60] See Inspection Générale des Finances, *Mission d'Analyse Comparative des Administrations Fiscales: Rapport de Synthèse*, May 20, 1999. The other countries that France was compared to in the Ministry of Finance study were Germany, Italy, Great Britain, Canada, Ireland, Sweden, Holland, Spain, and the United States.

générale des impôts (DGI), but he must make his payment to the treasury, which is in turn dependent upon another agency, the *Direction générale de la comptabilité publique* (DGCP). If he has two secondary residences and a parking space, for example, which fall outside the administrative district of his primary residence, he will receive four tax bills on his residences, each administered by a different tax center, and each payable to a different treasury. To those, he can add four property tax bills, administered by tax property centers; naturally, there will also be three bills for *redevance audiovisuelle* [a television tax], which are administered by a specialized service. These various taxes will be payable to the same treasuries as the residence taxes, with the exception of the *redevance audiovisuelle*, which is payable to a separate entity. But, if the taxpayer has to pay a luxury tax *(impôt sur la fortune)*, he must pay the main tax office, which depends not upon the DGCP but upon the DGI. Vehicle registration stickers, now obsolete, could be purchased in a *tabac* or at the main tax office (DGI), and always at the main office when payment was late or when the car was purchased during the year.[61]

Complexity has its costs. The Ministry of Finance report shows that the French tax collection system is the most costly: for every franc it collects, France spends 40 percent more than Great Britain, the Netherlands, Spain, Canada, and Ireland, whereas Sweden and the United States spend half as much as France does to collect their taxes. The reasons for this are many: overstaffing, excessive presence of offices across the country,[62] lack of computerization, and the existence of several administrations. The cost of tax collection in France is not due to the complexity of the tax code (that of the U.S., for example, is infinitely more complex), but to poor organization and mediocre service.[63] The number of civil servants and the advantageous remuneration they receive in comparison with their counterparts in other ministries has helped French tax collecting become the most expensive in the industrialized world. In a recent report, the *Cour des Comptes* castigated the Ministry of Finance for its "propensity . . . to take liberties with legislative and regulatory guidelines, notably in budget and accounting matters,"[64] whether with regard to the number of people employed or with regard to their remuneration.

Objectives of the Reform

After a devastating diagnosis of the tax system in France, a reform project was proposed by the Ministry of Finance. Its principal aim was to provide

[61] Bert, "La réforme de Bercy," 121–2.
[62] Inspection Générale des Finances, *Mission d'Analyse.*
[63] France has 65.5 offices for each million inhabitants, whereas Germany has 7.9, Canada 2.0, Spain 5.2, the U.S. 0.1, Ireland 36.1, Italy 16.6, the Netherlands 1.6, the U.K. 8.5, and Sweden 13.5. See Inspection Générale des Finances, *Mission d'Analyse.*
[64] Cour des Comptes, *La Fonction Publique,* 147.

better service to the citizen and to rationalize the organization of the fiscal bureaucracy. A considerable economy was expected to be made by simplifying the structure. An indispensable part of this aspect of the reform was the termination of the separation of imposition and collection of taxes. This could be done, as in other countries, by mechanizing the numero⁀s tasks of receiving and verifying tax forms, collecting taxes owed, and providing citizens with information all along the process. This kind of reform calls for centralization of offices, which increases the competence of tax officials, and the closing of numerous local offices where officials often have only a modicum of knowledge of the tax code.

The goal of rationalization was the creation of greater competence of the tax officials and greater specialization of the tax authorities. The most sensible way of doing this was not to separate imposition and collection, but to organize the bureaucracy according to a logic determined by the *type* of client (individual, small firm, corporation). This would mean that each bureaucracy would be thoroughly specialized, would be more competent and more helpful, and would allow the citizen to know where she needed to go for all her taxes. In order to accomplish this goal of simplification and the creation of a user-friendly tax authority, there needed to be consolidation among the various tax bureaucracies so that the country could possess what all other industrialized nations have: a single tax agency.

A project was drawn up by the Ministry of Finance that took into account the sensibilities of the two major bureaucratic agencies responsible for imposing and collecting taxes.[65] There would be a transfer of civil servants but not a reduction in their numbers. Jean-Pascal Beaufret succeeded François Villeroy de Galhau as director general of taxation, and both men took pains to reassure the civil servants that no abolition of posts or agencies would be required. They sought to make rationalization as palatable as possible. Both met a brick wall.

The Ultimate Failure

How, then, did a reform that was judged necessary, economically rational, and beneficial to the public meet such a disastrous fate? Can the cause be attributed to the authoritarian process of policy-making that has for so long allowed the authorities to prepare reforms in secret and present them on a take-it-or-leave-it basis to those concerned?[66]

---

[65] The *Direction générale des impôts* and the *Direction générale de la comptabilité publique*.
[66] See Pierre Muller and Yves Surel, *L'Analyse des Politiques Publiques* (Paris: Montchrestien, 1998), 110.

In fact, the government went to considerable lengths to seek legitimacy for this reform. It provided comparisons with other countries, thus hoping to pressure the unions and the politicians to take notice of France's backwardness. Second, it leaked these comparisons to the press, thus hoping to mobilize public opinion against the backwardness of the present structure. Finally, the government undertook to consult the public through a series of surveys. But it also involved the trade unions in all discussions, ever careful not to be accused of acting in an authoritarian manner.

The government thus offered its backing to the offices in the Ministry of Finance (the minister and the senior officials), who themselves were the initiators and engines of this reform. Yet, very quickly tensions developed between the two arch-rivals of the tax bureaucracy, the *directeur générale des impôts* and the *directeur générale de la comptabilité publique*. To this horizontal tension must be added problems of a vertical nature. Civil servants lower down in the hierarchy feared having to make efforts at obtaining new qualifications, or being squeezed out by automization. Hence, civil servants at the lower end of the hierarchy and those in the middle working in the provinces joined forces and opposed the reform, even though potentially there were numerous pecuniary inducements as well as relocation choices offered.

The opposition of the trade unions was yet another important factor in the failure of the reform. The two major trade unions, FO *(Force ouvrière)*, which opposed the single agency idea from the start, and SNUI *(Syndicat national unifié des impôts)*, which represents 25 percent of the tax officials and accounts for 44 percent of the votes, were hostile to the creation of an office for corporations and to the modernization of the offices that they feared would eventually reduce the number of civil servants in the tax bureaucracy. The unions found their positions threatened by the reform of the tax bureaucracy. Not wishing to be outdone by their base, they adopted a hard line against the reform.

The unions were able to mobilize local elected officials against the proposed reform. As the secretary general of the main trade union in the Treasury (FO-*Trésor*) put it: "At our urging, thousands of mayors have already mobilized to demand control of their tax office."[67] An SNUI official also avowed: "We have contacted all of the elected officials. They are furious. They were not consulted by the ministers either, who are not even elected."[68]

The local officials mobilized to put pressure on the Socialist Party, which then put pressure on the Socialist government to withdraw the reform. Pressure from below created a loud noise and, fearing the negative

[67] *Le Parisien*, February 28, 2000.
[68] *Le Monde*, March 11, 2000.

consequences (strikes, defeat in the municipal elections the following year), the prime minister withdrew the project.

Many factors account for the failure of the reform: the government's seeking to elicit the press, and mostly the financial and elite press rather than the popular press; the government's failure to recognize the fears of the trade unions (reduction in the number of civil servants, the closure of offices in rural areas, the favoring of the Paris region over the provinces); the announcement of the reform by the minister, which gave the appearance to the trade unions of a fait accompli; the refusal of the unions to countenance changes of the status quo; and, finally, the internecine conflicts of the tax agencies.

The trade unions, to be sure, did not hesitate to invoke the general principles of republicanism: "the equality of citizens before taxes,"[69] the dismantling of the public services, the creation of inequalities among regions and among categories of citizens (corporations vs. individuals). The FO trade union even refused the merger of the functions of imposition and collection on the grounds of respect for the "democratic and republican principles of our country."[70]

Confronted with these normative arguments, the reformers were unable to develop a sufficiently strong set of arguments that could compete with the "legitimacy" of the grand principles espoused by the opponents of reform. The reformers avoided presenting the case that reforms were based on the need for profitability and productivity. They even avoided arguing that the collection of taxes would be more efficient. They tried to place the "client" at the center of their case.[71] But the client as such cannot compete with the grand principles of republicanism and equality. In fact, reference to the "client" by the administration turned out to be counterproductive. As the Ministry of Finance's statement outlining the proposed reform observed: "In the eyes of a significant proportion of tax officials, the terms 'debtor' or 'subject' reflected better the grand aspect of their task than did that of 'client.' "[72] Anything smacking of "profitability" was attacked as being contrary to the principles of the Republic. This was the trade union's answer to the Ministry of Finance's own study showing that France had a more expensive tax-collecting system than other industrialized countries. The concept of a client is alien to any view that places the collectivity and the

---

[69] Interview with the secretary general of the SNUI, Christian Boulais, in *Le Parisien*, February 28, 2000.

[70] Interview with the secretary general of FO-*Trésor*, Gérard Mazuir, *Le Parisien*, February 28, 2000.

[71] "A Reform Which Puts, for the First Time, the Client at the Center of Its Logic," interview with François Villeroy de Galhau, director general of taxation, *Le Monde*, March 8, 2000.

[72] Ministère de l'Economie, des Finances et de l'Industrie, *Mission 2001: Construire Ensemble le Service Public de Demain* (Paris: Ministry of Finance, 1999). This document is known as the Bert-Champsau report.

attendant equality among its members at its center. Criteria of cost, productivity, and efficiency are seen as constituting a direct assault on the concept of the *service public*. Bert cites a tax official who observed that his agency "dealt not with clients but with subjects, to whom one had to apply the law in accordance with the dispositions of the public authority." In fact, at its congress in 2000, the FO approved a motion demanding that the term "client" be replaced by "administré."[73]

Lessons for Reforming the State

To what extent was the failure to pass this reform exceptional and to what extent was it representative of the fate of reforms in general in France?

POLITICAL RESPONSIBILITY

In the face of the recurrent failures to reform the French state—health care, pensions, education, taxes—the temptation is strong to blame the trade unions and exonerate the politicians. But failed reforms are a symptom of the failures of politics. Many placed emphasis on the absence of clout of the minister bringing the reform. It may be that the authority of Christian Sautter within the administration and in the eyes of the public suffered because of the comparison with Dominique Strauss-Kahn, his predecessor and former boss. Conversely, the reform efforts of Claude Allègre surely suffered from an excess of charisma and from media attention heaped upon a minister who had alienated a good number of the teachers: teachers became deaf to the projects and propositions of the minister. The two ministers may have lacked essential political resources, like the unction of universal suffrage and deep relationships with the party in power (the Socialists). They were stigmatized as technocrats removed from the realities and constraints of politics. What is less often mentioned is that they were left to twist in the wind by their own government. This was especially the case of the minister of finance.

A strong political will is a necessary, if not sufficient, condition for success. If the will of Sautter and Allègre was real, the investment of the prime minister was relatively weak, at least with respect to reforming the tax administration, which never appeared to be a priority for Lionel Jospin.[74] As a result, the opponents of reform had an important advantage. Underlining the political cost of reform—alienation of a important portion of the electorate—to the prime minister was more convincing than the need for the reform itself.

[73] Bert, "La réforme de Bercy," 114.
[74] "Une réforme à risque pour Jospin," *Libération*, March 7, 2000.

The various administrative reforms that have gone through in France clearly indicate how crucial a great political investment is to success: the reform of the French army, which proceeded under the direction of the president of the Republic, is a good example. Political engagement must be steady; it cannot be held hostage to cabinet reshuffling. The time allowed for the professionalization of the armed forces was fixed at six years to correspond with the length of the presidential mandate; this way, administrative sabotage, spurred by the fact that a minister's life is approximately two years, could be avoided. The successful reform of the telecommunications industry also shows the importance of sustained political commitment. From 1986, when the director general of France Télécom changed, to the company's appearance on the stock market in October 1997, the reform benefited from the consistent support of ministers Longuet (liberal), Quilès (Socialist), and Fillon (Gaullist).[75]

THE TRAP OF REGIONAL DEVELOPMENT

The question of regional development and the closing of local establishments contributed significantly to the failure of tax reform. The mobilization of locally elected officials and deputies had already foiled Jean-Pierre Chevènement's police reform of 1998, which sought to transfer certain rural precincts to the suburbs. With 36,000 townships, more than any other in the European Union, and 500,000 locally elected officials, any reform touching upon the closure or transfer of a local office becomes a political hot potato and a source of conflict, of mobilization. Every plan to close a maternity hospital gives way to protest involving the concerned employees, local inhabitants, and elected officials, and garners at least regional media coverage.

In the case of tax reform, the reformers did not know how to protect themselves against this pitfall, and even less how to gain from it. It was not until February 3, 2000, three weeks after the release of the 2003 mission report and more than fifteen days after the unions had reacted (at the urging of locally elected officials), that the minister of finance understood the stakes at hand. The director general of the tax bureau, François Villeroy de Galhau, and the director general of public accounting, Jean Bassères, reacted by sending a letter to their local representatives. Not only did their action come much too late, but they were sharing the communications they had had with local officials with directors and treasurers of local tax offices—people who, like the elected officials, had a vested interest in seeing the reform fail.[76]

[75] See Ezra Suleiman and Guillaume Courty, *L'Age d'Or de l'Etat* (Paris: Seuil, 1997).

[76] "Nous vous demandons de conduire dans les meilleurs délais tous contacts personnels avec les élus et toutes actions de communication nécessaire, selon les formes les mieux adaptées à la situation locale." Cited in "Les syndicats des finances freinent le recouvrement des impôts," *Le Monde*, March 16, 2000.

The reform of the armed forces, which was of a much greater scale in terms of regional development, was no doubt the only reform not to stumble over the question of local institutions. This was a result of the role played by the minister of defense, who had benefited greatly from the restructuring undertaken in the early 1990s. For example, the Ministry of Defense and the general leadership of the armed forces, in particular of the army, the most invested party, took a lesson from the 1989 "trauma of Barcelonette," in which the plan to dissolve the local regiment provoked substantial local mobilization. In turn, this uprising, which benefited from tremendous media coverage, reached the president of the Republic and led to the resignation of the minister of defense. From the moment the territorial reorganizations of 1996–2002 began, the leadership of the armed forces arranged to compensate the closed sites, and involved local officials in the process, several weeks and often several months in advance. Moreover, the scope of the military restructuring led to a new structure at the heart of the Ministry of Defense: the *Délégation aux restructurations*, the head of which is one of the close advisers of the minister.

UNIONIZATION AND THE ABSENCE OF AN OPPOSITION

If the failure of the reform illustrates the shortcomings of politics in reforming the state, it illustrates just as well the crucial role civil service unions play in this process. We have emphasized that FO is essentially a civil service union, for which every conflict with the government has major stakes: numerous examples come to mind concerning hospitals and social security. The recent attempts to reform the state have shown the role the unions play in blocking change. In effect, the civil service offers numerous perquisites to the unions. In the fight against Claude Allègre's reforms, the SNES, the primary union of secondary schools, played a decisive role.[77]

Conversely, the successful reform of the armed forces was clearly facilitated by the inability of the military to mobilize effectively. As one high military official joked, "We don't have the time to overthrow our minister." The example of the military is also interesting for what it says about unions. It is in the domains where the unions are the strongest that military reform has taken the longest, or been postponed or watered down (namely, military arsenals and naval construction).

Union influence in the process of reforming the state is also a result of the absence of opposition. In this respect France differs from Anglo-Saxon countries, in which citizen associations often play a significant role.

---

[77] Allègre attributes the primary responsibility for the failure of his reforms to the SNES. See Allègre, *Toute Vérité Est Bonne à Dire*.

Taxpayer associations are not well developed in France; they did not even have a recognized role in the unfolding of the tax reform plan. In the realm of education, where civil associations are no doubt the most powerful and well structured, Claude Allègre often expressed regret at the fact that parent associations had neither the ability nor the will to uphold the proposed reforms or to organize large protests. Generally speaking, this example illustrates a classic dilemma of collective action: it is easier to mobilize people to defend the status quo than to support reform.

Is it very risky for a reform movement that has a particular group at its center not to mobilize that group? If so, is a strategy that places "citizens against the agents" (in the case of tax reform) or "parents against teachers" viable?[78]

The absence of opposition to government unions is also a result of the marginal role the National Assembly plays in pushing state reforms that have important social consequences. Members of the Assembly often wear two hats: sworn enemy of public expenditure when they are in Paris; relentless defender of "their" maternity hospital, "their" regiment, "their" tax office when they return to their constituencies.

The weakness of civil associations is coupled with the absence of powerful research organizations that can make policy recommendations, offer a place for dialogue among high functionaries, politicians, and union leaders, and nourish independent expertise. France does not have "think tanks" and foundations. Therefore expertise remains largely concentrated in the hands of high functionaries and union leaders.

DEFINING THE TERMS OF THE DEBATE: PARTICIPATION AND MOBILIZATION OF AGENTS

One of the principle lessons of the failure of the reform lies in the inability of the interested parties to define the terms of the debate in order to foster a legitimate discussion on the objectives of the reform. This failure also follows from the inability to mobilize the agents likely to be affected in favor of the reform and from the difficulty in insuring the participation of the parties interested in elaborating the reform.

At an initial level, the failure to define the terms of the debate was a failure to identify the various interested parties and their positions. Moreover, the natural tendency of the reformers is to consider the interests of their opponents as simple, corporatist reflexes, when in fact the interests

---

[78] The only large mobilization of parents, which was exceptional because of its size, took place in 1984; parents were defending free schools against the minister of education, Alain Savary.

being defended are often legitimate, at least with respect to the agents.[79] This phenomenon is extremely important, given that reform must be seen in terms of interests (purchasing power, qualification, prestige, status) by those who are going to put the reforms in place.

The primary cause of the failure was the inability to mobilize administrative agents at all levels of the hierarchy. All it took to renew the dialogue between the unions and the ministry was for the new minister of finance, Laurent Fabius, to speak of reform-modernization. The concept of reform implies that things are not going well and that everything must be changed, which in turn negatively affects administrators: the work announced in the Mission 2003 humiliated numerous finance ministry functionaries.[80] The education example confirms this point: numerous teachers, many of whom were very favorable to important reforms, perceived the actions of Claude Allègre as an attack on their practices and professional ethic. The notion of modernization, by contrast, has a positive connotation; it denotes progress, improvement, reevaluation: "the results are correct, the work is good, but we can do even better." The army, for example, mobilized its entire personnel around a common project: the creation of an army of the future, of the best technology, an army for the twenty-first century. In large part, this explains the enormous success of the army's historic reform.

By the same token, the successful reform of the telecommunications industry was built around the challenge of international competition and the need to meet the demands of the technological revolution. In certain cases—France Télécom, Air France, the Banque de France—international economic and legal pressures play a critical role in spurring reform. Military reform also benefited from the need to meet international standards. In the domains of tax administration and national education,[81] no equivalent spur existed.

---

[79] In this respect the most ardent proponents of state reform, who are very often found in the high civil service, become, when their privileges are at stake, just as conservative and corporatist as the functionaries they castigate.

[80] From this point of view the publicity and use of the Lépine report by the top administration of Bercy had a devastating effect upon the morale of agents and their perception of the reform and reformers.

[81] I refer mainly to secondary education here. Higher education is unique, and it is no coincidence, therefore, that this part of the educational system, the one most tied up in international competition, has made the greatest reforms in the last few years.

PART III

CHAPTER EIGHT

DEPROFESSIONALIZATION: THE DECLINE
OF THE CIVIL SERVICE CAREER

THAT GLOBAL ADMINISTRATIVE REFORM turns out not to be global and not an American package that is readily shipped abroad and just as readily implemented does not mean that there are no universal tendencies pushing the administrative systems in particular directions. They may have been little noticed, but that is only because we have been looking at reforms that have been devised by specific people and pushed by particular institutions and countries. We naturally assume that these are, or ought to be, the (universal) changes taking place. In focusing our attention on proposals for reform that proclaim themselves as revolutionary, we neglect to look at endogenous forces that may in the end have a far greater impact and a far more universal influence than projects such as NPM. Indeed, the fanfare surrounding NPM, which owes more to an ideology that is projected by what appear to be a series of sometimes inchoate or unrelated reforms, has been a distraction from other forces that affect the future of bureaucracy more profoundly than the series of NPM reforms.

This is not to say that NPM has failed to have an impact. It has obliged public institutions in a variety of settings to be more sensitive to inefficiencies, costs, and the need to be more responsive and accountable. Important as these improvements are, they cannot be said to revolutionize national bureaucracies. Nor can they be said to have replaced one paradigm with another. Transformative changes sometimes come about undirected by movements making large claims. Consequently they remain undetected even if the trend they instigate becomes inexorable.

In this and the following two chapters, I turn to two powerful forces making themselves felt on administrative systems and on governance in nearly all democratic societies, though to varying degrees: the downgrading of the public service career and the increasing politicization of bureaucracies. These trends do not derive from proposals for a specific reform, do not follow prescribed principles of organization, and are not supported by a panoply of ideas that suddenly came into vogue. They are, for all this, no less real and are likely to have a deeper impact than NPM in the long run on the bureaucracy.

The Nature of Administrative Reform

The history of administrative reform is filled with ambitious projects and claims. While much ink has been spilled (and we have spilled some ourselves here and elsewhere) on the latest and most ambitious of administrative reform projects, the fact remains that administrative reforms rarely become reality. Few people have been willing to champion isolated or piecemeal reforms, but most are willing to stand behind and to lend their voice to vast projects of reorganization.

"The history of administrative reorganization in the twentieth century is a history of rhetoric," wrote March and Olson almost twenty years ago.[1] They concluded their analysis of administrative reorganization thus: "Despite the frequency and intensity of serious efforts, major reorganizations seem to have been largely unsuccessful. Most reorganization efforts produce some formal administrative change."[2] Much is often claimed for administrative reform projects. Much might even be claimed for their results, but that has more to do with the fact that there is generally a chorus of support from all political institutions for administrative reforms than concern with the actual accomplishments. As March and Olson observed: "In terms of their effects on administrative costs, size of staff, productivity, or spending, most major reorganization efforts have been described by outsiders, and frequently by participants, as substantial failures. Few efficiencies are achieved; little gain in responsiveness is recorded; control seems as elusive after efforts as before."[3]

And yet reforms do occur; changes do take place, and administrative structures have evolved over time.[4] But changes in administrative structures that are willed and that result from laws or decrees are not the only changes that occur in bureaucratic responsibilities, powers, and interactions in society. Nor are they necessarily the most important indicators of how the bureaucracy actually operates. Indeed, Woodrow Wilson noted in 1887 that there were bound to be certain organizational similarities in the ways bureaucracies evolved.

But the bureaucracy is also subject to extrabureaucratic influences. Practices that do not derive from laws or reforms get adopted, built upon, and developed until they become a "natural" way of operating. These evolving practices are not the product of a carefully thought out project. They occur for particular reasons at a particular moment and they gather

---

[1] James G. March and Johan P. Olson, "What Administrative Reorganization Tells Us about Governing," *American Political Science Review* 77, no. 2 (June 1983): 282.

[2] Ibid., 287.

[3] Ibid., 288.

[4] See J. G. March, "Footnotes to Organizational Change," *Administrative Science Quarterly* 17 (1981): 563–77; and March and Olson, "Administrative Reorganization," 281.

speed with each successive government. As March and Olson noted with respect to political institutions in general, "The long-run development of political institutions is less a product of intentions, plans, and consistent decisions than incremental adaptation to changing problems with available solutions within gradually evolving structures of meaning."[5]

What are the "evolving structures of meaning"? Clearly, they are not to be found exclusively within the bureaucratic structure. This institution merely responds, not in its structural aspects but in the manner it is used and in how it functions, to a multiplicity of both endogenous and exogenous forces. The bureaucracy is part and parcel of a larger political system. This being the case, it becomes, as Aberbach and Rockman note in their recent study of the American federal bureaucracy, "relevant to ask not only how the U.S. federal executive system is changing but also how American politics is changing. It is necessary . . . to note the ways in which the federal executive adapts to such changes in the political system as well as what forces in the political environment are working to change the nature of government—its operations, scope, and activities."[6]

I will turn later to the question of the relationship between the decline in the civil service career and the process of creeping politicization that now characterizes the civil service of nearly all democratic societies. We will also examine the relationship of these two phenomena to NPM. But it bears noting at the outset of this discussion that we are probably on firmer ground when referring to a convergence, or universalistic tendencies, with regard to the decline in appeal of the civil service as a career and to the increasing politicization of this career, than we are with reference to NPM.

NPM can be considered a universal paradigm only if the whole gamut of administrative reforms, from decentralization to reduction in public employment to agencification to entrepreneurship, is considered as constituting part of NPM. This is not the case with the public service career or with its gradual politicization.

Not only are these two phenomena easier to define, to spot, and to measure, they are also the consequences of changes that take place outside of the civil service proper. Indeed, the civil service neither wills nor desires them. It is subjected to them and it is powerless to hold them in check.

Equally important is the fact that because these changes come about as a result of changes in politics, governance, and society, analysts have either not spotted them, or have not attributed sufficient importance to them. In fact, as public administration has returned to the management fold, its specialists have tended to concentrate on specific reforms. These emanate

[5] March and Olson, "Administrative Reorganization," 292.
[6] Joel D. Aberbach and Bert A. Rockman, *In the Web of Politics: Three Decades of the U.S. Federal Executive* (Washington, D.C.: Brookings Institution, 2000), 4.

from and fit into "policy-making" that is directed at the pubic sector. It is understandable that specialists in policy-making and in public administration should wish to study reforms that emanate from political institutions.

Yet, changes come about not only through specific policies, and they are not always introduced by grand or spectacular reforms (NPM, SES, etc.). They may occur piecemeal. Or they may occur as a derivative of what takes place in other sectors, which explains why NPM has absorbed the energies of innumerable specialists, while other critical changes that risk transforming the public services in important ways have attracted scarcely any attention.

This is the case with the creeping politicization of the civil services of democratic countries. This will have a dramatic and lasting impact on the bureaucracy. It will affect its professionalism, its capacity to act, and, in the end, its role in society.

Decline of a Career

The civil service career probably no longer holds the appeal it once possessed. This is the case in practically all democratic societies. There are, of course, many reasons for this: the availability of alternatives in growing economies; the vast disparities in salaries between the public and private sectors, the possibilities for moving up within an industry, not just within a single firm; the opportunity to experiment with a variety of jobs in the private sector. All these factors are real and adversely affect the attractiveness of the civil service career. These are simply the market forces that operate in a capitalist economy and that account for shifts in the choice of careers.

Politicization of the bureaucracy cannot alone therefore be blamed for the declining appeal of the civil service career. Nonetheless, not only has this trend not stemmed the tide, but it has probably seriously and adversely affected the image of the civil service career. The declining appeal of this career is demonstrated by (1) the number of candidates seeking entry, (2) the number of those seeking to depart well before retirement age, and (3) the declining overall pool as well as the quality of the pool from which new applicants are selected.

It is not an accident that in certain countries—the United States, Britain, Australia—the desertion of the public service career by "the best and the brightest" is not a cause for alarm. In fact, there are few calls or proposals whose aim is to reverse the tide. In part this is because this shift is considered unstoppable and in part because the diminution in the prestige of the public service career is viewed in a positive light. Whatever contributes to weakening the bureaucratic instrument accords with the staunchest advocates of NPM. In other countries—Spain, France,

Japan—the desertion of the public service is viewed with varying degrees of alarm.

Let us look briefly at what has happened to the public service career in societies where this career was until very recently considered the most prestigious, and in the United States, where this career never was viewed as the epitome of success. The important issue is that the declining attractiveness of a public service career affects those societies where the central state has been an interventionist one and where therefore state service combined both power and prestige (Great Britain, Japan, France, Spain) as well as societies (the United States in particular) where the federal state was not particularly strong or interventionist (save during wartime) and where state service never attained the cultlike attractiveness that it possessed throughout the nineteenth and most of the twentieth centuries.

This convergence among states of varying cultural and state traditions is significant because of the long-term consequences it will have on the key instrument of the state. It is a convergence that is absent in the case of NPM.[7]

Japan

A career in the upper civil service has traditionally been regarded as highly prestigious in Japan. Only the best and brightest, often top graduates of the Law Faculty of the University of Tokyo, would become elite-track state officials, it was thought. In addition to social prestige, elite bureaucrats also possessed real power, even from a relatively young age. Furthermore, although pecuniary compensation did not compare favorably with private-sector pay, especially at junior levels, it was understood that elite bureaucrats would amply be compensated for their loyal service with cushy, well-paid jobs outside the state upon their retirement.[8]

[7] See Christopher Hood, "Contemporary Public Management: A New Global Paradigm," *Public Policy and Administration* 10, no. 2 (1995), 104–17; Jan-Erik Lane, ed., *Public Sector Reform: Rationale, Trends and Problems* (London: Sage, 1996); Jon Pierre, ed., *Bureaucracy in the Modern State* (Cheltenham, U.K.: Edward Elgar, 1995); and Tony Verheijen and David Coombes, eds., *Innovations in Public Management: Perspectives from East and West Europe* (Cheltenham, U.K.: Edward Elgar, 1998).

[8] It has to be noted that the Japanese elite bureaucracy rigorously practices early retirement. As elite-track officials compete to climb up the administrative pyramid, the losers get sidelined into outside jobs one by one. Moreover, once a colleague of the same or later "class" (entry year) reaches the apex, all the others take early retirement so that the sole winner becomes the most senior official in the entire ministry. This informal rule means that many elite officials start to leave the civil service in their late forties, and virtually all would retire by their late fifties.

Competition for a Career in the Elite Bureaucracy

Figure 8.1 presents the data on the competitiveness of the elite-track bureaucracy exam every five years since 1975.[9] Not surprisingly, the exam was the least competitive in 1990, at the peak of the bubble economy. The number of applicants sees a marked increase in 1995, but it is only in 2000 that the exam becomes once again as competitive as it was in 1975. Moreover, it never attains the same level of competitiveness as in 1980, despite the prolonged recession of the 1990s in Japan.

A yearly breakdown for the period between 1995 and 2000 shows that the number of applicants stagnated, if not declined, during the latter half of the 1990s (figure 8.2).[10] The level of competitiveness was maintained only by cuts in the number of successful candidates. There was some real concern in the ministries, especially from 1996 to 1998, as the number of applicants declined rather sharply in spite of the simultaneous rise in the unemployment rate. It was also during this period that public perception of the elite bureaucracy quickly deteriorated to reach a historic low, due to a series of bureaucratic scandals as well as to economic mismanagement.

The broad picture is much the same when we take a look at the data on the elite-track diplomatic exam between 1976 and 2000 (figure 8.3).[11] If anything, the bureaucracy's renewed difficulties, in drawing many applicants and maintaining the high level of competition in recent years, are even more clearly visible in the case of the foreign ministry (figure 8.4).[12]

Changing demographics, namely, the decline of the university graduate population, are also presenting serious challenges to the efforts of the state

[9] The data were drawn from Jinji-in (National Personnel Authority), *Komuin Hakusho* (White Paper on Public Servants), 2000, 374, except for 2000, which was obtained through the NPA Web site (http://www.jinji.admix.go.jp). This exam, *Kokka Komuin Isshu* (National Public Service 1st-Category), recruits most of the elite-track officials for all ministries, except for the Ministry of Foreign Affairs. (The Ministry of Justice is also somewhat of an exception in that many of its officials are prosecutors recruited through the bar exam.) The figures include all subcategories, namely, both first-category administrators (mostly of law background) and first-category technicians (trained in sciences or engineering). It should also be noted that only about half of those who passed the exam actually became bureaucrats. Candidates have to go through interviews in each ministry before they can really join the civil service.

[10] Ibid., 102 and 114. In contrast to figure 8.1, this gives the number of people who were actually hired after the interviews by the ministries.

[11] The elite-track diplomatic exam recruits the first-category officials for the foreign ministry. Unlike the elite-track exam for the home civil service, success in the diplomatic exam automatically means that the candidates are hired by the foreign ministry, and therefore there is no distinction between those who merely passed and those who were actually hired. The elite-track diplomatic exam used to have an academic qualification restriction until 1975; that is why, for the purposes of comparison, we have used the 1976 figure for this data set.

[12] The data are drawn from the Web site of the foreign ministry (http://www.mofa.go.jp).

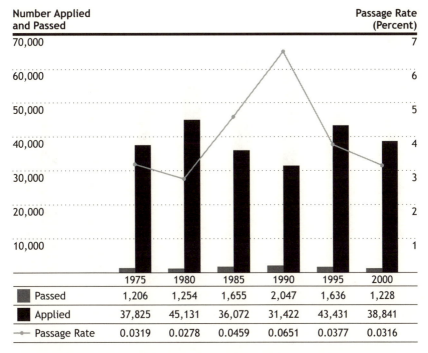

Number Applied and Passed	1975	1980	1985	1990	1995	2000	Passage Rate (Percent)
Passed	1,206	1,254	1,655	2,047	1,636	1,228	
Applied	37,825	45,131	36,072	31,422	43,431	38,841	
Passage Rate	0.0319	0.0278	0.0459	0.0651	0.0377	0.0316	

Figure 8.1. Elite-track bureaucracy exam, 1975–2000. Source: *Jinji-in* (National Personnel Authority), *Komuin Hakusho* (White Paper on Public Servants), 2000.

to recruit from the largest possible pool of candidates. It has to be pointed out, however, that what really preoccupies the ministries is the prospect that they might no longer be "entitled" to the supposedly best and brightest from the graduates of the Law Faculty of Tokyo University. This is because even among the elite-track recruits, the true crème de la crème, who are to monopolize the top positions of the ministries, are the first-category administrators, not the technicians. The Ministry of Finance, MITI, and other ministries, just like the foreign ministry, hire only about twenty new graduates as elite-track administrators per year, and they fiercely compete against each other for students that they have earmarked in advance through old-boy networks. The tarnished public image of elite bureaucrats in recent years, combined with the lure of often incomparably higher pay scales and potentially exciting careers in foreign multinational companies (which have strengthened their presence to replace weaker and stodgier Japanese firms of late) has been a source of concern to Japanese governments in recent years.

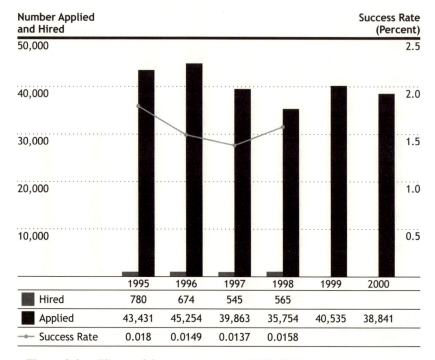

Figure 8.2.   Elite-track bureaucracy exam, 1995–2000, breakdown. Source: *Jinji-in* (National Personnel Authority), *Komuin Hakusho* (White Paper on Public Servants), 2000.

Mid-Career Departure

Early departure from the bureaucracy has long been common in Japan in the form of the so-called descent from heaven *(amakudari)*.[13] This phenomenon, in comparison with the *pantouflage* in France or the "revolving door" in the U.S., has the following characteristics: (1) reemployment positions are obtained and managed quasi-officially by each ministry; (2) retired officials generally gain reemployment in the sectors under their former employers' jurisdictions; (3) the moves refer to one-way, early

[13] For various accounts of *amakudari*, see Chalmers Johnson, "The Reemployment of Retired Government Bureaucrats in Japanese Big Business," in Johnson, *Japan: Who Governs? The Rise of the Developmental State* (New York: W. W. Norton, 1995); Kent E. Calder, "Elites in an Equalizing Role: Ex-bureaucrats as Coordinators and Intermediaries in the Japanese Government-Business Relationship," *Comparative Politics* 21, no. 4 (1989); Ulrike Schaede, "The 'Old Boy' Network and Government-Business Relationships in Japan," *Journal of Japanese Studies* 21, no. 2 (1995); and Koichi Nakano, "Becoming a 'Policy' Ministry: The Organization and *Amakudari* of the Ministry of Posts and Telecommunications," *Journal of Japanese Studies* 24, no. 1 (1998).

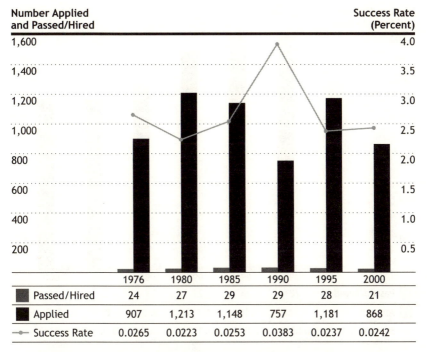

| Number Applied and Passed/Hired | | | | | | | Success Rate (Percent) |

	1976	1980	1985	1990	1995	2000
Passed/Hired	24	27	29	29	28	21
Applied	907	1,213	1,148	757	1,181	868
Success Rate	0.0265	0.0223	0.0253	0.0383	0.0237	0.0242

Figure 8.3. Elite-track diplomatic exam, 1976–2000. Source: *Jinji-in* (National Personnel Authority), *Komuin Hakusho* (White Paper on Public Servants), various years.

retirement of senior elite-track officials at the end of their career in their respective ministries. *Amakudari* is authorized and orchestrated by the ministries—in that sense, these are not really cases of mid-career departure from the bureaucracy, but, rather, more like "end-of-career departure."

Figure 8.5 better captures spontaneous mid-career departures from the bureaucracy as the data focuses on officials under the age of forty-five.[14] Again, not surprisingly, the mid-career departure rate reaches its peak at the height of the bubble economy in 1991. Although the rate goes down after the burst of the economic bubble, it then maintains a level that is slightly but consistently higher than in the mid-1980s, despite the prolonged economic recession and rising unemployment rate in Japan. The overall trend is much the same when we further limit our data to the male

---

[14] The officials included in this count are national public servants, who are categorized as *gyoseishoku I* (administrators I) in the pay system—these include not only the elite-track bureaucrats but also the clerical and secretarial personnel in ministry offices. The percentage given is calculated as the ratio of officials under forty-five who quit in a given year to the number of officials under forty-five employed in the previous year.

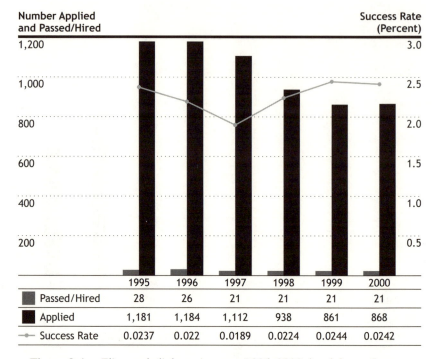

	1995	1996	1997	1998	1999	2000
Passed/Hired	28	26	21	21	21	21
Applied	1,181	1,184	1,112	938	861	868
Success Rate	0.0237	0.022	0.0189	0.0224	0.0244	0.0242

Figure 8.4. Elite-track diplomatic exam, 1995–2000, breakdown. Source: Ministry of Foreign Affairs.

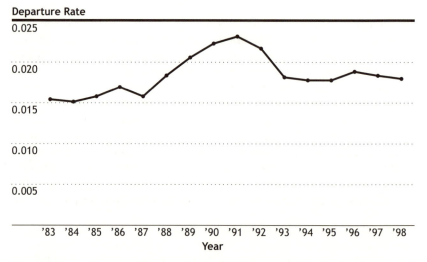

Figure 8.5. Mid-career departure (under 45). Source: *Jinji-in* (National Personnel Authority), *Komuin Hakusho* (White Paper on Public Servants), various years.

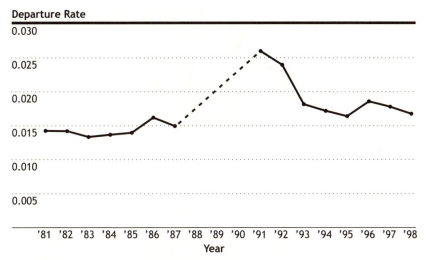

Figure 8.6.   Mid-career departure (male under 30). Source: *Jinji-in* (National Personnel Authority), *Komuin Hakusho* (White Paper on Public Servants), various years.

officials under the age of thirty (figure 8.6). The National Personnel Authority record does not provide data for this gender and age breakdown between 1988 and 1990, and one can only speculate that this may be because the departure rate got worryingly higher in these years. Indeed, in 1991 over 2.6 percent of male administrators under thirty prematurely left the civil service, nearly double that of 1983. With this gender/age group, too, in spite of the immediate decline after the collapse of the Japanese economy, the departure rate in the 1990s remained consistently higher than in the early to mid-1980s. To be sure, the rate is still not very high, but it is rather significant when one takes into account the sharply contrasting economic climates in the 1980s and 1990s: more bureaucrats are leaving the civil service today even though, generally speaking, it should be considerably harder to find a private-sector job.

Unfortunately, there are no data that are specific to mid-career departure of elite bureaucrats. Anecdotal evidence does suggest, however, that elite bureaucrats are at least as likely (if not more so) as those of lower categories to leave the bureaucracy.[15] There is a widely shared sense among young bureaucrats that it is often the more competent colleagues who jump off the boat prematurely to land on attractive private-sector jobs.

---

[15] See for instance, *Tokyo Shinbun*, November 20, 2000; and *Nihon Keizai Shinbun (Nikkei)*, November 30, 2000.

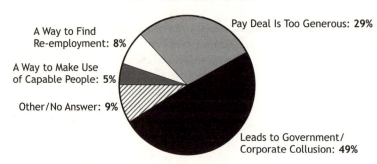

Figure 8.7. What do you think of *amakudari*? Source: *Asahi Shinbun*, May 15, 1994.

Amakudari

If a career in the higher civil service is losing its erstwhile appeal to both university graduates and junior officials, the increasingly bleak *amakudari* prospect is likely to play a part. As we have seen above, *amakudari* refers to postretirement jobs outside the state that ministries arrange for their elite-track bureaucrats, especially for the first-category administrators. Since civil service pay compares poorly with that in the private sector, especially at junior levels, the hefty pay package that *amakudari* commonly implied used to be considered almost an integral part of a career in the higher civil service, in which elite officials finally receive deferred financial rewards. In the past, when higher education was still a rare commodity, it was also a way to "recycle" capable former bureaucrats.

The Japanese do not look at *amakudari* so favorably today, as figures 8.7 and 8.8 show. Although *amakudari* has by no means disappeared,[16] it has certainly come to receive much more public scrutiny and criticism since it came to be known that *amakudari* was a background factor in many failures of government oversight in the 1990s.[17] There is now an army of prominent former top officials who have not been able to obtain lucrative second employment because of the hostile public mood.[18] There has been continuous debate over the introduction of stricter rules to restrict or ban *amakudari*, and a self-imposed moratorium has already been put in place in some ministries.

It used to make sense for ambitious young men to persevere the long hours and poor pay in the bureaucracy in the past, knowing that the ministry was going to look after and take good care of them when they retire. There is more temptation today to try one's luck in the corporate sec-

---

[16] Indeed, in some sectors (for instance, telecommunications) it is being expanded. See Nakano, "Becoming a 'Policy' Ministry."

[17] The HIV-contaminated blood scandal and the collapse of the banking sector, to name the most obvious.

[18] Top-ranking officials from the finance ministry, who used to have a range of positions reserved for them, have been notably frustrated. Many of them scrape by as university professors.

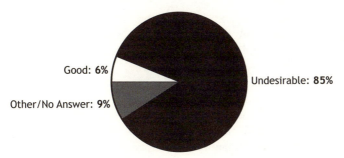

Figure 8.8.   Do you think *amakudari* is good or undesirable? Source: *Asahi Shinbun*, December 12, 1996.

tor by quitting the bureaucracy before it becomes too late or even not joining the civil service in the first place.

United States

The American federal bureaucracy has never had the prestige of the British, French, or Japanese bureaucracies. It made little effort to train or to recruit the most highly talented people. As a consequence, the desertion of the public service in recent years has not been a cause for alarm, nor has it led to a public debate or inspired politicians to come to the rescue of this institution.

Nonetheless, the trend has progressed so far that the National Commission on Public Service, which came to be known as the Volker Commission, sought to shake the country's complacency by referring to the state of recruitment in the federal bureaucracy as being in a state of "crisis," or, rather, what it called a "quiet crisis." The commission expressed concern that public service in the United States is "neither as attractive as it once was nor as effective in perceived needs."[19]

The reasons for this are, as we noted, multiple, but the fact itself is beyond dispute. A recent study by Paul Light on how the public career is changing confirms the Volker Commission's findings. While one might wish to debate some of Light's recommendations, his analysis of the decline in the attractiveness of the public service career is indisputable. He observes: "By the end of the 1980s, the gap between federal and private pay had widened, attacks on government by the media and political candidates were at an all-time high, the Office of Personnel Management had been weakened by a director who believed that mediocre was good

[19] National Commission on Public Service, *Leadership for America: Rebuilding the Public Service*, Report of the National Commission on Public Service (Washington, D.C., 1989), 59. The Volker Commission's conclusion has been challenged on the ground that it is not based on any meaningful data. See Aberbach and Rockman, *In the Web of Politics*.

enough for government, and the public had lost confidence in its elected and appointed leaders. At the same time, America's most talented citizens had lost interest in public service of any kind, and morale within the civil service was at a modern low."[20]

The sorry state of public service in the United States derives partly from the fact that we live in an age in which the younger generation seeks risk, innovation, money. Public service represents the antithesis of all this. The decline results also from the downgrading of the work that civil servants do. As the federal government now outsources most work, as the process of decentralization seems never to run out of steam, as the political stranglehold on the bureaucracy gets ever tighter, and, of course, as the salary disparity between the public and private sectors grows wider, public service is more and more bereft of competence. As Light puts it, "Simply stated, the government talent pool is draining out with less and less in the pipeline to replace it."[21] He suggests, in desperation, that "the first step is to declare a human capital crisis in government."[22]

All analysts of the American federal bureaucracy agree that the generally low prestige of the civil service has been aggravated in recent years by incessant attacks on this institution that have resulted in its downgrading in relation to other institutions. It should be noted here, though it will be emphasized in due course, that the undermining of the federal bureaucracy has gone far beyond the objective of rendering this institution less wasteful and more productive. The objective has been more political: to reduce the role of the bureaucracy in society. Program cutbacks insured this. As Levine observed: "Since 1981, budgetary cutbacks, program termination, and a general decline in program activism have combined to reduce the sense of achievement that prevailed during the 1960's. Few people who have contributed to the creation, development, and growth of a program can be expected to approach its retrenchment with equal enthusiasm. Nor is it reasonable to suppose that adapting organizations and programs to cope with conditions of austerity will strike many potential federal employees as a rewarding challenge."[23]

The nature and significance of the work of the federal government has thus been significantly transformed. The crisis that the Volker Commission and others have pointed to is only marginally tied to the disparity in pay scales between the public and private sectors. If the scope of the federal government has been markedly reduced, and if, as we shall see, politicization

---

[20] Paul C. Light, *The New Public Service* (Washington, D.C.: Brookings Institution, 1999), 3. See particularly chapter 3, "A Profile of the Profession," 42–102.

[21] Light, *The New Public Service*, 137.

[22] Ibid.

[23] Charles R. Levine, "The Federal Government in the Year 2000: Administrative Legacies of the Reagan Years," in *Agenda for Excellence: Public Service in America*, ed. Patricia Ingraham and Donald F. Kettl (Chatham, N.J.: Chatham House, 1992), 173.

has further discouraged potential recruits, then it follows that the crisis will be a permanent one. Indeed, it will no longer be seen as a crisis but, rather, will come to be considered the new state of affairs.

France

The public service career was for many years, during the nineteenth century and for most of the twentieth century, the most prestigious of careers in France. This was understandable, given the privileges enjoyed by those who reached the top, the opportunities for moving into other sectors (politics or business), and the possibility of cumulating several appointments simultaneously. In addition to all this, for those who remained in the bureaucracy the chances of attaining a top position became more distant as the graduates of the Ecole Nationale d'Administration came to create a monopoly on many of the top jobs in their ministries.

The past two decades have witnessed a precipitous decline in the attractiveness of the higher civil services as a career. In part this is due to the decreasing role of the *dirigiste* state. Privatization has not only reduced the state's role, but it has also left it with far fewer public sector positions to offer those who had exhausted their career possibilities within the administration proper. As the banks and the state industries were transformed to the private sector, the career possibilities, once there for the asking, soon disappeared. The European Union has also taken its toll. As powers were transferred from the national to the transnational level, the top civil servants could no longer aspire to lead in the same way they once did. Third, pay disparities between the private and pubic sectors have grown so wide that it is difficult now for most senior civil servants to resist the departure toward greener pastures. The consequence of these factors, and the fact that a career at the top of the civil service no longer assures a career beginning at the top in the private sector, has meant that civil servants who wish to leave the public sector must do so at an earlier and earlier age.

All this becomes quite clear when one examines the figures concerning those who would be preparing to become the next generation of higher civil servants. The number of those preparing for the entry examination into ENA has fallen from 1,374 candidates in 1995 to 995 candidates in 1999, a drop of 30 percent. At the Institut d'Etudes Politiques of Paris, those who prepare for the ENA exam have largely deserted this career path. In 1990 there were still 1,000 students clamoring to enter this preparatory class. In 1999 the number had dropped to 200. Moreover, the IEP's mission has itself changed over the past decade since in 1989 two-thirds of its students sought to gain their diploma in the "public service" section, whereas today that proportion has dropped to one-third.[24]

---

[24] *Le Monde*, November 3, 2000.

It is not only among the new generation of potential recruits that the civil service has become a less attractive career. Whereas for the postwar generation the civil service had gradually become a stepping stone to careers in the private sector, the current generation no longer seeks to make use of public service even as a stepping stone. A study by Bauer and Danic of one of the elite corps (the *Inspection des Finances*) shows that the rate of departure from this corps toward the private sector grew considerably during the 1980s.[25] Moreover, the acceleration of the departure rate accompanies the younger age at which these civil servants leave public service for the private sector. This accelerated departure rate coincided with the privatization of state enterprises.

That this phenomenon is relatively recent is shown by the fact that the departure from public service for the private sector was rare. In the decade following World War II only nineteen *inspecteurs des finances* left state service to join private firms.[26] In the wake of the privatization of state firms during the 1980s, the privatized firms merely replaced the state firms for the *inspecteurs des finances*.[27]

The change from the 1980s to today is seen by the fact that state service is no longer seen as attractive in and of itself and, more dramatically, is not viewed as even a necessary passageway to the private sector or to a political career. Both these factors mirror the trend that we observed in the Japanese case.

The reason for this desertion of the public service is similar to that shown in Light's survey of the public sector in the U.S. The disparity in salaries is certainly a factor. But the important factor remains the state's inability to provide sufficient room for action, innovation, and continuity. No sooner has work on a project reached completion than the civil servant comes face to face with an inevitable reality: the government changes and the project is dropped. This occurs in the best of cases. For the most part, the exciting projects and the room for innovation and risk all seem to fall in the private sector.

The growing politicization, the need to show overt partisanship to one party or another, has also discouraged civil servants from remaining in the administration. Since one can no longer succeed in a career without being almost overtly political, many civil servants leave the bureaucracy, and they do so early on in their careers so that they augment their chances of succeeding in their new careers. The available evidence indicates both that more civil servants of both the technical and nontechnical corps have departed from the bureaucracy over the past decade and that the age of those leaving tends to

---

[25] Michel Bauer and Dominique Danic, *L'Inspection des Finances: 16 Ans de Pantouflage, 1974–1989* (Paris: CNRS/Heidrick and Struggles, 1990).

[26] See Michel Bauer and Bénédicte Bertin-Mourot, *Les Enarques en Entreprise de 1960 à 1990: 30 Ans de Pantouflage* (Paris: Boyden Global Executive Search, March 1994).

[27] Bauer and Danic, *L'Inspection des Finances,* 25.

be younger. Fewer people compete to enter the higher civil service, and there are more departures as well as earlier departures. This is now a clear pattern.

Distrust of Public Servants

No sector can long sustain its standing or itself when it is faced with early departures from its ranks, when the talented pool of potential recruits shrinks, and when the standard of those that remain to be recruited declines. How can this trend be reversed?

Perhaps a preliminary question ought to be: Does anybody care? Do governments want to reverse the trend? The answers to these questions are not at all evident. Even if there has not been a systematic policy to render the public service career unattractive to the bright and talented, policies and practices have been put into place that have affected the recruitment of public services: low pay, the declining importance of the work, and, finally, the infringement, through politicization, of the principle of merit.

Public sector salaries can probably never keep pace with those of the private sector. But they have fallen substantially behind in recent years. This is the case in all democratic societies. But beyond this obvious and glaring disparity, there remains the fact that public service no longer carries with it such advantages as prestige and security of employment. The tendency everywhere has been to go beyond the public service for talent, for loyalty, and for the work itself (outsourcing or agencification).

Not only have governments not sought to reverse these trends, they have felt hamstrung by their own rhetoric. Why seek to recruit talented people when the order of the day is to downgrade the work and the institution? Why propose pay raises for public officials when the political rhetoric points to redundancy? Why encourage talented people to undertake public service as a career when the general belief is that risk and entrepreneurship should be the goals of all talented youth?

A leading scholar of public service has argued that governments are mistaken if they think that closing the pay differentials between the public and private sectors will make public service more attractive to those trying to decide whether to seek a career in the public service. Government cannot become more competitive, he argues, by offering more money. Government has to provide interesting work: "Pay is no doubt important as students consider first jobs, but it is far less important than the nature of the job itself. Young Americans are not saying 'Show me the money' so much as 'Show me the work.' And it is on that count that government is losing ground."[28]

Regardless of whether one agrees with the view that attributes such nobility to America's youth of today, the question remains: How can gov-

---

[28] Light, *The New Public Service*, 3.

ernment provide exciting work? Light argues that "government has an obligation to provide challenging work and the opportunity for growth, as do private firms and nonprofit agencies."[29]

It is not only by their rhetoric but also by their actions that governments have practically insured that they will have less and less interesting work to do and therefore to offer their civil servants. The attacks on bureaucratic inertia, incompetence, and waste have led to a demoralization of the institution. Indeed, the gradual dismantling of the bureaucratic apparatus has meant that the challenging work that governments did in the past is gradually being passed on to other nonpublic institutions.

The reforms that governments have undertaken, particularly privatization, outsourcing, and decentralization, have considerably reduced the scope of the public sphere. Many of these reforms were long overdue in some countries. But many of the projected reforms associated with NPM and the inexorable drive toward politicization have practically insured that governments will no longer hand over the interesting and challenging work to their public servants.

Governments have manifested a growing distrust of public servants. They have sought either to phase them out by placing them in positions lower on the hierarchical scale or to have them replaced by politically loyal officials. This has been done sometimes with considerable determination and sometimes more discreetly.

Civil servants everywhere perceive the decline in importance of their work and the decline in their influence. Aberbach and Rockman were able to conclude rather categorically: "One thing we can say for sure is that there is a remarkable fall-off in the perceived influence of senior civil servants, especially as seen by the senior civil servants themselves."[30]

All the available data on other countries suggests a similar pattern. This is not merely a question of perception. Power is today more diffused, so important decisions are no longer merely in the hands of national governments. International organizations and agreements all serve to limit the power of national governments. All these factors have constrained the power of national governments and, by extension, the power of their civil servants.

But these objective factors affect all advanced industrial societies. In and of themselves they would not necessarily lead to a desertion or scorn of the public sector. What serves to make the work "unexciting" and unattractive are the incessant attacks on the bureaucracy and its increasing politicization.

Everywhere the results are pointing in the same direction: greater control of the administrative machinery by the political parties; greater distrust of the more neutral, or politically unaffiliated, public officials; less scope for interesting and innovative work; and, in the end, a less competent bureaucracy.

[29] Ibid., 138.
[30] Aberbach and Rockman, *In the Web of Politics*, 117.

CHAPTER NINE

DEPROFESSIONALIZATION:
THE PROCESS OF POLITICIZATION

*"All party struggles are struggles for the patronage of office,
as well as struggles for objective goals."*
—Max Weber

THERE HAS LONG BEEN a debate on the extent to which bureaucracies should be instruments of the government of the day and the extent to which they ought to be staffed by professionals who are granted, or who may usurp, a certain degree of autonomy. This debate has attracted the likes of Weber, Schumpeter, Woodrow Wilson, and many other contemporary distinguished scholars and analysts. While debate may rage on among students of public organizations, it has for all intents and purposes been resolved in the world of practical politics. This resolution is of stunning importance.

Important as this development has been in today's democracies, it has been based on no blueprint; it has not been spearheaded by a proselytizing nation eager to export its practices; and it has not been a response to an intellectual fad or dogma. Unlike NPM, it has no doctrinal underpinning, and it was not ushered in by any reform.

The need to exercise government (or party) control over the bureaucracy has appeared simultaneously in many democracies. It will have a greater impact on shaping the bureaucracy, the executive branch, and the role of bureaucracy in society than will NPM. And taken together, NPM and politicization, each in its own way, have already contributed heavily to undermining the value of a professional bureaucratic apparatus.

Whereas the process of politicization could previously find no intellectual justification, since the strongest arguments were on the side of a professional, nonpolitical bureaucracy, today that is no longer the case. Political control of the bureaucracy has elicited ex post facto rationalizations. The politics-administration dichotomy, which in the past elicited innumerable analyses and debates, has now run its course. It was an issue that required debating so long as the principle of the dichotomy was generally believed to be positive for democracy.

Reassertion of Politics

It may appear paradoxical to claim that politics has reasserted itself after attempting to make it clear that the state, in the United States in particular but in other countries as well, has been systematically downgraded and its sovereignty undermined. If political choices assume a less important role, then it follows that the bureaucratic instrument's utility needs to be diminished. This may follow logically, but it is more apparent than real.

In reality, politics has assumed an ever-greater control over expertise and yet has systematically sought to diminish not only the autonomy but also the area of authority of the bureaucratic instrument.

The state is merely a multitude of organizations that can be considered as the instruments of the legitimately elected political will. Elections are still won by political parties on the basis of ostensible programs or manifestos. The bureaucratic instrument is ostensibly there to serve its political masters. No one doubts that the bureaucracies in all liberal democracies are being essentially guided by political authorities with mandates to deregulate, to privatize, and to reduce the weight of the state in the economy and in society. Over the past two decades few analysts have ventured to provide a picture in any national context of the usurpation of power by bureaucrats. Nor has a case been made for successful bureaucratic resistance to the clearly articulated objectives of governments to reduce the weight of the state in the economy and society of the advanced industrial nations.

Why does this need noting in view of the fact that bureaucratic subordination constitutes the essence of democratic governance and of the Weberian ideal-type dichotomy? The importance of the new form of bureaucratic subordination is that, while eradicating the fear of the reign of technocrats and experts, it does this not by assuring a professional, more or less impartial bureaucracy but by completely subjecting the bureaucracy to the will of the political majority of the moment. While the Weberian model of bureaucratic organization has therefore, at best, been modified or tinkered with in particular contexts, it has been vastly transformed where the relationship between politics and bureaucracy is concerned. Political dominance has been achieved not in spite of preserving thoroughly professional bureaucracies but rather through deprofessionalizing the bureaucratic instrument.

The politics-administration dichotomy is based on a division of labor that assumes the bureaucracy's loyalty to the government of the day as well as to the even-handed, professional implementation of policies. Bureaucratic subjugation to a political program or philosophy requires alternation in the bureaucracy to match alternation in governments.

For much of the postwar era, it was generally believed that politicians were no longer in control of public policies. They could neither obtain information nor evaluate the information they were able to obtain. Hence, public policies were essentially formulated and certainly implemented by experts. Some saw this as the greatest threat to democracy. Others regarded it as the dawn of an era when decisions would be made on a more rational basis.

Many years ago, Seymour Martin Lipset observed that the great struggle of the future would not be between capitalism and communism but between democracy and bureaucracy.[1] This concern was widely shared and analyzed. James Burnham's *The Managerial Revolution*[2] or Djilas's *The New Class*,[3] or J. K. Galbraith's concept of a ruling "technostructure"[4] all pointed to the growing importance of technocrats who had effectively usurped political power from legitimately elected politicians. Daniel Bell's *The Coming of the Post-Industrial Society* recognized the importance of technocrats, but viewed this as a positive development since decisions would henceforth be made on rational (that is, nonpolitical) bases.[5]

Rarely has a threat to democracy that caused so much alarm been found to have been as much of a chimera as this one. To the extent that a threat exists, it comes not so much from unaccountable, rational, apolitical technocrats operating in democratic states as from a bureaucracy that more and more finds itself controlled now by one governing party, now by another. All democratic governments seek to politicize the bureaucracy so as to maximize the use that can be made of this instrument. To be sure, this is usually carried out under the rationale of efficient management. What is scarcely ever made clear are the goals that this efficiency is expected to serve. As David Rosenbloom has observed, "In their zeal to promote visions of the public interest, American administrative reformers sometimes seek to remake the political system to serve the needs of better management rather than to develop better management to serve the purposes of the political system."[6]

How is the political system to be defined? Who defines what is best for it? Without getting bogged down in such debates, and without retracing the politics-administration dichotomy, it is possible to adopt a minimalist argument regarding the bureaucratic professionalism-democracy dichotomy. It will not do to argue that the Weberian model is incapable of approximating reality, because civil servants have both policy and administrative

---

[1] Seymour Martin Lipset, *Political Man* (New York: Doubleday, 1961).

[2] James Burnham, *The Managerial Revolution: or What Is Happening in the World Now* (Harmondsworth: Penguin, 1945).

[3] Milovan Djilas, *The New Class: An Analysis of the Communist System* (New York: Praeger, 1957).

[4] John Kenneth Galbraith, *American Capitalism: The Concept of Countervailing Power* (Oxford: Blackwell, 1980).

[5] Daniel Bell, *The Coming of Post-Industrial Society: A Venture in Social Forecasting* (New York: Basic Books, 1973).

[6] David Rosenbloom, "Editorial: Have an Administrative Rx? Don't Forget the Politics!" *Public Administration Review* 3, no. 6 (November–December 1993): 506.

roles, as Weber himself recognized. The Weberian argument was based on the *need* for professional civil servants, because such professionalism, even if it could not always live up to the high standards of neutrality, is a sustaining force of democratic government.

NPM and Politicization

The New Public Management seeks to do more than introduce efficient principles of management through the private sector. Rather, it aims to transform the nature of the relationship between the citizen and his state. The reform of the state or of its administration has undergone a transformation over the past three decades. Such reforms no longer merely concern specific policies for this or that sector. They now concern the entire administrative structure.

Bureaucratic reform aims today not merely to reform the bureaucracy but, according to the NPM, to undo the tie that has long bound a citizen to his state. The emphasis, and consequences, of the NPM philosophy is the undoing of the social contract that creates mutual obligations between state and citizen. The state's obligations to its "citizens," as they were once called in the U.S., or to its "*administrés*," as they were commonly and paternalistically called in France, have been redefined.

The citizen today has been raised or lowered in status, depending on one's point of view, by becoming a customer. She is the purchaser of services that the state sells. This requires administrative reform to center on the provision of services at "market" price: "Thanks to the free market philosophy, administrative reforms have changed from being policies involving the public sector internally to interventions aimed at improving the efficiency and effectiveness of services for citizens and, as such, policies external to the machinery of the state."[7]

But for NPM to gain the widespread support it sought and has received, it needed to be seen as (1) not politicizing the bureaucracy and (2) being politically neutral. Efficiency was its only goal and the entrepreneurial model merely the means to achieving this goal.

Can it be said that NPM, when implemented, does not affect in any way the politics-administration dichotomy? Put another way, do the practices of the NPM leave unaffected the complex relationship between political executives and civil servants? Or, alternatively, has NPM, which may not have been responsible for initiating the long process of gradual politicization, nonetheless helped speed it along the way?

[7] Sabino Cassese, "The Age of Administrative Reforms," in *Governing Europe*, ed. Jack Hayward and Anand Menon (Oxford: Oxford University Press, 2002), 117.

In order to answer these questions, it helps to keep in mind the *means* that underlie NPM. These involve competition within the public sector, competition with the private sector, and, finally, the contracting of public services to the private sector. This may not seem at first glance to be linked to the politics-administration relationship. Yet it cannot be so easily separated.

The next question that we have to ask relates to the goals of a government. What relationship does a government seek to have with its bureaucracy? As numerous studies have shown, governments seek commitment, loyalty, and support for their policies from the bureaucracy. This is entirely in keeping with the rules and requirements established at the outset for this institution.

How, then, has the creation of a new "spirit" of public service, or "modernization" of the state, or NPM (those are various labels that opening public bureaucracies to the winds of change have gone by in different countries) affected the process of politicization? There is no direct link between NPM and politicization. But, as we shall see, NPM has been a stimulus to a process that had already been under way.

I shall examine the process of politicization in a number of democracies. This is a process that is not always easy to define, but when it occurs it is difficult to miss. In some countries, it involves civil servants injecting themselves into the political arena. In others, it involves increasing the number of appointments from outside the civil service. In still others, it involves massive turnover in administrative personnel with changes in party government. Bureaucratic politicization has even found a new rationale, which has led to a redefinition of the concept of responsiveness.

Politicization: A Rationalist Perspective

Democratic governments are expected to be accountable to the electorate for their actions. The bureaucracy is expected to be accountable and responsive to the government and to the citizens. The second postulate leaves some room for debate since it is not clear to whom the bureaucracy is obliged to be more responsive.

It used to be accepted as an article of faith that a neutral bureaucracy served the general interest, or democracy, more effectively than a politicized bureaucracy. Politicians generally claimed that a neutral bureaucracy was important to the democratic order. And they were quick to criticize anything that appeared to involve political interference in the bureaucracy.

Times have changed. Once the process of politicization was clearly visible and seen as resulting from actions taken by politicians, it was not long before justifications were forthcoming. As always, the justifications came *after* the phenomenon could not be ignored. It was not suggested or hinted that politicization was a positive development *before* it developed. In all such cases, the justifications have arisen to support a need that has arisen and to which a solution has been developed. Hence, choices are seen as rational and those who make them are seen as maximizing their interests.

Consequently, the attempt to gain control of the bureaucracy by an elected government is no longer viewed as objectionable. In fact, it is now commonly argued that executive leaders, needing to consider their own reelection, their prestige, and their performance, feel a need to gain control of the instruments of governance. Writing of the American presidency, Moe notes that "the modern president is driven by these formidable expectations to seek control over the structures and processes of government. . . . What he wants is an institutional system responsive to his needs as political leader."[8] For Moe, the executive's "needs," as they are defined by the executive, suffice to justify the solution found. It matters little whether the executive in question was a particularly ideological one with a clearly articulated (or extreme) program, or whether this is a structural need that requires addressing and debating. It also matters little what the effects of fulfilling the need are on other institutions or on democratic norms.

An executive's desire for "an institutional system responsive to his needs as political leader" cannot simply leave a leader in a democratic society free to devise his own solution. After all, executive leaders have all kinds of needs, such as being less constrained, seeking more complete control of the bureaucracy, using arms of the bureaucracy (the judicial system, or the F.B.I.) to achieve specific ends. Self-defined needs and self-defined solutions always appear rational. This is quasi-tautological. It may address an executive's immediate need. It does not for all that make it "rational" or useful, or positive in a larger sense that takes account of the political system as a whole.

What is true of the American president is also true of other political leaders, if to a lesser extent. We will see that Thatcher and Blair in Britain, González and Aznar in Spain, Jospin no less than his center-right predecessor Juppé, and Schröder and Kohl in Germany all sought appointees on whom they could rely to make the bureaucracy responsive to their governments. And these are political leaders in countries with strong civil service traditions.

The concept of bureaucratic neutrality has come upon hard times, and its point of glory had long passed before any idea of introducing

---

[8] Terry M. Moe, "The Politicized Presidency," in *The New Directions in American Politics*, ed. John Chabler and Paul Peterson (Washington, D.C.: Brookings Institution, 1985), 239.

entrepreneurial injections into the public sector had appeared. But "modernization" or "reinvention of government" and NPM have sounded its death knell. Some scholars, like Moe and Maranto, have maintained that neutrality is not to be valued for its own sake. In fact, from the vantage point of those in power, the need is for efficiency and responsiveness and not for neutrality. Maranto suggests that the advantages associated with neutrality represent something of a "fiction."[9]

It may be that neutrality assures competence, even if it does not guarantee efficiency, innovation, and a freedom to dispense expert advice honestly. It was always thought to assure competence. While Maranto might argue that "federal executives under spoils were innovative [and] they were among the first managers of large scale enterprises in American history,"[10] others have gone perhaps further in suggesting that neither competence nor neutrality need be valued for its own sake. Why is this the case?

The answer is that a chief executive is responding to a set of incentives and not to the values of scholars of public administration. Moe maintains that a president "values organizational competence, to be sure, but what he seeks is 'responsive competence,' not neutral competence."[11] This is because "in the real world, they [presidents] . . . embrace politicization and centralization because they have no attractive alternatives."[12] If scholars seek to have presidents respect the neutrality of bureaucratic agencies and make appointments that accord with the criterion of professionalism, it is because, argues Moe, they subscribe to outdated academic ideas of how presidents should behave, ideas that are "entirely inconsistent with the way presidents have viewed their own incentives, resources, and constraints."[13]

Since no one would argue against competence and professionalism, or for what Derlien and Szablowski called, in the case of East Germany, "politicized incompetence,"[14] the key term for legitimating politicization is "responsive competence." In fact, this is probably what occurs in most societies, even in countries like France, Spain, and Germany. The pool of politicized civil servants is sufficiently large that party turnover poses few problems for replacement of officials with precisely the same type of politicized ("responsive") competence. In most cases there is a minimum of

[9] Robert Maranto, "Thinking the Unthinkable in Public Administration: A Case for Spoils in the Federal Bureaucracy," *Administration and Society* 29, no. 6 (January 1998): 623.

[10] Ibid.

[11] Moe, "The Political Presidency," 239.

[12] Ibid., 246.

[13] Ibid., 266.

[14] Hans-Ulrich Derlien and George Szablowski, "Eastern European Transitions: Elites, Bureaucracies and the European Community," *Governance* 6 (July 1993): 310.

competence, so we cannot speak of incompetent patronage appointments. Nonetheless, as Ingraham notes, "For public organizations, being controlled does not mean being effective."[15]

A recent study of the top civil servants in departments or ministries argues that although their role has evolved and they are no longer considered sage authorities dispensing wise advice to their ministers, they have not in fact become more politicized.[16] But politicization is defined in this work as "party political appointments," an extreme definition that allows for the argument that civil services are more or less as unpoliticized as in the past.

The Rhodes and Weller study bases its conclusion about the absence of politicization on the assumption that since all appointments to top positions in the ministry are made from the public sector, and almost none from the party, we can safely conclude that all turnover in personnel at the top of the bureaucratic hierarchy has therefore remained nonpoliticized. "In all these countries, the overwhelming majority of appointments are made from within the public sector. At so senior a level, few come direct from the private sector. So there is political involvement, but that does not make the appointments partisan."[17]

For the political, Rhodes and Weller substitute the personal, arguing that "it is more productive to move beyond the idea of politicization to a different idea, that of personalization."[18] This becomes a question of the compatibility of temperaments: "Departmental secretaries are selected and kept in part because of their style and approach, in part because of their policy preferences, and in part because ministers are comfortable with them."[19] But surely this is not the real question. The real question is: How does a minister feel comfortable with the top officials in his or her ministry if they are known not to share the same political views?

Let us take, again, two very different cases: France and the United States. In the case of France, one in which Rhodes and Weller adhere to a long-standing image,[20] it is possible to argue that there has been no politicization since almost all appointments are from within the civil service. Yet it

---

[15] Patricia Ingraham, *The Foundation of Merit: Public Service in American Democracy* (Baltimore: Johns Hopkins University Press, 1995), 131.

[16] See R.A.W. Rhodes and Patrick Weller, eds., *The Changing World of Top Officials. Mandarins or Valets?* (Buckingham: Open University Press, 2001). These officials are known by different titles in different countries: permanent secretaries in Britain, chief executives in New Zealand, *directeurs d'administration centrale* in France (though this refers to several directors within in a ministry).

[17] Ibid., p. 238.

[18] Ibid.

[19] Ibid.

[20] The editors also describe France in a rather picturesque way at every turn, calling it at one point the "Zanzibar" of their group of countries.

would be impossible to sustain this argument. The higher civil service in France remains in the hands of civil servants, and both the Left and the Right choose their team from the same pool. Yet that pool is now wholly politicized. The turnover in ministerial cabinets when there is a party turnover is close to 100 percent. The turnover in directorships of the central administration can be well over 70 percent after a government has been in power for more than two years.[21] The case of France is significant, as we noted earlier, because of a highly developed civil service tradition that all parties respect but all abuse. The civil service itself therefore now operates under different guidelines, the most important of which is that to rise to the top of the administrative hierarchy it behooves one to have strong links to a political party. This is a reality that cannot be ignored and that cannot be confused with level of "comfort" or "temperaments" or "personalization."

The only aspect of the civil service that has remained untouched has been the recruitment process. Higher civil servants continue to be recruited through the Ecole Nationale d'Administration and the Ecole Polytechnique. Once they enter the civil service, the new rules of the game have to be adhered to if one is to get to the top of the bureaucratic ladder.

In the United States, the top of the bureaucratic pyramid is almost exclusively reserved for partisan appointments. This includes not only secretaries, under-secretaries, and assistant secretaries but numerous other appointments that fall under this category, including judges and ambassadors. It is estimated that the president has approximately three thousand political appointments to make when coming into office. Indeed, the placing of party loyalists is one of the most important functions of the cumbersome transition process.[22]

The politicization of the civil service, and of bureaucracies that once experienced only minimal political interference, such as the diplomatic corps, has now gained intellectual respectability in the United States. This has come about through the realization that politicians are capable of exerting control over the bureaucracy and thus controlling agency loss.[23]

---

[21] See Ezra Suleiman, ed., *Bureaucrats and Policy-Making: A Comparative Overview* (New York: Holmes & Meier, 1984); Luc Rouban, *Les Attitudes Politiques des Fonctionnaires: Vingt Ans d'Evolution* (Paris: CEVIPOF, 1999); Luc Rouban, *Les Préfets de la République 1870–1997* (Paris: CEVIPOF, 2000); Jean-Patrice Lacam, *La France: Une République de Mandarins? Les Hauts Fonctionnaries et la Politique* (Bruxelles: Editions Complexe, 2000); Andre Mathiot, *La Vie Politique aux Etats-Unis et les Tendances Recents* (Paris: Cours de Droit, 1974–75). See also chapter 10.

[22] See Charles O. Jones, *Passages to the Presidency: From Campaigning to Governing* (Washington, D.C.: Brookings Institution, 1998), 103–33.

[23] See M. McCubbins, R. Noll, and B. Weingart, "Administrative Procedures as Instruments of Political Control," *Journal of Law, Economics and Organization* 1, no. 2 (fall 1987); and the rejoinder by Murray J. Horn and Kenneth A. Shepsle, "Commentary on 'Administrative

Executives need respond only to incentives that increase their power. Indeed, some scholars have thought it unfortunate that for a long time the "competition" between neutral competence and political leadership seemed to be won by the former. And neither bureaucratic officials nor students of politics could bring themselves to comprehend "that politicization and centralization might actually be highly positive developments."[24] These are considered positive developments because they fit in with the *needs* of executive leadership. They accord with "rational" calculations of a political leader; hence they are desirable. Yet, rationality from one actor's perspectives does not logically confirm desirability.

Why, then, have not all political leaders responded in like manner? Not even all American presidents have responded in the same way or been driven to politicize the bureaucracy to the same degree as Nixon did, albeit not very successfully, or Reagan, who did it very successfully. Chief executives in other countries have also faced the temptations of centralization and politicization, but they did not succumb to the same extent. What the rationalist perspective fails to recognize is that the drive toward a "political" solution to what is considered a political, as opposed to a managerial, problem entails costs, which explains why few chief executives have pursued it with the determination of either Nixon or Reagan.

All-out politicization is usually defended on the grounds that it makes executives more effective. First, there is no distinction made between short-term effectiveness and long-term damage. Reagan may have succeeded very well in controlling the bureaucracy, and the literature of rational choice analysts overflows with hero-worship bordering on idolatry when it comes to Reagan's accomplishments in this domain. Yet, no calculation seems to have been made of the costs of Reagan's actions in terms of future effectiveness or of the adverse effects on the competence of the bureaucracy. I know of no analysis that convincingly demonstrates that the drive of one chief executive to politicize the bureaucracy has successfully improved the responsiveness and efficiency of this institution for his successors.

Second, there is also no evidence that politicization increases impartiality in implementation and regulation by the bureaucracy. Effectiveness or political leadership may remain confined to executive orders and successful

---

Arrangements and the Political Control of Agencies': Administrative Process and Organizational Forms as Legislative Responses to Agency Costs," *Virginia Law Review* 75 (1989): 499–508. See also Barry R. Weingast and Mark J. Moran, "Bureaucratic Discretion or Congressional Control? Regulatory Policymaking by the Federal Trade Commission," *Journal of Political Economy* 91, no. 5 (October 1983): 765–800; Mathew D. McCubbins, "The Legislative Design of Regulatory Structure," *American Journal of Political Science* 29, no. 4 (November 1985): 721–48.

[24] Moe, "The Politicized Presidency," 265.

negotiations with Congress, but those may not translate into effective enforcement.

Finally, the rationalist perspective fails to take into account the declining morale, and hence declining competence, of the bureaucracy. If the successful actions of one president to politicize and control the bureaucracy render it less able to attract competent personnel, in what way can it be said that he has improved conditions of governance for his successors? In what way can this accord with criteria of leadership?

The rationalist argument, as I have indicated, does not begin with a view of what is likely to constitute good government in a democratic society. What we see, as some scholars have argued, is that behind the discourse on rationality and efficient management exists a "desire of governments to reestablish control over the civil servants which the institutionalization of the bureaucracy has largely deprived them of."[25]

All the arguments by the rationalists to support a president's desire to politicize the bureaucracy are advanced in the belief that this will ipso facto augment his political leadership and influence—a connection that needs to be better defined before it can even be proven—are ex post facto arguments. In other words, the arguments follow what chief executives have wanted to do or, in some cases, what they have done. They thus seek to justify actions that have already been undertaken.

Why is this significant? Because such arguments as a president's "needs" or his drive for "leadership" and "influence" were never offered or analyzed prior to the appearance of the phenomenon as a major issue. I am unaware of any seriously advanced argument prior to the Reagan presidency in the United States, or at any time in any European country, that made the case for politicizing the bureaucracy so as to facilitate the task of governing. It is, to be sure, not a case that can easily be made, because it would need to go beyond the declarative and vague assertions about the "exercise of leadership." It would have to take into account the process of governance in its totality, and would therefore have to take account of the costs that such an action entails. It would, above all, have to compare a politicized agency with a relatively unpoliticized one. This remains to be done.

Nonetheless, despite its evident weakness and its inability to define what constitutes "efficiency" and "leadership," this form of rationalist argumentation has provided an academic and intellectual respectability to bureaucratic politicization. It is an issue of considerable importance and merits debate and careful analysis, even if the case remains a weak one. I turn now to two distinct but nonetheless clear cases of bureaucratic politicization.

---

[25] Françoise Dreyfus, *L'Invention de la Bureacratie: Servir l'Etat en France, en Grande-Bretagne et aux Etats-Unis (18ème–20ème Siècle)* (Paris: La Découverte, 2000), 201.

One (the United States) has accomplished this through bypassing the civil service in the appointment process. The other (France) has limited appointments to civil servants while politicizing these officials, thus insuring professional (political) competence. In the next chapter I turn to less evident cases of politicization.

United States

Of all democracies with a civil service tradition, the U.S. is generally considered to be the one that has remained attached to a modified form of a spoils system or, at any rate, to be the country that has had the greatest dedication to circumventing the rules that govern civil service neutrality. This may turn out not to be wholly accurate when figures for politicization are examined closely. But it is undeniable that the passage of the Pendleton Civil Service Act of 1883 did not affect the view of future presidents that the bureaucracy was, and ought to be, an instrument of the legitimately elected administration.

How, then, to reconcile the main tenets of the Weberian requirements of a civil service (embodied in the Pendleton Act) with the needs of a political administration elected ostensibly on a political platform that it sees itself mandated to implement? On the one hand we find the basic requirements of a democratic state: neutrality, recruitment based on examinations, and promotions based on merit. On the other hand we find the need to respect the requirements of the civil service statutes and yet not render the bureaucracy the mere instrument of the legitimately elected administrations. This tension has existed throughout the twentieth century between the needs of chief executives and the need to respect the principles on which the modern bureaucracy was established.

With respect to the founding basis of the civil service in the U.S., there is scarcely the wide gap that some students of American politics attempted to establish between the U.S. and the European tradition. Although it has become an article of faith that the general interest does not exist in the U.S. because the basis of American democracy resides in group interests, the fact remains that the drive behind the Pendleton Act was precisely the principle of neutrality of public servants. The principle of neutrality was merely another way of affirming that public servants were recruited, rather than chosen, on the basis of professional qualifications to serve an interest that transcended party interests. A civil service career system came to be accepted as an indispensable component of a modern state.[26] In fact, as

---

[26] See Stephen Skowronek, *Building the American State: The Expansion of National Administrative Capacities, 1877–1920* (Cambridge: Cambridge University Press, 1982).

legal scholars like Robert Vaughn came to recognize, this view of the civil service "reestablished the premise that an employee was an agent for broadly defined public interests; it created special responsibilities; and it emphasized the importance of public employment, creating a moral calling for public service."[27]

Indeed, the United States, like all new states, including the states of Eastern Europe following the fall of communism, had to erect a structure that possessed a degree of professionalism. The transition from a politically controlled bureaucracy to one based on principles of professionalism was not an easy one. But without such a successful transition, as Skowronek has shown, the United States would not have been able to constitute an American state: "A state organized from the bottom up had to be reorganized from the top down. A state tied together by the procedures of the spoils appointment had to be reoriented around procedures of merit appointment. A state operated in the interests of party workers and party managers had to give way to the interests of a permanent civil service and a new intellectual cadre of independent professionals. The challenge of constructing a new governmental order informed every stage of the process of administrative modernization."[28]

While the battle for creating a modern administration was won, the tension between executive needs to possess a loyal instrument for governing and the need to preserve a nonpolitical administration has remained intact to the present. Richard Nixon's battle with the bureaucracy, his attempts to control the institution, and his vituperative views of its aims and power were unique in that he set out to create the first truly partisan or political bureaucracy. His attacks on the bureaucracy were strewn across many of the tapes that constitute part of the record of his presidency. "We have no discipline in this bureaucracy," Nixon told his aide John Ehrlichman. "We never fire anybody. We never reprimand anybody. We never demote anybody. We always promote the sons-of-bitches that kick us in the ass."[29] Nixon did not trust the bureaucracy and set himself the specific goal of trying to bring it under his control. If the Nixon case was extreme in that he was obsessive about control, the mistrust of presidents as different in their concepts of governance as Kennedy, Carter, and Reagan has been fairly stable. Each president has sought to mold the bureaucracy in his image.[30] Heclo well summarized the problem: "In practice the idea that

[27] Cited in Paul C. Light, *The Tides of Reform: Making Government Work 1945–1995* (New Haven: Yale University Press, 1997), 19.
[28] Skowronek, *Building the American State*, 209–10.
[29] Cited in Richard Nathan, *The Administrative Presidency* (New York: John Wiley & Sons, 1983), 53.
[30] See Ingraham, *The Foundation of Merit*, 92–111.

the higher civil service should be a resource for political leadership is still alien to Washington."[31]

The United States made giant steps toward the creation of a merit-based civil service through the Pendleton Act and equally important steps toward the exclusion of civil servants from political intrusion and repercussion through the Hatch Act of 1939. But the postwar period has seen constant attempts by both Republican and Democratic administrations to circumvent the spirit of a meritocratic civil service and to reform or, more precisely, to rewrite the Hatch Act so that the stringent demands it made on civil servants to stay clear from politics would be loosened.

The attempt to free civil servants from the constraints of political involvement has probably been more of a Democratic than a Republican project. President Ford vetoed a bill passed by Congress that would have extended the rights of civil servants to engage in political activity. A further attempt was undertaken by President Carter in 1977 to change the Hatch Act, though that was halted as a result of wrangling in the House.[32] It was left to President Clinton to sign a bill, in the first year of his presidency, that modified the Hatch Act and allowed civil servants to participate in partisan political activities.

The modification of the Hatch Act needs to be seen in tandem with the increasing politicization of the civil service. The president's distrust of the bureaucracy probably reached its apogee with Richard Nixon, who firmly believed that the federal bureaucracy was an essentially democratic institution, loyal to the New Deal and Great Society programs. It was not that Nixon was wholly mistaken. Rather, he saw a vast conspiracy among the bureaucracy, Congress, and an array of anti-Nixon forces in society. He went on the attack determined to have the bureaucracy at his command. Aberbach and Rockman describe Nixon's onslaught as the first time that

> an administration went on the attack against the bureaucracy it inherited and yet had done little at the outset to influence. Nixon's initial indifference to the bureaucracy was transformed into a monumental effort to control it when he believed his policy choices, as well as some of his more questionable tactics, were being resisted. . . . The efforts of the Nixon presidency to maximize bureaucratic responsiveness left their mark, despite Nixon's fall from grace. Others looked at what the Nixon presidency sought to do and paid attention to how it might be done more effectively.[33]

[31] Hugh Heclo, *A Government of Strangers: Executive Politics in Washington* (Washington, D.C.: Brookings Institution, 1997), 241.

[32] See André Blais, Donald Blake and Stéphane Dion, *Governments, Parties and Public Sector Employees: Canada, United States, Britain and France* (Pittsburgh: University of Pittsburgh Press, 1997), 81–85. See also Ingraham, *The Foundation of Merit*.

[33] Joel D. Aberbach and Bert A. Rockman, *In the Web of Politics: Three Decades of the U.S. Federal Executive* (Washington, D.C.: Brookings Institution, 2000), 32.

If Presidents Nixon, Reagan, and Bush were committed to the view that the federal bureaucracy needed to be made ever more responsive to the elected chief executive, President Carter, in his own way, contributed substantially, though no doubt unintentionally, to the process of ever greater politicization. From our viewpoint, the most important aspect of the Civil Service Reform Act of 1978 was the introduction of the Senior Executive Service. Among its various consequences was the ability of the president to increase the number of political appointments. It now seems indisputable that, whatever Carter's intentions, the ultimate result has been "to provide political leaders of the executive branch better tools with which to sculpt the senior civil service, especially agencies deemed critical to achieving policy objectives."[34]

In fact, it may well be that Carter's mission was not simply to make the bureaucracy more efficient. As Patricia Ingraham noted in her analysis of the Carter reform, the separation of the policy role of SES members from the classified service meant that the Senior Executive Service was placed "in a kind of buffer zone between the merit employees and the political appointees in an organization."[35] But one can see this "buffer quality, the mobility provisions, and the performance-award provisions of the SES as a sign of increased political direction and control of the Senior Executive Service. Virtually all the decisions in this regard would be made by political appointees; as the top executives in the organization, they technically supervised the members of the SES."[36]

The trend of the postwar era has been in the direction of political control of the bureaucracy. What Moe referred to as the "politicized presidency"[37] and applied to Reagan can be extended to Reagan's predecessors as well as to his successors insofar as the federal bureaucracy is concerned. The methods used by presidents for politicizing the civil service have varied, from Nixon's avowed attempt to bring the bureaucracy to heel to Carter's ostensible objective of creating a senior mobile service to Reagan's reduction of personnel through not killing political appointments at lower levels in the chain of command. The cumulative effect of the successive reforms and practices has been a greater politicization of the federal bureaucracy as well as an undermining of public service in general.

The available data show that the "administrative presidency" has been gathering momentum even as the total number of federal employees has been declining. "The total number of senior executives and presidential appointees grew from 451 in 1960 to 2,393 in 1993, a 430 percent

---

[34] Ibid., 35.
[35] Ingraham, *The Foundation of Merit*, 79.
[36] Ibid.
[37] Moe, "The Politicized Presidency," 260–72.

increase."[38] Every president in the postwar period has contributed to this process. Eisenhower felt that in order for him to insure that presidential orders were carried out, the proportion of political appointees to career civil servants had to be considerably increased. He introduced Schedule C, which allowed him to make appointments to policy positions from outside the civil service, a practice that almost all executive leaders in democratic societies have resorted to.

It is interesting to note that the desire to gain control of the bureaucracy was strong not only with a president used to a military hierarchy, such as Eisenhower,[39] but equally so with President Carter. Indeed, as Patricia Ingraham has shown, "President Carter . . . availed himself of a political initiative that Richard Nixon had not used: the increased use of Schedule C appointees. Where Nixon had turned to illegal manipulation of the merit system to increase the number of employees he deemed appropriately loyal, Carter turned to the policy-sensitive appointment system created by President Eisenhower."[40]

The politicization of the civil service through the aggressive use of Schedule C appointments continued unabated. Reagan used it to considerable effect to increase his hold on the bureaucracy. Bush, while putting a halt to the incessant attacks of his predecessor on the bureaucracy, nonetheless did little to reverse the trend. As Ingraham concluded: "Although President Bush did not increase the numbers of political appointments in some agencies, the total number of Schedule C appointments at the end of his term was still nearly double the nine hundred such appointments in place at the end of the Ford administration before the building began."[41]

It needs to be noted that politicization can be accomplished in more ways than one. While Nixon sought to make as many political appointments as possible and to have these appointments replace positions that had been reserved for civil servants, Reagan sought politicization through nonappointments, that is, through holding positions vacant. He also in-

---

[38] Paul C. Light, *Thickening Government: Federal Hierarchy and the Diffusion of Accountability* (Washington, D.C.: Brookings Institution, 1995), 7.

[39] Eisenhower learned quickly that giving orders to the civilian bureaucracy was different from giving orders to the military, despite Truman's belief that he would make the mistake of confusing the two: "He'll sit here, Truman would remark (tapping his desk for emphasis) and he'll say 'Do this! Do that!' *And nothing will happen.* Poor Ike—it won't be a bit like the Army. He'll find it very frustrating." See Richard Neustadt, *Presidential Power: The Politics of Presidential Leadership from FDR to Carter* (New York: John Wiley & Sons, 1980), 9, italics in original. Eisenhower turned out to be more bureaucratically savvy than Truman, and many others, gave him credit for. See Fred I. Greenstein, *The Hidden-Hand Presidency: Eisenhower as Leader* (New York: Basic Books, 1982).

[40] Ingraham, *The Foundation of Merit*, 99.

[41] Ibid., 103.

sured that the permanent civil servants would be excluded from the policy-making process. As Pfiffner notes, "Reagan appointees began their terms by systematically excluding career executives from policy-making deliberations based on the fear that they would try to undercut the administration policies if they were included."[42]

With the indisputable politicization of the federal civil service, a phenomenon that the appointments process and the makeup of the federal civil service show to be the case, there remain three issues that need to be taken up. First, how effective has politicization been? Second, what remains of the concept of neutrality as a basis for organizing the civil service in the U.S.? And third, what is the federal bureaucracy likely to resemble in the years ahead?

The incessant process of politicization has not produced the results that presidents had hoped for. All the studies of executive-bureaucratic relations have arrived at this conclusion, well summarized by Dunn: "In sum the 'solution' of adding more political appointees in order to achieve greater responsiveness from the bureaucracy has not worked, although elected executives are likely to continue to promote it as a solution. That they continue to think they need more political appointees despite the fact that the number of these appointees has been growing for many years suggests that this 'solution' is an ineffective tool for increasing political responsiveness."[43]

It has been suggested that American presidents have basically been barking up the wrong tree. Their quest to bring the bureaucracy under their total control is an illusion and, like all illusions, can never be attained. The bureaucratic machine is far too large and deals with an extraordinary number of issues that cut across agencies and departments, each with its own hierarchical structure. As Heclo concluded some years ago, "In a day-to-day sense only bureaucrats can control bureaucracy."[44] But the general distrust of the bureaucracy, particularly in the United States, means that politicians are not likely to use the bureaucracy for effective control. They are likely to continue adding additional layers of political appointees. It is a losing, if unavoidable, battle, for sooner or later politicians recognize the competence of civil servants who mostly clear signs and directives from their political chiefs. But as Light, Heclo, and others have shown, by the time politicians and political appointees recognize this, they also recognize

[42] James P. Pfiffner, "Political Appointees and Career Executives: The Democracy-Bureaucracy Nexus," in *Agenda for Excellence: Public Service in America*, ed. Patricia W. Ingraham and Donald F. Kettl (Chatham, N.J.: Chatham House, 1992), 50.

[43] Delmer D. Dunn, *Politics and Administration at the Top: Lessons from Down Under* (Pittsburgh: University of Pittsburgh Press, 1997), 26.

[44] Heclo, *A Government of Strangers*, 249.

that an opportunity for cooperation has been missed.[45] And the cycle begins all over again.

The concept of political neutrality that forms the basis of all bureaucracies and that accompanies professionalization was also an important rationale that underlay the Pendleton Act and the Hatch Act. But in the intervening years, not only has it suffered severe blows in practice, but its respectability as an organizing idea has also been dealt a blow. Indeed, it has been suggested that Americans have always had a hard time believing that people can act without interests. The attack on the concept of neutrality "proceeds from a philosophical base, which finds neutral competence difficult to describe and believe."[46] But there are consequences when neutrality is accorded little value. It has led to what Light has referred to as the "thickening of government": "Politicians must have their own people in positions of responsibility in agencies and departments. This belief leads to the practice of more appointments of those whose knowledge and experience are suspect; it can also cut people with that knowledge and experience out of the policy formulation loop. . . . This practice creates communication problems, making it difficult for politicians to provide political direction to civil servants and for bureaucrats to provide appropriate levels of information to politicians."[47]

Politicization, in effect, is one of the chief causes of demoralization of the civil service corps. This (as the following chapter will show) is not exclusive to the United States, which has gone furthest in the direction of politicization and which is also the first country to develop a justification for the process. However, analysts concerned with what Charles Levine has called the problem of "human resource erosion"[48] have generally concluded that the demoralization and desertion of the civil service have derived from "the politicization of the higher civil service and the most extensive use of central controls by OMB through the budget and regulatory review process to shape the policy agendas of departments and agencies."[49] But the true meaning of politicization in the United States is clear: "the increased numbers and importance of political appointees at lower and lower levels in the agencies and the increased direction of the agencies by the White House."[50]

---

[45] See Heclo, *A Government of Strangers*, 240–50; Aberbach and Rockman, *In the Web of Politics*, 119–30; Paul Light, "When Worlds Collide: The Political-Career Nexus," in *The In-and-Outers*, ed. G. Calvin Mackenzie (Baltimore: Johns Hopkins University Press, 1987).

[46] Dunn, *Politics and Administration at the Top*, 154.

[47] Light, "When Worlds Collide," 155.

[48] Charles R. Levine, "The Federal Government in the Year 2000: Administrative Legacies of the Reagan Years," in *Agenda for Excellence*, ed. Ingraham and Kettl, 174.

[49] Ibid.

[50] Ibid.

With neutrality, or at least approximate neutrality, no longer a value to be prized, the United States has essentially relegated it to the status of a nonissue. This has been accomplished by introducing the concept of entrepreneurial management. When a bureaucracy no longer has as its mission the serving of the common good, when it becomes merely an organization providing services, the issue of neutrality is effectively reduced to secondary importance. In fact, it has been argued that behind the discourse of rationality and entrepreneurialism as management lies "the desire of governments to reestablish their control over the civil servants which the institutionalization of the civil service has largely deprived them of."[51] Whether there is a direct link between NPM and politicization is not clear, since politicization has been a process that all governments have found beneficial. What is perhaps more evident is that NPM has facilitated the process of politicization since it sanctions above all the hiring of "entrepreneurial managers" from outside the confines of the civil service proper. It thus provides both a rationale and a justification for bypassing or undermining the civil service.

Finally, the politicization of the federal bureaucracy has also effectively reduced the importance of expertise. The addition of increasing numbers of layers, that Heclo alerted us to some twenty-five years ago and that Light has more recently documented, suggests that the shape of the federal bureaucracy is being transformed. As Light observes: "If current trends continue, the Federal hierarchy may eventually resemble a circle, with very few employees at the bottom, hordes of managers, supervisors, and technical analysts of one kind or another at the middle, and a vast coterie of political and career executives at the top. The rest of the traditional bureaucratic pyramid will still exist, of course, not filled by Federal employees, but by those who work for the increasing number of contractors, nonprofits, and state and local agencies that deliver services once provided above."[52]

Politicization is, of course, not the only reason for the "thickening" of government. But as a trend that has been unstoppable (and deemed undesirable by all administrations), the addition of political layers is clearly transforming the bureaucracy as well as the concept of what a bureaucracy is supposed to do. Seeing little hope in bureaucratic depoliticization, Heclo long ago proposed the creation of a corps of what he called "Federal Executive Officers," who would be "more changeable and mobile than bureaucrats but more institutional and enduring than political appointees,"[53] an idea borrowed from the British and French civil service traditions.

[51] Dreyfus, "L'Invention de la Bureaucratie," 201.
[52] Light, *Thickening Government*, 15.
[53] Heclo, *A Government of Strangers*, 249.

This did not, and probably could not, happen, as the SES experience has shown. First, the United States was founded on un-elitist ideas. Relying on one group over an extended period of time and for the sole reason that this group alone possesses certain attributes was not a view that the Founding Fathers could accept. This is what two authors have referred to as the "unsentimental view of public service" that the Founding Fathers shared: "The Founders of the American regime were stubbornly unsentimental in their view that the republic not be *dependent* on a highly virtuous citizenry led by disinterested governors. They were optimistic that the regime would produce many virtuous citizens and leaders, but did not seek to impose a political elite to oversee that process."[54]

The second reason that a professional corps of senior civil servants would be unlikely to see the light of the day in the United States has been the freedom that chief executives have sought to permit them to politicize the instrument of government. The drive for politicization, which derives not only from the need to exercise leadership, as Moe and others have claimed, but also from the need to reward party faithfuls and the party machine that made the conquest of power possible, simply means that values expressed in the Pendleton and Hatch Acts have been supplanted by others. Little analysis has gone into the consequences for governing of this development. Yet, the process of democratic governance was based on principles that were arrived at gradually and that were sometimes hard to win. Merit recruitment, security of employment, professionalism and expertise, neutrality—these all came about in the United States, as in other democracies, gradually and came to be considered as basic to democratic governance.

Changing the basis on which the bureaucratic instrument was founded cannot be accomplished without changing the governing process. If interest groups associated with the party in power have an open door to the bureaucracy, as is more and more the case, how are citizens expected to trust their elected leaders? Cutting waste is not what elicits the trust of political leaders and political institutions. It has become a means by which politicians distract attention from the increasingly politicized way of governing. In subverting the principles on which the bureaucratic apparatus was founded, our political leaders have insured citizens' distrust of their political institutions. No emphasis on "family values" or bowling in teams as opposed to doing so alone can ever compensate for the mistrust that is generated by the slippery slope of bureaucratic politicization that contem-

---

[54] Lloyd G. Nigro and William D. Richardson, "The Founders' Unsentimental View of Public Service in the American Regime," in *Agenda for Excellence*, ed. Ingraham and Kettl, 17.

porary democracies are traveling on. In short, the absence of a professional bureaucracy may offer short-term benefits to governments, but it also renders governments less able to carry out their duties. If democratic states cannot act effectively, democracy is inevitably fragilized.

France

France, like the United States, is one of those rare democratic countries where strong political attachments and state service go hand in hand. Also like the United States, the politicization of the administration is practiced though it is not openly recognized and accepted as a fact of life. The fiction of the nobility and neutrality of state service is preserved. In reality, a change in party government in France leads to changes in appointments in the bureaucracy in a fashion that is still unknown in most European countries, though recognized and accepted in the United States.

A Political Administration?

The phenomenon of politicization has had different connotations during different historical periods. In France, the debate has mostly centered on the period up to the end of the 1950s, a period since the creation of the Fifth Republic in the late 1950s, and on the particular role higher civil servants have played in politics. A historical perspective suggests that the problem of having a political administration figured strongly during the nineteenth century, first under the Second Empire, then during the first years of the Third Republic.[55]

The relationship between politics and administration since the beginning of the Third Republic has known four different phases. The first, between 1875 and 1940, functioned according to the Weberian principle of separation between administration and politics. The first years of the Third Republic, for example, were strongly marked by the practice of seeking loyalty from pro-republican civil servants in order to insure the implementation of republican measures.[56] In fact, what transpired from 1870 until the turn of the century was not dissimilar to what has been happening since the middle of the 1970s: administrative nominations often guided by partisan considerations.

---

[55] See Françoise Dreyfus, *L'Invention de la Bureaucratie*.

[56] See, for example, Jean-Pierre Machelon, *La République contre les Libertés? Les Réstrictions aux Libertés Publiques de 1873 à 1914* (Paris: Presses de la FNSP, 1976); Christophe Charles, *Les Hauts Fonctionnaires en France au 19ème Siècle* (Paris: Gallimard/Julliard, 1980).

The second phase, from 1945 to 1958 (the years of the Fourth Republic), was characterized by the distinction between administrative and political domains. This was made possible by the advent of a generation of civil servants that gained legitimacy by its previous involvement in the Resistance. The involvement in politics by high civil servants was not approved of, in part because the structure of the partisan game was still a favorite of those in power and in part because the position of high civil servant in the context of the reconstruction and modernization of French society gave these civil servants unprecedented importance and visibility.[57]

The third phase, from 1959 to the beginning of the 1990s, saw the evolution of the administration-politics relationship, in the double sense of the technocratization of the political profession and of the politicization of top administrative posts. It is helpful here to distinguish between two trends that are often conflated. First, beginning in 1959, access to political posts (minister, then national representative, finally party representative) was given to high civil servants who were targeted and promoted by the entourages of General De Gaulle and Georges Pompidou. These civil servants rose in the ranks as a result of their technical-administrative ability and because they had not been "perverted" by the political games that had prevailed up to that point.[58] This technocratic movement first affected the Gaullists, then the liberal Right surrounding Valéry Giscard d'Estaing, and finally the Socialists after François Mitterrand's designation, at the Epinay Congress of 1971, as head of the Socialist Party. The second trend emerged clearly after 1970: nominations to the top positions in the civil service and to the top positions in state-run industries were more clearly guided than before by partisan considerations. Choices were made among civil servants who had accumulated the classic attributes of the public servant—in other words, membership in a technical or administrative *grand corps* and partisan relationships. This politicization movement, confirmed during the change of power in 1981 when the Left came to power, can be explained in part by the competition at the heart of the Right coalition between *gaullo-chiraciens* and *giscardiens*; and in part by the long hold on power of these two center-right movements that made the careers of a large number of civil servants who were later to be excluded by the Left.

Finally, since the 1990s, discussion of the politicization of the administration has given way to a new rhetoric of the state-in-crisis. Nominations still proceed largely along political lines, but this practice no longer raises much concern—not only because it is now accepted or tolerated but

[57] See Delphine Dulong, *Moderniser la Politique. Aux Origines de la 5ème Rèpublique* (Paris: L'Harmattan, 1997); and Henri Rousso, ed., *De Monnet à Massé* (Paris: Editions du CNRS, 1986).

[58] See Bastien François, *Le Régime Politique de la 5ème République* (Paris: La Découverte, Coll. Repères, 1998).

because the nature of the debate surrounding the state has changed. The question is no longer the politicized administration or the "witch hunts"—which have been relatively "humanized" during the period of cohabitation. At issue now is brain flight to the private sector. In effect, it is probably preferable to hire a high civil servant who is loyal to serving the state over one who will use the connections gained while in public service in order to leave it.

The institution of a Weberian-style bureaucracy in the complex post-Empire political context—the imposition of republican values on an administration that was more or less Restorationist or Bonapartist—led to the recruitment of civil servants with certain values. In the same way, if the problem has shifted since 1960, it is because the function of the administration can only be seen with respect to its distance from politics. In other words, mixtures of people who serve the state and people who serve a cause or a party are seen, on a normative level, as a menace to the smooth functioning of the state. The role of technocrats comes into focus: they are valued because they remain apart from politics; they place more value instead on serving the state and on bureaucratic rationality.[59] And, in effect, the political advancement of high civil servants by General De Gaulle and Michel Debré, which followed a strategy of delegitimizing the "old notables," created the conditions for a repoliticization of the administration of the French state.[60]

It is generally understood that a politicized administration is an administration run by civil servants whose nominations are—ability aside—the result of proven loyalty to those in political power. This is the definition we have used throughout our crossnational analyses.

The vast majority of civil servants do not claim to have pronounced or obvious political affiliations. Even those who serve in ministers' staffs (in ministerial cabinets) refuse the idea that they owe their position to their political affiliation. They prefer to rationalize that working in a cabinet is a professional necessity, and that they are doing nothing more than serving the state.

Two elements have long structured the discussions surrounding the politicization of the administration. The first comes back to the ideological divide between the two political camps, a divide that helped give great visibility to those civil servants who publicly chose to affiliate themselves with a party. To commit oneself in this way was not without professional consequences—the high civil servants of the Left during the 1970s are a good example. They placed their values ahead of their career. The second

---

[59] Dulong, *Moderniser la Politique*. See also Vincent Dubois and Delphine Dulong, *La Question Technocratique* (Strasbourg: Presses Universitaires de Strasbourg, 1999).

[60] François, *Le Régime Politique*.

element concerns the centrality of the state in French society and the fact that, as a result, serving the state while also serving the party in power allowed certain civil servants to accelerate their careers to the top. It allowed them to hope for nominations to prestigious posts in public or nationalized industries. Such pragmatism incited public servants to "play the game" according to which passage through the political-administrative center, a ministerial cabinet—for example—would open the doors to a central position.

Politicization: A Noncodified Practice

It is generally accepted that the politicization of the higher level public service is a movement that originated in the mid-1970s, borne out of the competition between the heirs of Gaullism and the holders of the liberal Right, followers of President Giscard d'Estaing. This movement was amplified with the transfer of power to the Socialists in 1981[61] and continued in 1986, 1988, 1993, 1997, and 2002.

Politicization can be defined in two ways: first, it can be measured objectively, by the number of public employees whose assignments correspond directly to the assignments of government leaders—more than five hundred since the reform of 1985—and the avowed fact that newly installed governments use this prerogative to designate high civil servants who are "close," "loyal," or have been activists in the party.

On another level, politicization can be understood subjectively, which is to say that there is a consensus among members of the administrative elite that politicization exists, and that access to positions of power in the administration (and, more generally, throughout the public sector) is directly tied to partisan considerations. This sentiment does not necessarily take the form of explicit partisanship, however, but the result is still the placement of individuals. One of the chosen practices of high civil servants is to assume strict neutrality—"I am not a partisan, I have never been a partisan, I am a doer"—all the while following a professional path, like a stint in a ministerial cabinet, that attests to a partisan preference.

The problem posed by the close relationships between the high civil service and the political class is less their existence than the fact that they are not formally regulated. As distinguished from a spoils system, what governs the system in France is nothing less than *le fait du prince*. The problem is in fact twofold. First, there are the "discretionary" appointees in the administration—approximately five hundred positions to be filled by the

---

[61] See Pierre Birnbaum, ed., *Les Elites Socialistes au Pouvoir* (Paris: Presses Universitaires de France, 1985); and Monique Dagnaud and Dominique Mehl, *L'Elite Rose: Qui Gouverne?* (Paris: Ramsay, 1988).

government. The risks associated with these nominations are limited, since all are known entities: the list of these positions is published, making it possible to identify those high civil servants who have posts that are directly related to their political affiliation and those who do not meet the technical qualifications of their post.

Second, and far more risky, is the fact that the politicization of the administration is gradually permeating the secondary ranks, particularly the subdirectors and those below them, the *chefs de service*.[62] In these cases, appointments are not directly political, but they are part of a system of influence in which ministerial cabinets—and therefore the high civil servants who work in them—follow closely what is happening in their ministry and apply direct pressure on the choice of appointees.

Civil servants today feel under pressure to cultivate relationships in the political arena, and therefore to play the game of politicization. The typical higher civil servant may well follow a career which puts him/her at the head of a division of a ministry by the age of forty. Practically the only way to ascend the hierarchy by this age is to affiliate with a political party. Luc Rouban reports that between 1985 and 1997, "40 percent of central administration directors had an explicit political affiliation [and] nearly 20 percent among them passed through a ministerial cabinet such as those of Matignon and Elysée."[63] Rouban adds that "politics is becoming a means of promotion and is replacing the professional regulation of careers. A majority of civil servants are brought up as political administrators, thus, fuzzying the line between the world of public service and the world of politics."[64] The case of France with regard to the politicization of its higher civil service is, as we have seen, hardly unique.

Political and Administrative Transfers of Power

The practice of naming new directors of the central administration after a transfer of power has been amply documented: between 1986 and 1988, for example, more than 80 percent of them (out of a total of 160) were replaced; this figure went down to 45 percent in 1988 and increased again to 55 percent in 1993.[65] This practice applies not only to transfers of power between

---

[62] Danièle Lochak, "La haute administration à l'épreuve de l'alternance," in Birnbaum, *Les Elites Socialistes au Pouvoir*. See also Danièle Lochak, "Les haut fonctionnaires et l'alternance," paper delivered at the Association Française de Science Politique, February 7–8, 1991.

[63] Luc Rouban, *La Fin des Technocrates?* (Paris: Presses de Sciences Po, 1998), 41. See also Jacques Chevalier, "La Gauche et la haute administration dans la 5ème République," in *La Haute Fonction Publique*, ed. Jean-Luc Bodiguel and Jean-Louis Quermonne (Paris: Presses Universitaires de France, 1982).

[64] Rouban, *La Fin*, 42.

[65] Ibid., 38.

TABLE 9.1
Professional Background of Directors of Central Administration (percent)

	1984–85	1988–89	1993–94
Same Ministry	26.4	21.3	22.1
Cabinet	31.9	28	11.6
Public Enterprise	2.8	9.3	14
Private Enterprise	5.6	5.3	5.8
Other Corps	4.2	13.3	14
Finance Inspectorate	0	1.3	5.8
Director from Another Ministry	8.3	5.3	4.7
Member of a Grand Corps	2.8	5.3	9.3
Director in Same Ministry	5.6	1.3	2.3
Ministry of Foreign Affairs	12.5	9.3	4.7
Paris and Paris Region	0	0	5.8

Source: Luc Rouban, "The Senior Civil Service in France," in *Bureaucratic Elites in Western Europe*, ed. E. Page and V. Wright (Oxford: Oxford University Press, 2000), 70.

political parties but also when the prime minister changes within the same party. Thus Pierre Bérégovoy in 1992 and Alain Juppé in 1995 replaced most of the directors named by Edith Cresson and Edouard Baladur.[66] These replacements can happen in stages, though the most sensitive administrations (those that are the most political, in other words) are the fastest ones to change. These are the administrations—finance, interior, justice, foreign affairs, and education—in which it is urgent to have a loyal director.

The widely accepted hypothesis that serving in a ministerial cabinet is a typical form of political and career advancement for a high civil servant has been called into question in recent years. It may be necessary in fact to refine this hypothesis. All ministerial cabinets do not propel a career in the same way. There are differences among ministries. The rank of the higher civil servant in the ministry is also a factor.[67] It seems clear that the posts of director or co-director of a cabinet or special adviser in the Ministries of Economy and Finance, and of Industry, lean more toward the development of a career in the semipublic or private sector. The officials who occupy

[66] Ibid., 39.
[67] See Pierre Mathiot and Fréderic Sawicki, "Les Membres des cabinets socialistes en France (1981–1993) recrutement et reconversion," *Revue Française de Sciences Politiques* 49 (February–April 1999).

these posts are usually experienced civil servants, endowed with a network of connections, for whom working in a high-level cabinet post (often after having held less important cabinet posts) is a passageway out of public service. For younger civil servants, however, working in a cabinet represents a rung on the professional ladder. Occupying posts of responsibility in ministries less concerned with economic affairs improves the chances of being nominated to a prestigious public post—ambassador, regional prefect, etc.

Outside Nominations to the Corps

The custom of the politico-administrative system and the civil servants' use of political networks take on a particular form in France, when they combine to introduce appointments of outsiders to the *grands corps*. Until now, the politicization discussed so far has referred only to those civil servants who, on account of their political ties and professional interests, manifest loyalty to a particular political camp in order to further their career.

The problem can be seen from a slightly different angle when we examine the case of civil servants who are named to a corps by a government decree. For example, nearly 10 percent of the members of the *Conseil d'Etat* were named *au tour exterieur*, that is to say, for reasons directly related to their political affiliation. Twenty such nominations to the *Conseil* were made between 1988 and 1993, and 30 such nominations were made to the *Cour des Comptes* during the same period, 22 to the *Inspection Générale de l'Education Nationale*, 11 to the *Inspection des Finances*, and 29 to the *administration préfectorale* (of which 15 were prefects). During the same period, we also find evidence of the nomination of 224 civil administrators.[68]

This practice was reinforced by the decision made in 1984 to allow access from *le tour exterieur* to the corps of inspector generals of a ministry. This measure contributed to transforming the inspectorate corps of ministries into sinecures for the politicized civil servants after an electoral defeat of the party to which they had given their loyalty. Two major categories of employees benefit from the *tour exterieur*: high civil servants who are able to move to more prominent posts—from civil administrator to a major corps, for example—and loyalists without professional status who are, in a sense, rewarded for their devotion.

The Place of Enarques

The proportion of *énarques* in ministerial cabinets between 1984 and 1997 was between 22 and 36 percent. These percentages were not uniform

---

[68] Christian Rigault, *Les Cabinets Ministériels* (Paris: LGDJ, 1997).

TABLE 9.2

Distribution of Each Corps (percent)

	1984	1989	1996
Civil Administrator	55.7	54.7	42.2
Council of State	9.8	9.1	8.8
Court of Accounts	4.9	5.6	9.8
Prefectoral Corps	0.8	5.2	4.9
Finance Inspectorate	7.4	6.9	8.8

Source: Luc Rouban, *Les Enarques en Cabinets 1984–1996* (Paris: Cahiers du *CEVIPOF*, no. 17, 1997).

across all sectors of the government. The ministerial cabinets of the Ministry of Economy and Finance, and of Matignon (the prime minister's staff), for example, included, respectively, 48 percent and 41 percent *énarques*.[69] If we expand our analysis to include all civil servants, the picture becomes somewhat different since the proportion of civil servants in the cabinet between 1984 and 1997 was around 70 percent, as compared to 90 percent between 1958 and 1984. This decrease came at the benefit of non–civil servants (party loyalists, appointees from the private sector). It also confirms the loss of influence of two categories of civil servants who were prominent during the Fourth Republic and during the 1960s: *normaliens littéraires* and *polytechniciens*. And their loss was the *énarques'* gain.

If ENA seems like a rite of passage for the majority of civil servants in the ministerial cabinets, we notice an important trend since the beginning of the 1980s: the number of *énarques* who enter the prestigious administrative corps (*Inspection des Finances, Conseil d'Etat, Cour des Comptes, Corps diplomatique*) are less likely to serve in ministerial cabinets than the other *énarques* (those who did not enter the grands corps). This was the case for the 1984–1997 period.[70]

It seems evident that for members of the prestigious administrative corps, working in a ministerial cabinet does not have as much professional utility as was the case in the past. But it remains necessary for civil administrators and, by extension, for "internal" *énarques*. With respect to the super-elite[71] of the major corps, career advancement has depended more

[69] Luc Rouban, *Les Enarques en Cabinets 1984–1996* (Paris: Cahiers du CEVIPOF, no. 17, 1997).

[70] Jean-Michel Eymeri, *La Fabrique des Enarques* (Paris: Economics, 2001).

[71] The expression is taken from Michel Bauer and Bénédicte Bertin-Mourot, *Enarques en Entreprise* (Paris: Boyden-CNRS, 1994).

and more, and earlier and earlier, on the private sector. Large corporations have developed a great demand for higher civil servants. They are not so much looking for technical specialists as for generalists of the highest order who, because of their connections and intimate knowledge of how the state functions, are needed and are qualified to hold high-level positions in these corporations. The privatization of many large firms since the mid-1980s has encouraged many young civil servants to leave the administration before even having served in a ministerial cabinet. A great demand for those young officials was closed off in the administration and a great demand for their services was created in the private sector. This explains the desertion from public service, even in a country like France, that we discussed in chapter 8.

The Relationship of High Civil Servants to Politics

Another way of comprehending the politicization of the administration is to measure the political involvement of higher civil servants. In his work on *énarques* in the ministerial cabinets, Rouban found that 31 percent of members of ministerial cabinets have clear political attachments but that this is the case of only 24 percent of *énarques*.[72] He adds that this involvement assumes less the form of militant partisanship than of participation in *clubs de réflexion*, and is what we can therefore call "expert involvement."

In their work on the Socialist cabinets of 1981–1986 and 1988–1993, Mathiot and Sawicki calculated that 52.8 percent of the group they studied belonged to the Socialist Party, a considerable difference from the percentage in the first legislature (60.2 percent) and the second legislature (41.0 percent).[73] Of those who participated in the "circle of experts," 47.2 percent were members of ministerial cabinets. When considering access to cabinet posts, Mathiot and Sawicki estimated that partisanship was a marginal factor (15.8 percent of their sample) compared to the variables "personal connection with the minister" (33 percent) and "friendship" with one or more members of the cabinet (35 percent).

The relation between higher civil servants and politics is more complex than appears at first glance. Access is more likely to be the result of personal connections than of political involvement. Higher civil servants do not always have to demonstrate an activist's involvement in a party. All they need do is participate in certain circles and maintain friendships with their colleagues in politics in order to be promoted. They are not asked to share the same ideas and political visions but, rather, to be loyal and competent. The higher civil servant, then, is one who commits himself more to

[72] Rouban, *Les Enarques en Cabinets.*
[73] Mathiot and Sawicki, "Les membres."

a political leader (or to a friend) than to a particular cause or party.[74] Thus the number of high civil servants engaged in politics has not changed significantly since the 1970s. What has changed, however, are the access routes to political-administrative posts. Since the end of the 1980s, high civil servants have been less willing to assert their political preferences. Instead, their political involvement is instrumental, in the sense that they participate and cultivate personal relationships insofar as this will advance their administrative career or help them in the private sector. The personal and the political merge in a convenient manner in France.

Another way to approach the question of the relationship between high civil servants and politicians is to observe what is commonly called the technocratization of politics—in other words, the movement to political action of people initially involved in the high civil service. Among other important leaders, President Jacques Chirac and former Prime Minister Lionel Jospin belong to this category of *énarques* who moved on to politics. The fact that France is unique among liberal democracies in this respect can be misleading. First of all, among the approximately 500,000 elected French officials, the number of elected civil servants—several scores—is relatively small. In France there are many more farmers, artisans, and schoolteachers who have been elected than *énarques*. This conclusion is insufficient, though, because it does not take account of the type of electoral mandate. When we consider the most important elective offices in France, we see that the proportion of high civil servants increases—they comprise nearly 10 percent of deputies, for example. This has been the case since the 1970s: high civil servants are the most highly represented professional group in the National Assembly, nearly equal to the number of lawyers and secondary school teachers.[75]

If we consider those who occupy ministerial portfolios, the figure is even more striking: Since Chirac's first government, in 1974, the proportion of civil servant ministers has approached 50 percent,[76] of whom the majority are *énarques*. The one significant difference between the Right and the Left in this regard is that the Left recruits more of its high civil servants from the universities. For the most part, however, ENA is the passageway par excellence to the seat of political power. This explains in part why ministerial cabinets remain largely the preserve of the higher civil service: a minister trained at ENA is going to rely upon his younger peers.

[74] Ibid.

[75] See for example, Pierre Mathiot, "Le nouveau profit des députés," *Le Figaro*, June 4, 1993.

[76] Ezra Suleiman, "Les élites de l'administration et de la politique dans la 5ème République: homogénéite, puissance, permanence," in *Le Recrutement des Elites en Europe*, ed. Ezra Suleiman and Henri Mendras (Paris: La Découverte, 1995), 37–39.

Politicization: The Banalization of an Issue

Even a quick look at the literature on the politicization of the French administration over the last thirty years reveals that since the 1980s there has been little debate on this subject. What was at issue then was the claim of a political movement to a hegemonic control of the levers of power through the use of the civil service. The political debate was fueled by the domination of the Gaullists, including the 1974 election of Valéry Giscard d'Estaing, who raised questions about these practices before having recourse to them. The Left roundly criticized the Right for hoarding power.

The Left's arrival to power in 1981 and the various changes of parties in power after 1986 contributed to the toleration of a practice that had caused serious conflict in the 1970s. The work of a number of scholars shows how the change of power in 1981 reinforced the tendency of politicians to name close friends and loyalists, often from the highest levels of the administration, to important administrative posts and to the top positions of a newly enlarged state sector.[77] In some ways, this realization put an end to the study of elites. Was it interesting any longer to study the subject once all government parties began to do the same thing?

Cohabitation, which allows two chief executives to share the important administrative appointments, has had a paradoxical effect: the party in power was no longer in a position to name loyalists to the top posts in the administration. Since power is often shared between the president and the prime minister, appointments to top positions tend to reflect the sharing of power of two opposing political forces. In other words, the number of positions for which it was possible to rely solely on bureaucratic qualifications has decreased considerably. Today, all nominations are willy-nilly political.

Politicization is no longer a contentious issue in France. This may be due to the recentering of politics, which has created a situation in which "political" higher civil servants no longer make particularly ideological decisions. This relative homogenization of public service is accentuated by the fact that, across party lines, higher civil servants have very similar social and educational backgrounds. As the saying goes, "There is nothing that resembles an *énarque* of the Right more than an *énarque* of the Left!" In fact, it is no longer merely the fact that higher civil servants have come to

---

[77] Birnbaum, *Les Elites Socialistes au Pouvoir*, and Chevalier, "La Gauche." One of the reasons for the failure of administrative reform to make much headway in France is precisely because the importance of civil servants in political life. See Philippe Bèze, "Bureaucrats and Politicians in the Politics of Administrative Reform in France (1988–1997)," in *Politicians and Administrative Reform*, ed. B. Guy Peters and Jon Pierre (New York: Routledge, 2001), 47–60.

dominate in ministerial cabinets and governments and to make claims to the highest administrative positions based on their political affiliations; equally noticeable is the growing practice of civil servants becoming candidates and being elected to national offices. In the 2002 legislative elections, a quarter of the candidates for the National Assembly were civil servants, and slightly over 25 percent were elected.[78]

A second explanation revolves around the role of higher civil servants. What is at issue today is less their party affiliation than what is seen, in the eyes of public opinion, as their excessive influence. The political or politicized civil servant is less stigmatized than the technocrat who is seen using his position to make political decisions.

A third, and probably the most important, explanation has to do with a structural transformation of the role of high public service in the administration of state action. The increasing development of authorities peripheral to the state—the European Commission, local and regional authorities— has led to a questioning of the role of the state and of its public officials. As a result, the career strategies of civil servants have changed. Serving the state no longer seems like the best way to advance one's career, and the rewards of public service have decreased along with the shrinking authority of the state. Instead of cultivating relationships with important politicians, it seems a surer bet to cultivate the business world, to use the skills and connections acquired in public service to enter the private sector.

If the politicization of higher civil servants is not widely debated now, the reason is that it is now an accepted facet of French public life, though one that seems to have been overshadowed by a new "reality," namely, the pull of the private sector.

State service in France has, despite its history and past prestige, experienced the same decline and denigration, the same politicization, the same loss of prestige and authority as has occurred in a number of other advanced industrial democracies. The loss of standing and prestige has no doubt been accelerated in France by the inability to institute meaningful reforms in the public sector, which has contributed to giving an image of backwardness to this sector. Public service thus no longer represents dynamism, power, or prestige.

---

[78] See Mariette Sineau and Nicolas Catzaras, "La politique se fonctionnarise," *Libération*, June 11, 2002; and Anne Cheyvialle and Christine Ducros, "Le parti de l'entreprise est majoritaire à l'Assemblée," *Le Figaro Entreprise*, June 24, 2002.

CHAPTER TEN

THE END OF THE NONPOLITICAL BUREAUCRACY

T
HE MOVEMENT toward a politically controlled bureaucracy has been led in the democratic world by the United States. It is there that the process finds its strongest expression in practice, and it is there that its intellectual justification has been developed. Where else can one expect to find public administration specialists, social scientists, or even the occasional public official engendering a debate on the merits of the spoils system?[1] Although Maranto seeks to make a number of arguments based on administration in the nineteenth century, on innovation, and on corruption, others have simply maintained that it is "rational" for leaders to want to have a bureaucracy that loyally carries out their policies. Yet, asserting the rationality of a phenomenon is not proof of rationality, nor can it put an end to a debate.

In none of the other countries that we have studied, from those that have adopted fairly ambitious public sector reform to those that have chosen a more conservative, or modest, path toward the reform of their public sector, has a government sought to make a case for the advantages of politicization. The language of responsibility, accountability, and responsiveness is uniformly invoked. The need for innovation, dynamism, and attention to client (that is, citizen) needs is also universally echoed. All these, it is implied, can be achieved by a professionally competent bureaucracy, which does not need to be replaced by a politicized bureaucratic apparatus.

Now, echoing beliefs in a professional, neutral bureaucracy does not mean that this takes pride of place in the hierarchy of a government's needs. In fact, governments have more and more come to realize, as we shall see, that there are basic inconsistencies in their requirements. An innovative, dynamic bureaucracy may be, to some extent, incompatible with contemporary methods of recruitment and promotion. Similarly, a politically responsive bureaucracy is likely to be in conflict with the objective of a neutral bureaucracy.

---

[1] See Robert Maranto, "Thinking the Unthinkable: A Case for Spoils in the Federal Bureaucracy," *Administration and Society* 29, no. 6 (January 1998): 623–43. See the debate in the same issue and Maranto's rejoinder, "Rethinking the Unthinkable: A Reply to Durant, Goodsell, Knott, and Murray on 'A Case for Spoils in Federal Personnel Management,'" *Administration and Society* 30, no. 1 (March 1998): 3–13.

Responsiveness

When the bureaucracy is called upon to be more "responsive," this may be a call to greater responsiveness to the citizens or to the people's representatives, whether in Congress or in the executive branch. If it is the former and if this implies better service in the post office or in the Bureau of Motor Vehicles, no client is going to raise objections. But responsiveness to the public rarely means only an efficient, friendly face behind the counter. Most often, it is necessary to distinguish among clients. Citizens have conflicting needs. Who should the bureaucracy listen to? On what criteria should its decisions be based? Should it listen to those who shout loudest, to those who are the most generous in financing politics, to those who exercise influence in the governing party or in the Congress?

It has been suggested that the bringing of bureaucracy into the political fray has required it to become "hyperresponsive," that is, to "respond to political demands whether or not those demands are consistent and whether or not they are expressed through politically legitimate channels."[2] Efficiency, therefore, comes to be associated with quick but selective responsiveness.

What of responsiveness to political leadership on which rationalist arguments of governance are based? When the bases for a professional bureaucracy were developed, they had as much to do with democratic governance as they did with the bureaucracy itself. Schumpeter, for example, was only interested in what bureaucracy could contribute to a democratic order. He saw the existence of a professional, nonpolitical bureaucracy as one of the foundations on which a democratic polity needed to rest. To politicize a bureaucracy, whatever advantages this may offer to a government, entails serious risk for a democratic polity. Even those who have studied the American bureaucracy and found it to be a reasonably responsive institution have sometimes raised fears about the degree of politicization. As Aberbach and Rockman have noted: "There are greater dangers in any reform that concentrates exclusively on responsiveness to political leadership. Without a sense of the civil service's independent responsibility to uphold legally constituted institutions and procedures, political control of the bureaucracy can easily go too far. Any single-minded commitment to executive energy is likely to evolve into arbitrary power."[3]

Again, it is only in the United States that there has developed the notion, not to say a coherent argument, that politicization brings a whole set of advantages to modern-day governance. In fact, Light speaks of "the

[2] Kenneth J. Meier, "Bureaucracy and Democracy: The Case for More Bureaucracy and Less Democracy," *Public Administration Review* 57, no. 3 (May–June 1997): 196.

[3] Joel D. Aberbach and Bert A. Rockman, *In the Web of Politics: Three Decades of the U.S. Federal Executive* (Washington, D.C.: Brookings Institution, 2000), 244.

vision of a permanent civil service unencumbered by politics"[4] as belonging to the past.

Governance Today and Democracy Tomorrow

The argument that political control of the bureaucracy is a necessary and understandable requirement of political leadership is not difficult to comprehend. All governments desire the bureaucracy to be an extension of the government and loyal to its agenda.

What might facilitate the task of governing today may not be what strengthens the foundations of democracy in the long run. This is one aspect that the rationalist view fails to take into account. What works for one government because it is ostensibly a rational choice will also work for the successor government. Yet, these "rational choices" for governments may be of little benefit to the democratic polity. What is good for a government may not be synonymous with what is good for democracy. As Ronald Moe observes in another context, "The political interests of a particular presidency and the institutional interests of the presidency are not necessarily congruent."[5] Presidents in the Unites States, and political leaders in other countries, have devoted considerable energy to seeking short-term benefits through controlling the bureaucracy. As Moe puts it, "The institutional capacity and legitimacy of the presidency has been weakened as presidents, beginning with Richard Nixon, have deliberately chosen to ignore the public law basis of one polity and of governmental management and have sought instead to control the executive branch through administrative fiat."[6]

European governments that have moved toward a greater degree of politicization have been loath to follow the American example, which tends to set "a layer of incompetence between elected officials and the career bureaucracy."[7] The continental practice has instead politicized the bureaucracy in an effort to preserve expertise.

Ending a Monopoly

While American political executives tend to demonstrate a disdain for bureaucratic experts, their European counterparts have tended to undermine

[4] Paul C. Light, *The Tides of Reform: Making Government Work 1945–1995* (New Haven: Yale University Press, 1997), 18.

[5] Ronald C. Moe, "The 'Reinventing Government' Exercise: Misinterpreting the Problem, Misjudging the Consequences," *Public Administration Review* 54, no. 2 (March–April 1994): 118.

[6] Ibid.

[7] Meier, "Bureaucracy and Democracy," 197.

the monopoly of senior administrators on the top posts in the bureaucracy. In the British case, while the permanent secretaries in the departments have remained civil servants, seeing changes taking place as having little effect on them,[8] the fact remains that employment through contracts has been the single most important part of the civil service reforms.[9] With some exceptions that may not remain permanent, the reforms in Britain have effectively withdrawn the monopoly of civil servants on positions within the bureaucracy.

While the abolition of a monopoly does away with a degree of expertise, that expertise may or may not be easily replaceable. Hence, continental European countries have preferred to adhere to their longstanding civil service traditions and to rely on the expertise that lies within them. They have not for all that avoided politicizing the experts and eroding the concept of bureaucratic neutrality.

The European process of injecting politics into the bureaucracy has been a slow one, and in no case have the brutal attacks or attempts at takeovers by the executive branch that characterized the Nixon or Reagan endeavors been observed in Britain, France, Germany, or Spain. Yet, in all these countries, and even in Japan, there can be observed the beginnings of a break with earlier traditions and even the acceleration of a trend that has been in the making for some time.

I turn now to an examination of the embryonic process in several countries that constitutes the beginning of the reversal of a strong civil service tradition, a tradition that has been in the making for two centuries and that culminated in the acceptance of an essentially nonpolitical, professional bureaucracy. The signs of reversal are observable even if they are not as indisputably in clear focus as they are in the United States or in France.

Japan

All democracies do not necessarily take the same road or travel at the same speed when it comes to politicization. Although I have spoken of a "process" of politicization suggesting perhaps an ineluctability, it may be more accurate to refer to the increasing pressures on bureaucracies to come under the control of party governments.

One country that has so far resisted the pressures of politicization is Japan, although, as we shall see, some changes have occurred that signal a break with past practices. But we need to bear in mind that Japan has largely been a single-party democracy since the end of World War II. The

---

[8] See R.A.W. Rhodes, "United Kingdom: 'Everybody but Us,' " in *The Changing World of Top Officials: Mandarins or Valets?* ed. R.A.W. Rhodes and Patrick Morey Weller (Buckingham: Open University Press, 2001), chap. 5.

[9] Dreyfus, *L'Invention de la Bureaucratie*, 201.

absence of party competition that generally leads to alternation in power has been absent in Japan. This in turn left the LDP "weak" in both institutional and ideational terms.

Political Appointment of Nonbureaucrats

Politicization can take several different forms: (1) increased political appointment from outside the state bureaucracy (e.g., spoils system); (2) party-politicization of elite career bureaucrats (i.e., party loyalty as a key for internal promotion); and (3) ascendance of formal and informal political advisors from outside the state bureaucracy, including "spin doctors" and think tanks (i.e., loss of monopoly in policy advice).

Japanese politicians have been severely constrained by law and custom on matters of political appointment to government posts. In fact, the only political posts available for an incoming government to fill were the premiership and other cabinet posts (up to twenty), plus the political vice-ministership.[10] This meant that the total number of appointments that a new government could make was only about forty-four.[11] In fact, even the prime minister could only appoint four loyal political supporters to his staff—the chief cabinet secretary, two deputy chief cabinet secretaries, and one personal secretary.[12]

There has been a mounting call for the reinforcement of political control over government in the 1990s. The number and status of political vice-ministers were somewhat enhanced, and this trend led to legislation in 1999 stipulating that from January 2001, coinciding with the reorganization and mergers of central ministries, the post of political vice-minister would be upgraded to deputy ministership,[13] and new positions of "minister's political officers" (MPOs) were to be created as well.[14] This

---

[10] One each per ministry, with the exception of three economic ministries, namely Finance, International Trade and Industry, and Agriculture Ministries, which got two. The lack of any real work or influence of political vice-ministers was such that they had often been referred to as "appendices." The chief cabinet secretary (a cabinet minister) was also assisted by two political deputies.

[11] In addition, each minister brings in one personal secretary, but his/her policy influence is normally nonexistent. They are often referred to as "bag carriers."

[12] The Prime Minister's Office is staffed by one more (administrative) deputy chief cabinet secretary (the highest bureaucratic position), four more administrative secretaries (always one each from the Finance, Foreign, and International Trade and Industry Ministries, and the national police agency), and a host of career bureaucrats, most of whom are on temporary loan from other ministries.

[13] The realigned ministries were to get between three (Cabinet Office) to one (Ministries of Justice and Environment, and defense agency) deputy minister each (two for all the other ministries).

[14] The Cabinet Office; the new, giant Ministry of Public Management, Home Affairs, and Posts and Telecommunications (its official English title!); the Ministry of Land, Infrastructure, and Transport (another giant, public-works ministry); and the Foreign Ministry are to have

would bring the new total of junior ministers to forty-eight. But since the number of cabinet ministers was to be cut down to fourteen (up to seventeen "in special circumstances"), at the same time the overall maximum total of political appointees under the new regime would be sixty-five.

An important cabinet reshuffle in December 2000 prepared the new team of cabinet and junior ministers that was to make the transition the following month. Prior to the reshuffle, however, there was a general expectation that a number of former bureaucrats might be appointed to be MPOs. As it turned out, the preliminary list of MPOs for the first government under the new ministerial arrangements consisted solely of junior elected politicians, but it remains to be seen whether the original intent of the reform—to enhance the political control over government bureaucrats—would really be upheld, even in the short run. The fact is that neither the LDP nor the bureaucrats have ever been keen on the idea of increased political appointments. The 1999 reform was only adopted in order to placate the then coalition partner, Ichiro Ozawa's Liberal Party, which has since moved to the opposition camp. The bureaucrats' resistance to increased political appointment is understandable. The LDP, on the other hand, would rather have its junior Diet members continue to be busily engaged in constituency service or in Diet management as foot soldiers in committees, rather than in policy formulation, as MPOs are supposed to be, especially if this was to annoy the bureaucrats.[15]

Another component of the ministerial reorganization of January 2001 was the creation of the Cabinet Office, which resulted from a merger of the existing Prime Minister's Office, the Economic Planning Agency, and Okinawa Development Agency, with the aim of strengthening the leadership role and the central coordination capacity of the prime minister.[16] Since the prime minister had been severely constrained in the past by the lack of loyal officials, the new Cabinet Office was obliged by law to draw on competent people from outside the bureaucracy as well as from inside. Out of the 1,200 officials in the Cabinet Office, the original idea was to recruit some 100 from without, including some senior appointments at the bureau-chief level. In the end, only 24 outsiders were expected to be brought in to occupy full-time positions in the Cabinet Office.[17] The highest-

---

three of these political officers each; just one for the Justice and Environment Ministries; and two each for the rest.

[15] See *Asahi Shinbun*, October 29, and November 8, 2000.

[16] The Cabinet Secretariat, too, was to be reorganized and enhanced. For instance, three new posts of assistant deputy chief cabinet secretaries were being created, although the first appointees were expected to be bureaucrats.

[17] See *Asahi Shinbun*, December 27, 2000. Nine of these were joint appointments (for instance, professors of national universities). The overall total including the part-timers was to be 130.

level outside appointment was for the director in charge of the Economic and Fiscal Council, which is responsible for the broad outlines of budget formation. This crucial post was to be given to an economist from Tokyo University, who also happened to be a former bureaucrat of the Economic Planning Agency, and who was therefore going to rejoin his former colleagues at the council secretariat. In fact, this and other appointments were not really "political" appointments, because the search had been led by bureaucrats, not politicians. It is not surprising that the people who were hired consisted mostly of friendly regulars of government councils, many of them pet academics of bureaucrats.

It is easy to see why the career bureaucrats are reluctant to lose high-ranking positions to outsiders. The ruling LDP, as a perennial governing party, save for a brief interlude in 1993–94, has always relied on the bureaucracy for policy advice, and thus simply does not have any independent outside network of policy experts that it can tap into. In addition, two features of the civil society in Japan need to be taken into account. First, Japan still lacks the extensive array of think tanks and NGOs that would give politicians, as is the case in the United States and Great Britain, access to sympathetic policy analysis. Second, lifetime employment remains the norm even today, especially among high-flyers in both the public and private sectors. There is no incentive for successful people from the private sector to take a temporary leave for a spell in the bureaucracy.

There is now a plan in the LDP-led government to extend outside appointments to other ministries as well so that those ministers can add political appointees to their staff.[18] Although the pressure for political appointment appears on the increase, the parasitic nature of the LDP has so far allowed the bureaucracy to slow down the process with considerable success.

Party Politicization of Elite Bureaucrats

It is no secret that the Japanese elite bureaucracy has always had conservative political inclinations, even though the public front of a neutral civil service was relatively easy to maintain, thanks to the complete absence of alternation in power over almost four decades. An indication of its broad identification with the LDP can be found in the fact that, until the mid-1990s, virtually all of the bureaucrats-turned-politicians (who were numerous) entered politics with an LDP label. Even though this indicates a form of uniform politicization, it seems fair to say that party identification was generally restrained. The ministries also largely retained their autonomy over personnel management and promotion, although loyalty to the powerbro-

---

[18] The idea was approved by the cabinet on December 1, 2000, but this would require further legislation, and it was not certain how committed the LDP was to this idea.

kers inside the LDP was assumed to be a requirement of high-ranking officials. The LDP leadership did have veto power over senior appointments,
but overt meddling with bureaucratic promotion remained nevertheless an
exception rather than the rule. Nonetheless, the Japanese bureaucracy has
been an integral part of the Japanese ruling coalition and an integral part of
the society's elite networks. It is what Pempel referred to as "integration
without polarization."[19] Ellis Krause, more recently, has observed that the
strengths of this institution are also closely tied to its weaknesses: "Its elite
recruitment and internal *esprit de corps* also produce its factiousness; its autonomy from politicians in economic policy-making is made possible by a
great degree of partisan polarization in non-economic areas; its national interest goals are not only constrained, but also achieved, even defined, by
dense informal networks with private societal groups."[20]

There was no major upheaval when Morihiro Hosokawa's seven-party
coalition government took over from the LDP in 1993. Some of the new
ministers were completely lacking in government experience and so were
obliged to rely on the advice of the senior bureaucrats already in place.
Moreover, key ministerial posts were occupied by those who had bolted
from the LDP with Ozawa. In one publicized case, a close aide of Ozawa,
who was appointed minister of international trade and industry (and himself a former MITI official), openly intervened in a senior appointment,
but that was the only such case.

Perhaps a more significant development for party politicization of the
bureaucracy was that the LDP was no longer the only party in the center-
right. Bureaucrats would soon enter politics with Ozawa's blessing,
through what is the Democratic Party of Japan today, or via the LDP.

Nevertheless, the LDP's spell in opposition, which lasted a year, was too
short to leave a lasting impact on party politicization of elite bureaucrats.
There was one case, however, where the perceived closeness of certain bureaucrats with Ozawa and his political allies led to significant consequences. Of course, very close personal ties between conservative political
leaders and elite bureaucrats were nothing new in Japan, but the backdrop
of alternation in power was. While the LDP was in opposition, the leadership of the Ministry of Finance teamed up rather openly with Ozawa, the
new political master of Hosokawa government.[21] In particular, the Min-

---

[19] T. J. Pempel, "Organizing for Efficiency: The Higher Civil Service in Japan," in *Bureaucrats and Policy-Making: A Comparative Overview*, ed. Ezra Suleiman (New York: Holmes &
Meier, 1984), 78.

[20] Ellis S. Krause, "Japan: Divided Bureaucracy in a Unified Regime," in *Bureaucracy and
the Modern State,* ed. Jon Pierre (Brookfield, Vt.: Edward Elgar, 1995), 137.

[21] See for instance, Koichi Nakano, "The Politics of Administrative Reform in Japan,
1993–1998: Toward a More Accountable Government?" *Asian Survey* 38, no. 3 (March
1998): esp. 294–95.

istry of Finance invited the wrath of the LDP over the 1994 budget, particularly as the LDP strongly resented the "cold" and "arrogant" attitude
of the Ministry of Finance now that it was in opposition. Inconveniently
for the Ministry of Finance, the LDP was back in power supporting a
Socialist prime minister in coalition by June 1994. The then secretary-
general of the LDP was so angered by some Ministry of Finance leaders
that they were banned from his office for some time. Incurring the dis-
pleasure of the LDP turned out to be extremely damaging for the Finance
Ministry since it lost crucial protection from its political masters at a time
when it came under unprecedented criticisms ranging from economic
mismanagement that led to various charges of corruption and scandals.[22]

It bears emphasizing, however, that Japan has yet to see the emergence
of openly "pro-LDP" or "pro-Socialist" bureaucrats who vie for fast promotion thanks to their party identification and loyalty. Even the demotion
or firing of bureaucrats who are disliked is still rather rare, although politicians can and do veto or delay the appointment of these officials at times.

Political Advisors

Morihiro Hosokawa, the first non-LDP prime minister in thirty-eight
years, was also the first to bring an advisor with him to office in 1993. In
this instance, however, his one advisor (a close political aide) had no legal
status and remained unpaid. Subsequent legislation formalized the
arrangement, and made it possible for a prime minister to appoint up to
three advisors from outside the bureaucracy. To be sure, no prime minister has ever utilized all three posts,[23] and the appointment of advisors was
never extended to other cabinet ministers.

All Diet members, including ministers, are also entitled to a subsidized
"policy secretary." This provision was meant to strengthen the policy-
making capacity of politicians, but in practice these policy secretaries are
usually no different from the bag-carrying personal secretaries of old.

Of course, all ministers have always been able to receive the advice of a
host of governmental advisory councils. The actual nature of these advisory councils varies considerably,[24] but ministers have invariably had only
nominal control over them, and they do not normally get to pick their

[22] It may be argued that this was one of the reasons why the Finance Ministry was ultimately unable to defend its organizational integrity, and lost much of regulatory control over
the financial sector to what is now the Financial Services Agency.

[23] As of January 2001, the prime minister could appoint up to five advisors, but Mori, the
first prime minister under the new regime, appointed only one.

[24] See Frank J. Schwartz, *Advice and Consent: The Politics of Consultation in Japan* (New York:
Cambridge University Press, 1998) for a well-informed account of advisory councils.

members.[25] A partial exception to this rule occurs when the prime minister gets to create a high-powered council directly under his leadership.[26] The best example of such a council was the Second Provisional Council on Administrative Reform (*Rincho*) during Yasuhiro Nakasone's premiership in the 1980s that privatized Japan's national corporations. It appears to be the case that recent prime ministers (from Hashimoto to Obuchi to Mori) have shown an increased appetite for such high-profile councils, with the undoubted expectation that they would help to shore up their leadership (or at least appear to). Their real impact on policy has ranged from relative success to quiet failure.[27]

Spin doctors and think tanks, two other aspects of policy advice that are prominent in the United States and Great Britain, are not nearly as important in Japan. In fact, the very concept of "spin" simply has not entered the Japanese vocabulary as yet, and press secretaries are virtually nonexistent. To a large extent, this is because Japanese politicians, including ministers, have long been protected by the cocoonlike "closed shops" of press clubs.[28] On the other hand, independent policy think tanks are still relatively few in Japan. Most of those that do exist tend to have ties either with a government ministry or with major financial *keiretsu*.[29] The few that are truly independent are not infrequently little more than ephemeral vehicles for powerful individuals.

A Creeping Politicization?

Despite some real challenges to the morale, integrity, and autonomy of the bureaucracy, politicization has been relatively subdued in Japan so far. The LDP, Japan's perennial governing party except for a brief interlude in 1993–94, has always relied on the bureaucracy to govern and to stay in power. While their relationship is by no means tension-free, the LDP has generally been more interested in staying in power and in enjoying the fruits of power than in confronting the bureaucracy with a coherent policy

[25] Bureaucrats commonly decide who gets appointed to join these councils, and sometimes even control the proceedings as well. At other times, civil society actors, such as industry associations, trade unions, or academic experts, may play crucial roles.

[26] See Schwartz, *Advice and Consent*, chap. 3.

[27] Relative successes include the Decentralization Promotion Commission, and the Administrative Reform Conference, which Hashimoto himself led.

[28] See Laurie Anne Freeman, *Closing the Shop: Information Cartels and Japan's Mass Media* (Princeton: Princeton University Press, 2000) for a detailed account of Japan's prevalent press clubs.

[29] The think tanks that are backed by financial institutions naturally tend to focus on such things as economic forecasting.

program of its own. Bureaucrats would help the LDP live, and it would let them live in turn. The LDP's raison d'être has essentially been to hold on to power. Much less important has been the use to which it puts this power.

Ever since its foundation in 1955, the LDP has always been an extremely broad church, earning itself a nickname as a super catch-all party. While broadly conservative, its membership has ranged from center-left liberals to old-style right-wingers who never came to terms with the defeat of war. Lacking a coherent ideational backbone, even its electoral platforms have usually been crafted with extensive help from the bureaucrats.

The LDP's institutional coherence has also remained rather weak. Factions and *zoku* (policy-sector "tribe") politicians embody the fragmented and decentralized structure of this party. The party president, who is usually also the prime minister, is at best only one of the party bosses. Party structure is virtually nonexistent at the constituency level, and each politician relies on his/her personal support groups for electoral campaigning, where personality and pork barrels feature more prominently than policy ideas.

Party competition in Japan, at least until recently, did not present any realistic prospect of alternation in power, allowing the perennial governing party to stay in power without having to forge some real party coherence. If politicization of the bureaucracy commonly occurs through the need of political parties to make their electoral promises come true in the face of potential bureaucratic resistance, or through the need of finding employment for political sympathizers who helped craft the winning campaign platform, neither of these pressures really existed for the LDP in the past. Indeed, it may be argued that, to the extent to which these pressures are now being felt by Japanese political parties, this new development is largely due to the increased party competition and the real possibility of alternation in power in post-1993 Japan. And genuine party competition is likely to speed up the process of appointing the "faithful" and "loyal" civil servants.

Britain

We have already seen some of the spectacular changes, sometimes known as "Raynerism" or "Thatcherism," that were imposed on the civil service. Perhaps in no country outside the United States was the civil service the object of such virulent attacks by its own executive chiefs. Thatcher's visceral hatred of the civil service is well known and has been well documented. It had little to do with inefficiency and waste, and much to do with the welfare, Keynesian-Beveridgite policies that the civil service did so much to put in place. In addition, it was run by a privileged class that constituted an obstacle to change and that represented the consensus that had brought Britain to such depths.[30] With such views, it was not surprising that Thatcher would seek not to work with or respect the civil servants that epitomized the consensus that she was seeking to overturn.

Civil servants in Great Britain have never been politicized, nor did they become so under Thatcher, at least not politicized in the American, Spanish, French, or Italian modes. They were not asked to play political roles. They continued to steer clear of the overtly political institutions and forces. In fact, as Clifford and Wright note, "At no moment was there a purge or an attempt to appoint political allies to the civil service. The Conservative government never felt the need to introduce into Whitehall ministerial cabinets or staffs composed of civil servants favorable to the Conservative party."[31] Political control in Britain, then, did not involve the need to assure the responsiveness of the civil service by appointing at the top, as Nixon had done, or by appointing at different levels, as Reagan had done, people who shared their views and agendas.

The objective of the Conservative Party, in particular of Thatcher, was in reality not different from that of other executives determined to render the bureaucratic apparatus responsive to them. Having been elected by universal suffrage, all executives quite understandably feel they have a mandate to carry out a program. The bureaucracy has to be a loyal instrument for the carrying out of this mandate.

Thatcher accepted to some extent Rayner's view that "Whitehall was rich in officials wishing to probe and to innovate who found themselves smothered by the system."[32] Perhaps she would never have expressed such a kind view of the "class" that she so thoroughly detested. But since there was no question of wholesale removals of personnel or the introduction of any kind of a spoils system, whether of the American or French variety, Thatcher sought to change the system rather than merely those who manned the civil service. And in so doing, she broke the final link of the civil service to the original principles on which it had been based.[33]

How, then, did Margaret Thatcher proceed to politicize the civil service? First, she did so through the method put into practice by Reagan,

[30] See Peter Hennessy, *Whitehall* (London: Fontana Press, 1989), 589–635.

[31] Christopher Clifford and Vincent Wright, "La politisation de l'Administration britannique: ambitions, limites et problèmes conceptuels," *Revue Française d'Administration Publique* 86 (April–June 1998): 268.

[32] Hennessy, *Whitehall*, 596.

[33] For a discussion of the Northcotte-Trevelyan ideas, see the discussion in Bernard S. Silberman, *Cages of Reason: The Rise of the Rational State in France, Japan, the United States, and Great Britain* (Chicago: University of Chicago Press, 1993), 350–62.

which consisted of essentially reducing the functions, size, and budgets of the bureaucracy. The measure of privatization brought down the number of civil servants from 762,000 in 1976 to 481,000 in 1998.[34] Clearly, the more Thatcher succeeded in rolling back the state, the less the civil service would have to do.[35]

The second method through which Thatcher aimed at weakening the higher civil service and gaining greater political control was through the ambitious reform of the "Next Steps" program. A parliamentary committee called the reform "the most ambitious attempt at Civil Service reform in the twentieth century," which Robin Butler, a former head of the civil service, said was an accurate depiction.[36] Butler characterized this reform as one that aimed at "changing the organization of the service from an essentially horizontal basis of large, monolithic departments sharing common staff conditions, pay and grading structures and working practices, to a much more vertical basis of small, core policy departments each with its own Executive Agencies."[37]

The creation of agencies is, as we have already seen, the way Britain chose to get around the constraints of the civil service system. These agencies are headed by agency chief executives and not by traditional civil servants recruited through the competitive examinations. It remains the case that 60 percent of the agency chief executives are still civil servants. However, 40 percent are not. As Robin Butler put it, "We no longer have the expectation that civil servants should be recruited directly after education."[38] This has allowed the recruitment of people from outside the service. Indeed, civil servants in England, unlike in most countries, no longer have a civil service ministry. This was abolished by Thatcher shortly after she became prime minister.

The third aspect of politicization in Great Britain involves nominations. Whereas the hallowed tradition of the British civil service has been the permanence of the top civil servants in a ministry (both during government changes and during party government changes), there have been serious inroads made into reducing the power of these officials. The Next Steps program, as well as other reforms introduced by Thatcher, had as one of their aims the assertion of political control over the administrative machine.

---

[34] R.A.W. Rhodes, "New Labour's Civil Service: Summing-Up Joining-Up," *Political Quarterly* 71, no. 2 (April–June 2000): 152.

[35] This is, as I have argued, the political objective of NPM in the United States.

[36] Robin Butler, "The Evolution of the Civil Service—A Progress Report," *Public Administration* 71 (autumn 1993): 400.

[37] Ibid.

[38] Ibid., 402.

It is the case that all governments that come to power after a lengthy period in the opposition fear that the civil service will be too closely identified with the previous regime and will thwart the program of the new government. What Thatcher believed in 1979 was no different from what Attlee or Wilson were warned of when they became prime ministers. But all governments have made their peace with the civil service, and few governments had reason to complain of disloyalty or, worse still, sabotage. Thatcher, who already had her set of grievances against the civil service, was taking no chances, if only because she accused the civil service of sharing the consensus ideology that not only characterized the Labour Party but also a good part of her own party. Besides, as Hennessy observed, "Always ready to exempt those who served her closely, Mrs. Thatcher nonetheless detests senior civil servants as a breed."[39]

Did Thatcher politicize the civil service? Some analysts have taken the view that she wanted a completely tamed civil service and ended up creating a civil service that is "a thoroughly Thatcherized satrapy."[40] Clifford and Wright have also pointed to some of Thatcher's nominations that they claim were inspired by political considerations.[41] Others have argued that there has so far not been "overt *politicization* of appointments to the senior Civil Service."[42] Rhodes observes that the issue of politicization did not die with the resignation of Thatcher: "When New Labour appointed fifty-three political advisers, compared with thirty-eight under the previous government, it threw petrol on the dying embers of the politicization debate, as did the (abandoned) attempt to appoint Jonathan Powell, Blair's chief of staff, as his principal private secretary (a post normally filled by a civil servant). . . . Some senior civil servants fear that, with open competition and contracts, the era of political appointments to the top job is already with us."[43]

Whether Thatcher began the process of politicization and whether this process has speeded up under New Labour should not get tangled up in issues of definition. What appears abundantly clear is that Thatcher successfully stormed a citadel, one she considered to be not so much a partisan institution as a privileged, docile, consensus-loving institution. In so doing, she deprived the higher civil service of its claim on particularly important jobs and its right to a monopoly over the top policy-making positions. Several consequences have ensued from the reforms that have been at times imposed on, and at times willingly agreed to, by the civil service.

[39] Hennessy, *Whitehall*, 592.
[40] Cited in Rhodes, "New Labour's Civil Service," 158.
[41] Clifford and Wright, "La politisation de l'administration britannique," 274–75.
[42] Rhodes, "New Labour's Civil Service," 158, italics in original.
[43] Ibid.

What was accomplished in the Thatcher years has been reinforced by Tony Blair's government. Blair has centralized decision-making by seeking greater control over Whitehall. Not only has policy-making been centralized in the prime minister's office, but the Treasury has asserted its control over the ministries by forcing them to adhere to spending targets that are now negotiated every three years instead of the previous annual negotiating procedure. The process of centralization has come to be known as the replacement of the "percolator with a *cafetière*," that is, "strong pressure from above, infusing the policies and actions of the department below. . . . The big decisions are no longer hammered out around the committee tables"[44] but by the prime minister's office. The consequence of this has been for the chief executive to rely on a few trusted aides and to reduce civil servants' input into policy-making. And since policy formation is now separated from policy implementation, the role of the civil servant has been drastically reduced. The result led to what has been seen as "a cultural revolution."[45]

Second, the creation of agencies inevitably opened up the civil service to non–civil service nominations. Whether agencification was, or turned out to be, a form of politicization is immaterial. What matters is that it brought to an end the monopoly that the civil service had come to enjoy over the top positions in the state apparatus. It also brought to an end the monopoly that the civil service enjoyed as a "political advisor."[46]

In seeking non–civil servants as managers, the governments of the past twenty years have effectively done away with the civil service monopoly and created a new form of patronage. It has, in effect, transformed the role of the civil servant into a manager. The aim has been to make the civil service more efficient, but, more importantly, it has been to make the civil service more in tune with or responsive to the government of the day, an obsession of every U.S. president. Since the higher civil servant has lost his role as a policy initiator, he no longer dares propose policy initiatives to his minister. He tends to spend more of his time being asked to put out fires. As one permanent secretary put it, "Management? My job isn't management. The Secretary of State comes in and says 'I'm in a hole! Get me out of it!' That's my job."[47]

The insistence on responsiveness leads inevitably to, in one form or another, politicization or, at any rate, a form of deprofessionalization. One of the most serious consequences of this is that "there is no clear dividing line between policy and operations," and this undermines "ministerial

---

[44] *The Economist*, August 21, 1999, 47.

[45] Ibid.

[46] Ibid., 159.

[47] Cited in Kevin Theakston, *Leadership in Whitehall* (New York: St. Martin's Press, 1999), 258.

accountability to Parliament by helping ministers avoid blame. In short, British government has undergone a significant decrease in political accountability."[48]

Third, the political takeover of the civil service in Britain has affected morale in much the same way that has been the case in the United States. As Theakston observed, "There is now less group self-confidence within the mandarinate than there was forty or fifty years ago, a factor which has an important bearing on the leadership task in Whitehall."[49]

Finally, again as in the United States and France, the politico-managerial role has left civil servants exposed in the same way, as Theakston notes, that politicians are exposed. Indeed, the "higher public profile"[50] of civil servants has allowed politicians, as Rhodes notes, "to take the credit when the policy goes well but to blame the chief executive when things go wrong."[51] In the pre-Thatcher years, the chief merit of higher civil servants was described by Sisson as their "nonentity," by which he meant their essential nonexistence insofar as the public was concerned.[52]

It is true that civil service "nonentity" or anonymity went hand-in-hand with the doctrine of ministerial responsibility. But could ministers logically be held responsible for everything that occurred in their ministries? Did this not tend to induce civil service irresponsibility? This explains why the Next Steps program placed as a priority not only the delegation of managerial and budgetary power with the delivery services but, equally important, as Hennessy put it, "quash[ing] the fiction that ministers can be genuinely responsible for *everything* done by officials in their name."[53]

The reforms of the civil service over the past two decades are yet to be evaluated. Privatization, deregulation, and agencification have not been able to stem the degradation of British public services. It may be that the tide against anything connected with the state has been stemmed: for the first time in two decades, the major parties competed over which would spend more to restore confidence in public services. The decline of public services can be linked to the practice of deprofessionalization of public service and to the denigration of all public functions. This is a direct consequence of NPM.

It has been suggested that Thatcher did not select people merely because they shared her political beliefs. "Rather, people were selected because they fitted in, in some way or other. Mrs. Thatcher asked 'are they one of us?' But she did not mean, 'are they conservatives?' She wanted

---

[48] Ibid., 159.

[49] Ibid., 257.

[50] Ibid., 259.

[51] Rhodes, "New Labour's Civil Service," 158.

[52] C. H. Sisson, *The Spirit of British Administration* (London: Faber and Faber, 1959).

[53] Hennessy, *Whitehall*, 620, italics in original.

a style of action; the can-do manager."[54] This may well have been the case, but the disdain for public servants in general, the substitution of criteria for recruitment and promotion, the ambiguity of "are they one of us?"—all this has come to involve a change of mentality that has occasioned the beginning of politicization of the civil service, more subtle that what occurs in other countries, but real nonetheless. Dreyfus, who has studied the British reforms closely, concluded that the effect of the Thatcher reforms has directly attacked the principle of neutrality, but that in the end, these reforms "seem to have as their effect, even if this is not openly avowed, the return to a patronage, or worse still, a clientelistic system."[55]

But even analysts who see considerable continuity between the pre-Thatcher era and today have observed that the reforms in the civil service since 1980 have created the twin dilemma of "a fragmented civil service and politicization."[56] The first occurs because of the dispersion of responsibilities within and across departments. How does coordination in the midst of decentralization take place? With regards to politicization, "the dilemma is to reconcile a permanent, anonymous, neutral bureaucracy with the pressures from politicians for appointees who can deliver on the government's promises."[57] Because it is a telling commentary on current trends, I quote at length one of Rhodes's interviewees, himself a high-ranking member of the civil service:

> I am pessimistic about the future of the non-political civil service. I think it is in its last five or seven years. I think it will survive until after the election. I would not be confident it would last another parliament. I mean there is a perfectly respectable argument that ministers are entitled to look for a degree of commitment to their policies from their principal advisers that is incompatible with a non-political service. On the other hand I think there are great strengths in our system. Somebody has to ask the skeptical questions. I don't think it has happened yet though I think there is a bit of a shadow there. Some of the younger officials see their future lying in demonstrating their passion for politics. That is natural. A thrusting young guy of 40 or something, to show yourself enthusiastic about government that looks as though it is going to be there for another seven, eight, nine years, it is a very natural thing to do. So that is why I am gloomy about it.[58]

---

[54] R.A.W. Rhodes and Patrick Weller, "Conclusion: Antipodean Exception, European Traditionalism," in Rhodes and Weller, *The Changing World*, chap. 8.

[55] Dreyfus, *L'Invention de la Bureaucratie*, 254.

[56] R.A.W. Rhodes, "United Kingdom: 'Everybody But Us!'" in Rhodes and Weller, *The Changing World*, 149.

[57] Ibid., 150.

[58] Ibid.

No country has come close to the United States in making a case for politicization. Not only do politicians in the U.S. not shrink from declaring their
preferences for their "own people," but they have found allies capable of providing the necessary intellectual arguments for their case. That this does not
occur in other countries does not mean that their political systems do not
practice it. Even if governments in Britain have been measured in their attempts to replace civil servants with their own appointees, the fact remains
that, as Rhodes and Weller, who do not share the view of increasing politicization in the British Civil Service, observe: "The efforts of ministers to
reassert control over the civil service is a common feature of recent public
reform in Westminster systems. Under New Labour, there has been a notable
increase in political advisors to 78, especially in the No. 10 Policy Unit."[59]

Germany

"The classical bureaucrat . . . has never been as important in Germany as foreign students of Max Weber have come to think," concluded two German
scholars after having studied the German bureaucracy closely in the 1980s.[60]
In line with their conclusion, the civil service in Germany is generally considered to be less neutral than the civil service in Britain. Unlike in the
British system, civil servants in Germany are allowed to be members of political parties. Career crossovers from the civil service to politics and back
again are accepted and even encouraged. Moreover, German law permits
ministers, using political criteria, to hire and fire bureaucrats for the two top
positions within the federal ministerial administration. Nonetheless, the civil
service in Germany is far less political than its American counterpart, since
the German bureaucracy is firmly based on promotion within a career system and has not experienced an influx of outsiders into its ranks.

Without disputing the generally accepted view of the relative nonpoliticization of the German civil service in comparison with that of other democratic polities, we nevertheless need to account for changes over time
within the German system itself. The aim of this discussion is to allow us
to answer the question of whether the civil service in Germany has become
more politicized in the postwar era.

The German civil service system, which has been aptly described as
a "career system with loopholes,"[61] has without doubt become more

---

[59] Ibid., 115.

[60] Renate Mayntz and Hans-Ulrich Derlien, "Party Patronage and Politicization of the
West German Administrative Elite 1970–1987—Toward Hybridization?" *Governance* 2, no.
4 (1989): 396.

[61] Hans Ulrich Derlien, "Repercussions of Government Change on the Career Civil
Service in West Germany: The Cases of 1969 and 1982" *Governance* 1, no. 1 (1998): 55.

politicized on the two elite levels of the federal bureaucracy. We have strong evidence suggesting that politicians are making increasing use of one of the loopholes in the civil service career system, namely, the right to send elite bureaucrats on temporary retirement and promote political allies. Moreover, we expect this trend to continue and be self-reinforcing according to a logic that has been termed "patronage cycles."[62] Since similar arrangements for temporary retirement exist at the Länder level, politicization of the bureaucracy at the state level is likely to mirror that of the federal level. Second, there is reason to conclude from an analysis of promotion within the German bureaucracy that there is a "chimney-effect"[63] triggered by the politicization of the elite civil service. The chimney effect means that civil servants in lower ranks of the bureaucracy, where the procedures for hiring and firing have fewer loopholes, will have stronger incentives to emphasize their party preferences and develop their political skills than do civil servants in a system that is neutral all the way to the top. A third aspect pointing to the increasing politicization of the bureaucracy in Germany derives from the increasing reliance of politicians, both on federal and Länder levels, over the last decade on networks other than the traditional bureaucracy for advice.

The debate concerning the relationship between politicians and bureaucrats in Germany has centered mostly around two concepts. First, should the concept of politicization be understood as the growing importance of party affiliation over expertise or seniority for determining appointments to the higher civil service? If so, what effect does this have for the career patterns of civil servants?[64] Second, should it be viewed as the consequence of hybridization, which refers to the blurring of the distinction between politicians and civil servants? Hybridization generally means the similarity in background and training that bureaucrats and politicians receive. It also refers to the interchangeability of the two careers, as well as to the convergence in role-perceptions of politicians and bureaucrats.[65] As in our analysis of politicization of other countries, our evidence for politicization relies on the use and abuse of temporary retirements, the recruitment of outsiders, civil servants' own perceptions of politicization, career crossovers

---

[62] Mayntz and Derlien, "Party Patronage," 400.

[63] Derlien, "Repercussions of Government Change," 55.

[64] See, for example, Joel D. Aberbach, Robert D. Putnam, and Bert A. Rockman, *Bureaucrats and Politicians in Western Democracies* (Cambridge: Harvard University Press, 1981); and Hans-Ulrich Derlien, "Compétence bureaucratique et allégeance politiques en Allemagne," in *Le Recruitement des Élites en Europe*, ed. Ezra Suleiman and Henri Mendras (Paris: La Découverte, 1995).

[65] See Mayntz and Derlien, "Party Patronage," 384–404; and Joel D. Aberbach, Hans-Ulrich Derlien, Renate Mayntz, and Bert A. Rockman, "American and German Federal Executives—Technocratic and Political Attitudes," *ISSJ* 123 (1990): 3–17.

(from the civil service into politics), role-perceptions of civil servants and politicians, and the use of advice from outside the civil service.

Temporary Retirement

In Germany, state secretaries and division heads (*Ministerialdirektoren*)— the two top positions of the federal civil service—can be fired at the whim of the minister in office. More precisely, a minister has the right to remove civil servants holding these positions by sending them into temporary retirement. The minister also exercises considerable discretion regarding whom he or she appoints, though those holding the two top positions must be career civil servants or meet the civil service requirements. The 150 bureaucrats who occupy, or who aspire to occupy, one of these two top positions are therefore to a large extent dependent upon political or personal bonds with the minister for being promoted or for maintaining their position. Reflecting their close relationship with politics and politicians, elite bureaucrats in this special category are called political civil servants (*Politische Beamte*). The legal institution of political civil servants is old, dating back to 1852, and is in itself not a reflection of increasing politicization in Germany in the postwar period. However, there is clear evidence that political affiliation has become more important as a criterion for holding a position as a political civil servant. That is, ministers have during the last thirty years made increasing use of their discretionary powers when hiring or firing political civil servants.

The most dramatic changes in the top positions of the bureaucracy have taken place following the three major changes in government in 1969, 1982, and 1998. Derlien's data show that the replacement rates of political civil servants increased with each of the three main changes in government. When Helmut Schmidt's SPD-led government took office in 1969, his government replaced 33 percent of the political civil servants. The CDU-led government under Helmut Kohl replaced 37.5 percent of them when they entered office in 1982. By comparison, the recent government takeover by Gerhard Schröder's coalition of the SPD and the Greens in September 1998 led to the replacement of 52.2 percent of the political civil servants.[66] The high replacement rate after the last government change was partly made possible by the special circumstances surrounding the change of governments in 1998. It was the first time in the postwar period that there was a complete change in government. All previous governments had included the FDP. In addition, it was the first time that the Greens joined a government. The high replacement rate of political civil

---

[66] Hans-Ulrich Derlien, "Personalpolitik nach Regierungswechseln," in *Regieren nach Wahlen*, ed. Hans-Ulrich Derlien and Axel Murswieck (Opladen: Leske & Budrich, 2001), 51.

TABLE 10.1

Party Membership of Political Civil Servants and Subdivision Heads,
1970–1987 (percent)

Party	Year	State Secretary	Division Head	Subdivision Head
CDU/CSU	1987	61.5	47.2	17.8
	1981	0.0	8.9	10.0
	1972	0.0	13.6	13.0
SPD	1987	0.0	7.5	22.2
	1981	60.0	37.8	24.3
	1972	42.9	25.0	14.1
FDP	1987	7.7	9.4	8.9
	1981	0.0	13.3	11.4
	1972	42.9	2.3	3.5
Nonmember	1987	30.8	35.8	51.1
	1981	40.0	40.0	54.3
	1970	14.3	14.3	69.4

Source: Renate Mayntz and Hans-Ulrich Derlien, "Party Patronage and Politicization of the West German Administrative Elite 1970–1987—Toward Hybridization?" *Governance* 2, no. 4 (1989): 388.

servants cannot only be explained by the special circumstances surrounding the 1998 coalition, because there is sufficient evidence to show that the increasing importance of party affiliation within the civil services preceded the 1998 change in government.

Table 10.1 shows party membership according to position as state secretary, division head, and subdivision head between 1970 and 1987. Unlike the first two positions, subdivision heads are not political civil servants and are thus not subject to temporary retirement. In 1972, 42.9 percent of the state secretaries belonged to the main governing party, the SPD, and by the end of the term the number of SPD members among state secretaries had increased to 60 percent. No state secretaries were members of the CDU/CSU in 1972 and in 1981. Similarly, no SPD members were state secretaries in 1987. Complete government dominance of the highest rank in the civil service was also the case in 1998 when nineteen state secretaries belonged to the SPD and five were recruited from the membership lists of the Greens.[67]

Similar to our observation about state secretaries, table 10.1 shows that party affiliation was important for division heads as well. However, at the position below state secretaries the exclusion of civil servants from the

[67] Derlien,"Personalpolitik nach Regierungswechseln," 42.

opposition party was *not* absolute between 1970 and 1987. In 1981, 37.8 percent of division heads were members of the main governing party, the SPD, while 8.9 percent belonged to the main opposition party, the CDU. By contrast, in 1987, as many as 47.2 percent of the division heads were members of the main governing party (CDU), and only 7.2 percent were members of the main opposition party (SPD). For the special category of political civil servants, there is therefore evidence that the governing party not only has felt entitled to select party sympathizers, but that this was done to a large extent prior to the 1998 change of government.

A growing degree of politicization among top bureaucrats is made possible, on the one hand, by more extensive use of the legal provision to send political civil servants into temporary retirement, or through other ways that involve interruption of the careers of civil servants. On the other hand, selective promotion to positions that become vacant or efforts to bring in outsiders reinforce the trend toward politicization. Derlien reports that there has been a general decline in uninterrupted careers of all civil servants to the extent that by 1999 less than one-third of political civil servants had uninterrupted careers.[68] Moreover, studies of government changes in 1969, 1982, and 1998 show that the use of temporary retirement increased both for state secretaries and division heads. During the first SPD government, thirty-three state secretaries and division heads were temporarily retired. In 1982 the number of temporary retirements reached forty-two, while in 1998 the comparable number was as high as sixty-five.[69]

The importance of temporary retirement as a means of allowing a government to bring in its "own people" is shown by a comparison of the political civil servants with the subdivision heads, who cannot be sent on temporary retirement. Table 10.1 shows that more subdivision heads were members of the opposition party (SPD) than of the government party (CDU) in 1987. The same trend was true for subdivision heads in 1970. An equal number were members of the opposition party (CDU) as of the government party (SPD). However, selective promotion, or new subscription to the SPD's party lists, worked over time to bring subdivision heads into line with the party in government. The percentage of subdivision heads who were members of the main governing party increased from 11.1 percent in 1970 to 24.3 percent in 1981. In 1981 the SPD members also clearly outnumbered members of the opposition party in the nonpolitical civil servant category of subdivision heads. This evidence suggests that politicization is taking place also at the level of bureaucrats who hold the rank below the political civil servant category.

---

[68] Hans-Ulrich Derlien, "Unorthodox Employment in the German Public Service," *International Review of Administrative Sciences* 65 (1999): 13–23.

[69] Derlien, "Personalpolitik nach Regierungswechseln," 48.

We should expect that administrations at the Länder level develop according to the same "patronage cycles" as the federal administration, since all of them, except Bavaria, allow temporary retirement for top ministerial positions, heads of regional authorities, and heads of police. Moreover, a civil service reform in 1997 allowed for probation appointment for top jobs in both federal and Länder administrations, and this exacerbates political influence over final appointments. As Derlien points out, however, probation appointments affect mostly about one thousand headmasters and university chancellors—positions where responsiveness to politicians is generally considered of minor importance in modern democracies.[70]

Outside Recruitment

Instead of—or in addition to—selective promotion, recruiting outsiders is an important way for politicians to insure that they are able to work with party loyalists. According to Goetz, the political support units are the most common avenues into the top positions in the German bureaucracy for outsiders (*Seiteneinsteigern*). Political support units grew in size and importance in the period from the 1970s to the 1990s.[71] The Press and Information Office, the Office for Cabinet and Parliamentary Affairs, the Minister's Office, and personal assistants are usually included in the political support units. Most often these offices are situated outside the organizational hierarchy of the civil service, and recruitment to them thus usually takes place outside the formalized selection procedures.

Although the entrance criteria are restrictive, it has been shown that these regulations are "easily circumvented by offering the new recruits the status of ordinary public employees (*Angestellte*) rather than civil servants, with the flexibility that employment contracts governed by general labor law afford."[72] Press spokesmen are often recruited by such circumvention of the rules. They are usually professional journalists who get hired as public employees. But outsiders face some hurdles if they wish to be integrated into the civil service after having worked for a particular minister. There are restrictive guidelines, adopted by the Federal Personnel Committee (*Bundespersonalausschuss*), regarding the admission of outsiders into the civil service. In general, an outsider receives a rank and a wage level below that which is given to a career civil servant holding the same function. The restrictive entrance criteria, along with the restrictions on promotion of outsiders, are part of the explanation why there was no

[70] Derlien, "Unorthodox Employment in the German Public Service," 13–23.
[71] Klaus H. Goetz, "Acquiring Political Craft: Training Grounds for Top Officials in the German Core Executive," *Public Administration* 75 (1997): 753–75.
[72] Ibid., 766.

increase in the number of outsiders who were brought in when the government changed in 1969, 1982, and 1998. In all three cases, about 20 percent of the top bureaucrats were brought in from the outside.[73]

Perception of Politicization

German civil servants believe in increasing numbers that the civil service has become more politicized. Derlien and Mayntz have shown that in 1987 more than eight out of ten civil servants in the federal administration thought that the bureaucracy was either definitely or to some extent politicized. This total number had increased from 55 percent in 1970 to 86 percent in 1987. The perception of politicization extended beyond the ranks of political civil servants. In fact, a larger percentage of the lower ranks perceived politicization than those of higher rank. Almost 94 percent of civil servants below the rank of subdivision head perceived politicization in 1987, whereas the corresponding number for state secretaries was 84 percent.[74] It is possible that the civil servants of higher ranks felt more restricted when answering the question about politicization, and that the higher percentage noted in the lower ranks thus is an artifact of the questionnaire. Another possible explanation is that the rank effect is a sign of politicized promotion. Thus, it may be that the civil servants in the lower ranks felt the selective promotion strategies more strongly than the political civil servants, since they had not yet managed to reach the top positions in the system. Regardless of how we interpret the rank effect, the proportion of civil servants who perceived the system as politicized in 1987 is considerable. Moreover, there is evidence that the number who admitted that they perceived politicization had increased, although the data may not be completely comparable since it was gathered by different teams using different samples.[75]

The data on perceived politicization tend to confirm the gradual politicization of promotion procedures. These data also indicate that civil servants have tended to become more comfortable with the political aspect of their jobs. From 1970 to 1987, the number of civil servants who said that they liked the political side of the job very much increased from 45 percent to 78 percent.[76] Interestingly, Aberbach et al. found that when they com-

---

[73] See Derlien, "Personalpolitik nach Regierungswechseln," 40–57; and Derlien, "Repercussions of Government Change," 50–78.

[74] See Mayntz and Derlien, "Party Patronage," 370.

[75] The first study was conducted by Robert Putnam, and the second study was conducted by Renate Mayntz and Hans-Ulrich Derlien. The earlier Putnam study was published as "The Political Attitudes of Senior Civil Servants in Britain, Germany and Italy," in *The Mandarins in Western Europe*, ed. Mattei Dogan (New York: John Wiley, 1975).

[76] Mayntz and Derlien, "Party Patronage," 394.

pared the attitudes of the German civil servants to those of American civil servants, the German bureaucrats were in general less technocratic and more concerned with the political side of their job than their American colleagues. Sixty-one percent of the German civil servants disagreed with the statement that "in policy-making it is essential for the good of the country that technical considerations be accorded more weight than political factors," while 49.5 percent of the American civil servants took this view.[77] The studies of perceptions of politicization and attitudes toward the political side of the job are further evidence showing both that political affiliations and considerations have been growing in importance over time across several ranks in Germany and that these attitudes are remarkably strong even when compared to those in the U.S.

Social Background and Training

When we investigate the social backgrounds of civil servants in Germany we find much less change. A study by Derlien shows that most civil servants and politicians come from homes where the father was a civil servant or an entrepreneur. No civil servants come from homes where the father was an unskilled worker.[78] The distinctly elite structure of the family background of both most politicians and most civil servants is not special to Germany. Aberbach, Putnam, and Rockman found the same elite structure in all the countries that they studied in 1981—Britain, France, Germany, Italy, the Netherlands, and the U.S.[79] The difference between civil servants and politicians was similar in the different countries studied by Aberbach et al. In all cases, the social background of civil servants was more distinctly elitist than that of politicians. In the case of Germany, Derlien found that there had been a slight increase in the number of civil servants who came from worker and entrepreneurial families in the period between 1969 and 1983.[80] This evidence means that the difference between the backgrounds of politicians and bureaucrats narrowed somewhat in Germany.

An analysis of the educational background of politicians and civil servants shows that there was a convergence in the period between 1950 and 1983. In 1983, about 65 percent of politicians and civil servants had an educational background in law, whereas in 1962 as many as 72 percent of civil

---

[77] Aberbach et al., "American and German Federal Executive," 9.

[78] Hans-Ulrich Derlien, "Recruitment, Careers, and Role Understanding of the Political and Administrative Elites in Germany," unpublished paper prepared for a conference at the Observatoire du Changement Social en Europe Occidentale, Poitiers, April 5–7, 1994. See also Derlien, "Competence bureaucratique et allégeances politiques en allemagne," in Suleiman and Mendras, *Le Recruitement des Elites en Europe.*

[79] Aberbach, Putnam, and Rockman, *Bureaucrats and Politicians in Western Democracies,* 55.

[80] Derlien, "Repercussions of Government Change," 71.

servants had an educational background in law, and as few as 53 percent of politicians had a law degree. The number of both politicians and bureaucrats with an educational background in economics increased, whereas the number of politicians and bureaucrats who had a background in engineering decreased.[81] Compared to bureaucrats in the U.S., the uniformity of the backgrounds of German bureaucrats stood out starkly. The U.S. administration had a sizable group of civil servants with training in science, medicine, social science, business, and public administration, in addition to lawyers and economists. Whereas the two latter groups add up to about 80 percent of the educational background represented in the German bureaucracy, they made up only 39 percent of the American bureaucracy.[82] One important difference between politicians and bureaucrats in Germany remained: while the number of politicians without university education was significant, almost all civil servants in Germany had a university education. This difference is likely to narrow even if it does not disappear, because university education is one of the entry requirements to the German bureaucracy.

It is sometimes argued, with some justification, that analyses of bureaucratic elites tend to focus too much on the educational and social background of civil servants. Goetz argues that this makes us lose sight of an important variable that shapes the relations between politicians and top bureaucrats in Germany. He calls this variable "political socialization on the job" and maintains that it influences the capacity of civil servants to think politically. The Chancellery provides one important ground for learning the political game, and this especially during times when that institution has come to assume the kind of importance within the political system that it did under Adenauer and Kohl. Due to socialization on the job, civil servants who have been in the Chancellery become well versed in politics regardless of whether or not their educational or social background differs from that of politicians.[83] This is particularly the case of the top officials in ministries in Britain, France, and Spain.

Career Crossovers

An additional way for bureaucrats to become politically socialized is provided by a longstanding tradition in the German higher civil service of granting bureaucrats extended unpaid leave (*Beurlaubung*) to serve one of the political parties in Parliament. As table 10.2 shows, eighty-two higher

[81] Derlien, "Recruitment, Careers, and Role Understanding." See also Derlien's "Compétence bureaucratique," in Suleiman and Mendras, *Le Recruitement des Elites en Europe*, 64–90.

[82] Aberbach et al., "American and German Federal Executive," 7. See also Bert Rockman, "Continuité et changements: Les élites politiques et administratives américaines," in Suleiman and Mendras, *Le Recruitement des Elites en Europe* 229–42.

[83] Goetz, "Acquiring Political Craft," 753–75.

TABLE 10.2
Top Civil Servants on Leave to *Bundestag* in 1996

Department	Number of Civil Servants
Chancellery	4
Foreign Affairs	8
Interior	11
Justice	2
Finance	10
Economics	14
Agriculture	2
Labour	4
Transport	3
Post	—
Defence	5
Health	1
Environment	4
Youth and Family	3
Development	1
Construction	1
Education and Research	9

Source: Klaus Goetz, "Acquiring Political Craft: Training Grounds for Top Officials in the German Core Executive," *Public Administration* 75 (1997): 768.

federal civil servants were on such leave in 1996. Most of them came from the Ministries of the Interior, Finance, Economics, Education and Research, and Foreign Affairs. Forty-five of these civil servants worked for the leading party in power, CDU/CSU, eleven worked for the coalition partner, FDP, and twenty-six worked for the main opposition party, SPD. The civil servants on leave were mostly from the three highest positions of the federal administration. In such cases, all civil servants are expected to return to their posts within the administration after their time in Parliament, and most of them do so within four years.

Several incentives lure civil servants to take a period in Parliament. First, the CDU/CSU and FDP offer higher pay than the service salary scale.

Second, civil servants are able to use the time in Parliament as a way of increasing their chances for promotion. On the one hand, working for a parliamentary party is a clear declaration of political allegiance. On the other hand, a period in Parliament may be seen as a way to obtain the political skills needed for the top positions of the German bureaucracy. For bureaucrats who are members of the opposition party, taking time off in Parliament may be considered an attractive way to get out of a position in a ministry that the civil servant either does not like or where he or she feels offers little prospect for promotion. Parliamentary civil service for German higher civil service is akin to service in a *cabinet ministériel* of a French minister. It permits integration into the top political-administrative network and it hones the official's political skills.

We should not, however, overemphasize the magnitude of career crossovers in the German civil service. Although crossovers between political and civil service careers are permitted, and even encouraged, when it comes to service in Parliament there is no evidence so far that this arrangement has become more popular among civil servants. There is no doubt, however, that serving in Parliament is one of the factors that facilitate politicization of the bureaucracy in Germany, since it is clearly work in the service of a political party and it is therefore a politically socializing experience.

Role-Perception

Neither similar social backgrounds nor career crossover make politicians and bureaucrats indistinguishable from one another. First, civil servants express categorically that they think that their job differs from that of politicians. Second, the working day of a bureaucrat remains distinct from that of the politician. Most bureaucrats perceived their role as different from that of politicians in 1970 and 1987. Moreover, the perceptions were strikingly similar at the two different points in time. The only trend that can be discerned from the data shows that civil servants in 1987 were more aware of the different roles of politicians and civil servants. While 15.6 percent of the civil servants answered that they perceived the role of top civil servants and politicians as nearly similar in 1970, less than 11 percent of civil servants perceived their roles as relatively similar or nearly identical in 1987. The increased tendency to distinguish between politicians and bureaucrats appeared in the answers of parliamentary politicians, too, when they were asked the same questions.[84]

The perception of the distinct roles of politicians and bureaucrats is further supported by data on typical working days of politicians and bureau-

[84] Mayntz and Derlien, "Party Patronage," 394.

crats in Germany. Although both politicians and bureaucrats mentioned that they spend most of their time in meetings, only civil servants emphasized that a large part of their working day is spent on studying records and doing conceptual work. By contrast, politicians said that they spend most of their time on external contacts, constituency work, and appearance in Parliament.[85]

Outside Advisors

Since the 1990s a development has occurred in Germany and elsewhere that allows politicians to either increase their influence over civil servants or to bypass them. This involves the practice of the use of networks other than the one around the traditional civil service for advice on government reform. Unlike in the decades preceding the 1990s, advisors have to an increasing degree come from business administration schools, management consultancies like Roland Berger and McKinsey, and the private Bertelsman Foundation, which since 1987 has sponsored research and experimentation on public management reform.[86] Before 1990, the network of advisors was characterized by continuity. They came from and circulated between the Ministry of the Interior, the Graduate School of Administrative Sciences in Speyer, and the Federal Civil Service Academy. The composition of the federal government's reform commission "Lean State," which started working in 1995, was an example of the government's decreasing reliance on traditional civil service networks. Out of a total of eighteen members, only two—a mayor and a former political civil servant—had a traditional public administration background. By contrast, three members were from the business sector, including a consultant from Roland Berger.[87] The increased use of advisors from outside the normal civil service network is also taking place on the levels of Länder and local government. Derlien portrays the change in Bavaria in polemical language: "Most disturbing to traditional observers, the Bavarian government, normally a guardian of traditional values, the monopoly of jurists and clean public service, recently published the draft of a public service *Leitbild* in order to create a 'corporate identity' for the 'Unternehmen Freistaat Bayern,' following the example of Siemens and advised by a management consul-

---

[85] Ibid., 496.

[86] The use of outside consultants by ministries for purposes of reorganization and ostensibly for learning to deliver services better is now a growth industry in all countries.

[87] Hans-Ulrich Derlien, "Bureaucracy and the Public Service as Objects and Agents of Reform," unpublished paper prepared for the British-German workshop "Comparing Public Sector Reforms in Germany and the United Kingdom," Humboldt Universität zu Berlin, June 12–14, 1997, 7.

tant."[88] The change in network of advisors is still ongoing and has not yet replaced the old network based on the traditional civil service circles. However, it is fair to conclude from these recent developments that German politicians seem increasingly willing to replace their advisors from the civil service with other professionals. In the long run such a practice is likely to enhance the influence of politicians over civil servants. In this trend Germany is no different from Britain, Spain, and Japan.

Conclusion

Derlien's characterization of the bureaucracy in Germany as a "career system with loopholes" has been useful for our analysis of politicization. The system is career-based in the sense that it favors those who follow the traditional path of career civil servants. The predominance of career bureaucrats is shown by the lack of growth of recruitment of outsiders and the relatively stable educational and social background of top civil servants. However, politicians have made increasing use of the loopholes in the system by taking advantage of the arrangement of temporary retirement to an increasing degree. Civil servants' right to hold membership cards in political parties, to show their allegiance by work in Parliament, and to develop political skills in central offices facilitate the process of politicization. Derlien was able to conclude that although politicization was not a new phenomenon in Germany, "the extent to which it has been done during the last two decades, and the frankness with which it is admitted, is new."[89] We have also found evidence that politicization is also taking place in the ranks below the rank of political civil servants. Moreover, the most recent change in government confirms the evidence from previous governmental changes, which suggested that a series of patronage cycles had been put into place. According to the dynamic of such patronage cycles, every major government change brings about more rather than fewer changes in the top civil service positions. Finally, the loopholes of the civil service system in Germany may be getting larger. By showing increasing interest in getting advice from outside the traditional civil service circles, German politicians are developing a new way to increase their influence over the traditional bureaucracy. In light of our discussion, it is safe to conclude that the German bureaucracy has become more politicized in the postwar period and that, in spite of important constraints, there is no evidence suggesting that the trend is likely to be reversed.

[88] Ibid.

[89] Hans-Ulrich Derlien, "Public Administration in Germany: Political and Social Relations," in *Bureaucracy and the Modern State: An Introduction to Comparative Administration*, ed. Jon Pierre (Brookfield, Vt.: Edward Elgar, 1995), 89.

Spain

Like Britain and France, Spain possesses a venerable administrative tradition. Its hallmarks have been, as the Napoleonic tradition would imply, hierarchy and a strong sense of esprit de corps that helps to separate it from the world of competitive politics. In view of the tumult of Spanish politics in the twentieth century, the relationship between politics and administration admits of no categorical conclusion that would cover the entire period. Much work has been carried out on both the central and regional levels in recent years.[90] The available evidence indicates that a trend exists in the direction of an unmistakable subordination of the bureaucracy to politics.

Political Appointments in the Central Administration

Different political criteria are at work in the appointments process: party membership, proximity to party, sharing a party's ideology. Purely political appointments are those that are made not on the basis of any expertise but rather on the basis of political affiliation.[91] This does not imply that expertise is necessarily absent.

Different terminological expressions are used to refer to those who occupy these positions. I refer to "positions of political appointments" because this is the most accurate description of those who are appointed from outside the civil service.[92] The term "high-level position" is often used in Spanish regulations. Reference to this designation is made in the Act on the Juridical System of the State's Administration of 1957, which grants the Council of Ministers the authority to define "high-level po-

[90] See Carlos Alba Tercedor, "Administración y Política," in *Política y Sociedad: Estudios en Homenaje a Francisco Murillo Ferrol*, vol. 1 (Madrid: Centro de Investigacionas Sociológicas y Centro de Estudios Constitucionales, 1987), 493–513; Carlos Alba, *Revue d'Administration Publique*; Rafael Banón Martínez, "Burocracia, Burócratas y Poder Politico," *Información Comercial Española* 522 (February 1977): 34–47; Miguel Beltran Villalba, *La Acción Pública en el Régimen Democrático* (Madrid: Centro de Estudios Políticos y Constitutionales, 2000); and "Las Administraciones Públicas," in *Entre Dos Siglos: Reflexiones Sobre la Democracia Española*, ed. J. Tusell, E. Lamo, and R. Pardo (Madrid: Alianza, 1996), 265–95. See also J. Matas Dalmases, *Las Elites Políticas de la Administración. Los Altos Cargos de la Generalitat De Cataluña* (Barcelona: Escola d'Administración Pública de Catalunya, Centro de Estudios de Derecho, Economía y Ciencas Sociales, 1996); A. Mesa, *Administración y Altos Cargos de la Comunidad Autónoma Vasca* (Madrid: Centro de Investigaciones Sociológicas, 2000); and S. Parrado, *Las Elites de la Administración Central (1982–1991). Estudio General y Pautas de Reclutamiento* (Sevilla: Instituto Andaluz de Administración Pública, 1996).

[91] See Mesa, *Administración y Altos Cargos de la Comunidad Autónoma Vasca*; and Jimenez Asensio, *Altos Cargos y Directivos Públicos* (Onati: Instituto Vasco de Administración Pública, 1996).

[92] It is the expression used by Adela Mesa.

sitions" and to confirm appointments. This category came to be defined as including the undersecretaries, general directors and civil governors. This list was subsequently modified by the "Real Decreto" 1558/1998 Act, which introduced an intermediate position between the ministers and undersecretaries of state: secretary of state.

Before the Spanish constitution was ratified in 1978, the expression "high-level position" was used to refer to the intermediate levels between ministers and civil servants. The constitution blurred the distinction among these positions by giving the members of government and the high-level positions equal consideration.

Neither Act 10/1983, on the Organization of the Central Administration, nor Act 6/1997, on the Organization and Functioning of the States General Administration, allayed this confusion. The first used the expression high-level position, but it did not distinguish between the political level and the political-administrative level; the second did not distinguish between the influential agencies and ordinary ones.

In the Spanish system, top political positions are filled by appointment, through acts known as "Reales Decretos." There are three levels of these positions: ministers, who are appointed by the president;[93] subministers,[94] including secretaries of state (SE), undersecretaries (SbS),[95] and general secretaries (SG); and directors general (DG), who are members of top-level agencies and who include technical general secretaries,[96] general directors, directors of the minister's cabinet, and presidents of autonomous agencies.

The fact that appointments to top positions are increasingly in the hands of politicians indicates the extent to which the executive branch controls the state machinery. The process of politicization of administrative structures is, as in the other countries, a complex phenomenon, though it is possible to discern trends.

Control over the Organization

The number and distribution of top government positions are of great importance to any government since these positions control the administration's decision-making processes. Unless there is a specific rule to reduce the number of posts subject to political appointment, members of a government will try to expand the size of the political sphere at the expense of civil servants in the same way as some American presidents have sought to do. One way to analyze this phenomenon is simply to count the number of posts. A

[93] Section 98.1 of the Spanish constitution; section 2 of Act 50/1997.

[94] Section 8.1 of Act 10/1983.

[95] According to Section 15 of Act 6/1997, the undersecretary ("subsecretario") must be appointed from among career civil servants.

[96] According to Section 17 of Act 6/1997, the technical general secretary ("secretario general técnico") must be appointed from among career civil servants.

TABLE 10.3
High-Level Positions in Spanish Central
Administration, 1938–73

	SbS	DG	Total
1938	4	35	39
1943	5	25	30
1957	12	89	101
1965	18	100	118
1969	17	91	108
1973	12	76	88

Source: J. Gómez and S. Parrado, *Ciencia de la Adminstración*, vol. 2 (Madrid: UNED, 2000), 280.
Note: SbS = subsecretaries; DG = directors general.

more precise analysis, however, introduces a qualitative element: in theory, the positions that are closer to members of the government share more control over the decision-making process than less elevated positions do. If, then, politicization does take place, at what level does it occur?

In order to examine this phenomenon in the Spanish context, we need to look three distinct periods: 1939–1975, the period of Franco's dictatorship; 1975–1978, the period of democratic transition; and the present period.

From 1939 to 1975, the governmental system was a centralized one, directed from Madrid. During this period, in the absence of political parties, the bureaucracy controlled access to top political positions. As a result, the extent to which there was an increase in the number of positions of political appointment is of little significance. Still, the bureaucracy was not a single, cohesive group; rather, it was a conglomeration of government agencies. These agencies acted on behalf of political parties that wanted to control access to power.

The period of Franco's regime can be divided into three different stages with respect to the number of positions of political appointment (see table 10.3). The first stage was one of isolation and autarchy in Spain and dates from the end of the Spanish Civil War in 1938 to 1957. During this period, the number of political appointees was small. The number of top positions, excluding those in ministries, falling in the "political" category ranged from twenty-four to seventy. Between 1957 and 1972, Spain was undergoing an economic boom and the number of positions of political designation nearly doubled from the previous period. Then, in 1973, the number of positions of political appointment began to fall off again.

There is no data available from 1975, the year the political transition to democracy began, to 1978, the year of Franco's death and the year the

TABLE 10.4
High-Level Positions in Spanish Central
Administration, 1973–2000

	SE-SbS-SG	DG	Total
1973	12	76	88
1983	52	179	231
1986	64	206	270
1989	65	209	274
1991	78	227	305
1996	53	217	270
2000	53	200	253

Source: J. Gómez and S. Parrado, *Ciencia de la Administración*, vol. 2 (Madrid: UNED, 2000), 280. Data for the year 2000 was calculated from the Boletín Oficial del Estado (Diario Oficial del Estado).
Note: SE = state secretaries; SbS = subsecretaries; SG = general secretaries; DG = directors general.

Spanish constitution was ratified. This was a period of profound political change, in which power was concentrated in the Unión de Centro Democrático (UCD), a political party founded primarily by civil servants and top appointees of the previous regime.

The ratification of the Spanish constitution in 1978 had two crucial implications for the political-administrative system: the proliferation of political parties and the decentralization of power to the Spanish provinces (Comunidades Autónomas, or CCAA). In the 1980s, many functions previously carried out by the central government in Madrid were transferred to the seventeen autonomous regions. At the same time, the welfare state was expanding, creating in turn an expansion of the administrative structure, one which applied both to the CCAA and to the General State Administration (AGE).

As table 10.4 shows, the decentralization of the 1980s and 1990s was not accompanied by a reduction in the size of the bureaucracy. From 1982 to 1996, the Socialist Party (Partido Socialista Obrero Español, or PSOE) was the dominant party in the governing coalition. After 1996, the right-wing Partido Popular (PP) governed with the support of the nationalist parties before winning a parliamentary majority.

The number of political positions increased from 231 to 305 between 1983 and 1991 (table 10.4). This increase is explained not only by the expansion of the welfare state but also by the fact that the Socialist Party was powerless during Franco's regime and until 1978. The first Socialist government of 1983, therefore, had to find people whom it could trust and in whose hands it could place political power. The Socialist government immediately replaced 80 percent of the political-administrative elite, keeping only forty-four people who had occupied important positions in the UCD government.

The PSOE tried to reduce the role of directors general. As a result, under the party's control the number of secretaries of state and general secretaries increased. As we can see from table 10.4, the number of secretaries, undersecretaries, and general secretaries was four times greater in 1983 than it was in 1973, whereas the number of directors general only doubled.

When the Partido Popular came to power, it reduced the number of positions of political appointment. It had promised to do so during the campaign when it criticized the Socialists for having increased the size of the bureaucracy. Still, the process of reducing the number of top political-administrative positions proved difficult.[97] It might have been possible to combine the responsibilities of several directors general or state secretaries, but it was feared that, had this occurred, the new ministers might have acquired too much power.

As a result, as the data show, the reduction of political positions, although significant, was not as widespread as had been promised. A more significant reduction took place at the level of secretaries of state, undersecretaries, and general secretaries, whose numbers decreased from seventy-eight in 1991 to fifty-three in 1996.

The Political Party and the Corps of Civil Servants

The important question is whether the government controls access to top administrative positions or whether only career civil servants can be appointed to these positions. This is the enduring issue in all political-administrative relations.

The transition period, as well as the first democratic governments, was under the control of the centrist Unión de Centro Democrático. The party had in its ranks many higher civil servants. During this period, civil servants monopolized the top positions in the bureaucracy, and they eventually came to control the party itself.

It was expected that when the PSOE came to power in 1982, this state of affairs would be reversed and party members would be appointed to political-administrative positions. But this did not occur. Approximately one-third of all political appointees who occupied top political-administrative positions between 1982 and 1991 belonged to the Socialist Party prior to occupying their position. Among the positions closest to the min-

---

[97] Because the term "high positions" was never clearly defined, it was difficult to know the precise number of those considered falling into the political-administrative category.

isters, this figure was as high as 49.7 percent, whereas among directors general, it was 30.2 percent. Party affiliation was higher among government officials appointed during the first Socialist government of 1982 (45.6 percent) than it was among those appointed in 1991 (32.4 percent).[98] Equivalent data is not available for the Partido Popular, though the party's tendency, particularly after it obtained a majority in Parliament, was to appoint people who were already closely affiliated with the party.

The distribution of political positions among the different branches of the administration is instructive.[99] During Franco's regime, 91.9 percent of the undersecretaries and directors general belonged to a single administrative corps. During the first years of the regime, there was a high ratio of military men in government, but by the 1960s this ratio had decreased significantly.

During the Socialist period, the civil service corps monopolized many of the appointments to top positions: 66.2 percent of the positions at the second level of the administration (secretaries of state, undersecretaries, and general secretaries) and 78.2 percent of directors general. Twenty percent of the political appointments in this period, generally at the second level of the top positions, came from outside the corps, whether from the private sector or from the political arena.

During the period of control by the Partido Popular, state lawyers *(abogados del estado)*, diplomats, and engineers have received a greater share of political appointments than they did in the previous period, while finance inspectors and university professors have had a less significant presence. In this period, there was still a tendency to have top positions occupied by the prestigious corps of the higher civil service.[100]

Consultants and Political Advisors

Consultants and political advisors, known as contingent personnel, are also politically appointed. The reason consultants and political advisors are considered to be contingent personnel is that, despite their being political appointments, their bond is with a particular politician and not with the administration itself. Thus, their appointments depend on a minister and last only as long as the minister himself remains in power.

As a result, contingent personnel do not have to meet any formal requirements to be appointed. Only their fidelity to the politician who appoints them matters. Hence, they are quintessential political appointments. The main difference between civil service appointments and "pure"

---

[98] See Salvador Parrado Déez, "Las Elites Político-administrativas del Estado Central de España" (doctoral thesis, Madrid, 1995); and Jose Antonio Olmeda Gómez and Salvador Parrado Díez, *Ciencia de la Administración*, vol. 2 (Madrid: UNED, 2000).

[99] The prestigious civil service corps in Spain have traditionally possessed a standing, advantages, and power akin to the *grands corps* in France.

[100] Asensio, *Altos Cargos y Directivos Públicos*, 295.

TABLE 10.5

Evolution of Contingent Personnel in the State Administration

	1992	1993	1994	1995	1996	1997	1998
Contingent Personnel	417	427	434	448	421	413	340

Source: Calculated from annual data in *Intervención General de la Administración del Estado* (IGAE).

political appointments is the role each plays. Those who occupy the high civil service positions have the major responsibility of heading the administrative agencies, whereas consultants and political advisors are there to support the politician who appoints them. The latter play a role akin to that of members of ministerial cabinets in France.

The data in table 10.5 show that the number of contingent personnel increased between 1992 and 1995, when it reached its highest point. It then began to decrease until 1998, when it rose again. The decrease in the number of contingent personnel is not a result of any restriction put on this type of personnel; it is, rather, the result of the privatization of many public enterprises, which began with recent Socialist administrations and continues today. The importance of these pure political appointments can be seen from the role they have come to assume in the office of the presidency of the government (prime ministership).

The data in table 10.6 show that there was no reduction in the number of contingent personnel in the prime minister's staff. The practices adopted varied during the centrist, socialist, and center-right periods.

During the centrist period, Suarez, the first prime minister of the new democratic regime, did not create his political-administrative structure. He had a cabinet and a group of special consultants, who subsequently became counselors of the president of the government (*consejeros del presidente del gobierno*). The advisory function was subsequently given over to the cabinet.[101]

Under the prime ministership of Calvo Sotelo, the position of state secretary adjunct to the president (*secretario de estado adjunto*) was created, as were the positions of general state secretary (*secretario general del estado*),[102] studies director (*director de estudios*),[103] and technical cabinet of the president of government (*gabinete técnico del presidente del gobierno*).[104] The posts of general secretary of the president's cabinet and director of organization were both eliminated.

[101] It was restructured by means of Act 2761/1977, Section 1, June 28; the advisory function was established by Royal Decree 2158/1978, Section 2, September 1.

[102] Part of the category of undersecretary.

[103] Part of the category of director general.

[104] Part of the category of director general.

TABLE 10.6
Evolution of Contingent Personnel in the Office of the Presidency

	1992	1993	1995	1996	1997	1998
Presidency	162	173	174	155	160	163
% of total	38.8	40.5	38.8	36.8	38.7	47.9

Source: Calculated from annual data in *Intervención General de la Administración del Estado* (IGAE).

When Felipe González came to power, he initiated a major restructuring of the Office of the Presidency. Directly under him stood the General Secretariat, the State Secretariat for Relations with the Spanish Parliament (*Las Cortes*), and the Legislative Coordination; in 1983 the Office of the Government's Spokesman (*Oficina del Portavoz del Gobierno*) and the Ministry of the Presidency (*Ministerio de la Presidencia*) were also added.

The coming to power of the center-right political party, Partido Popular, has occasioned a profound restructuring of the Office of the Presidency. There is a new Ministry of the Presidency, which subsumed the Ministry of Relations with the Spanish Parliament, the Government Secretariat, and the Ministry of the Spokesman. Where there previously existed eight cabinet departments, there are now only five. Recently, the Ministry of the Spokesman has reappeared and the Ministry of the Presidency has become stronger.

Conclusion

The number of political appointments increased during the socialist period and then remained steady despite the privatization of public enterprises and the transference of responsibilities from the central government to the provinces. The number of contingent personnel has remained constant except in the Office of the Presidency, which has experienced a significant increase in such posts.

Spain appears to have adopted practices that greatly resemble those of France, where civil servants, closely linked to, even if not actual members of, political parties, come to occupy top political-administrative positions. To be sure, they are civil servants. But they have also been chosen for their political loyalties. This phenomenon has been referred to as "personalization" rather than politicization,[105] though by the definition we have employed, it suggests an unmistakable trend toward politicization. Careers are made in the civil service (and often subsequently in politics) on the basis of loyalty to a political party.

[105] A debate on this issue has long existed. See David Richards, *The Civil Service under the Conservatives 1979–1997: Whitehall's Political Poodles* (Brighton: Sussex Academic Press, 1997).

CHAPTER ELEVEN

CONSTRUCTING A BUREAUCRATIC APPARATUS
IN EAST-CENTRAL EUROPE

THE DEVELOPMENT of democracy in European societies and in the United States did not occur in the absence of a more or less professional bureaucracy. It would be well-nigh impossible to find an analyst of political development and of democratic institutions who has sought to advance the idea that democracy came into being, or would have been consolidated in a shorter time span, in the absence of a competent state bureaucracy.

Yet, in view of the influence of NPM in all its various guises and of the mounting antistatist fervor in many Western democracies, one central question needs to be addressed: If today's consolidated democracies can come to regard the state bureaucracy as being largely superfluous, does it follow that a fledgling democratic state, fresh out of the shackles of authoritarian rule, can dispense with the need for a professional, or at least largely competent, bureaucracy?

Since the overthrow of communism, Eastern and Central European states have passed through two phases: illusory belief that the construction of a professional bureaucracy was dispensable and recognition of the need to begin the process of developing such a bureaucracy. That most countries newly liberated from communism went through the first phase before succumbing to "reality" is not difficult to understand. Many of the states of what we today consider consolidated democracies had at various times in their history experienced traumas that raised questions about how the coming order was to be established. In no case was a new democratic order envisaged that did not include bureaucratic structures. Governmental authority cannot be exercised without professional state structures, and democratic legitimacy cannot be attained without such an instrument.

What happens to the main instrument of governing when a regime is overthrown? Is the bureaucracy purged? Or does the new regime govern with those who served the old order? Are bureaucratic institutions revamped as a country moves from authoritarianism to democracy?

Many new regimes, whether democratic or authoritarian, have had to confront this familiar problem from the moment the old order was overthrown. It was Marx who called for smashing the bureaucracy—that instrument of the bourgeoisie—once the revolutionary force took power. Lenin subscribed to this view but had to wait several years before purging the Russian bureaucracy of the last vestiges of its bourgeois elements. His need for a state machine to carry out immediate reforms was greater than the need to purge this machine upon taking power.

To take a very different example, when Clement Attlee became prime minister of Britain's first postwar Labour government, he was repeatedly warned that he would be unable to govern with what was essentially a conservative bureaucracy long accustomed to serving conservative governments, a "representative bureaucracy" that represented not society but the ruling elite. Despite being urged to replace the higher civil servants, however, Attlee did not attempt a purge. Indeed, he subsequently claimed to have received loyal service from the higher civil service.

In recent times different French governments have had to face the problem of bureaucratic loyalty. The Vichy regime saw a large segment of the bureaucracy adapt rapidly to the Pétainist regime, whereas the Liberation forces had to sanction some of those who had served Vichy. But even in the postwar years, there was no major purge of the bureaucracy. When the left-wing government came to power in France in 1981 after twenty-three years of uninterrupted right-wing rule, it planned to make massive personnel changes in the bureaucracy. After the initial tremors and some changes in personnel at the top of the bureaucratic pyramid, however, all major reforms that threatened the structure, personnel, and promotion processes were abandoned.

Although all revolutionary governments plan to overthrow existing bureaucratic structures and replace an ostensibly hostile personnel with a new partisan elite, radical change rarely occurs and the pace of change is almost always slow. For the most part, the case of Eastern Europe conforms far more to this pattern than to the pattern of China after the accession of the communist forces in 1949, when scores were settled rapidly, brutally, and without regard for immediate consequences.

Why, then, in the case of more gradual and nonrevolutionary changes were plans to effect mass change so quickly shelved? In large part, the answer is related to (1) the fear of creating further instability, (2) the need to reassure the society of certain continuities, and (3) the absence of a counterelite.

In an examination of regime changes and their impact on the bureaucracy in France, Germany, and India, Graham Wilson observed that reality very quickly sets in for the new political leaders and "accommodation is reached."[1] As Wilson notes, either a bureaucracy can be an initiator and implementer of policy, or it can be a mere implementer, as occurs under regimes that set clear policy directives. By and large, new rulers come to terms with the bureaucracy: "The French example suggests more clearly

[1] Graham Wilson, "Counter Elites and Bureaucracies," *Governance* 6 (July 1993): 433.

that counter elites may be forced today more than in the past to come to terms with bureaucracies. The increased scale and complexity of government has made it even less plausible than in the past to pull up a bureaucracy by the roots and plant a new one. The larger and more complex government is, the greater the attraction of maintaining its machinery intact, as in India."[2]

Reform and Stability

In the wake of a revolutionary change of regimes (or governments, as in the case of the Socialists coming to power in Spain in 1982, or the French Socialist Party taking the reigns of power in 1981), the new rulers face two often contradictory tasks. First, they need to distinguish themselves immediately from their predecessors by taking radical steps to fulfill the longing of their supporters for reforms long sought and long promised while the party was in opposition. Second, they need to minimize the degree of instability so as to avoid discouraging those who run the key economic, social, and administrative institutions. Severe political instability also leads to capital flight and to an acute decrease in investments, and it ultimately creates a new set of problems that ends up requiring further drastic action on the part of the new government. New, drastic actions in turn only serve to heighten the prevalent instability, as happened in France in 1981–1982, when "strong party pressure . . . compelled the government to continue its innovation campaign in the face of waning authorization and dwindling resources, thus producing increasingly disappointing and counterproductive results."[3]

In the case of Eastern Europe, since there had not been any meaningful competitive elections prior to the collapse of the communist regimes, there were no clear reforms or mandates for reform that could serve as guides for the new governments. By any measure, however, the revolutionary change created what some analysts have seen as "policy windows," that is, opportunities for major policy innovations.[4] What were the priorities set by the new governments?

On the whole, these priorities were determined in part by the rejection of the old order and in part by the international context in which the transition from communism to democracy took place. It hardly needs emphasizing

[2] Ibid.

[3] John Keeler, "Opening Windows for Reform: Mandates, Crises, and Extraordinary Policy-Making," *Comparative Political Studies* 25 (January 1993): 66.

[4] See John Kingdon, *Agendas, Alternatives, and Public Policies* (Boston: Little, Brown, 1984).

that "successful dismantlement of the old order does not guarantee a democratic outcome."[5] Furthermore, it is not clear to students of transitions what it is that guarantees such an outcome.

The priorities set by the new regimes in Poland, Hungary, and the Czech Republic have generally included the dismantling of the centralized state apparatus. Among the particular policies advocated were privatization and decentralization. Consequently, the most important policy in the economic area was the movement away from central planning and regulation toward market-oriented economies. In the administrative area, the most important policy was not the restructuring and revitalization of the central administration but, rather, the devolution of power toward subnational governmental units. These policies reflect a rejection of the old order characterized above all by centralized bureaucratic power that served neither democracy nor efficiency. As Lena Korlarska-Bobinska notes about Poland, there is an "absence of any conception of the role [that] the state should play in social and economic life besides a very general call for the reduction of its role."[6] There is nonetheless a recognition that the state is responsible, in Leszek Bakerowitz's words, "for the construction of a new economic system."[7]

A reduction in the role of the state, the policy followed in the countries of Central and Eastern Europe for reasons already explained, has also had the consequence of not according the reform of the state the attention it deserves. As Peter Drucker observes, "downsizing" is not synonymous with reforming or "reinventing" government: "By now it has become clear that a developed country can neither extend big government, as the (so-called) liberals want, nor abolish it and go back to nineteenth-century innocence, as the (so-called) conservatives want. The government we need will have to transcend both groups. The twentieth century megastate is bankrupt, morally as well as financially. It has not delivered. But its successor cannot be "small government." There are far too many tasks, domestically and internationally. We need effective government—and that is what the voters in all developed countries are actually clamoring for."[8]

Effective government requires developing a competent bureaucratic apparatus, and the first step toward achieving this goal is recognizing the

[5] Russel Bova, "Political Dynamics of the Post-Communist Transition: Comparative Perspective," in *Liberalization and Democratization: Change in the Soviet Union and Eastern Europe*, ed. Nancy Bermeo (Baltimore: Johns Hopkins University Press, 1992), 118.

[6] Lena Kolarska-Bobinska, "The Role of the State in the Transition Period," unpublished manuscript, 2.

[7] Cited in Lena Kolarska-Bobinska, "The Role of the State: Contradictions in the Transition to Democracy," in *Constitutionalism and Democracy: Change in the Soviet Union and Eastern Europe*, ed. Douglas Greenberg et al. (Baltimore: Johns Hopkins University Press, 1992), 301.

[8] Peter Drucker, "Really Reinventing Government," *Atlantic Monthly*, February 1995, 61.

need to train professional public employees. But it is quite likely that an additional deterring factor, besides wanting to avoid all association with the old order, was that in the context of complex transitions the institution of a new order appears as a luxury that the new rulers can ill afford.

A new regime is always under pressure to demonstrate that it is in control, that it is enforcing change, and that it will produce rapid results: "To establish a professional and impartial civil service is a long-term endeavor in any country. . . . Enforcing civil service legislation, building civil service institutions and developing personnel management systems are all investments from which countries can hardly benefit in a very short-term perspective."[9] This was a dilemma that confronted all the countries of Eastern and Central Europe. Many of the "consolidated" democracies—France, Germany, Spain, Japan—faced the same dilemmas either after the war or after the end of authoritarian rule. But they did not face these pressing issues in the face of a worldwide movement that offered a panacea.

Undoing the State: Privatization and Devolution

The reduction of state power, considered to be part and parcel of democratic transition, is being accomplished through two measures: privatization of state enterprises and devolution of state power to local authorities. Both these trends are not unfamiliar to the countries of Western Europe, where since the early 1980s the reaction to statism has led to the privatization of state industrial and financial enterprises[10] and to decentralization of administrative authority.

The privatization of industrial enterprises has been the chief element of the economic reforms in Eastern Europe. The extent and modalities of the privatization process have not been uniform across Eastern Europe. But regardless of the methods adopted, it remains clear that the governments of the former Soviet bloc have sought to end the command economy through the sale of state enterprises.[11]

Privatization did indeed remove from the payroll a substantial number of state employees and state organizations responsible for running sectors of the economy. But in every country a new structure has to be created to administer the privatization process. In the Czech and Slovak cases, the process fell to the Privatization Ministry, the Federal Finance Ministry, and the Federal and Republican Funds of National Property. In Poland, a

[9] Staffan Synnerstöm, "Civil Service Development in Central and Eastern Europe," *Public Management Forum*, OECD, vol. 5, no. 2 (March–April 1999): 3.

[10] See Ezra Suleiman and John Waterbury, eds., *The Political Economy of Public Sector Reform and Privatization* (Boulder, Colo.: Westview Press, 1990).

[11] See R. Frydman et al., *The Privatization Process in Central Europe* (London: Central European University Press, 1993).

Ministry of Ownership Transformation was created and was charged with selecting and overseeing the transfer of ownership. Hungary, which already possessed a less controlled economy prior to the overthrow of the Communist Party, did not create a Ministry of Privatization and was able to maintain a relatively decentralized privatization process that assigned responsibility for initiating the process to enterprise managers. There is, however, a State Property Agency (SPA), created in 1990, that oversees all privatization and that is headed by a minister without a portfolio.[12] As in Western Europe, the process of privatization in Eastern Europe also entailed either the creation of a new bureaucratic agency or supervision of existing agencies. It is also likely, as in some West European cases, that privatization will eliminate the agencies and personnel that ran the state enterprises but will require setting up regulatory agencies. This is particularly likely with enterprises that remain largely monopolistic. In the case of the privatization of gas, water, and telecommunications in Great Britain, the government of Margaret Thatcher had to resort to the creation of additional regulatory agencies for these privatized firms.[13]

If the transition to democracy implies a reduced role for the state in the economy, even more does it imply a reduced role for the state in administration and policy-making. It has been an article of faith that reform of the state bureaucracy has largely been synonymous with its diminishing role. The state reduces its role by delegating greater functions to local units. One study of the reforms of public administration in Hungary, confined almost entirely to the devolution of power, even went so far as to warn about what it calls the "artificial comparison . . . according to which the central state administration organs are inefficient and undemocratic because they are instruments of state intervention, while the local and regional self-governing units are the truly democratic ones, the latter, therefore, should be the repositories of state authority and should have most state tasks transferred to them."[14]

In the Czech and Slovak Republics restructuring public administration has also largely meant altering the relationship between the center and the periphery. Thus the Czech Republic abolished the level of region, the intermediate administrative level between the central administration and the district level, of which there had previously been seven. There were three such regions in Slovakia, and these too were abolished. There are now seventy-one districts in the Czech Republic and thirty-six in Slovakia. The

---

[12] Ibid.

[13] Jeremy J. Richardson, "Pratique des privations en Grande-Bretagne," in *Les Privatisations en Europe: Programmes et Problèmes*, ed. Vincent Wright (Paris: Acte Sud, 1993).

[14] *The Reform of Hungarian Public Administration* (Budapest: Hungarian Institute of Public Administration, 1991), 15. For further information on decentralization in Hungary, see *Public Administration in Hungary* (Budapest: Hungarian Institute of Public Administration, 1992).

only difference between the Czech and Slovak administrative structures is that the latter has a subdistrict level.[15] In Poland the reorganization of the administrative structure has resulted in the granting of greater autonomy to local governments: "The twofold subordination of local government under the Communist Party bureaucracy and the directives of central government has been broken."[16] In fact, the local government law drastically restricts central authority over local authorities.

In Poland, Hungary, and the Czech and Slovak Republics, the reforms of the organization of the state apparatus have been largely concerned with altering the balance between the center and the periphery. The report by Hesse and Goetz concludes that "in sum . . . local governments and administration in Poland have gone through major upheavals during the past years. The territorial organization of local governance has remained largely unchanged, but there have been far-reaching functional, political, administrative and financial reforms which have begun to transform the role of the local level in the governance of Poland."[17] But it is not only administrative structures that are changed in the devolution of central powers and functions. Lurking in the background are some profoundly political repercussions that may threaten the very structure of a state initiating such reforms.

The devolution of state authority to local units may in particular contexts lead to the rise of strong regional sentiments, as has occurred in Western and Southern Europe. Hesse and Goetz observe that in the Czech Republic there has long been a movement for "the re-establishment of some form of regional government for the historical lands of Bohemia, Moravia, and Silesia. . . . Should those regions be reconstituted, it is most probable that they will have the character of self-governing entities, i.e., they would not be part of state administration."[18]

The postcommunist phase of the transition to democracy has been influenced by the ideology of the previous regime and by the global context within which transitions took place. The concordance of both led in a single direction: loosening the hold of the state on the economy and on the society. The first implied the policy of privatization; the second led to the devolution of central administrative power. Both policies have received loud applause, though it is the policy of privatization that has received by far the greater attention. Only the modalities of the move to a market

---

[15] J. J. Hesse, ed., "Administrative Transformation in Central and Eastern Europe," *Public Administration* 71, special issue, nos. 1 and 2. See also J. J. Hesse and K. Goetz, "Public Sector Reform in Central and Eastern Europe: The Case of the Czech and Slovak Federal Republic," unpublished report, Oxford and Geneva, July 1992, 31–32.

[16] Hesse and Goetz, "Public Sector Reform in Central and Eastern Europe," 37.

[17] Ibid., 39.

[18] Ibid., 33.

economy have been debated ("shock therapy" versus "gradualism"). To be sure, the regimes of 1989 in Eastern Europe were not the same as those of the 1950s or the 1960s, which explains why the communists of the 1980s have been able to return to positions of authority in Poland, Hungary, Romania, and even in the Czech and Slovak Republics. As Przeworski noted:

> By the seventies, repression had subsided as the communist leadership became bourgeoisified, it could no longer muster the self-discipline required to crush all dissent. Party bureaucrats were no longer able to spend their nights at meetings, to wear working class uniforms, to march and shout slogans, to abstain from ostentatious consumption. What had developed was "goulash communism," "Kadarism," "Brezhnevism," an implicit social pact in which elites offered the prospect of material welfare in exchange for silence. And the tacit premise of this pact was that socialism was no longer a model of a new future, but an underdeveloped something else. . . . We [did not understand] how feeble the communist system had become.[19]

Feeble though the communist system had become, it remained associated with the party-bureaucratic state. Its organization in the transition phase had to be associated with the "undoing" of a strong state apparatus. And yet, if the task facing Central and Eastern Europe is, as Janos Simon believes, nothing less than what Karl Polyani called a "Great Transformation," then it does not necessarily follow that the undoing of the state's capacity is the ideal solution. Simon argues that the transition process in Central and Eastern Europe is essentially a more complicated one than it was in Latin America and Southern Europe, because in the former set of countries it is the entire model of social reproduction that needs to be transformed. The task before these countries is "not only the democratization of an authoritarian political system (as was the case in other transitions), but also the carrying out of a thorough transformation of the economic and political systems."[20]

How is the Great Transformation to be carried out? What mechanisms are to be put into effect to ensure the delivery of services and the efficient execution of the extractive tasks that all states perform? How is the state to break with its habits of serving an ideology or a class or a political movement? How, in short, is the state to develop a stable, professional bureaucracy subject to the rule of law and capable of applying the law?

---

[19] Adam Przeworski, "Eastern Europe: The Most Significant Event in Our Time," cited in Hans-Ulrich Derlien and George Szablowski, "Eastern Europe Transformations: Elites, Bureaucracies, and the European Community," *Governance* 6 (July 1993): 306–7.

[20] Janos Simon, "Post-Paternalist Political Culture in Hungary: Relationship between Citizens and Politics during and after the Melancholic Revolution (1989–1991)," *Communist and Post-Communist Studies* 26 (June 1993): 227.

One of the most striking aspects of the transition process in Central and Eastern Europe was the absence of recognition, at least in the essential phase of the transition, that a professional bureaucracy is crucial to both the consolidation of the democratic process and the imperatives of economic development. As Frydman and Rapaczynski note, the transfer of state assets to the private sector does not obviate the need for a neutral state. Rather, it renders it all the more necessary. "Privatization," the authors observe, "is a transfer of valuable resources from the control of some parties (state bureaucrats) to others, and one of the primary effects of this transfer is to enfranchise owners and make them more powerful, not merely in the economic, but also in the political sense. This in turn means that the new owners are as likely to make a political use of their new resources as they are to use them in a more conventional, economic fashion."[21] What needs to be guarded against, in other words, are the "effects of the privatized resources that might create new and ever more successful forms of rent-seeking behavior."[22]

Building a Professional Bureaucracy

"The habits of communist bureaucracy run counter to Weberian principles such as the rule of law, meritocracy, or professionalism," observes Jacek Kochanowicz.[23] But what of the postcommunist regimes? Have they been more inclined to create a professional bureaucracy that transcends political loyalty?

The bureaucracy remains a critical institution because it is both a necessary institution in a democracy as well as the indispensable instrument of the state. Kochanowicz summarizes the role that the state needs to fulfill and the important functions that a state bureaucracy carries out. He observes that the market economy is just as much in need of a "strong state" as a nonmarket economy. The state is needed to set norms and regulations by which society can function. In effect, the state has a modernizing role to play.[24] Consequently, a "revitalized and reoriented state capacity is crucial to the success of both market-oriented reforms and consolidation of democracy."[25]

It is worth raising the question of what might have occurred in Western Europe had the state not played the role of instigator, orienter, and planner

[21] Roman Frydman and Andrej Rapaczynski, *Privatization in Eastern Europe: Is the State Withering Away?* (New York and Budapest: Central European University Press, 1994), 175.

[22] Ibid., 175–76.

[23] Jacek Kochanowicz, "Reforming Weak States and Deficient Bureaucracies," in *Intricate Links: Democratization and Market Reforms in Latin America and Eastern Europe*, ed. Joan M. Nelson (New Brunswick, N.J.: Transaction, 1994), 202.

[24] Ibid., 197–203.

[25] Joan M. Nelson, "How Market Reforms and Democratic Consolidation Affect Each Other," in Nelson, *Intricate Links*, 78.

in the years following World War II. The most accurate and best description of the economic policies undertaken by European governments in those years remains Andrew Shonfield's.[26] Schonfield showed that the spectacular economic results achieved in Western Europe following the devastation of the war were due largely to the role assumed by the state and its bureaucracy. Through the combination of a market economy and "indicative planning," the economies of Western Europe were able to achieve full employment and increased productivity.

The states were able to do this because (1) they assumed control of a key economic mechanism, the credit sector, through the Ministries of Finance and the Treasuries, and (2) they had at their disposal professional bureaucratic structures run by competent, well-trained officials. Both factors allowed for orientation of investments that were expected to meet production targets. And, finally, states had the means at their disposal to assure order in recently ravaged societies.

The states of Western Europe were expected to play a role in orienting investments. The French Planning Commission and the way in which the state furnished itself with a cadre of highly qualified officials were soon being imitated in Italy, Great Britain, and Germany. The existence of a competent, even elitist bureaucracy was an indispensable complement to economic growth and to democracy, even if bureaucratic stability was often called upon to compensate for political instability.

The countries of Central and Eastern Europe cannot, of course, be expected to follow the path taken by their neighbors in Western Europe. In the first place, the world in which they find themselves struggling to develop economically and to consolidate economic institutions is vastly different from the one that existed in 1945. It is a much more competitive one, and one in which the number of competitors has substantially increased.

Second, the ideological shift within the successful cases of economic growth today precludes an important role for the state. The term "indicative planning" implied a model that offered an alternative to uncontrolled market allocations and to Soviet planning, and gave an important role to the state. Today, such a model, or such a term, would be met with opprobrium. Not surprisingly, as Kochanowicz notes, of all the state functions, whether rectifying the environmental devastation caused by the communist regimes, investing in human capital, or managing the national debt, "by far the most controversial concerns industrial policy—where industries need a push from a development-promoting state in order to compete internationally."[27] Behind this controversy lies an ideological conflict that

---

[26] Andrew Schonfield, *Modern Capitalism: The Changing Balance of Public and Private Power* (London: Oxford University Press, 1965).

[27] Kochanowicz, "Reforming Weak States and Deficient Democracies," 199.

questions the role of the state, a conflict that had been absent in the countries of Western Europe after the Second World War.

Third, the countries of Eastern Europe have been left to their own devices to a far greater extent than were their Western neighbors in the postwar period. They have not benefited from a Marshall Plan. Nor did they have an immediate need to insure the existence of a professional bureaucratic structure to administer such a plan. Besides, the international organizations that exist today to help Eastern European societies develop their economies—IMF, the World Bank, the Bank for European Reconstruction and Development (BERD), the European Union—tend to dictate economic policies.

These are all powerful factors that explain to a very large extent the difficulties faced by Eastern European societies in their quest for economic growth and democracy. What is surprising, however, is that these countries have not chosen to tackle problems that are within their power to resolve. The development of a central bureaucratic structure that is built on Weberian principles and that is administered by professional officials requires no negotiations and compromises with international organizations. It would allow the state to avoid the pitfalls of privatization that lead to the excessive power of new "rent seekers," reduce corruption in the decision-making process, and ultimately strengthen the legitimacy of the state. Despite these immense advantages and possibilities, states in Central and Eastern Europe did not accord priority to this task. This may be because postcommunist regimes were, as Schöpflin notes, "expected to play a near impossible role" of both safeguarding social welfare and initiating and guaranteeing freedom. The state was also expected to take a neutral stance and to neglect its own bureaucratic interests. "In the circumstances these expectations could not be fulfilled. Not only were existing tasks all but insuperable, but the entire communist and precommunist legacy pointed in the opposite direction and, after all, the overwhelming majority of those involved in the state administration under postcommunism acquired their bureaucratic habits under the culture of communism."[28]

Reforming *Ancien Régime* Bureaucracies

Despite these handicaps, the countries of East-Central Europe have not entirely neglected the restructuring of their public bureaucracies. But the legislative follow-through has been slow in coming.[29]

---

[28] George Schöpflin, *Politics in Eastern Europe 1945–1992* (Oxford: Blackwell, 1993), 280.
[29] Jak Jabes and Staffan Synnerström, "La réforme de l'administration publique dans les pays d'Europe centrale et orientale," *Revue Française d'Administration Publique* 70 (April–June 1994): 275.

Bureaucratic reform has largely been limited, as we noted, to the devolution of power. Indeed, devolution and bureaucratic reform have become almost synonymous. Jan Kubik notes, for example, that "Poland carried out the most comprehensive administrative reform in east central Europe thus far. As a result local communities were burdened/blessed with a number of administrative prerogatives and responsibilities."[30] Such far-reaching reforms have been undertaken in Hungary and in the Czech and Slovak Republics. But Kubik recognizes that such ambitious reforms of politico-administrative units themselves come to have an impact on the state's capacities, "I would also argue," he writes, "that decentralization which led to the decoupling of central and local fields, worked against substantivists' political ambitions."[31]

Altering the balance of power between center and periphery sidesteps the need for bureaucratic reform. The importance of such a reform is stated succinctly in the mission statement of the OECD's SIGMA (Support for Improvement in Governance and Management of Central and Eastern European countries): "The governments of Central and Eastern European countries (CEECs) are in an unprecedented situation. They have to build up democratic systems of governance and transform to market-oriented economies simultaneously. But they must do this without experienced political/administrative elites, without mature structures to mediate and aggregate interests, and without appropriate social, legal, and constitutional frameworks."[32]

"The idea of public service as understood in developed countries is absent" in Eastern Europe, states another recent OECD report. Public service is simply held in "low esteem." In addition, the developing private sector offers more pecuniary advantages, so that public service comes to be reserved for those unable to "make it" in the private sector. This is the case today in Hungary, Poland, Romania, and the Czech Republic. The OECD report goes on to note that the "concept of a professional and apolitical public service is slow in gaining acceptance around a region where for decades politics pervaded every decision throughout society, not just in the administrative realms."[33]

No serious attempt has been made thus far either to make wholesale changes in bureaucratic personnel or to prepare a new bureaucratic elite to manage the bureaucratic apparatus. It is rare, as we noted earlier, for a new regime to proceed to make wholesale changes in bureaucratic personnel.

---

[30] Jan Kubik, "Post-Communist Transformation in East Central Europe: Dual (Political-Economic) or Quadruple (Political-Economic-Administrative-Cultural)? A Study of Cieszyn, Silesia, Poland," unpublished manuscript, 1994, 10–11.

[31] Ibid., 40.

[32] OECD, *Sigma* Mission Statement, 2.

[33] SIGMA, *Bureaucratic Barriers to Entry: Foreign Investment in Central and Eastern Europe* (Paris: OECD, GD 94, 124, 1994), 16–17.

"In general," notes Graham Wilson, "in the modern state the arrival of a counter elite in power does not result in immediate radical changes in the bureaucracy. The counter elite may remove a significant minority of the bureaucracy, but the remainder stay on giving adequate if not enthusiastic service. The report of officials who have endangered their careers or lives by resisting a new regime is not very high."[34] But it is not merely the potential resistance of the bureaucrats of the *ancien régime* that is at stake. It is the willingness of the new regime to maintain those who served the old order. Why is this the case in Eastern Europe?

First, the nonviolent nature of the revolutions in Eastern Europe dictated that the settling of scores would be kept to a minimum. The refusal of the regimes to hold accountable the elite of the communist regimes extended to the bureaucracy.

Second, in none of the countries of Eastern Europe was there a counterelite ready to assume the reins of power. Those most responsible for fighting the former regime, the dissidents, were immensely influential in bringing down communism. But they were ill prepared to assume the reins of the state. Indeed, it is astonishing to see how little they count for in the new world they did so much to pave the way for. Timothy Garton Ash explains it this way:

> With remarkable speed, the intelligentsia has fragmented into separate professions, as in the West: journalists, publishers, academics, actors, not to mention those who have become officials, lawyers, diplomats. The milieus have faded, the "circles of friends" have dispersed or lost their special significance. Those who have remained in purely "intellectual" professions—above all, academics—have found themselves impoverished. Moreover, it is the businessmen and entrepreneurs who are the tone-setting heroes of this time. Thus, from having an abnormal importance before 1989, independent intellectuals have plummeted to abnormal unimportance.[35]

The dissidents always had a natural ambivalence about holding power, in part, no doubt, because they could not embrace Weber's "ethic of responsibility" and in part because the "coffee shop" and "the circle of friends" are more conducive to awakening a public to a ruthless regime's abuses than to managing a society in which "technical" knowledge—law, economics, managerial skills—are prized.[36]

It has been argued that wholesale purges were unnecessary in countries such as Poland and Hungary, where the communist regime was in any case

---

[34] Graham Wilson, "Counter Elites and Bureaucracies," 433.

[35] Timothy Garton Ash, "Prague: Intellectuals and Politicians," *New York Review of Books* 12 (January 1995): 40.

[36] See ibid., for an interesting discussion of Vaclav Havel's relationship to power.

undergoing major changes. In these countries "an incremental replace-ment of elites had already taken place during the dying stages of the old regimes."[37] Klaus von Beyme distinguishes between the model of "regime collapse" and the "erosion of power" model. In the former, a geronto-cracy that refused to renew itself by integrating younger party activists led to the collapse of the regime. This was the case in East Germany, Czecho-slovakia, and Romania. In the latter case, as in Poland and Hungary, there was a gradual renewal of the communist elites in the 1980s, but even here mobility was restricted so that those below the top echelons of the bu-reaucracy had no qualms about switching sides when the communists were deposed.[38]

What to do with the officials high up in the hierarchy of the bureaucra-cies was the subject of endless debates. In fact, these debates consumed so much time that they came "to take priority over pushing needed reforms." Rather than mass replacements or purges, what occurred was something that has been referred to as "elite conversion."[39]

In no country in Central and Eastern Europe, with the exception of the GDR, were there wholesale changes in the bureaucratic personnel, Indeed, except at the top, the changes in bureaucratic structures and per-sonnel have been kept to a minimum. Graham Wilson concludes the spe-cial edition of the journal *Governance* devoted to this very issue thus: "We may look forward in years ahead to seeing whether the expectation that in modern states the need for bureaucracy outweighs distaste for the past be-havior of bureaucrats, or whether drastic changes in bureaucratic person-nel occur; so far, there have been few instances of radical personnel changes."[40] The political elite experienced a far greater renewal than did the bureaucratic elite, and this was the case in almost all the countries of the region. In Hungary, for example, over 95 percent of those in the 1990 legislature were first-time members: "Many of the new insiders were out-siders in the communist era, most of them were simply non-players."[41] The explanation for the relative stability of bureaucratic elites and the renewal of political elites is to be found in the availability of replacements.

Access to a political career is relatively simple in societies which suddenly experience an explosion of political parties. The number of parties competing

[37] Klaus von Beyme, "Regime Transition and Recruitment in Eastern Europe," *Gover-nance* 6 (July 1993): 411.

[38] Ibid., 413.

[39] Jacek Wasilewski, "Hungary, Poland and Russia: The Fate of Nomenklatura Elites," in *Elites, Crises and the Origins of Regimes*, ed. Mattei Dogan and John Higley (Lanham: Rowman and Littlefield, 1998), 165.

[40] Wilson, "Counter Elites and Bureaucracies," 436.

[41] Thomas F. Remignton, ed., *Parliaments in Transition: The New Legislative Politics in the Former USSR and Eastern Europe* (Boulder, Colo.: Westview Press, 1994), 33.

in the elections of 1991 and 1992 varied from eleven in Albania to forty-five in Hungary, sixty-seven in Poland, and seventy-four in Romania.[42] No particular skills are called for, and what is required can be acquired on the job. The job is also relatively unconstraining. To be a bureaucrat is vastly different: it requires skills and a high tolerance for routine, anonymity, and subordination. While many were flocking to take up politics, few were seeking to join the bureaucracy.

In short, the regimes can scarcely afford to disturb the only structures that they can use as instruments. It is not at all certain that political leaders who topple regimes have the patience for the process of governing. But in all cases, the new leaders must rely to a large extent on those who served the previous regime. Nonetheless the question raised by Kolarska-Bobinska remains valid: "Can the old bureaucratic structures implement change in the social order to the extent necessary to bring about a system that is a result of negotiations among various interests and social forces?" She observes that "there has been no essential change in the personnel in the state administration at lower levels because of a lack of experts and professionals. How many persons, and in what posts, must be replaced if the bureaucracy is to be inspired with a new spirit?"[43]

The GDR and a Reunified Germany

In the countries that were governed by the Communist Party, many members of the old *nomenklatura* either began a conversion in the years preceding the demise of the communist regimes or adapted to the new regimes. But in all those countries, as in all postrevolutionary situations, there existed a political "elite vacuum."[44]

In most cases, this vacuum was filled with a combination of a degree of elite circulation and the old (transformed or co-opted) *nomenklatura*. This does not imply that the relatively kind treatment of the old elite does not pose political and moral problems, as the case of the Lustration Law in the Czech Republic shows. This law prohibits former high officials of the Communist Party from occupying positions of authority for a period of five years. The application of this law, which involves decisions about whether to fire people currently holding office or to refuse to hire qualified people, is generally recognized as problematic.

Vaclav Havel proclaimed that it was possible to reconcile politics and morality and that all one needed was "tact, the proper instincts, and good

---

[42] *The Economist*, March 13, 1993.
[43] Kolarska-Bobinska, "The Role of the State in the Transition Period," 309.
[44] Derlien and Szablowski, "Eastern European Transitions," 311.

taste." In fact, he said that he had discovered "that good taste is more useful here than a degree in political science." No sooner had he uttered these
words than "fate played a joke on me. It punished me for my self-assurance
by exposing me to an immensely difficult dilemma." This dilemma was the
Lustration Law, which many have considered a "morally flawed" law passed
by a "democratically elected parliament."[45] Havel decided to sign the bill
and then asked Parliament to amend it.

Havel's dilemma was a moral one: the law did not sufficiently guarantee
the civil rights of those who would be affected. But there was a practical
side, one that was likely to render the law difficult to apply: the demand for
competence, relative as this may be, meant in effect that the vacuum could
not be filled by a readily available new elite.

The only case where the old elite was removed is found in the GDR, but
this was also the only case where an alternative elite was immediately available. Moreover, as Klaus von Beyme notes, of "all the East European
countries currently in transition, only East Germany does not need to
change its political and economic systems simultaneously."[46] Nonetheless,
East Germany, like the other Eastern European states, did undergo a revolution, one that meant a new state and new institutions. During this
process the economies and most public functions have to continue to operate, which is why no wholesale purges of bureaucracies take place. This
was also the case in the early phase of the transition in the GDR.

The GDR entered an entirely different phase when reunification with
West Germany occurred. It was not merely that reunification dissolved the
GDR. It was that the reality of unification gave the decision-makers an additional and unique opportunity: elite transfer. This term refers to a wide
and broad deployment of Western public servants drawn from the Bonn
government, from the Western state (Länder) governments, from Western
municipalities and Western specialized agencies and institutions to the
new administrative structures of the Eastern regime.[47]

Koing shows in his study of replacement of the old East German
nomenklatura that from the beginning of the unification process, civil servants from the West were being shuttled to Berlin by the hundreds to keep
the administrative machine running. Subsequently, with the transfer of
civil servants from the West to the East, what had been a temporary
process became permanent. Consequently, as Koing concludes, "It can be
safely said that West Germans are represented in all administrative branches
and in all public service ranks."[48]

---

[45] Cited in Ash, "Prague: Intellectuals and Politicians," 37–38.

[46] von Beyme, "Regime Transition and Recruitment of Elites in Eastern Europe," 410.

[47] Klaus Koing, "Bureaucratic Integration by Elite Transfer: The Case of the former GDR,"
Governance 6 (July 1993): 389.

[48] Ibid., 391.

Following the reunification of Germany, the new rules that went into effect permitted the dismissal of officials for a large number of reasons (lack of qualifications, violation of human rights, cooperation with the Stasi, administrative reorganization). Thus, a former bureaucracy that was characterized by what Derlien has referred to as "politicized incompetence"[49] was replaced. In fact, a study by Ursula Hoffman-Lange concluded that "the elite changes that occurred in eastern Germany after 1989 were much more extensive than those which took place in western Germany after 1945."[50]

Although several factors may explain the successful replacement of the East German elite, one stands out: the availability of alternative elites. This also explains why the political elites have experienced a greater degree of new entrants in all East European countries than have the bureaucratic elites. The existence of what Derlien call "the reservoir of new elites" and the concomitant "elite import"[51] distinguished the case of the GDR from the other countries that experienced a transition to democracy. Competence is always in short supply, and the new political leaders have to confront the urgent task of reforming political institutions while keeping economic institutions running. If administrative incompetence or loyalty to a party-bureaucratic state is to be replaced by a competent bureaucracy based on the rule of law, then measures need to be taken to develop a system of recruitment and training of public officials. The post-transition period may be able to make do with the relics of the bureaucratic apparatus of the *ancien régime*, but what of the future? How will the needs of a democratic, industrial welfare state be administered? More pertinently, have the countries of Central and Eastern Europe been hesitant to link the consolidation of their democratic regimes with the creation of a professionalized bureaucratic structure?

The transition has given rise to considerable debate on constitutional issues, economic reform, and the relationship between center and periphery. Absent from these debates has been the creation of professionalized bureaucratic structure. There are both cultural and political reasons for this failure.

The cultural hurdles concern the fact that public service has never been accorded much importance. In fact, its longtime association with the Communist Party has made it an object of scorn. It was a politicized bureaucracy, substantially incompetent and known for its arbitrariness. That this remains the general attitude toward the bureaucratic apparatus may not be surprising. What is surprising, however, is that the political elite itself has been slow to recognize the importance of setting in motion a process of developing a bureaucratic structure that has a legal basis and that is characterized by professionalism. What Hesse and Goetz observe

---

[49] Derlien, "Compétence bureaucratique."

[50] Ursula Hoffmann-Lange, "Germany: Twentieth-Century Turning Points," in Dogan and Highley, *Elites, Crises and the Origins of Regimes*, 179.

[51] Derlien, "Compétence bureaucratique," 66.

for the Czech and Slovak Republics applies to the other countries of Eastern Europe. These countries have not been able to formulate and implement policies that could be expected to result in major improvements in the personnel sector. The steps that have been taken have principally been directed at alleviating some of the most pressing short-term difficulties, but have failed to tackle more deep-seated structural problems. Moreover, there is little indication that, in adopting measures concerning particular elements of personnel policy, sufficient thought has been given to their interlinkages. In other words, isolated steps, without reference to a more comprehensive reform design, have predominated.[52]

None of the countries of Central and Eastern Europe at first sought to develop a civil service statute akin to anything that exists in the Western democracies. The development of these statutes was long in coming, and while they may be questioned today in some Western democracies, they remain important elements in an orderly process of recruitment that privileges competence over patronage. In most of the East European countries there remains an absence of civil service statutes. For a long time, even "the idea of a public service as such [did not] really have a basis in law."[53]

Civil service statutes in the West recognize a legal basis of employment for public servants that is separate from the labor laws that obtain in these societies. They regulate rights and duties, provide protection, and set salary scales for all public servants. There have been discussions and drafts of laws in Eastern Europe that are moving toward the creation of a unified civil service. In the absence of such laws, ministers organize their ministries according to their own wishes. Hiring is done by the individual ministry, and party politics predominate in the process.

A professional bureaucracy requires competent civil servants, and tomorrow's bureaucracies will be the result of the measures taken today to train higher civil servants. Efforts in this direction have not gone very far. "It is difficult," writes Lazlo Keri, "to find a trace of an overall concept in the selection and appointment process of executives."[54] Even less is it possible to find a policy that facilitates the training of those who will run the state apparatus in the years to come. In Poland and Hungary schools exist for the training of middle-level civil servants, but neither carries much prestige or has made progress toward creating a cadre of high-ranking officials.

The OECD has sought to encourage the creation of a SES (Senior Executive Service) group within the bureaucracies of the East European countries. While the American SES reform never materialized in the way that the reformers intended, there are variants of the model (the German model of *Beamtpolitische,* the ENA model in France). The logic behind

[52] Hesse and Goetz, "Public Sector Reform in Central and Eastern Europe," 42.

[53] Ibid.

[54] Lazlo Keri, "Decision-Making of the Government from the Point of View of Organizational Sociology," unpublished manuscript, 89.

the creation of a senior civil service elite is that such a reform would strengthen the bureaucracy, would professionalize it, and would increase the morale of the entire structure because it would show those lower in the hierarchy that the government now valued this institution. But this is unlikely to happen, at least in the near future, because, as two OECD officials have noted, politicians are not interested in issues that affect the bureaucracy, and neither is the public.[55]

The creation of a professional cadre of senior civil servants is considered crucial for the efficient working of the government structure because the task of coordination would be facilitated. There are few functions today that can be totally carried out within a single ministry. The policy-making process depends on the capacity of the governmental and bureaucratic machine to coordinate both the making of policy and the implementation of policies. This now represents a new challenge to the bureaucracies of the East European countries, and one for which they are only now beginning to prepare themselves.

Establishing a Civil Service

Although no attempt was made to overhaul civil service procedures and recruitment, the countries of East-Central Europe made attempts during the 1990s to establish a civil service that could be distinguished from the wholly politicized bureaucracy that existed under communism.

The countries of East-Central Europe took different paths, and accorded different priorities, to the creation of a civil bureaucracy. Although Hungary was the first to introduce a Civil Service Act—it did so immediately after the fall of the communist regime—Poland and the Czech Republic took various measures to improve the quality of their civil service, even if they hesitated to pass a civil service statute.

In Hungary, work on the reform of administration began in 1988, that is, before the fall of the communist regime. Between 1989 and 1992 the Hungarian Parliament adopted twenty-two key resolutions concerning public administration.[56] One of these was the Act on the Legal Status of Civil Servants, which was the result of a two-year parliamentary debate. Later, several amendments were added. The most important of these were introduced in 1995, as part of 1995–1996 administrative reforms. There were also different decrees used by local governments to regulate particular basic areas of the civil service.

The issue of the role of bureaucratic structure in the political transformation in Poland was publicly discussed in the very beginning of the

[55] Jabes and Synnerström, "La réforme de l'administration publique," 275.

[56] I. Balazs, "The Transformation of Hungarian Public Administration," in Hesse, *Administrative Transformation*, 76.

1990s. Politicians as well as commentators were well aware of the potentially hampering role of the administrative structure. In his first speech to the Polish Parliament as prime minister, Jan Olszewski said in September 1991, "Our state is threatened by paralysis caused by disorder in public administration and its inability to carry out its basic tasks."[57] There was a popular consent about the necessity of the radical reform, as the patterns of the bureaucratic "behavior" (i.e., operating in the conditions of "freedom from the law and from popular control")[58] were obviously threatening for the implementation of democratic institutions. At the same time, there was a lack of political consensus on the shape of the reform. After the 1991 election the political context in Poland became unstable due to the fragmentation of the Parliament, which also contributed to the "paralysis" of the bureaucracy: "Before elections or when there is an imminent change in government, a particular problem arises: virtually all activities come to a halt, matters are not taken care of and there is no response to pressure."[59]

After three years of preparatory work, the post of the Government Plenipotentiary in Charge of Public Administration Reform was established in Poland in October 1992. One of the main functions of this official was to propose measures and coordinate works on the reform of administration.[60] This reform was intended to begin the process of introducing the Civil Service Law. Work had begun on this project in 1990, and in the period 1993–1995 several drafts of the act were prepared. However, they were never voted by the Parliament.[61] The final version of the act was voted as the Law of the Civil Service on December 18, 1998, and came into force in January 1999.

The Polish attempt to establish a professional, largely depoliticized civil service took the better part of a decade to accomplish. The first Civil Service Law of July 5, 1996, established the Office of the Civil Service, which came into being in January 1997. But the act led to further discussions, opposition, and amendments. It at the very least established the foundations for what had come to be recognized as "one of the most important institutions of the democratic state."[62] A new version of the law was presented to Parliament in April 1998 and was voted into law on December 18, 1998. This was again amended and then superceded by the Law of August 16,

[57] J. Letowski, "Polish Public Administration between Crisis and Renewal," in Hesse, *Administrative Transformation*, 1.

[58] Ibid., 8.

[59] Ibid., 3.

[60] M. Kulesza, "Administrative Reform in Poland," in Hesse, *Adminstrative Transformation*, 34–35.

[61] J. J. Hesse, "Rebuilding the State: Public Sector Reform in Central and Eastern Europe," in *Public Sector Reform: Rational, Trends and Problems*, ed. Jan-Erik Lane (London: Sage, 1997), 138. See, in particular, Republic of Poland, *The Law on Civil Service of 18 December 1998*.

[62] Office of the Civil Service, "Civil Service in Poland" (Warsaw, December 2000), 6.

1999. In January 2000 the Civil Service Council had begun to function and the new competitive recruitment system came into being.[63]

In the Czech Republic the discussion about the reform of the civil service began before the dissolution of the Czechoslovak federation. The initial attempts undertaken in 1991, at the time of the existence of CSFR, focused on adaptation of the Labor Code for the need of a civil service, so that it reflected the specificity of the employees' relation to the state. However, these projects were soon abandoned, as there was a need for more thorough reform. The first Klaus government expressed the intention of creating legal regulations of "the status of state administration." The policy statement made by the government in 1992 was followed by the attempts of preparing the draft Civil Service Act. The Office of the Government of the Czech Republic established a working group for civil service reform. As in Hungary and Poland, the main focus of this work was the transformation of the existing structure, inherited after the communist state, into an efficient, well-qualified bureaucratic organization. Thus, the act was planned to regulate the rights and duties of public servants, as well as the career structure and entrance requirements. Although the first part of the results of the working group was ready before June 1992, the government never reviewed it. While this draft was never voted on by the Parliament, the attempts to prepare it indicate that in the Czech Republic "administrative reform has been put firmly on the political agenda, and that its significance for democratic government and successful economic transition was acknowledged"[64] immediately after the emergence of the independent Czech Republic. It should also be noted that as much as 90 percent of the normative acts adopted between 1990 and 1992 primarily concerned public administration, its rights, duties, and organizational structures.[65] By January 1995, the draft of the Civil Service Act and drafts of implementation acts were submitted, but again the government, for political reasons, did not review them.[66]

Concerns about the role of the civil service in the political transformations of the Czech Republic were reflected in the public statements made by politicians. For example, President Vaclav Havel stressed numerous times the importance of a well-functioning bureaucratic organization for the development and consolidation of a new democratic state (as, for example, in his address to the Chamber of Deputies on March 14, 1995). He also called for the creation of a civil service ethos similar to that which obtains in the

[63] Ibid., 9.

[64] O. Vidlakova, "Administrative Reform in the Czech Republic," in Hesse, *Administrative Transformation*, 70.

[65] R. Pomahac, "Administrative Modernization in Czechoslovakia," in Hesse, *Administrative Transformation*, 62.

[66] O. Vidlakova, *Civil Services and State Administrations. Country Report: The Czech Republic* (SIGMA, 1999), available online at http://www.oecd.org/puma/sigmaweb/acts/civilsevice/cscountryreports.htm

Western democracies.[67] The Klaus government also declared in July 1996 its intention of introducing a Civil Service Act in order to determine the status of civil servants, their duties and rights, and especially to stress the significance of their political independence. The basic principles of this draft were different from the previous project, in that the latter abandoned some of the elements of a career system as well as the principle of a permanent civil service. Further work on this project was suspended, partly due to the opposition of the civil service itself, and partly because of budgetary problems. The new government committed itself in 1998 to pursue the civil service project. At this writing, the bill being developed is planned for implementation in 2003.[68]

In all three countries the stress of reforms was put on the principle of legalistic neutrality and impartiality. The necessity of creating politically independent administrative agencies was slow to be recognized in view of the subordination and dependence of this institution on the Communist Party. The Czech Republic, Hungary, and Poland took special measures to insure that the new civil service was "detached" from its earlier communist networks. All three countries implemented screening laws, which in all three cases gave rise to acrimonious debates.

Screening laws had a twofold purpose. First, they were aimed at dismantling the *nomenklatura* "clique" and to cutting the ties between the officials and their former comrades who were presently involved in politics or in private enterprises. At the same time they were meant to contribute to the creation of an ethos of a "professional with clean hands." They aimed to create a new image of the civil service, one that showed a transformed institution that would inspire confidence. Probably the most extensive and radical measures were implemented by the Czech Republic. The Lustration Act was passed at the end of 1991. As a result, secret service collaborators, Communist Party officials, members of the People's Militia and paramilitary units were banned from major political and business posts for five years. In 1995 the effect of the law was extended until the end of 2000.[69] Despite the radical character of the law, it did allow for exceptions "in the interest of the state." The law permitted certain people who possessed rare qualifications to be employed despite their deep involvement with the previous regime.[70]

Hungary is often used as an example of the "moderateness" of the screening process that was employed. The Lustration Law passed by the Hungarian Parliament in March 1994 initially applied to people holding

[67] Ibid., 5.

[68] O. Benda, "Reforming the Czech Civil Service," *PMF. Public Management Forum* 5, no. 2 (1999): 19.

[69] N. Letki, *Lustration: Towards the Consolidation of Democracy?* Unpublished master's thesis, CEU, Warsaw, 1999.

[70] A. Tucker, "Paranoids May Be Persecuted: Post-Totalitarian Retroactive Justice," *Archives Européennes de Sociologie* 40 (1999): 81–82.

major public posts, including state-owned companies. The basis for dis-qualification was collaboration with the communist civil service. However, the Hungarian Constitutional Court decided that parts of this law were un-constitutional. As a result, its scope was narrowed to public officials who take oaths before Parliament or the president.[71] The moderation of the lus-tration process in Hungary makes it an example of the policy of leniency to-wards former communist officials. Two of the three judges assessing the law for its constitutionality turned out to have a "lustratable" past. In addi-tion, twelve top politicians (including prime minister Gyula Horn) refused to resign from their office despite their "secret service" past.[72]

The Polish method of dealing with the communist legacy differed from the Czech and Hungarian methods. Screening had been a controversial is-sue since 1990. Before the dissolution of the Parliament in 1993, several versions of the screening law were ready, yet Parliament did not manage to review them. Work on lustration laws slowed down during the 1993 post-communist coalition government. But the opposition parties managed to outvote the coalition and pass the lustration law involving screening of all top state officials as well as heads of the state radio and television stations. The law was enforced in mid-1998 and has sought to screen for collabo-ration with the communist secret service. The peculiarity of the Polish so-lution consists in the fact that civil servants are not necessarily disqualified because of their involvement with the previous regime, but can be dis-qualified for giving false statements about their involvement. This came to be labelled "lustration lies."[73]

The manner in which reforms of the civil service were conceived, develop-ed, and introduced in different countries in Central Europe depended on the importance that each country attached to the civil service function. The prime concern of Czech politicians and legislators was the civil service's "lack of val-ues, as well as an excessive retrograde conservatism which is listless and de-fenseless against the external pressures of 'progress' unleashed by politi-cians."[74] The principle guiding Hungarian reformers was the continuity of legality. Consequently, a greater stress was placed on the reform of the civil service without undue preoccupation with the past. Finally, Polish discus-sions about the reforms of the bureaucratic structure focused on this insti-tution's involvement in current politics. The consequence of this led the Polish authorities to stress "the assumption that administrative agencies ought to remain neutral towards the cases brought before them. Their be-havior is expected to be guided strictly and exclusively by the law."[75] The

[71] Letki, *Lustration: Towards the Consolidation of Democracy?*

[72] K. McKinsey, "Poland: Decommunization Process Tackles Communist Past," *RFE/RL Report* (July 1998), available online at http://www.rferl.org

[73] N. Letki, *Lustration.*

[74] Pomahac, "Administrative Modernization in Czechoslovakia," 61.

[75] Letowski, "Polish Public Administration between Crisis and Renewal," 9.

Polish screening act stigmatizes not the fact of collaboration with the communist secret service but the attempt to hide this fact. Legislators thus stressed the importance of transparency and professionalism of civil servants.

The civil service acts in both Hungary and Poland show that the legislators sought to create a professional, impartial, effective bureaucratic structure. The introduction to the Hungarian act states that "the precondition of democratic public administration generally esteemed by the society is that public affairs be conducted by impartial public officials neutral to party politics, operating legitimately and possessing up-to-date special knowledge," while the main objective of the Polish law is the creation of the civil service "to insure professional, reliable, impartial and politically neutral execution of tasks of the state." Both acts regulate the issues of conditions of remuneration and employment. Both contain provisions regarding the independence and impartiality of civil servants. Hungarian civil servants are thus not permitted to engage in the activities of political parties, while in Poland this ban extends also to trade unions. Officials cannot be guided by their individual or group interests and cannot act in ways that interfere with the normal functioning of their office, like engaging in strikes or protests. In the Czech Republic there are no restrictions regarding membership in trade unions or participation in strikes and protests. Czech civil servants can also be members of political parties, although in the case of some groups (customs officers or policemen) different regulations apply.

The acts in all three countries specify in a detailed way the recruitment criteria and the training procedures. In Hungary, Poland, and the Czech Republic, civil servants are appointed on the basis of their skills. The public employment system is considered a career system, and officials are rated on the basis of their professional performance, although there are special selection procedures for entry that apply to the apex of the bureaucratic pyramid.

In all three countries particular emphasis is placed on the training and qualifications of civil servants. In Poland, a general, multilevel training plan was prepared, which was intended to supplement civil servants' own professional expertise. Similar measures were adopted in Hungary, where the civil service had come under strong criticism for its lack of expertise. The 1999 reform was aimed specifically at improving performance and efficiency of the civil service.[76] In both Poland and Hungary emphasis was placed on centralized guidance and funding, as well as on the creation of standardized and unified measures for the assessment of qualifications and professional achievements in all sectors.[77] In the Czech Republic the emphasis has been different: training

---

[76] Z. Hazafi and Z. Czoma, "Civil Service Reform in Hungary," *PMF. Public Management Forum* 5, no. 2 (1999): 7.

[77] P. Keraudren and H. van Mierlo, "Reform of Public Management in Hungary: Main Directions," in *Innovations in Public Management*, ed. T. Verheijen and D. Coombes (Cheltenham, U.K.: Edward Elgar, 1998), 147.

is not regulated centrally, but particular ministries and their departments organize training for their own employees. All three countries placed particular emphasis on training in foreign languages, mostly due to prospective membership in the EU. There are even certain positions for which knowledge of at least one foreign language is the condition of entry.

As an answer to the challenge of improving the quality of the civil service, Poland founded in June 1991 the National School of Public Administration, modeled after the French Ecole Nationale d'Administration. Its goal is to train public servants. The degree received from NSPA is considered adequate for a high-level position in the service. But even such a school cannot guarantee competence. In Hungary, the School of Public Administration was founded in the early 1980s. As one analyst noted, "Hungarian practice has not been completely adapted to the principle applying in most western countries of treating public administration as a professional activity in its own right, requiring specialised qualifications in higher education."[78]

Currently, Poland has around 105,000 civil servants employed in the state bureaucracy (excluding local governments), out of whom 561 are appointed at the discretion of the government. In comparison, in the Czech Republic in 1997 there were around 90,000 civil servants in the state administration, and an additional 70,000 were employed in local governments. In Hungary in 1997 there were only around 50,000 civil servants employed in the state administration, with an additional 40,000 in local governments. These numbers were relatively unchanged between 1994 and 1997 in Hungary. In the Czech Republic total employment in the state administration increased from 77,000 in 1994 to 90,000 in 1997, and from 43,000 to 70,000 in local governments.[79]

Conclusion: Bureaucracy in the Transition Phase

The transition to democracy in Central and Eastern Europe is associated with a departure from a repressive state whose chief instrument was a large, politicized, and arbitrary bureaucratic apparatus. Not surprisingly, the transition process in all democratizing Eastern European societies has been preoccupied with divesting the state of its all-embracing role in the economy and in society.

While any transition to a democratic order needs to concern itself with creating political competition, establishing a new constitutional order, and separating civil and political society, it remains the case that no society is

[78] A. Baka, "The Framework for Public Management in Hungary," in Verheijen and Coombes, *Innovations*, 137.

[79] Sources: for Czech Republic, see O. Vidlakova, *Civil Services and State Administrations. Country Report: Czech Republic*; for Hungary see G. Jenei, *Civil Services and State Administrations. Country Report: Hungary*, both available at http://www.oecd.org/puma/sigmaweb/acts/civilservice/cscountryreports.htm

conceivable without a bureaucratic apparatus. Just as the nation-state is the dominant form of territorial organization, no state operates without the instrument of a bureaucracy.

Democracy requires more than an apparatus. It calls for the development of a competent, legally based, accountable, and professional bureaucratic structure. Creating such an institution has evidently not been a central preoccupation in Central and Eastern Europe. The new regimes were, at least in the period immediately following the fall of communism, inevitably reacting to the critical instrument used by the old order. Paradoxically, the instrument of political power (the vast network of bureaucratic institutions) was the object of far more suspicion, mistrust, and derision in the postcommunist era than was the locus of power (the party) during the reign of communism. In part this is because of the omnipresence of the bureaucracy, with its multiple police and security forces, in the daily lives of citizens. The reappearance of the party politicians also poses less of a threat than does the reappearance of bureaucrats because the former participate today in the political process without enjoying the monopoly they once possessed. Yet another factor helps drive the antistatist or antibureaucratic fervor of the democratizing societies: the global context within which the transition is taking place. This context, defined mostly by a reaction to statism and to state intervention in the economy, is also characterized by deregulation and privatization of state assets, even of services long provided by the state. Within this global context there is inevitably a considerable degree of emulation, or bandwagoning. Emulation, notes John Ikenberry, "is an important process by which policies spread because states tend to have similar general goals. All states are interested in doing better rather than worse; they prefer economic and political success to any alternatives, and the experiences of other states provide lessons and examples of how success might be achieved. The guiding rule is: copy what works."[80]

It has become evident by now that the study of postcommunism requires a new vocabulary and a new approach. At the same time, it invites us to reconsider classical principles that have been long entrenched in our liberal tradition. It shows, for example, that less state power does not always mean more freedom. On the contrary, a weak state might be a serious obstacle to the success of economic, political, and social reforms. Liberalization cannot succeed under conditions of state collapse or inefficient bureaucracy. Administratively weak states prove to be incapable of implementing reform. As Holmes and others have noted, liberal rights are difficult to implement without effective, administrative, and adjudicative authorities. That is why it is time to reconsider the role of bureaucracy in the transition of democracy.[81]

---

[80] G. John Ikenberry, "The International Spread of Privatization Policies: Inducements, Learning, and Policy Bandwagoning," in Suleiman and Waterbury, *The Political Economy*, 103.

[81] Stephen Holmes and Cass Sunstein, *The Cost of Rights: Why Liberty Depends on Taxes* (New York: W. W. Norton, 1999).

CHAPTER TWELVE

THE POLITICS OF BUREAUCRATIC REFORM

"If administration is to reach full stature and functional maturity, it should no longer be viewed as a branch of government but rather as an integral and vital part of the whole interacting democratic system. It should be, not merely subject to or controlled by government, but an active agent in implementing, supporting, and realizing democracy."
—A. C. Millspaugh

I HAVE ARGUED in this book that bureaucracies, like all institutions in democratic societies, require reforming and need to evolve and adapt to the changing needs of society and to management techniques. Bureaucracies are financed by citizens and they need to act with parsimony, efficiency, and accountability. The central question becomes how adaptation is to occur so that the public is served in a more efficacious way and that would-be reformers are not permitted to destroy an institution that remains central to the functioning of democracy.

I have also indicated that reforms need to aim at improving the functioning of the bureaucratic machine and not at destroying it. Bureaucratic organizations develop dysfunctions, inefficiencies, and degrees of autonomy. They develop bureaucratic interests independent of the larger organization, or of the society, of which they are a part. Vigilance for keeping them on track is an enduring problem, and it is this problem that politicians and management specialists need to address. Attempting to place the blame for all sorts of ills—citizen alienation, mistrust of public institutions, withdrawal from active participation in the life of the community—on the shoulders of the bureaucratic apparatus is a misdiagnosis that ultimately results in administering the wrong medicine to the patient.

Trust, as most political theorists of democracy agree, is a critical ingredient in the consolidation and operation of democracy. But trust is itself dependent on the application of the rule of law and on the conduct of political institutions. Political authorities have always needed to increase and to improve the capacity of states to consolidate embryonic democratic institutions. This is perhaps the one indisputable lesson that the history of political development teaches us.

Democratic institutions in the consolidated democracies needed the support of an authoritative state in order to flourish. The history of democracy in France, Britain, Germany, Japan, and the United States has shown that no state could exercise authority without a judicial system to insure rights and without an array of institutions, the most important of which was the establishment of a tax bureaucracy.[1]

If a bureaucratic apparatus was needed to develop and consolidate democracy, does it follow that this same institution is equally necessary at a "late stage" of democratic development? This is the central question that remains to be addressed.

Mass Democracy and Government Reform

The older democracies have grown confident about the durability of their political systems and have prospered economically. In the process they have seen democratic practices and expectations evolve considerably in the course of the twentieth century. Not only have there been substantial additions to the democratic club, but the ideas and practices of citizen involvement in society have also been dramatically altered.

The elitist view of democracy accorded elections paramount importance. Elections were neatly separated from governing. The first involved all adult citizens, while the second was the province of the few. Schumpeter maintained that citizens should vote and not try subsequently to dictate policies or to tamper with the governing process. The next election would provide citizens the opportunity to make their judgments.[2] Huntington saw a threat to democracy in citizen participation. Political stability would be threatened were citizens to place demands on the political system that the system could not handle.[3] Expectations would overload the political institutions and pose a threat to their existence.

Perhaps the clearest statement of the dangers of participation came, paradoxically, from the influential and pioneering study *The Civic Culture*. In a work that provided a mass of empirical evidence on the ideal civic culture, the authors were content to argue that such a culture ultimately depended on the *illusion* of participation. Acting on the belief that they could influence the political process would constitute a serious menace to political institutions.[4]

---

[1] See Niall Ferguson, *The Cash Nexus: Money and Power in the Modern World, 1700–2000* (New York: Basic Books, 2001).

[2] Joseph Schumpeter, *Capitalism, Socialism and Democracy* (New York: Harper, 1949).

[3] Samuel Huntington, *Political Order in Changing Societies* (New Haven: Yale University Press, 1968).

[4] Gabriel Almond and Sidney Verba, *The Civic Culture: Political Attitudes and Democracy in Five Nations* (Princeton: Princeton University Press, 1963).

Political practices over the recent decades make the views that the success of democracy is dependent on restrictive notions of citizen participation pretty much relics of the past. There has even occurred a rapprochement in the views of the Old Left and the New Right: both consider the view that democracy consists of periodic elections that leave little role to the citizens in the periods between elections to be outdated. "Part-time democracy"[5] is now considered merely another term for elitism, which our age seems to have rejected unambiguously.

What, then, is full-time democracy, and how has this concept affected the bureaucratic instrument? Even if it would be difficult to find a definition of "full-time" democracy that most theorists would agree upon, it nonetheless remains clear that it involves greater citizen participation and it recognizes that with this greater participation differences in society need to be accommodated.[6]

Citizen participation, whether in communitarianism or in "civic republicanism," is now viewed not merely as an inevitable development to which concepts or theories of democracy have to adapt but as necessary and integral to any definition of democracy. Witness the return of neo-Tocquevillianism in the rediscovery of voluntary associations as the indispensable ingredient of a democratic order.[7] Citizen involvement either strengthens democracy by the build-up of "social capital," or it allows for an equality of involvement in a collective enterprise. In either case, the involvement and participation of citizens in the political process means that a permanent and unambiguous line of demarcation between citizens and rulers, or between society and politics, is effaced. As Ronald Dworkin puts it:

> A community can supply self-government in a more collective sense—it can encourage its members to see themselves as equal partners in a cooperative political enterprise, together governing their own affairs in the way in which the members of a college faculty or a fraternal society, for example, govern themselves. To achieve that sense of a national partnership in self-government it is not enough for a community to treat citizens only as if they were shareholders in a company giving them votes only in periodic elections of officials. It must design institutions, practices, and conventions that allow them to be more engaged in public life, and to make a contribution to it, even when their views do not prevail.[8]

[5] The phrase used by *The Economist*, December 21, 1996.

[6] See Amy Gutmann and Dennis Thompson, *Democracy and Disagreement: Why Moral Conflict Cannot Be Avoided and What Should Be Done about It* (Cambridge: Harvard University Press, 1996).

[7] See Putnam, *Bowling Alone*.

[8] Ronald Dworkin, "The Curse of American Politics," *New York Review of Books*, October 17, 1996, 23.

Participatory democracy ("power back to the people") is the antithesis of elitist democracy. It is practiced on a daily basis and in many ways: through lobbying for or against public policies, through a variety of organizations, through referenda, and even through assuming functions and roles once thought to be the exclusive responsibility of the central government.

The possibility of an "overloaded" government threatening to collapse under the weight of excessive citizen demands becomes irrelevant in a society that seeks to give "power back to the people." The very concept of governmental responsibility, like the notion of a collectivity, gets transformed. Hence the role of the bureaucracy becomes more and more superfluous.

Indeed, in a decentralized society where citizens take on the responsibility for organizing their own community, the concept of government overload is superfluous. There appears to be a convergence of views among a variety of groups or philosophies—communitarianism, civic republicanism, builders of social capital—all of which suggests that citizen action and responsibility are an effective replacement for governmental actions.

While citizens may assume ever greater responsibilities for the conduct of the affairs of their community, they lose their status as citizens in a community with a collective interest and obtain that of a customer. This transformation has vast implications for the organization of the society in general and the bureaucracy in particular.

Bureaucracy and Alienation

That citizens hold politicians in low esteem, that they are dissatisfied with the way democratic institutions work, that they are disinclined to participate actively in the life of community, that they mistrust political leaders, that we live in a world characterized by a popular culture of bad government, all this is scarcely deniable. Whether this is the consequence of a "cultural shift" or whether it is merely the consequence of the accumulated failures of political leadership matters little. What matters is believing that undermining the instrument of political authority is the answer to all these problems.

Even politicians who would genuinely like to see the government operate more efficiently believe that setting the bureaucratic house in order will reverse the mistrust that citizens feel toward their political system: If only citizens can come to feel that the government is not wasting their money, they will return to trusting it, to trusting one another, and to rekindling their community spirit. In other words, making government more efficient, or substantially reducing its functions, is the antidote to alienation. Most of these claims derive from a series of non sequiturs. Here is President Clinton linking government reform and trust:

> The central tenet of every democracy in the end is trust. . . . We have a performance deficit that has led to a trust deficit. The profound sense of alienation so many people feel in our country has got to be heeded. . . . So in the end, this is about more than dollars, it's about more than the pain of filling out these forms. It's even about more than making you happier and more productive on the job. It's about whether together we can restore the trust of the American people in their government. If we can reestablish that trust, we can regenerate opportunity, we can restore a sense of community in this country, we can make other people willing to take responsibility for their own actions because we are doing it and we are setting an example.[9]

This statement, with all its eloquence, its lack of aggressiveness toward the bureaucracy, and its apparent logic, well summarizes the confusion that reigns about the consequences of governmental reform. Clinton somehow managed to link the "reinvention of government" with personal responsibility, with restoring "opportunity" (for what?), with a "sense of community." He even equated the state's sense of responsibility with an individual's. Vice President Gore was more categorical: "There is no way to re-establish confidence in government and confidence in ourselves as a free nation unless we can dramatically change the way the federal government works."[10]

Why does our confidence in our freedom, or our trust in government or in one another, depend on the kinds of reforms (some managerial, others involving mostly transfers of functions of the federal government to outside contractors or to state governments) that Clinton and Gore were promising? They merely followed Reagan and others who had attacked, more aggressively, the government's role. They did not stop at wishing to make government more cost-effective. Nor did they stop at attempting to apply the "reinvention principles" of changing the bureaucrats' incentives and turning the bureaucrat into an "entrepreneur." They carried through their own program of slimming down the federal government.

In the end, the attacks on the federal government, whether with a hammer or with a velvet glove, achieved none of the grandiose goals of reducing alienation, creating a sense of community, increasing participation, or increasing trust in government. These noble objectives were merely invoked

[9] Bill Clinton, "Remarks by the President and Vice-President at REGO Event, GSA Warehouse, Franconia, VA," *Weekly Compilation of Presidential Documents*, vol. 29 (October 8).

[10] Al Gore, "Creating a Government That Works Better and Costs Less: September 1994 Status Report," A Report of the National Performance Review (Washington, D.C.: Government Printing Office, September 1994). See also Al Gore, "The New Role of the Federal Executive," *Public Administration Review* 54 (July–August): 317–21.

to justify the reduction in the role of the government. Clinton and Gore learned that politicians who live by denigrating the functions they were elected to perform end up denigrating politics, public service, and the functions they assume.

Because politicians have developed slogans such as "It's the people's money not the government's" or "Let the people decide" or "Government is the problem, not the solution," they have come to view this form of sloganeering as providing a fully developed philosophy for exercising political authority. There is simply no evidence that reducing a central government's functions increases people's trust in government or people's trust in one another.

In fact, the opposite may well be the case. The politicians and political movements that advocate the denigration of political authority and the reduction (or abolition) of the instrument of state authority have in fact done little more than advocate denigration of the political function. Incessant attacks on the governmental institutions have added up to an avowal of the impotence of politics and have thus encouraged the mistrust of all political authority, debates, motives, and decisions. In short, by attacking the very functions that they are elected to carry out, politicians have increased alienation from politics and mistrust of politics and political institutions. This has been particularly the case in the United States, though other countries have begun, if only gingerly, to follow suit.

Reforming Society or Reforming Bureaucracy?

The public debate about bureaucracies is a muddled one. As James Q. Wilson observed:

> Liberals who want the government to play a larger role in society often either minimize the problems created by bureaucratic rule or assume that problems can be solved by simply spending more money, constructing better facilities, hiring better people, or vesting the clients of these agencies with more rights. Conservatives who want the government to play a smaller role in our lives taunt liberals for their misguided optimism about the nature of bureaucratic rule and urge that bureaucracy be curtailed, but often they apply their critique of bureaucracy inconsistently: "Let us have fewer welfare offices but a bigger army."[11]

It has long been recognized that citizens would like to pay less taxes and receive greater benefits from their government. But when a government sets about changing the way it functions and the way it responds to citizen demands, questions need to be raised about the goals of government.

---

[11] James Q. Wilson, *Bureaucracy* (New York: Basic Books, 1989), 10.

Wilson is no doubt right when he says that that "there is no free lunch in politics or in economics. You can have big government, or you can have government that is easy to deal with and flexible in its management of complexities and problems. But I doubt you can have both."[12] Since it is not possible to have both, it becomes all the more important to ask *whom* the government serves in either case.

No reform of government, and least of all one that seeks to "reinvent" how government works, can be examined merely as one that involves innocuous management techniques. Government reforms involve policies, as do all reforms and government measures, and all policies generally have a constituency of supporters and opponents. In the case of government reinvention it is the voice of the supporters that has been heard. Opponents were neutralized by the presentation of the reforms as responding to citizen (or client) needs, as involving empowerment and competition and cost-cutting.

Still, as Caiden has noted, "All public administration is political; it is an instrument of politics and political values dominate. . . . [P]ublic management cannot be divorced from politics and political culture. Rarely is poor management in the public sector the outcome of purely managerial reasons and a bureaucratic culture."[13] In other words, public administration reform, like all reforms, has its winners and losers. No analysis has yet been undertaken to examine just who the main beneficiaries of the reinvention reforms have been.

It has been suggested, by Caiden and others, that the winners are those who want to distract the public by claiming to save it money while they continue raiding the public purse. This includes not only the rivalrous military services, the enormous farm and industrial subsidies, and the pork barrel expenditures, but also the widespread abuses of the public purse by a host of well-organized interests. In the end, argues Caiden, those who seek to reform the public bureaucracy "do not tell us how they will overcome a prevailing political (and administrative) culture of self-serving, of exploiting public office and public purse self-interest, in which politicians and lobbyists, contractors, and public employees, too, participate unmindful of the consequence for the country."[14] Others have associated the panoply of reforms with the conservative forces who wish to protect their welfare and who use the reinvention concepts as their weapon. As Christopher Pollitt notes: "Managerialism is the acceptable face of new right thinking concerning the state. It is an ingredient in a *pot pourri* which can attract

---

[12] James Q. Wilson, "Reinventing Public Administration," *Political Science and Politics* 27, no. 4 (December 1994): 673.

[13] Gerald E. Caiden, "Administrative Reform—American Style," *Public Administration Review* 54, no. 2 (March–April 1994): 126.

[14] Ibid., 128.

support beyond the new right itself. For that wider constituency 'better management' sounds sober, neutral, as unopposable as virtue itself. Given the recent history of public-service expansion the productivity logic has a power of its own which stands independently of the political programme of the new right."[15] Even a sympathetic (if critical) observer of government reinvention, James Q. Wilson, has noted that any governmental reform has to confront the crucial question of "what is it that government *ought* to do, and what is it that it *can do*." He goes on to observe that government cannot be "reinvented in any serious way without rethinking what it is government ought to do."[16] Yet nowhere is that question treated, either by the Gore Report or by supporters of the reforms or by analysts of the reforms.

The reason that this central question is eschewed by both reformers and supporters is not difficult to understand. More surprising is the fact that public administration has not seen fit to tackle it. But we can surmise that since public administration has come to consider itself part of "managerial studies" and not part of political analysis or political theory, its interests in assessing political benefits and losses and public policy outcomes have become secondary or nonexistent.

Reforms and the Public Interest

If American specialists of public administration have been reluctant to examine government reforms in terms either of a theory of governance or in terms of winners and losers, this does not imply that these reforms cannot be analyzed in this way. As a public policy, government reforms result from the interplay of contending forces and from a prevailing perspective on the role that the state and its administration ought to play. Bureaucratic reforms must therefore be analyzed as any governmental policy is analyzed.

Perhaps because American society is conditioned by markets, nothing is more natural than ending up with winners and losers. In such a context, administrative reform is one public policy to be fought over and to bend in line with the interests of some groups. To be sure, the winners may not obtain the whole trophy, but enough will have been gained by simply having a particular course set.

While the reformers may talk about "responsibility," "freedom," "self-confidence," "opportunity," "community," and "trust," they rarely discuss how their reforms will address the government's responsibility to the

[15] Christopher Pollitt, *Managerialism and the Public Services: Cuts or Cultural Change in the 1990's*, 2nd ed. (London: Blackwell, 1996).
[16] Wilson, "Reinventing Public Administration," 672.

public. Cynicism about politics does not result from routine government inefficiencies but from the fact that politics scarcely accords much importance to the public interest. The public space has considerably shrunk in the United States, and when that occurs there is no longer a trust that the government is the impartial ombudsman looking out over society's interests.

This is the fundamental reason that America's new ideas about organizing government, or reinventing it, did not become a best-selling export product. NPM never became a paradigm inspiring a universalistic package of reforms because other countries understood the ills of their public administrations in varying ways and went about correcting them through a variety of means.

Once there was a general understanding that states were not well suited to own industries, banks, and insurance companies, the privatization process spread like wildfire.[17] Similarly, once it became clear that just as the economy could not be centralized and neither could politics, the reforms aimed at decentralization and devolution followed a universal path. The decline in the number of public employees followed naturally from the sale of public assets and the decentralizing of central government offices.

Yet, even these reforms were carried out in markedly different ways and to very different degrees. There was an aspect of policy emulation, as well as an aspect of policy learning.[18] But beyond these reforms, there was no NPM paradigm.[19] The main reason for this was not due merely to Japanese, French, or German conservatism, which have often been contrasted with American dynamism and penchant for experimentation, but to the priority that these societies have historically accorded the public space in society. Seeking to preserve the public space is seeking to preserve as cohesive a society as possible in the face of growing group and individual demands. No doubt this reasoning has even prevented some necessary reforms from being undertaken in these societies.

The loss of the public space in the United States has been allowed to go to a point where nostalgia has set in for the days of old when there was a greater feeling of belonging and of community. Administrative reform is even presented as a way of recapturing "community," when in fact it can do nothing of the sort because it involves further abdication by the federal government of its role as the guardian of national norms. In numerous policy areas (education is a prime example), the absence of a national policy or national guidelines and norms has left the country severely handicapped.[20]

---

[17] See Suleiman and Waterbury, *The Political Economy of Public Sector Reform.*

[18] See Richard Rose, *Public Employment in Western Nations* (Cambridge: Cambridge University Press, 1985).

[19] See Christopher Hood, "Contemporary Public Management: A New Global Paradigm?" *Public Policy and Administration* 10, no. 2 (summer 1995): 104–17.

[20] On the lack of federal involvement in education, see Leon Botstein, "What Local Control?" *New York Times,* September 19, 2000.

Administrative reform in the United States has been presented not merely as a panacea for the functioning of the bureaucracy but also as a panacea for energizing the democratic process, and for creating "connectedness" and community. Is it any wonder, then, that, as one writer noted, "Administrative reform breeds more cynicism than efficiency and effectiveness"?[21] In what way is disengagement from associational life and participation in the life of the community to be remedied by administrative reform? Putnam's *Bowling Alone* is taken as evidence of the growing disconnectedness of the American citizen with his/her fellow-citizens and with his/her community. But *Bowling Alone* is not concerned with the impact of this phenomenon on our political institutions, nor does it discuss the role that our political institutions ought to play in regenerating "social capital" or a sense of community. Putnam addresses the important issue of participation in promoting democracy, but he does so in a non-political manner. In fact, Putnam does not discuss the issue of the decline in the public space in the United States or link it to the decline in social capital.[22]

The government has been instructed to treat all who have recourse to its services as clients. The citizen has been encouraged to view himself as a client purchasing the government's services. What incentives does such a perception provide for participation in associational life? Citizens can develop social capital. Clients are only interested in efficient services at the lowest price. Clinton and Gore were thus seeking contradictory goals through their reinvention of government program: they asked citizens to become clients and they wanted them to behave as citizens connected to a larger community. They wanted to introduce market criteria into the halls of government, yet they hoped that citizens would be committed to the public good. Nothing in the reinvention literature addresses the issue of the public good or the public interest. "Whatever happened," asks one writer, "to the virtues of public interest, guardianship, integrity, merit, accountability, responsibility, and truth?"[23]

European societies, as well Japanese society, may well need to do more to transform their bureaucracies into less costly institutions. They may well need to do more to break the hold of vested bureaucratic interests that have prevented the application of sorely needed reforms. But with the possible exception of Britain[24] (though even in this case a change in policy appears on the horizon), they have approached bureaucratic reform with

---

[21] R.A.W. Rhodes, "The Hollowing Out of the State: The Changing Nature of the Public Service in Britain," *Political Quarterly* 65, no. 2 (April–June 1994): 138.

[22] Putnam, *Bowling Alone*. See particularly the concluding chapter.

[23] Caiden, "Administrative Reform—American Style," 128.

[24] See Chris Painter, "Public Service Reform: Reinventing or Abandoning Government?" *Political Quarterly* 65, no. 3 (April–June 1993).

caution, in large part because of the concern for the preservation of the public space. The United States, having abandoned the public space or any notion of the public interest, has been able to regard administrative reform as merely another public policy area where policies are determined by the interplay of market forces. It now takes a war for Americans to feel connected to one another.

The Future of Bureaucracy

The central themes of this study have been (1) a concern for overzealous attempts to transform (or to undermine) the bureaucratic apparatus and (2) the trend in contemporary democracies of conceiving of the bureaucracy as, and turning it into, an instrument of the governing political party of the day.

In the case of attempts to undermine the bureaucracy we have seen that these are often masked as "necessary reforms." But these "reforms" are most often the consequence of political movements that seek to undermine political authority in general. I have suggested that diluting political authority constitutes a severe danger to the health of democracy.

The trend toward the politicization of the bureaucracy is not the consequence of designed reforms. It does not seek to undermine political authority. On the contrary, the objective of governing elites is to instrumentalize the bureaucracy so as to achieve political goals. Yet, curiously, both specific reforms to change or undo the bureaucracy and the instrumentalization of the bureaucratic machine by political authorities end up denying the state the professional public servants needed to effect much of the work that the public at large expects of their government. The events of September 11, 2001, have led to some rethinking of the programs advanced over the past two decades on the role of the federal government in the U.S.

The bureaucracy will thus remain a more or less professional instrument of politics. Does its role and does its organization need to remain unvaried? Must a bureaucracy that accompanied the development of the state continue to play the same role once that state has matured by establishing political authority, durable political institutions, and sufficiently widespread political attitudes?

These questions have become particularly pertinent in recent years, in view of the fact that there are two opposing views of development theory today: the need for a bureaucracy in the construction of a state and of a democracy, and the market (IMF) theory that essentially maintains that markets will allow states to develop in the absence of a strong state authority.

The market theory of development may be better suited to a strong, consolidated democracy than to an emerging democracy. The West, particularly the United States, today advises emerging democracies to forgo the building of authoritative institutions and to rely on the market and on civil society.

Yet, the historical development of the U.S., Britain, France, Japan, Prussia, and, in recent times, Korea, Taiwan, and India indicates that the development of bureaucratic authority accompanied and facilitated the development of the state and the subsequent development of democracy. Why, then, suggest a path of development to emerging democracies that no consolidated democracy followed?

This may be the result of a confusion between the need for a professional bureaucracy at different stages of development. If political development requires a professional democracy, is it possible to envisage a consolidated democracy with a less-than-Weberian bureaucracy?

This has been the issue that inspired this work and that underlies much of the analysis it contains. Clearly, the need for a professional bureaucratic apparatus and for a strong state authority that is accountable, limited, and responsible cannot be foregone. The historical evidence for this conclusion is overwhelming.

With regard to advanced, developed, participatory democracies ("strong" democracies), it may be possible to envisage a less central role for the state. Many of the reforms we have described in contemporary societies suggest that the importance of the bureaucratic machine can and has been diminished. It may well be reduced further, as citizens claim a greater role for themselves and as they come to replace what the central authorities once provided.

But, even with the inexorable trend of democracy, the state remains the main guardian of order, of security, of social harmony, and a source for engendering trust. These functions no doubt require a leaner, more efficient, and less costly bureaucratic apparatus. But they require an apparatus nonetheless. Trust in and professionalism of political authority—what Weber called the "impersonal" aspect of bureaucratic authority—remain ingredients of a democratic order.

INDEX